Lillian Hellman

the image, the woman

William Wright

SIDGWICK & JACKSON
LONDON

Lillian Hellman

First published in Great Britain in 1987
by Sidgwick & Jackson Limited
1 Tavistock Chambers, Bloomsbury Way
London WC1A 2SG

First published in the USA in 1986 by Simon & Schuster, Inc

ISBN 0-283-99446-0

Printed and bound by Butler and Tanner Ltd
Frome, Somerset.

To Barry Raine

ACKNOWLEDGMENTS

Of the over one hundred and fifty people I spoke with during the two years I spent researching this book, the lives of some were deeply entangled with Hellman's; others only brushed it. All of them, however, particularly those individuals mentioned below, contributed an essential piece of the puzzle and will better understand my gratitude when they become aware of the complex and contradictory whole, the thousands of other "pieces" into which theirs had to be integrated.

I also want to make special mention of those people—not many, but more than the usual number—who wished their help to remain anonymous. They have not only my thanks but my sympathy for their conflict, and my admiration for permitting their privacy-protecting impulses to give way to a desire to see an important story told correctly. I hope they feel the result justifies having decided in my favor.

Of those I spoke with, my special thanks to Renata Adler, Joseph Anthony, Ambassador Lucius Battle, Howard Bay, Mary Ellen Bigelow, Rabbi Murray Blackman, John Bloomgarden, Frances Schiff Bolton, John Malcolm Brinnin, Robert Brustein, McGeorge Bundy, Muriel Gardiner Buttinger, Ray Calamaro, Don Congdon, Edward Cooke, Rebecca Cort, Cheryl Crawford, Richard de Combray, Jane Fonda, Yolande Fox, Leon Friedman, Dr. George Gero, Stephen Gillers, Ruth Goetz, Milton Goldman, Albert Hackett, Thomas Hammond, Kenneth Holditch, Sidney Hook, Kim Hunter, the late Ralph Ingersoll, Diane

Johnson, Kevin Kelly, Lady Keith, Catherine Kober, Nancy Kramer, Joseph Lash, Richard Layman, Richard Lederer, Alfred Lemmon, Harry Levin, David Levine, the late Ambassador John Lodge, Eileen Lottman, David Lowe, Scott McKay, Mary McCarthy, Jo Hammett Marshall, Roger McNiven, Marion Meade, John Melby, Ann Haber Miller, Kathleen Harriman Mortimer, Howard Moss, Margo Mumford-Jones, Natalia Murray, Lester Osterman, Marjorie Osterman, John Painter, Austin Pendleton, Eleanor Jackson Piel, George Plimpton, Joseph Rauh, Eugenia Rawls, Anne Revere, Flora Roberts, Peter Rogers, Dorothy Samuels, Alvin Sargent, Arthur Schlesinger, Jr., Budd Schulberg, Betsy Seidman, Irene Selznick, Lola Shumlin, Robert Silvers, Mrs. Richard Simon, Carly Simon, Randall Smith, Helen Asbury Smith, Winston Smith, Stephen Spender, Harold Taylor, Howard Teichmann, Helen Gould Tierney, Diana Trilling, George Trow, Abbott Van Norstrand, Nan Werner, Hugh Wheeler, Ann White, Richard Wilbur, Burke Wilkinson, Mrs. William Wyler and Fred Zinnemann.

I also want to thank Simon and Schuster editors Frederic Hills and Burton Beals, who, in addition to having borne the usual editorial crosses with exceptional grace and sensitivity, played devil's advocate or devil's prosecutor for my absent subject in order to test and, it was hoped, strengthen my appraisals of the pricklier controversies.

PREFACE

N THE EVENING of January 16, 1986, a play called *Lillian* opened at the Ethel Barrymore Theater in New York, a few blocks from the theater in which a half century earlier Lillian Hellman propelled herself into the American cultural scene with the success of her first play, *The Children's Hour. Lillian* was a one-woman show in which the writer William Luce and the actress Zoë Caldwell created a portrait of Lillian Hellman based on the playwright's three memoirs and a series of interviews on public television. For a writer to be the subject of such an autobiographical monologue was in itself a rare accolade and placed Hellman in an elite that included Mark Twain, Oscar Wilde and Gertrude Stein. And Hellman did not have to wait as long as the others; her Broadway canonization came eighteen months after her death.

The reaction of the newspaper critics to *Lillian* was unanimous. None quarreled with Hellman as a subject for evening-long focus; all criticized the dramatization for presenting only one side of her, the side that was tough, principled and courageous. Apparently they knew, as many in the audience knew, that there were other less praiseworthy sides to this complex woman. They also had reason to believe that the events and encounters she described in the memoirs of her long and productive life were not necessarily true.

Had the play appeared ten years earlier, few would have questioned its validity. Two of Hellman's three memoirs had just enjoyed long runs on the best-seller lists without a murmur that they contained exaggerations, distortions or worse. The last memoir, *Scoundrel Time*, Hellman's account of her confrontation with the House Committee on Un-American Activities, provoked vociferous controversy but it always remained within the bounds of political disagreement. To be sure, she was accused of self-aggrandizement and of bending the truth to bolster her opinions, but it was not until the last five years of her life that her overall honesty came under a series of attacks. In January 1980, on national television, Mary McCarthy, a higher-ranking intellectual than Hellman but a less successful writer, accused her of being a persistent liar. Hellman responded with a $2,225,000 lawsuit against McCarthy. The litigation was on its way to trial when Hellman, with the reflexes of a playwright, diverted public attention from the rancorous and degrading argument to a more arresting bit of drama. She died.

For many, the cloud of doubt that had gathered over Hellman and because of her death was left undisturbed, only heightened curiosity about a woman with an array of claims to prominence, many of them beyond the reach of skeptics. She had written more hit plays than any other female playwright, all of them on serious themes. Only a small handful of American dramatists of her period—Eugene O'Neill, Arthur Miller and Tennessee Williams—are revived as frequently. Her three memoirs had not only broad sales, but were widely praised for their literary quality. Three of her six screenplays, written during Hollywood's *premier cru* years of the thirties and forties, are considered classics and were produced in collaboration with such film giants as William Wyler, Bette Davis and Samuel Goldwyn. She counted among her friends many of the most prominent people of her day. Her three-decade bond with that brilliant writer and enigmatic man Dashiell Hammett would, in itself, have assured her a place in the period's literary lore.

Interwoven through her variegated creative and personal life were passionate political convictions that placed Hellman at the center of the labor turmoil of the 1930s, the progressive movement of the 1940s and, as a victim, the radical witch hunts of the 1950s. Her sympathy for Communist Russia dominated her political vision and had such hurtful consequences, both before and after the McCarthy years, that, while the wisdom and clarity of her views could be questioned, her sincerity could not.

Hellman had a talent for placing herself at the scene of momentous events: Germany during the rise of Nazism, Russia during the purge trials, Spain during the civil war, the Russian front during World War II and Yugoslavia soon after Tito broke with Moscow. While other literary figures are forced to tint lackluster histories, Hellman was beneficiary of as colorful a background as America can offer: Southern Jewish forebears, some rich and avaricious, others poor and eccentric. As a child, she commuted between a New Orleans boardinghouse and Manhattan's Upper West Side. In her early twenties she circled the glamorous fringes of New York publishing and Hollywood filmmaking until she leaped to major prominence at the age of twenty-nine with the brilliant success of her first play. Her thirty-year career as a dramatist was punctuated with theatrical milestones and monumental feuds. She was not pretty, but her style, intelligence and frank sexuality led to more than casual involvements with two Broadway producers, a publishing giant, a diplomat, some millionaire businessmen and, among others, an unemployed longshoreman— all during her liaison with Dashiell Hammett. Indeed, her life had so much well-documented color, drama and achievement, it would seem to require no embellishment. Yet, according to her critics, embellish it she did in fashioning her memoirs with a skillful blend of fact, fiction and pure fantasy.

Hellman would hardly be the first American literary figure to indulge in touching up an unsatisfactory reality. It has gone on happily since Hawthorne inserted the "w" in his name, Whitman added six children to his family tree and Faulkner complained that his wife wasn't interested in his work. But if Hellman was not alone in truth-doctoring, she was definitely alone in the way she was publicly excoriated for it. Perhaps her rare and enviable combination of commercial and artistic success made her a tempting target. Her politics, extreme and rigid, may have brought her further enmity. Or her own combativeness may have provoked a compensatory aggression, just as her well-publicized moral displays made denigrators eager to catch her in a compromise. There was also the possibility that she had gone much further than others in manufacturing myths. Whatever the reason, the Lillian Hellman persona was tarnished by the suspicion that she was not the woman she claimed to be.

Even before her death, the life that had received such extensive and artful examination by the person who lived it seemed to need examination of a different sort, an impartial search for the truth behind the legend. That search would lead, after a thorough study of the memoirs, to lovers, friends, enemies, professional colleagues, widely scattered correspondence and manuscripts, a half century of interviews and news items. The picture that emerged was different in many significant ways from the portrait Hellman had painted of herself. The memoirs abounded in the self-aggrandizing fabrications she had been accused of, but she had also omitted episodes that did her credit and enhanced the sweep of her life. Both her frequent excursions from the rigid confines of nonfiction and her quirky omissions raised questions that defied simple answers. What was the reality behind her romance with Hammett—and what was the extent of his influence on her plays? Was she, in fact, a member of the Communist party—an allegiance she denied? Had she ever known Julia, whom she claimed as her closest friend in her memoirs' most famous chapter? And what, finally, were the reasons that compelled her to distort the circumstances of an already extraordinary life?

The real Hellman was a woman far more complex and controversial than the paragon of *Lillian*. Funny, tough, courageous—but also temperamental, obstinate, dogmatic and, at times, unscrupulous. She abounded in contradictions: fierce loves and fiercer hatreds, grand gestures and petty acts of vindictiveness, dogged adherence to principle and underhanded maneuvers, rock-hard strength and frightened vulnerability. Her life as she really lived it proved to be much more intriguing than the Hellman of the memoirs, much more dramatic than that of any character in her plays.

1

L ILLIAN HELLMAN was born into an auspicious set-
ting for theater. Her home for the first six years of her life was the
character-rich boardinghouse run by her father's two unmarried
sisters. The backdrop was the New Orleans of 1905, a combination of Old South, Creole France and ragtime America. At the
time of her birth on June 20 of that year, Hellman's father, Max
Hellman, was struggling to establish a shoe-manufacturing business he had set up on Canal Street with a stake from the wealthy
family of his wife, Julia Newhouse. The Hellman boardinghouse
where Max brought Julia to live was at 1718 Prytania Street in a
tattered fringe of the fashionable Garden District.

The Hellman sisters were remarkable women of robust character and lively personality. One of them, Hannah, worked most
of her adult life as a secretary for the telephone company, but had
a nearly equal hand in running the boardinghouse. Jenny was a
big woman, tall and heavy, given to flash rages. She was the more
dominant of the two. Both were strong-willed women with sharp
humor. They took no nonsense from their boarders, saving instead
their sympathies and tolerance for their brother, whom they wor-
shipped, and, to a lesser degree, for his wife and only child.

Of the four adult Hellmans living in the house, the most imposing was Max. He was born in New Orleans to Bernard Hellman and Babette Kochland Hellman, both of whom had come to Louisiana from Germany in the wave of emigration following the uprisings of 1848. Bernard had served in the Confederate army, heroically according to Max and his sisters, but as an office-bound quartermaster according to some unwanted research by a teenage Lillian. With no formal education beyond high school, Max, like his sisters, undertook to educate himself, and to an impressive degree he succeeded. Years later his daughter would contrast her father's erudition with her mother's lack of it, even though Julia Hellman had attended Sophie Newcomb College in New Orleans. Max shared with his sisters a sense of humor that was sufficiently askew to exclude, on occasion, everyone not born a Hellman, even his wife—but not his daughter. He also shared with Hannah and Jenny a talent for blunt, direct talk, which would echo later in Lillian Hellman's life, first as an element in her affinity for Dashiell Hammett and later in her writing.

Julia Hellman emerges with less clarity from her daughter's recollections of her childhood. Lillian Hellman admits to an exasperation with her mother, who lacked the high spirits of Max and his sisters and is portrayed as a vapid, dreamy sort of woman who docilely accepted not only the hardships her marriage to Max introduced into her pampered life, but eventually his infidelities as well. To the small degree in her recollections that Lillian Hellman allows her mother a personality, it seems bubbleheaded to the point of derangement. While professing affection, Hellman portrays her mother as an amiable fool.

In a magazine article about race relations, Hellman would later tell a story from her childhood concerning an episode in the Attalla, Alabama, train station in which her father threw himself on two roughneck white boys who were intent on raping a young black woman. In the confusion after the melee, Max Hellman hustled Lillian and the black girl onto the train, which had just arrived, then looked around frantically for his wife. As the train was about to pull out, he spotted her. She was still at the scene of the fight, the rednecks bearing down on her, blithely repacking the black girl's suitcase, which had broken open in the scuffle. Hearing her husband's cries, she smiled and waved.

In another episode, related in her memoir *An Unfinished Woman,* an Italian housepainter working at the Hellmans' New York apartment quizzed Julia about her daughter's eligibility for marriage. The man's questions were explicit enough for the barely teenaged Lillian to understand full well, but her mother missed the point completely. It is at the abrupt conclusion to this story that Hellman states flatly, "My mother was dead for five years before I knew that I had loved her very much."

A theme that recurs in Hellman's plays is the destructive havoc that can be caused—inadvertently, to be sure—by simple, loving natures. A suggestion of this paradox seems to exist in her ambivalent portrayal of her mother. By her protestations of love for her mother, Hellman seems to be telling us that she is all right, she has proper daughterly feelings. At the same time, while imparting to her mother goodness, gentleness, kindness, she makes it clear that her mother caused problems for those she loved. In Hellman's later writings, she gives a woman of almost sublime nobility her mother's name: Julia.

In contrasting her father's family with her mother's, Lillian Hellman would refer to the Hellmans as intellectual, energetic Jews relatively new to America, while her mother's family were established Alabamians of wealth and position. The Hellmans' Jewishness is referred to often, that of the Newhouses, never. The assumption arises that her mother's family was gentile, an assumption reinforced by the common knowledge that the non-Jewish Hubbard family in Hellman's play *The Little Foxes* was based on her mother's relatives. It is unlikely that Hellman deliberately created this impression. When in her first memoir she wrote of being asked by way of application to a youth group in Germany in 1929 if she had any Jewish connections, she commented, "I had no other kind that I knew of."

Although Lillian Hellman included a good deal about her mother's immediate family in her memoirs and, if they indeed inspired the Hubbards, immortalized them in *The Little Foxes,* she tells nothing of their background. In fact, both sides of her mother's family were representative of a fascinating yet little known aspect of American history: the quick rise during the nineteenth century in the deep South of a number of Jewish families from immigrant poverty to mercantile power.

Of her mother's family, Hellman tells us only that they were from Demopolis, Alabama, moved to Cincinnati for a time, then to New Orleans. She later speaks of visiting them at their homes in New York City. While this was true of her grandmother's generation, it suggests a nomadic existence for the family in general that is misleading. First, the "Newhouses" weren't really Newhouses; the dominant members of her mother's family were named Marx. Lillian Hellman's maternal grandmother, Sophie Newhouse, was born Sophie Marx. The family gatherings would have been with Sophie's brothers—all Marxes—among them the memorable "Uncle Jake" of *An Unfinished Woman* who was a successful banker in Demopolis and later in New York. Like Regina Giddens in *The Little Foxes*, Sophie Newhouse had a different married name, but she was a pivotal figure in a formidable clan: the Marxes.

In the same way that the fictional Hubbards congregated at the home of their sister Regina, talking and scheming about money, so did the Marxes congregate at the home of their sister, Sophie Newhouse, to discuss the same thing. Sophie's husband, Leonard Newhouse, the only link the Marxes had with that name, had been a wholesale liquor dealer in Demopolis, where he died eight years before his granddaughter Lillian was born.

While there is no reason to believe that Sophie, like Regina, had a hand in her husband's death, an odd suggestion of foul play elsewhere in the family has since emerged. When a public building that had stood nearly a century across the street from the Newhouse Demopolis home was demolished in the 1950s, a beam was found in the basement on which someone had written, "Mrs. Newhouse did not die of natural causes."

It is unlikely that Lillian Hellman's grandmother is the lady in question, since she lived in New York for many years before dying there. It could have been Hellman's great-grandmother or one of her great-aunts. Or it might have been scrawled there by a bored young Lillian on a family visit.

Sophie and Jake were two of the ten children of Isaac Marx, who came to Demopolis from Germany in 1840. The Newhouses, also German, came a short time later. Both families established themselves first in Mobile, then moved up the Tombigbee River to Demopolis just after the Civil War. The town was not picked at random by either family. It had been founded in 1817, not by the Anglo-Irish cotton planters who settled so much of Alabama, but by Frenchmen who emigrated after Napoleon's defeat. Because Demopolis was situated on two rivers and was linked by water to Mobile and the Gulf of Mexico, it received more itinerant traffic than other towns of comparable size. As a result, Demopolis, in the nineteenth century, prided itself on being more worldly, more tolerant and more spirited than other small southern towns. As the immigrants moved out of crowded Mobile and headed up the rivers in search of less competitive and less staked out areas for enterprise, Demopolis was an appealing prospect.

A good many of these mid-nineteenth-century settlers in Alabama were Jewish. Henry Lehman, the first of the future banking family to emigrate from Germany, arrived in Mobile in 1844 and by 1850 was able to abandon his peddler's wagon for a dry-goods store in Montgomery. Having saved enough to bring two brothers from Germany, he called his firm Lehman Brothers; this would grow into one of the nation's major financial institutions. Joseph Seligman, the founder of the first of the great American-Jewish dynasties, took a slightly different route. After making a successful start in Pennsylvania, he moved his operation to Mobile in 1841 when a younger brother returned from a selling trip with irresistible tales about the business prospects in Alabama.

While Lillian Hellman's forebears, the Marxes and the Newhouses, did not fare as spectacularly as the Lehmans and the Seligmans, both families, in the three decades from 1844 to 1874, rose quickly from poverty to affluence. With Demopolis as his base, Lillian Hellman's great-grandfather, Isaac Marx, also started out as a peddler, graduating after a few years to his own dry-goods store. In the 1860 census of Marengo County, he was listed as a merchant with a net worth of $23,000, an amount that put him comfortably into the middle class.

After the Civil War, Isaac and his sons were even more prosperous, suggesting unsavory, and perhaps unfair, parallels with Marcus Hubbard of *Another Part of the Forest*, Hellman's second play about the Hubbard clan. Marcus is depicted as profiteering from the war and finally betraying the Confederates for money. Whether or not this was invention, there is no doubt that Hellman felt disgust at the manner in which her wealthy relatives made their money. She at one point speaks of their having grown rich from the "borrowings" of poor Negroes, citing that as one of the causes of her radicalism.

Hellman's feelings about this side of the family, however, were clearly mixed; she also says that it was only after writing *The Little Foxes* that she was able to resolve conflicting feelings about money itself. But when she speaks of the trappings of her relatives' wealth—jewelry, cars, servants—the derisive tone does not conceal a manifest pride. Later, when staging her plays, Hellman would have fierce arguments with directors who sought to portray the Hubbards as nouveau vulgarians. She insisted that, in the years following the Civil War, these merchants, nouveau or not, were often the most urbane, elegant people in town. She had no use for their ethics, but their linen and silver, she wanted it known, were impeccable.

While all of Isaac's sons did well, it was his oldest son, Jacob, Lillian's Uncle Jake, who flourished most impressively. After succeeding in a number of small businesses, Jake started the Marx Bank in Demopolis, which prospered, and following the pattern of many other ambitious latecomers to the South, he wanted to try his luck on a larger field. He sold his bank and moved to New York, where he had further successes in banking. He died in New York in 1926, when his twenty-year-old grandniece was married to Arthur Kober and living in Paris.

His sister Sophie, two years younger than he, married Leonard Newhouse, who also did well, if less spectacularly than Jake, but well enough to leave his wife a wealthy woman when he died in 1897. Jake managed her inheritance, and when he moved to New York she followed. It is her grandmother Sophie's Manhattan apartment that Hellman describes in *An Unfinished Woman* as having servants' halls and "lovely oval rooms."

If Sophie Marx Newhouse inspired Regina Giddens, then her wily and prosperous brother Jake Marx was undoubtedly the model for Ben Hubbard. He clearly made a strong impression on the young Lillian. When he discovered that she had sold a watch he had given her in order to buy books, he was amused and told her that she had spirit, that she wasn't "made of sugar water like the rest of them." Mild as Lillian's crime was—cashing in a gift to buy something else—Jake's reaction would still suggest a rather broad, Ben-like definition of "spirit."

In later years, drama scholars, perhaps embarrassed and perplexed by the strong impact made on them by *The Little Foxes*, sought to justify their approbation by awarding the play important historical and sociological themes. One of the most frequent was that the piece encapsulated the South's transformation from an agrarian to an industrial society. But the Hubbards in *The Little Foxes* and *Another Part of the Forest* are merchants, with Leo perhaps a hint of the bankers to come. The play makes no mention of their having an agricultural present or past. Their stores were supported by the cotton economy, to be sure. Unlike the planters, however, these merchants were positioned to liquidate abruptly and switch to whatever business changing conditions or more promising opportunities suggested. *The Little Foxes* is not a depiction of a central element of the Southern economy, but a small, highly specific aspect.

The Hubbards, like their nonfiction counterparts, were seeking to move on from their stores and small-town banks to bigger things. In the Hubbards' case it was to be manufacturing, but with the Marxes, as with the Lehmans and the Seligmans, it eventually would be banking. They were also eager to get to other places. Regina's yearning for Chicago would not have been typical of a plantation belle.

It is true that momentous economic changes were occurring in the United States as the Hubbard family gathered at Regina's house for dinner in 1900. The changes opened up vast opportunities and the exciting aroma of quick killings hung over the country. But because these people—the Hubbards as well as their real-life counterparts—were not directly representative of the major shift, and because their story follows quite precisely the timing and patterns of Lillian Hellman's grandparents' generation, it appears that she used the historic events to illuminate her characters rather than her characters to illuminate historic events.

Hellman would write two plays about these maternal relatives before she would look to her father's side of the family for source material. The characters in *Toys in the Attic* are clearly patterned after her father and his two maiden sisters, and the characters in *The Autumn Garden* started out being equally close until Hellman, in later drafts, upgraded the boardinghouse and eliminated one of the sisters. It would be a mistake, however, to assume that she identified more closely with her mother's family. The opposite seems to have been the case. She was a Hellman, she lived with Hellmans, she was poor with Hellmans. These other people, with their different names and different living styles, were fascinating and alien—fair game to write about. It was surely not only their strong dramatic potential, but her perplexity about them—an admiration tinged with hostility—that drove her first to the Marxes as subject matter.

By the time Lillian was five years old, Max's New Orleans shoe business was doing well enough for him to move his wife and daughter into their own house at 1829 Valence Street. The independence was brief. The following year, 1911, Max's business failed. In a try for a fresh start, he took his family to New York City. Referring to the bankruptcy in later years, Hellman would say that it was caused by her father's partner, who absconded with the company funds. If so, Max Hellman's partner was not only crooked but silent; the New Orleans business directory of the time lists Max as president and sole owner of the Hellman Shoe Company with no mention of a partner. In *An Unfinished Woman* Hellman says only, "When I was about six years old, my father lost my mother's large dowry."

Max's decision to move to New York was probably prompted by his rich in-laws having moved there a few years before, but if winning a second chance as a family-financed entrepreneur was his motive, it did not succeed. Whatever the cause of the bankruptcy, it seems to have discouraged Sophie Newhouse and her brothers with Max as an investment prospect. Although they would lend Max money when he needed it, they would never again set him up in business.

Max spent the remainder of his working life employed by various companies, mostly as a salesman. For a number of years he did well enough to support a niche in the urban middle class, but he would always retain the stigma of a loser in the eyes of his smug Newhouse-Marx in-laws. Although she never said so, Hellman may very well have developed some of her enmity toward her rich relatives, and toward the rich in general, by this condescension to her adored father.

Because the first years in New York were shaky, Max made periodic retreats to his sisters' boardinghouse in New Orleans which had moved to a larger house farther out on Prytania Street (number 4631). He liked visiting his sisters and being pampered by them. While staying in their house he could also be sure of three solid meals and an abundance of familial attention for a daughter who was turning out to require more than the average amount of supervision. ("I was a prized nuisance child," Hellman later admitted.)

This recourse developed into a pattern for Lillian and her mother: six months each year in New York and six in New Orleans, sometimes with Max and sometimes without him. The timing was based, not on the season, Lillian's school semesters or vacancies in the boardinghouse, but rather on Max's convenience. Although that would be determined by finances and work, for the most part the suspicion arises that what started as an economic necessity eventually came to be used for personal expediency by the never fully domesticated Max.

New Orleans was not always the depository for his wife and daughter. For briefer periods, Max would sometimes leave them with relatives in a number of southern towns—such places as Memphis, Macon, Yazoo City—an exigency Hellman attributes to her father's "restlessness," but which may also have been connected with selling trips. Of all her childhood moving about, Hellman has no hesitancy in naming New Orleans as her favorite stopping place. New York meant harder schools, isolation with parents who needled each other, and ponderous family dinners at her grandmother Sophie's where the talk, to Lillian's annoyance, was inevitably about money. She would suggest in later writings that her distaste for money talk stemmed from a lack of interest in the subject. If so, her childhood disinterest would become an adult preoccupation with money both in her life and her writing. A more probable reason for her dislike of money as a topic at her grandmother's dinners was that she belonged to the one group at the table that didn't have any.

Compared to New York, New Orleans held out variety, fun and adventure for the young Hellman. It meant seeing her two colorful aunts, whom she adored; they in turn had little difficulty transferring a portion of their adoration for their only brother to his only child. New Orleans meant lavish nightly dinners that Hellman, looking back after a lifetime of serious eating, claimed fine French restaurants would have trouble equaling: abundant fresh seafood—shrimp, crab, crayfish, both river and gulf fish—as well as wild duck, quail and pheasant (three birds for a dollar) from Negro hunting-season violators who regularly came to the Hellman sisters' back door.

New Orleans also meant living among her aunts' middle-class boarders, generally a motley and eccentric group who could offer much of interest to a curious child. It is relatively rare for a seven- or eight-year-old, with parents intact, to live intimately with a random succession of adults. If this cast of characters who paraded through Lillian's childhood didn't develop in her a penchant for observing humankind, it at least provided models against whom she could compare her own adults. And it is clear from details about these sample humans remembered by Hellman a half century later that her interest in them was not limited to their dinner-table self-projections. When Nathanael West, bored as manager of a Manhattan hotel where Hellman lived in 1933, enlisted her to help open guests' mail, she in all likelihood had experience in such fringe-benefit snooping at her aunts' boarding-house.

An even stronger influence on Hellman and her future attitudes toward the people she encountered was her favorite of the two aunts, Jenny. By every description Jenny was a remarkable woman—large, heavy, pretty—and with a volcanic temper. Jenny had little use for most people outside her immediate family, particularly her boarders, whom she openly ridiculed with a brand of teasing that sometimes cut cruelly. Families in which intelligence is high and money low often affect attitudes of disdainful superiority to the people their bad financial luck places them among. Jenny was no exception, her disdain aggravated even further by the Hellman sisters' dependence on the money their boarders brought into the household and the obligation to cater to their pettiest needs.

Albert Hackett, the screenwriter who was a five-decade friend of Lillian Hellman's, once summed up a Hellman dispute with a prominent director. "The thing you've got to remember about Lilly," he said, "is that she is basically contemptuous of most people." Others have remarked on Hellman's assumption that the people one encounters are probably fools unless rapidly proved otherwise. Whatever the origins of her contempt reflex, it was an attitude that hung heavily over the Prytania Street boardinghouse, and nowhere did it find a more formidable manifestation than in the mean tongue of Hellman's beloved Aunt Jenny. Reminiscing years later, Hellman said, "I loved and admired Jenny and saw things too much through her eyes."

Schools in New Orleans demanded little effort from Lillian; she could coast for six months on what she had learned in Manhattan, then scramble to catch up when she returned north. In New Orleans she often cut classes and used the time to pursue her own reading program in a fig-tree hideout she fashioned for herself, or wander out to explore her part of New Orleans, which always offered some diversion. She could walk down to the Mississippi to see the boys no older than herself swimming naked, pay five cents for a Mae Marsh film at the New Dixie Theater, or watch the annual parade of Confederate Veterans march up Canal Street.

If nothing special was happening, Hellman could be entertained for hours by the day-long street action: hand-cranked hurdy-gurdies, Cajun vendors hawking in their rasping blend of English and French, the horse-drawn milk wagons with their galvanized tin tanks at which housewives would line up to fill their pitchers. If she sat on a curb, she could count on a conversation with a "white-wing," one of the white-clad street cleaners; or from anyone passing by, she could hope for a lagniappe—the custom of giving treats to children, even unfamiliar children. That alone put New Orleans ahead of New York. For some reason she doesn't offer, at about age twelve she turned against the Mardi Gras parade and informed her parents she would never go again.

In her memoirs, Hellman relates only a small number of childhood episodes, all occurring in New Orleans. They are character-establishing parables told with great vividness and telling detail. For both reasons—their vividness and their small number—the stories have been repeated in interviews and articles about Hellman over the years until they have taken on the mythical quality of George Washington's cherry tree. For all their charm, there is little reason to rank them any higher than George's cherry tree as hard-edged history. Undoubtedly, in all of these stories there are elements of truth upon which Hellman embellished. It is not an uncommon practice among literary figures, but Hellman's embellishments are so vivid that they linger in the mind and court skepticism. In a sense she is a victim of her own dramatist's skills.

At times Hellman also gives us enough information to construct our own pictures, some of them lovely indeed. For instance, she writes of outfitting her fig-tree bower with various comforts and conveniences, among them a nail in the tree trunk on which she hung her dress. Putting it all together we get the following scene: young Lillian cradled in the arms of a fig tree, above the street life of 1914 New Orleans, intently reading a book too old for her while she sipped a bottle of red soda pop, dressed only in her underwear.

There is a remarkable succinctness in the small bits Hellman does tell us about her early years, a brevity of words that smacks of one who wants to tell you everything important but who dreads boring you. After a terse presentation of the complicated, lifelong relationship with her first black nurse, Sophronia Mason, Hellman then writes: "Sophronia was the first and most certain love of my life."

Her recollections of her father are presented in greater complexity. While Sophronia was the only figure in her childhood to remain above criticism, there is no doubt that Hellman, as a child at least, idolized her father. Max's humor and impulsiveness, as well as his temper and sharp tongue, made him a commanding presence among the adults in the Prytania Street boardinghouse, particularly to his young daughter, who frequently infuriated him, sometimes impressed him, but mostly amused him with her bright curiosity and stubborn courage. Lillian basked in the focus of this paragon who, compared to his mousy wife, his workhorse sisters, and their seedy tenants, sparkled like a technicolor swashbuckler somehow misplaced in a black-and-white, hard-times crowd scene.

Hellman's feelings for her mother seem to have swung between annoyance and pity. Other elements besides Julia's weak-

ness put distance between mother and daughter. Julia was a
lovely woman and she was a lady, two things the prized nuisance
child knew she would never be. But, as the young Lillian's capacity developed for understanding nuances of behavior, she
came to appreciate more and more her mother's refined eccen-
tricities. What she had angrily dismissed as weakness and irres-
olution, she began to see as the dignity of resignation.

While Hellman's maturing sensibility seemed to bring with
it a growing understanding and sympathy for her mother, it also
brought a gradual disillusionment with her father. She could not
avoid seeing Max's high-handed treatment of his devoted wife
and sisters, whom he exploited without compunction. That he
was at least partly to blame for the loss of his business that cost
them their house and forced his wife and daughter to move frequently also came to be acknowledged by Hellman with advancing age. When she learned of her father's infidelities, the
idol fell resoundingly.*

While Hellman, by her own account, may have made adjust-
ments as she grew older to her parental allegiances on moral
grounds, she was indelibly her father's child on more emotional
ones. Max was lively, earthy, outspoken and—above all—fun. Julia
was refined, quiet and sad. For good or evil, Max was a perpetra-
tor; his wife was a victim. But if feelings of love for her mother
were working their way to the surface, the anger at her seen-
through father was being buried. It is very possible that her disillusionment with her idol revealed itself only in the rages, sporadic and generalized, that Hellman admits started at a young
age and plagued her throughout her life. Whatever the analysis,
there is no doubt that Hellman's relationship with her father is a
key to so many of the strong personality facets that defined her
in later years.

But throughout much of her childhood, the father-daughter
relationship was idyllic. In the midst of the congested household
on Prytania Street, Max and Lillian established a snobbish little

---

* It is ironic that this drama, the disintegration of an idolized father, a
disintegration climaxed by a discovery of infidelity, would be the theme of
Death of a Salesman, the play that forty years later enabled Arthur Miller
to demand that Lillian Hellman and a handful of others admit him to their
fraternity of major American playwrights.

cabal; as often happens when one member of a cabal is found to have strong outside allegiances—in this case tawdry and illicit ones—the perceived betrayal is harsh and unforgivable. Hellman could more readily excuse her father's caddish behavior toward her mother and aunts, but when she found herself in their sorry company of the betrayed, she wasn't ready to abandon her soul-mate and turn on him, so had to put her outrage somewhere else.

Her outrage would later find an outlet in her political radi-calism, and, like most radicals, Lillian Hellman would have a life-long distrust of authority—not authority in general, but the au-thority under which *she* found herself. No matter what others might say or what evidence to the contrary—after all, she had been there and *knew*—she was unshakable in her conviction that those governing *her* were prone to hypocrisy, baseness and treach-ery. The spectacle of exploited blacks and ruthless commerce undoubtedly launched her radicalism on an intellectual level; her betrayal by Max may well have provided its fierce energy.

2

UNTIL HELLMAN was sixteen and left New Orleans for good, half of her childhood was spent in Manhattan. In later interviews, however, she spoke extensively about New Orleans as her girlhood setting, little about New York. The southern city was, for the young Lillian, an adventurous sabbatical from the norm, which for her was New York. It is also possible that her New York milieu—middle class, Upper West Side—came to be seen by her as less colorful than the more yeasty city origins of some of her playwriting contemporaries—the slum poverty of a Clifford Odets or a Moss Hart, for example.

She once told a friend that she did not much care for cities. In the 1950s, however, when she ran into financial problems, it was not her Manhattan town house she sold, but her Westchester farm. From the age of twenty-nine, when she first became self-supporting, she would maintain a Manhattan base until her death fifty years later. Her childhood home, the Hellman family's Manhattan apartment, where Lillian lived from age six until her marriage in 1925, was on the tenth floor of a building on West Ninety-fifth Street, not far from the more impressive homes of her Newhouse and Marx relatives. The neighborhood was solid and safe. Max became a traveling salesman for a clothing manufacturer, and would continue in that line of work until he retired.

The New York half of Lillian's year was occasionally enlivened with excursions to Atlantic City and visits to houses in Westchester County and the Catskills rented in the summers by her wealthier relatives. The years when Max could afford it, he sent Lillian to summer camp for two months. One of the few adventures to emerge from the New York portion of her childhood occurred during World War I, when she was about twelve. Hellman and a girl friend decided to assist the country's war effort by stalking German agents. (There is no evidence that Hellman then, or ever, gave much thought to her own German origins.) The two girls felt certain agents could be detected by their suspicious way of walking Manhattan streets. In one day they reported four spies to the police, who were not grateful for their patriotic vigilance.

Hellman attended Public School 6 on Manhattan's West Side where she was considered wild by both the faculty and her friends' parents. She and her best friend, Helen Schiff, would cut classes for no better reason than a prolonged period of freezing weather, which made possible long walks on the frozen Hudson. Just on principle they would stay out past the time they were supposed to be home. Even in those pre-high school days, Hellman smoked, and would often go to Helen's apartment for forbidden cigarettes. If Helen's mother came into the room, Hellman airily tossed the cigarette from the high-story window. Her reputation for unruliness spread; at one point the school principal warned Mrs. Schiff that Hellman was a bad influence on her daughter.

She was even more rebellious in New Orleans, which was the scene of Hellman's most vivid childhood episodes. Perhaps the most memorable of them was her recollection in her memoirs of her rage, at age fourteen, brought on by an oddly mild dispute with her father that ended with her running away from home. Although the triggering disagreement (Max's demand to know the name of the boyfriend, a lock of whose hair Lillian had placed in the back of a new watch) was conducted on a high level of dignified reserve, Hellman was infuriated by the affront to her pride, and a rich array of consequences flowed from her decision to run away from home. In the three-page account of a forty-eight-hour period, Lillian experienced the following:

1. She vomited from her bedroom window.
2. She saw a policeman on St. Charles Avenue and hid in a museum-quality doll's house.
3. She slept for the night on "a tiny Madame Récamier couch."
4. She tried to buy a train ticket.
5. She discovered and explored the red-light section of Bourbon Street.
6. She was yelled at in French by a whore.
7. She prowled the French Market, where an old man called to her, then exposed himself.
8. She cadged two doughnuts from a vendor acquaintance.
9. She went to sleep behind a bush in Jackson Square.
10. She was awakened by two rats staring at her.
11. She urinated in her dress.
12. She pounded, screaming, on the doors of St. Louis Cathedral.
13. She tried to tear off her dress at the railroad station.
14. She had her first menstrual cramps.
15. She was spotted in the ladies room by a cleaning woman who ran off to report her.
16. She escaped to a Negro neighborhood.
17. She rented a room by telling a landlord she was part Negro.
18. She was found and taken home by her father.

In such a remarkable concentration of events, some of Hellman the dramatist was at work, perhaps even more of Hellman the screenwriter. But it is a greater tribute to her skills as a memoirist and the respect her prose commands that she was able to make this tale so palpable, vivid and—most amazingly if it is read with the slightest skepticism—believable. She seems to have compressed the noteworthy events of an entire childhood into one action-packed montage, and instead of responding with disbelief, we relish the story while applauding her storyteller's tempo and economy.

If some great-aunts and -uncles gave Lillian Hellman her most memorable characters, the Hubbards, others played a sizable role in forming her own. The first portrait in *Pentimento* is of an Aunt Bethe (Hellman is vague, even contradictory, about the relationship, but in all probability Bethe was a much younger sister of her paternal grandmother, Babette Hellman) whose flaunting of sexual convention Hellman credits with enabling her own sexual liberation some years later. Abandoned by her husband, Bethe lives in sin with a number of men. Her behavior, viewed as scandalous by the Hellman family, fascinates the young Lillian, who sees Bethe first as a symbol of sexual passion—but later, writing after a five-year marriage and a thirty-year affair, she also sees her as the one who opened up the alternative sexual possibilities for a rebellious nature that was looking ahead with growing alarm at the contractual imprisonment implicit in marriage.

"It was you who did it. I would not have found it without you," the young Lillian says to Bethe. "It" for Hellman may have been her sexuality in general, but it is more likely she was crediting Bethe with showing her sexual arrangements other than the confinement of matrimony. Hellman did marry—but only once— and as a young woman she embarked on a career of casual sex and intense love affairs that was remarkable for its energy, diffuseness and longevity.

Another chapter of *Pentimento* is devoted to Hellman's Uncle Willy, the husband of her great-aunt Lily (a younger sister of Sophie Newhouse). Willy's role in Lillian's development is more routine than Bethe's: he was her first erotic crush. Nothing comes of it, although Hellman tells us that in later years, after she had become a renowned playwright, Willy said to her, "It's time you and I finished what we have already started." Willy is the forceful no-nonsense type of man that Hellman favored later on— a man who, like Hammett, had in his past a strong hint of violence, perhaps murder. The Willy chapter suggests a degree of wish-fulfilled fantasizing in Hellman's recollections. The suspicion is strong that if Willy left unresolved sexual yearnings in the teen-age Lillian, she resolved them in her memoirs a half century later.

Although the regular half years in New Orleans stopped when she was sixteen, Hellman continued to make occasional visits there until she married at twenty-one. On one of these later stays, she was joy-riding one night with two boys in a borrowed car when they were stopped by the police for drinking while driving. Because of the rough manner in which they were treated, Hellman later wrote, she developed a lifelong dislike of "cops." On another occasion, she credits a different incident with starting this same aversion to authority, which, whatever its source, would remain strong.

Both in New Orleans and New York, Hellman enjoyed a generous degree of freedom, but was still considered rebellious and unruly by her parents. At a particularly exasperating moment of her teens, Max Hellman told his wife that when his shoe business failed, the worst economy made by the family was dismissing their black nurse, Sophronia, who was the only one able to control Lillian. Max believed his daughter would have turned out more tractable had she grown up under her discipline. Max would also show a jealous resentment of Sophronia's unique power over Lillian. But if he brooded overlong on his failure as a disciplinarian, and Sophronia's success as one, he might have reminded himself that Sophronia had succeeded only in bringing to heel the six-year-old Lillian. Even this formidable black woman might have had trouble with the fourteen-year-old version.

It is, of course, Hellman herself who repeatedly tells us what an impossible child she was, and admits to no limits to Sophronia's powers. An aging Hellman had audible fights with a disciplining character of her imagination called "Nursie." But while she is drawing on a child-nurse relationship frozen in place by a 1911 bankruptcy, she would respect, and in a sense fear, Sophronia until she died.

From her earliest days in the fig tree, Hellman was a rapacious reader, claiming that she was trying to escape from a world of real adults she didn't understand to a world of book adults she understood no better but who at least had the virtue of seeming to be of a different species from her aunts' tawdry boarders. When Hellman was sixteen, she started keeping a "writer's book" which she calls "a mishmash, the youthful beginnings of a girl who hoped to write." She also dashed off several love poems at the time of her crush on Uncle Willy. In high school in New York, she wrote a column briefly for the school newspaper titled "It Seems to Me, Jr.," a self-conscious parody of the then popular Heywood Broun column.

After several years of dropping in on Public School 6, Hellman attended with somewhat more regularity first Hunter then Wadleigh high schools, both on Manhattan's East Side, graduating from the latter (now Martin Luther King High School on Amsterdam Avenue) in 1921. She blames her drab school record on her frequent moves, but admits she was an unenthusiastic student. At Wadleigh, she had her first and, as far as is known, her only fling at acting when she was cast as the villainess in a mystery thriller called *Mrs. Gorringe's Necklace*.

Hellman says she was fifteen when she graduated from high school, but the records would indicate she was a month shy of seventeen. The same year, 1922, she started classes at New York University. She had hoped to go to Smith along with her friend Lois Jacoby. But Max, after considering Goucher, decided he could not afford four years at a distant college. Perhaps her disappointment dulled Hellman's enthusiasm for college, or perhaps it merely permitted the inevitable rebelliousness to erupt sooner than it might have at the college of her choice. In those days the Washington Square branch of N.Y.U. fit into the fourth floor of an office building. There was another more prestigious branch uptown, but it did not accept women.

A fellow student at N.Y.U. recalls her first impression of Hellman: "very homely and very unhappy." Although the girl and Hellman did not become friends, she had lunch with Hellman one day at a restaurant called The Crumperie run by two English ladies. Hellman spent the entire meal complaining about N.Y.U., saying it was just a factory set up to make up the university's uptown deficit.

Another student there at the time, Ann Haber, recalls Hellman vividly. Both girls smoked, which was only permitted in a special lounge. There Ann would see Hellman each day and exchange gossip. Hellman impressed her as being reserved and "not show-offy," yet projecting a lively personality and a sharp mind. Even so, Haber admits to being surprised by her later emergence as an important writer; she saw no sign of that kind of talent at N.Y.U. Indeed, Hellman seemed to have only the usual college-girl preoccupations. Once she asked Haber if she knew a certain boy. Haber said she did.

"Would you go out with him?" Haber didn't think so.

"You would if you saw his car," Hellman said knowingly. "It's a Stutz."

Both girls sat next to each other while taking an exam for a survey course on world theater. Hellman whispered to Haber to shove her paper over so she could see it. Haber did, but let Hellman know she didn't approve. While she copied answers, Hellman explained: "I know what *I* think about the plays, but for the test I have to know what the *instructor* thinks about them."

Neither source for this period in her life claimed to be close to Hellman and one admitted to not liking her, so the negative cast to both testimonies means little. But Hellman herself later admitted she was a lackluster student who would occasionally come alive for a particular course—Renaissance Art or World Literature—but quickly settled into a contemptuous lethargy. It was not a propitious time in her life and she might well have been expelled if she hadn't dropped out after two years. By her own account, Hellman's parents were so pleased at her decision to leave college that they rewarded her with a trip through the Midwest and the South accompanied by her mother. When she returned to New York, she took a course on Dante at Columbia.

The undisciplined child was giving way to the floundering adult. But the assets Hellman was bringing to the adult world were far from negligible: a sharp mind and an upbringing among bright, quirky, plain-speaking people on one side, rich, tough, and aggressive people on the other. Hellman knew she was smart and resilient and that she had a sense of humor. Although no beauty, she was nevertheless an agreeable physical presence— reddish-blond hair, a good figure (particularly her legs) and bright eyes. She was short—five feet, four inches—and had a tight upper lip that gave her a cute look of athletic eagerness. But her appeal was based on more than her individual physical assets. As a young woman, Hellman exuded a strong sexual aura that, for many men, amounted to far more than the sum of her specific attributes. She also had a sexual directness that was a half century ahead of its time.

Throughout her life, in fact, Hellman managed to combine a tough, "masculine" intelligence with a "feminine" coquetry some women considered not just incongruous, but demeaning. One longtime female friend said with exasperation, "With that brain and that talent and that accomplishment, put a good-looking man in front of her and she instantly became . . ." mocking a Southern accent ". . . Miss Lilly of New Orleans."

Whatever her secret—and the combination of all her physical and intellectual attributes probably *was* the secret—Hellman had no trouble winning men even before she became famous—to rule out one of the more cynical explanations. The package did not succeed with everyone, however. Several of the people who knew her in these early years, both women and men, insisted she was "ugly." Her photos of that period would tend to deny such a harsh verdict, despite a large, crooked nose and rather thick eyebrows.

Whether because of her sex appeal, brains or personality, Hellman got around socially. In fact, it was through a social event that Hellman, with only two years of college and no professional qualifications, was propelled quite suddenly into the literary major leagues. At a party one evening in the fall of 1924, she fell into a long conversation with a somewhat ponderous and thoughtful man, Julian Messner, who was a top editor at Boni and Liveright, then New York's most exciting publishing house. Messner was impressed with Hellman's intelligence and knowledge of literature; at the end of an evening's conversation, he offered her a job.

While it is not difficult to imagine that Hellman, who was then only nineteen, would make such an impression, it is certainly remarkable that she would be present at an informal gathering that included one of the city's top book editors, and that the editor, who could have had his pick of hundreds of better-educated, better-looking young women, would offer Hellman a job on the spot. The reason for such impulsive quirkiness lies to a large degree in the extraordinary nature of the Boni and Liveright firm.

Publishing until the early nineteen twenties had been an upper-class Protestant preserve, family-owned cabals of old-boy editors who did their pipes-and-sherry literary ruminating in book-lined offices, usually with fireplaces and, up until the end of the nineteenth century, usually in Boston. The good men of Boston's Houghton Mifflin and Little Brown and later the New York firms of Dodd Mead, Doubleday, E. P. Dutton, Harper and Brothers, G. P. Putnam's, Charles Scribner's and a few others dutifully published such solid crowd-pleasing authors as Kathleen Norris, Booth Tarkington and Edgar A. Guest—all the while harboring the silent gloom that American letters had been on a downhill slide since the golden age of Longfellow, Hawthorne and Ralph Waldo Emerson.

Of course, there were distinguished exceptions to this middlebrow outpouring, but too often the more adventurous books they published were begrudging experiments or downright flukes, as when Nelson Doubleday returned from Europe aghast to find that in his absence Frank Norris had pushed through to publication Theodore Dreiser's *Sister Carrie,* which Mr. Doubleday struggled to cancel on moral grounds.

B. W. Huebsch and Alfred Knopf had already broken the gentile monopoly of publishing by the time Horace Liveright, also a Jew, entered the field in 1917 (Albert Boni sold out to him in 1918). Within a very few years the Boni and Liveright company was clearly the most dynamic publishing house in America and, in terms of posterity's verdict on its authors, the most important. Foremost among the reasons for its success was that Horace Liveright was the first publisher to concentrate on the new and bold American writing that was springing forth in those years following World War I and which was still regarded with skepticism by the established houses.

Between 1917 and 1930, Liveright published new works by Sherwood Anderson, William Faulkner, Ernest Hemingway, Hart Crane, Ezra Pound, T. S. Eliot, Eugene O'Neill, Theodore Dreiser, Nathanael West, E. E. Cummings and many more of almost equal distinction. Liveright initiated the Modern Library series; when he sold it to Bennett Cerf to repay a loan to his father-in-law, it gave birth to Random House. Through Richard Simon, who once worked there, Simon and Schuster was another one of the publishing houses to evolve from Boni and Liveright.

Apart from its epoch-making list of authors, another reason for the company's fame was the personality of Horace Liveright himself and the Roaring Twenties zaniness of his operation. When Hellman went to work for him in 1924, Liveright was a dashing, mercurial thirty-eight-year-old publisher and occasional theatrical producer. With his John Barrymore good looks and his Jay Gatsby panache, he seemed cut on the mold of the new style of leading men—casual and natural—then coming out of Hollywood. His enthusiasm for good writing was genuine, but his quick success brought with it a megalomaniacal impulsiveness. It was rumored that anyone with an idea for a book could walk into the Liveright offices and emerge with a $500 advance—and probably with a number of shots of bootleg whiskey, which was an essential component of the firm's simplest transactions.

A clubhouse air permeated the Liveright offices in a brownstone at 61 West Forty-eighth Street (later torn down to make way for Rockefeller Center). The flight of wooden stairs that rose from the street to the parlor floor main offices clattered throughout the day with a stream of traffic that might include Theodore Dreiser, Dorothy Parker, Sherwood Anderson or any of a number of writers in need of an advance, advice or a drink—or any number of attractive young women of marginal literary interest. The locked office door was commonplace and understood by all.

Such privileges were enjoyed only by Liveright and his top editors, many of whom had bailed Horace out of tight financial spots and become co-owners of the company. A clear social distinction existed between them and the "staff"—the younger editors and clerks who, like Hellman, worked on the two upper floors. These distinctions, however, blurred at party time, which could strike without warning. The annual suspensions of hierarchy, which in most companies awkwardly mark Christmas parties, might occur twice a day in the Liveright firm. Adding to the leveling confusion was an absence of privacy. Walls were often mere partitions and phone conversations quickly became common knowledge. Everyone from Julian Messner to the switchboard operator knew which editor was cheating on his wife and the degree of Horace's hangover on any given morning.

Aside from the frequent impromptu parties, the firm had many planned ones. Sometimes these were stately affairs aimed at enhancing the Liveright prestige in the literary world; at other times they were free-form bashes aimed at enhancing the editors' sexual opportunities. Hellman, who later categorized them as "A" and "B" parties, came to be included in both. Liquor consumption and late arrivals, including crashers, often transformed an "A" into a "B" during the course of a party.

A firm with such a reputation for high jinks as well as literary preeminence had no trouble finding bright young people with brains and taste to do their typing and filing. And as usual in such bargain-minded compacts, the salary was for the clerical work; whatever literary acumen the beginners possessed was expected to be thrown in for nothing. Inevitably, the young hopeful found himself or herself in a race to establish editorial prowess before the higher-ups discovered clerical incompetence.

While the Liveright editors respected Hellman's intellect, her own tales of office foul-ups indicate that she was losing the race.

In such precarious editorial jobs, one way to ward off disaster, perhaps even make a name for yourself, is to champion a manuscript that the editors come to admire as well. It is a risky business; if the reverse should happen—should the editors despise a book you praise—it can unleash dangerous reflections on your basic compatibility. But Hellman stuck her neck out and recommended a number of books of good quality and doubtful commercial prospects—although her claim that William Faulkner's *Mosquitoes* was one of them is highly unlikely. Hellman left Liveright in 1925 and *Mosquitoes* was published in 1927 by Liveright, which earlier had published Faulkner's first novel, *Soldier's Pay*.

Her editorial judgment, however, was fallible. The highly successful novelist MacKinlay Kantor would occupy the upper portion of Hellman's Manhattan town house several decades later. On his living-room wall he had a framed letter from his landlady dating from her Liveright days, rejecting a novel and concluding with the sentence "You will never be a writer, Mr. Kantor."

Around the Liveright office, Hellman was known as bright, fun and sharp-tongued—serious about books and not too serious about important editors. There was a family feeling in the Liveright operation and Hellman was quickly embraced into it. There was also a casualness about office procedures, hours, sleeping on the job that suited Hellman's abhorrence of regimentation to a degree that raises questions about how long she would have lasted in a more orthodox business operation.

Author Louis Kronenberger, who would work for the firm after Hellman left and who would later become, briefly, her lover, and a lifelong friend, speculated that because Liveright was so far from a model boss, he did not care for model employees. If an unconventional employee was his criterion, Hellman would have appeared to be his ideal. The fact is, she never got close to him. Then, too, because of the speed and entanglements of Liveright's life, it is remarkable that he was aware of her at all, but, according to her memoirs, he was.

In *An Unfinished Woman,* Hellman writes that she became pregnant while working for Horace Liveright. She would eventually marry the man responsible—Arthur Kober—but she did not wish to do so with either of them under that sort of pressure, so she had a back-room abortion in Coney Island. Although she admits to being shattered and terrified when she returned the same afternoon to her family's apartment, the episode is sluffed off in a few lines and quickly forgotten.

The picture that Hellman creates of her generation's sexual liberation in this and other vignettes is rather matter-of-fact. And she makes a point of linking her experience to that of other young women of her age, all of whom, she says, had either slept with a man or pretended they had. She makes a distinction, however, between her age group and the traditional flapper, whom she places at five years her senior. Unlike the flappers, who Hellman says were shocked by their new freedom and so set out to shock others, Hellman, as a standard-bearer for the post-flapper rear guard, seems to have been quite blasé about the brazen new world her older sisters had created. By 1925, smoking, drinking and free love were commonplace, she implies, and while her age group partook of the license, they did it with little gusto and certainly no sense of daring. It is possible that Hellman really was as calm as she claimed over the trauma of abortion that would cause book-length agonies in female writers fifty years later. Or perhaps she was bravely reliving these youthful dramas from the perspective of a woman who was approaching the end of a peril-filled life.

The Liveright experience had a lasting effect on Hellman. She had been exposed on a daily basis to publishing decision-making in a place where those decisions would have an enduring impact on American literature. Adventurous and idealistic as Horace Liveright was, he was still a businessman, and while his primary motivation was to publish books of quality, he had to keep one eye on the market. Bright young people of Hellman's age and bookish bent are inevitably highly judgmental readers—Hellman was certainly one—but their judgments are rarely tempered by any considerations other than their own new and fervent artistic standards. To experience at close range the other consideration—Will this fine piece of work bankrupt us?—was an important exposure for a young woman who would soon make an assault on perhaps the most commercial medium of all. In writing her plays, Hellman's motive was never to make money solely by entertaining or flattering her audience. But neither did she ignore commercial requirements as she served up her three-act indictments.

There was another by-product of the Liveright experience that may have been more important still to Hellman's development as a writer. For avid young readers like her, with the potential and silent yearnings to write, it is often corrosively daunting to read work they recognize as superb. They may get a distorted picture, certain to intimidate, unaware of the bad books that may have preceded the one they are reading, or of the embarrassing first drafts, or of the substantial contribution of the editor. The tyros see only the pristine finished product, forbidding in its unapproachable excellence. Thus the tendency is to assume that the person who brought this work into existence is some sort of god-kissed genius who bears little resemblance to ordinary mortals, and certainly none at all to oneself.

At Liveright, Hellman had a chance to see firsthand the all-too-mortal foibles of first-rank authors: the edited pages, the requests for rewrites, the rejections. But most important of all, she saw the god-kissed themselves, the supermortals whose work was rocking the nation's literary arbiters. Perhaps nothing is so salutary to the fledgling ego than to see a recognized genius close up—sputtering inanities, drinking too much and clutching secretaries. The hopeful would not be normal if the spectacle didn't prompt thoughts of "If him, why not me?"

Hellman once wrote that during her college years she had been, like most talented young people, a terrible mixture: "opinionated and impressionable, arrogant and scared to death." Much of the negative side of those contrasts may have evaporated in the boozy, wacky air of Boni and Liveright, where people of talent could feel very much at home.

3

T HE YEAR 1925 was a triumphant one for American literature. It saw the publication of Scott Fitzgerald's *The Great Gatsby,* Sinclair Lewis's *Arrowsmith,* Hemingway's *In Our Time,* DuBose Heyward's *Porgy,* Ezra Pound's first *Cantos. The New Yorker* magazine was founded. Even with her low-level editorial job, Lillian Hellman, who was then twenty years old, was a member in good standing of the Boni and Liveright "club," and therefore at the center of the literary excitement. Yet, rather than basking in a spot any would-be writer would envy, she left it to get married.

It was an odd decision, not only because of what she was giving up but because of what she was giving it up for. Arthur Kober was a genial, physically unprepossessing man about Hellman's age, who worked as a theatrical press agent, at one time sharing an office with Hellman's subsequent director, Herman Shumlin, when both men worked for the legendary Broadway producer Jed Harris. Kober also wanted to be a writer, but was a long way from establishing himself in a writing career. When he eventually did, it was a career of a considerably lower order, in terms of ambition, than the one Hellman would achieve.

Kober was neither a man with intellectual or artistic pretensions nor was he impelled to write by anger or idealism. He
aspired only to capture the charm and the humor of the zany
ethnic world from which he came—New York's poor Jews—the
world he knew well and took delight in. While Hellman's plays
would make her one of the American theater's most serious voices,
Arthur Kober, in books, plays and sketches for *The New Yorker*,
would become a folk artist of the Bronx and the Catskills.

Not only were their aims as writers far apart, but in many
other ways Kober and Hellman were opposites. He was easygoing
and accommodating, she stubborn and quick to anger. He was
friendly and accepting, she was aloof and judgmental. Later on,
when Hellman indulged her romantic impulses, her preference
was for tall, thin men—dark, if possible. Kober was short and
stocky. "Not fat," a later girlfriend insisted. "He was quite solid."

While part of Hellman condemned the wealthy, upper-
middle-class element in her background, another part took pride
in it. Kober's background was altogether different. He came from
the very special brand of poverty that abounded on Manhattan's
Lower East Side early in the century. As a child, he told Hellman,
he lived in a building that had one bathroom for six families. His
parents, like many others in that neighborhood, dreamed of the
day when they could move to the Bronx and leave behind the
squalor of Rivington and Orchard streets. The disparity in their
backgrounds would be more dismissable if Kober's upbringing
had left a political anger that blended with Hellman's own radicalism. That was not the case. Politically she did not swing to the
far left for several more years; he never did.

Hellman later wrote that when she became pregnant by Kober
she would not let pregnancy force her into marriage. Given the
many incongruities between them, why then did she marry Kober?
Some of Hellman's friends of later years who also knew Kober belittled the relationship, even referred to the marriage as "a disaster." But no one who knew Arthur and Lillian while they were
married felt theirs was a serious mismatch. On the contrary, they
were considered well suited. People who liked them both knew
that Hellman needed the tolerance and forbearance that Kober
could muster better than most. Another indication of their underlying compatibility was that Hellman remained friendly with

Kober throughout her life and generally spoke of him with affection. There is also reason to believe their physical relationship was strong enough to survive their divorce.

Certainly a strong sexual attraction existed between Hellman and Kober, but the more relevant reason for their marriage lies in Kober's personality. If Hellman would show a taste for tall men, she would show an equal penchant for decent, likable men—a category, by all accounts, that included Kober. The lovely nature that informs his short stories was immediately evident in the man himself. His upbeat cheerfulness was certainly an additional attraction for Hellman. In those years, as indeed until the end of her life, she loved to laugh and enjoy herself. At the same time, there were commanding elements of her personality—anger, moral indignation, self-criticism—that stood between her and relaxed good times. Kober had a soothing, ameliorative effect on Hellman—who refers to herself in those years as "a strange and difficult girl."

Hellman also speaks of herself at that time as "a jumble of passivity and wild impatience." Not only could Kober untangle the jumble and make Lillian laugh; he was also not the sort of man to try to motivate her or bend her to his will. As both Max Hellman and Sophronia Mason could have told him, that was the wisest course with Lillian.

Friends remember Arthur and Lillian Kober as an "adorable" and "fun-loving" couple, much given to pranks and jokes. Because of that, and perhaps because they were both small in stature, others recall them as "a couple of kids." They were popular, enjoyed a busy social life, were fond of cardplaying, particularly poker and bridge, and had a penchant for parlor tricks. One stunt in particular occurred at their group's gatherings with ritual regularity. When a party had reached a certain level of hilarity, Kober would cry out, "Lilly! Let's do our trick." He would then crouch down and Hellman would climb on his back. As he straightened up, she would raise one arm, brandishing an imaginary torch. The others had to guess what the Kobers were portraying. After a number of predictably rude remarks, someone would mercifully call out "The Statue of Liberty" and the party would proceed.

Kober's pranks also had an offhand ingenuity. Once, sitting at a café table with a friend, he doodled a few figures on a sheet of paper—a dog and two adults—then signed the drawing "Arthur Kober." He presented it to his companion, who marveled at how precisely the sketch captured the style of James Thurber. Looking mysterious, Kober took back the drawing and crossed out the first two letters of his first and last names. "That's who I really am," he said.

If marriage was the reason Hellman left Liveright, she freed herself for the honeymoon and little else. Shortly after settling down with Kober she was looking for work, and she frequently visited the Liveright offices, sometimes to cadge a lunch from Julian Messner or Louis Kronenberger. Hellman wanted to ask Messner for her old job back but did not do so for fear he would refuse. Her pessimism was based not only on her previous record of efficiency, but also on her perception of the firm's precarious future. Indeed, Horace Liveright would soon lose control of his company and go to Hollywood as a producer for Paramount. When his Hollywood contract was not renewed, he returned to New York and died a poor and broken man in 1933. His successors at the publishing house were unable to rescue it from his freewheeling management.

Through contacts of Kober's, Hellman did get a job doing publicity for a Broadway revue called *Bunk of 1926*, which closed soon after it opened, but which gave her a first taste of working in the theater. Next she wielded her Liveright credentials to get herself assignments reviewing books for the *New York Herald Tribune*, for which she was paid $4.70 per review. Her first professional writing appeared in September 1926—a review of two books: *Our Doctors* by Maurice Duplay and *The Unearthly* by Robert Hickens—and showed indications of the critical bite and high standards that would mark her later work. She wrote other reviews in October and November and dabbled with some short stories, but abruptly dropped her fledgling career when Kober, through a friend, was offered a job in Paris as an editor of a new British-American literary periodical called *The Paris Comet*, which was to have its first issue in October 1927.

It was another remarkable piece of luck for an aimless young woman who knew she was intelligent, perhaps talented, but who was living on jobs her husband had turned down and who had almost no idea of what she wanted to do with her life. At Liveright she had convinced herself, and in all likelihood her bosses, she was not cut out for the regimentation of an office. Marriage had provided a very brief refuge. But even with a husband, the days still had to be filled. Going to live in Paris had the appearance at least of "doing something." Because she had never before been to Europe, in a sense it was.

Arthur and Lillian Kober moved into a small hotel on the Rue Jacob off the Boulevard St-Germain, hard in the middle of the intellectual excitement of the Left Bank. Both were American, both aspired to be writers in Paris in the 1920s, a time and place that have since been bequeathed to Ernest Hemingway and Gertrude Stein, as well as to their compatriots Ezra Pound, Hart Crane, e. e. cummings and Djuna Barnes. But much of lasting significance was going on there at the time that had nothing to do with American writers. In the visual arts there was the ascendency of dadaism and cubism; in literature, writers like André Gide were exciting more admiration among Americans than the American writers excited among the French. Even radical politics was having one of its periodic moments of broad acceptance. A group of French writers and artists banded together under the name "Surrealists" to protest publicly their government's repression of Algerian rebels.

Although Hellman found herself in a center of ferment, she expressed little interest in literature, art or politics in letters to friends written at the time, or in her memoirs written many years later. Oddly, she does mention them in the last writing before she died. In *Maybe*, a novella with a strongly autobiographical setting, she alludes to the intellectual and artistic turmoil in Paris when she was a young bride there but admits that she was not part of it. Only later, when she herself was famous, would she encounter in Paris Hemingway, Stein, Malraux and others of literary and political prominence. Instead of plunging into the city's intellectual upheavals the young Kobers settled into Paris like resident tourists—seeing the obvious sights, experimenting with the food and complaining about the complaining nature of the French.

During the day Hellman polished her stories and had several of them published by *The Comet*, later dismissing them as "lady-writer" stories ("The kind where the man puts down his fork and the woman knows it's over. You know"). But neither of the Kobers worked very hard at anything. For the most part they seem to have had a pleasant time living in cheap Left Bank hotels, dining in tiny *prix fixe* restaurants and socializing with other young Americans of no particular artistic bent, over late-evening coffees at Le Dôme in Montparnasse—a part of town the poet Max Jacob referred to about this time as a "sink of iniquity."

Mutual friends brought Hellman together with Janet Flanner who, as Genêt, had recently started her "Letter from Paris" for *The New Yorker*. Hellman liked Flanner and was particularly gratified that the more established woman remembered her book reviews for the *New York Herald Tribune*. Although they would remain lifelong friends, Flanner was too caught up in her work to be much help to Hellman in making something of her Paris life.

Throughout their marriage, Arthur Kober seemed disinclined to regiment his wife, to bring her to heel. Nowhere was this more strikingly manifest than in the freedom he granted her to stray off or, when it was necessary for him to move, to lag behind. Since fate had landed her in Europe, Hellman used her freedom to see as much of it as her finances allowed. She came to dislike Paris and grew eager to escape it. Kober, instead of fretting about his wife's restlessness, actually encouraged her jaunts and helped subsidize them.

Her favorite place was northern Italy, where she thought the people the handsomest she had ever seen, and the scenery, especially in the lake district, ravishing. She holed up for a few weeks in the small town of Stresa on Lake Maggiore ("cheaper and just as beautiful as Como," she wrote a friend), where she won enough money gambling to extend her trip. At Stresa, she also had a one-night affair with an Englishman who, with his wife, was staying in the same hotel, preying on what they took to be rich travelers.

On the French Riviera next door to Nice, Hellman "discovered" the fishing village of Villefranche, describing it to an American friend living in Paris as if it were a place unknown to the rest of the world. If that was still possible in 1925, it would not be so much longer. Down the coast a few kilometers at Cap d'Antibes, Gerald and Sara Murphy, Americans who were deeply involved in the literary and artistic life of Paris, and who would later become good friends of Hellman's, were moving that summer into Villa America to put the French Riviera indelibly on the international map as a summer playground.

But Europe itself soon palled for Hellman. Even with the unusual freedom to do what she liked, including sleeping with other men without worrying about her husband, she grew even more restless. After about six months she left Kober in Paris and returned to New York to live with her parents on West Ninety-fifth Street.

It was probably during this sabbatical—it was definitely during her marriage to Kober—that Hellman met and fell in love with a bright, egotistical young would-be writer named David Cort, who would later become the foreign editor for the yet unformed *Life* magazine. Cort and Hellman had a passionate affair that continued after her divorce from Kober and into the period of her relationship with Hammett. They also corresponded feverishly. The Hellman half of the correspondence was later read by a good number of people when Cort, in a curious spasm of caddishness and legal naiveté during the 1970s, set out to publish her letters. Hellman threatened to sue. The letters met a sorry fate. In his last years, Cort lived alone in a welter of disorder, doggedly refusing any housekeeping help. When he died, his family hired a woman to clean his apartment, and the trash bin was her solution to the impossible stacks of papers and magazines. Among them, the family believes, were Hellman's letters. According to those who had read them, they were not only full of romantic passion but a good bit of the other kind as well. Hellman even went so far as to decorate the margins with erotic drawings.

Cort was as determined to broadcast the affair as Hellman was to bury it. He wrote a roman à clef, again read by a number of people but also lost, about his involvement with Hellman that was spun around the Arthurian legend. If it is hard enough to think of Hellman as Guinevere, it is even harder to think of Kober as King Arthur, although it is possible—and here the dates grow murky—that King Arthur was Hammett. Cort's motive was neither money nor eagerness to capitalize on Hellman's fame. The experience was for him, as it would be for so many of the men involved with Hellman, a high point of his life, and he could never let it go.

Oddly enough, the Cort affair had no apparent effect on Hellman's marriage to Kober. She seemed to thrive on such emotional legerdemain and showed a singular ability to put an intense involvement on "hold" while she went off in a totally different direction, an ability she would put to frequent use during the Hammett years. At the time she left Paris to return to New York, the Kober marriage was running aground on its own, but helped into inertia by petty problems such as Hellman's aversion to Paris and her frustration because, to the French, her New Orleans patois was a source of amusement rather than communication.

Such irritations might have evaporated had Hellman felt she was using her time to some purpose. On the contrary, for her, Paris came to symbolize her lack of direction. Adding to the frustration, she knew it would be impossible for her to find a job, let alone a direction, in Paris or anywhere else in Europe. Yet in a letter from New York to friends still in Paris, she wrote how much she missed Kober and how the separation was not a good idea. She vowed to come back soon—she later changed her mind about going back at all—and she told the friends (Isador and Helen Schneider—he was also a Liveright alumnus) that when she arrived they must support her in return for which she would "clean, sweep, cook, sing, fornicate and sew."

However raucous, Hellman's appeal for assistance suggests that she was contemplating returning to Paris, but not to Kober. Or perhaps she was joking about her probable need for support, even if she were to live with her husband. But she ended her letter on a note of serious self-evaluation, deploring how "unarranged" her life seemed to be and how many aspects needed "clearing up and settling for good and all." She then added: "I am only just starting to accept the all too obvious fact that I have grown up."

Kober, who shortly followed his wife back to New York, appears to have accepted the fact that she had not.

4

BACK IN AMERICA, Lillian and Arthur Kober settled into a rented house in Douglaston on suburban Long Island, he to resume his career as a press agent for Marc Connelly's *Green Pastures*, she to read, play afternoon bridge, cook elaborate New Orleans meals and, occasionally, seal herself off for hours of frenzied writing. The product, more short stories, she deemed bad enough to excuse her from a writing career.

Losing her one justification for not taking a job, Hellman felt again the exasperation of her pointless existence. This time her dissatisfaction was shared by Kober, who agreed she should go to work; he had come to acknowledge that whoever it was he had married, she was not a suburban homemaker. Once again he culled his theatrical connections to find her a job. The one he turned up was happenstance, but it probably pointed Hellman toward her future more than any of her other happenstance jobs. She became a play reader for Anne Nichols, the author of the 1922 box-office phenomenon *Abie's Irish Rose*, who had switched to producing.

Hellman would later claim that, while reading for Nichols, she discovered Vicki Baum's highly popular play *Grand Hotel*. "Discovered" in this case meant that Hellman read the play and recommended it to her boss. But since *Grand Hotel* was eventually put on by another producer (Herman Shumlin, who would soon figure importantly in Hellman's life), it still had to be "discovered" by a good many other people—among them Arthur Kober—before finding its way to the stage. When Nichols decided against producing it, Kober tried unsuccessfully to raise money to produce it himself. Hellman's enthusiasm for the play may well have been instrumental in finally getting it produced. Nichols and Baum were among the very few successful women playwrights at that time. Within a few years, Hellman would surpass them both.

When Nichols's producing operation proved short-lived, Hellman took jobs, all brief, reading for other producers. Again she relied on her popular and gregarious husband to find these posts for her, admitting that she was not good at either finding jobs or keeping them. Eventually exhausting the New York possibilities, she took a position Kober had turned down: doing publicity for a stock company in Rochester. Leaving Kober in Manhattan, Hellman worked in the upstate New York city for four cold months in the winter of 1928–29. Either the job made few demands or she didn't respond to them; by her own admission, she spent most of the four months reading and playing bridge. She also hinted at having had an exotic romance to help pass the time by dining with a leader of the local underworld. It would not be the only time Hellman boasted of gangster chums; she later listed Mafia capo Frank Costello as an occasional dinner date.

Once again Hellman's skill as a gambler enabled her to escape—not only from Rochester theater flackery, but from a marriage that seemed to be commanding less and less of her attention. She won enough money from the bridge players of "Rochester society" to give herself a summer in Europe. Saying farewell to Kober, who had apparently reconciled himself to a correspondence marriage, Hellman wandered around the Continent, then, liking Bonn, decided to stay there with the vague idea of continuing her education. The open-ended nature of her plan cast an even stranger light over her marriage, which now seemed casual to a point of nonexistence. It might be assumed, in fact, that both Hellman and Kober had given up on their marriage, except that they invariably got back together—as they would in this instance.

When she eventually left Kober for Hammett, it would be inappropriate to say their marriage failed, but rather, that one of their separations succeeded—the first caused by a third party.

The summer in Germany went well. Hellman made a number of friends, all bent more on pleasure than on education—which was her mood as well. Bonn was a tranquil university town and she would have gone ahead with her study plans if she had not been brought up short by the alarming political currents that were swirling through Germany in the summer of 1929.

Hellman was not particularly political at this point in her life. She was, however, an intelligent young Jewish woman who had attended college in New York, who had worked with a major publishing house and who within a few years would define herself in terms of her antifascism. Yet in her memoirs she writes that she considered joining the Nazi party—or, more precisely, one of its youthful affiliates—in Bonn. Her explanation is that she did not recognize it for what it was, but rather took it to be a socialist youth organization. By her own account she was recruited by a Nazi student group, and, thinking she was "listening to a kind of socialism" she "liked" and "agreed with," she discussed joining. This bizarre development miscarried when she was asked, by way of clearing up technicalities, if she had any Jewish connections. The spirited give-and-take that followed led to a revulsion on both sides—but on Hellman's it was of a force sufficient to propel her out of Germany the next day. In *Scoundrel Time* she writes, "Then for the first time in my life I thought about being a Jew."

Hellman's naiveté about the many guises of Nazism and its menace is less easy to credit than her belated awareness of a fact of birth that has dominated other existences. Her Southern background and her family's weak sense of ethnic identity perhaps permitted such obliviousness. In both large cities and small towns in the American South, Jews were isolated and clannish only if they chose to be. The Newhouses and Hellmans did not choose to be. Almost nothing was made of her family's Jewishness either by her relatives or the many non-Jews with whom she had contact. New York produced the same result for the opposite reason; most of her friends and all of her relations were Jewish. Being the norm, it was little noticed.

That her family's ethnic background would have any effect

on her life came as a shock to Hellman, and she was quick to re-move herself from any place where it did. Abandoning the idea of continuing her education, she returned to New York, to her hus-band and to the Depression. Her next major move came about al-most immediately, caused not by Hellman's restlessness, but rather by a development in Kober's career that not only affected her—it totally changed her life.

At a time when an alarming number of Americans were losing their jobs—February 1930—Kober was offered the best one of his career: to go to Hollywood to write film scripts. Only two years before, with the release of *The Jazz Singer,* the movies had started talking. The flash success of this technological innovation rocked the film business. Producers were desperate for writers and, having exhausted the skimpy local supply, were importing them from the East by the club-carload. Kober was hired at a junior writer's sal-ary of $450 a week, modest by Hollywood standards,* but far more money than either he or Hellman had seen before.

Hellman was not enthusiastic about moving to Southern Cali-fornia with her husband, even with the promise of a life of sunny ease, year-round tennis, and the glamour of the movie business. Kober set off alone, Hellman promising to follow shortly. Instead, she stalled and delayed for several months—probably because of David Cort—before finally boarding a train and grimly heading off for active duty as a Hollywood wife.

Kober, who was cautious by nature, was unsure if he would last in Hollywood, so had rented "down"—a one-room apartment on Sunset Boulevard, which would be Hellman's first Hollywood address. Shortly after her arrival, however, the couple moved into the Garden of Allah, the legendary complex of twenty-five bunga-lows on Sunset Boulevard that had served at one time or another as temporary home for a lengthy roster of film stars from the Marx Brothers to Greta Garbo. It came to be even more noted, however, as the Hollywood refuge for such East Coast literati as Scott Fitzgerald, Robert Benchley, John O'Hara, Dorothy Parker and George S. Kaufman.

* Even though this salary was low, Kober was in distinguished company; in 1932 William Faulkner, with *As I Lay Dying* and *The Sound and the Fury* to his credit, was paid $500 a week by MGM.

An image has grown up over the years that the Garden of Allah was a budget residence for brainy but unrich talents, a zany hostelry that made up in color what it lacked in *luxe*. It indeed had color—the swimming pool saw as much sex between celebrities as any public facility with the exception perhaps of the Twentieth Century Limited. But it was no bargain. To live at the Garden—for actors or writers—was a well-understood signal that the career was thriving.

When it became clear to the Kobers that their Hollywood stint was going to last for more than a few months, they rented a house, a simple one in the Hollywood hills. They hired a cook (an ex-actress) and settled into a pleasant social life with other young Easterners, most of whom were as wryly disdainful of Hollywood as the Kobers—and equally pleased to be riding out the Depression on movie-studio salaries.

Like the Kobers, many of their group had come from more "legitimate" cultural enterprises such as publishing or the New York theater, and as a result had the inevitable condescending attitudes toward Hollywood's claims to creative importance. At the same time, they were aware of the motion-picture industry's daffy excitement and its glamour. They were even willing to grant it a potential for worthwhile products.

Although Hollywood, then as now, had a rigid caste system— the $1,500-a-week writers did not mix with the $500-a-week writers—Hellman and Kober, just barely in the lesser category, found that they shared it with others who would turn out to be among the most brilliant and talented people ever to work in films. Laura and S. J. Perelman were close friends, along with Laura Perelman's brother, Nathanael West, who had had a *succès d'estime* in New York with his first novel *The Dream Life of Balso Snell* but who had made no money from it and was then hanging precariously to his perch as a bottom-level screenwriter.

Also part of the group were Marion and Nunnally Johnson (he would shortly be the town's highest paid screenwriter) and Sam and Bella Spewack, who later wrote a number of successful Broadway comedies, as well as the book for *Kiss Me Kate*. The Kobers also saw a good deal of George and Ira Gershwin, a friendship that would seem to deny the rigidity of the caste system since the genius of the Gershwin brothers was even then acknowledged across America. Although their success placed the Gershwins in a far higher Hollywood echelon than the Kobers, Ira and Arthur had been close friends in New York, and such sentimental considerations occasionally permitted a certain amount of discreet category hopping.

At first the Hollywood time passed pleasantly enough for Hellman. During the day she would lie in the sun reading, sometimes meeting other wives for lunch, perhaps followed by bridge or tennis. At night, couples would get together to play cards, see a film or explore Los Angeles night spots—everything from low-life dives to the private and exclusive Clover Club where the stars and moguls gambled for high stakes. Whatever the program for the evening, the Kobers and their friends would convene at the Brown Derby for a nightcap. There, sitting in a booth one night, his wife and friends chattering around him, Kober, feeling his drinks, slumped in his seat and looked grimly profound. "I'm glamorous," he said to no one. "I'm a Hollywood writer drunk in the Brown Derby and that makes me glamorous."

The Kobers quickly adapted to the California tradition of dedicated hedonism. With several other couples, they rented a beach house in Santa Monica, using it for nothing more than changing and showering after a day at the beach, which says much about the low-rent modesty of 1930 Santa Monica. Several of the wives decided to take up polo and found a man to instruct them. Never determinedly athletic, Hellman sat out that phase with a book. But eventually she grew disgusted with herself for sitting out more than just polo. She decided to find a job, but the best she could do—even with Kober's contacts—was as a reader at MGM at $50 per week. Each day she drove from her Hollywood house to the MGM studios in Culver City, where she sat at a desk in a large room full of other readers. Among them was Lester Cole, who later became a highly successful screenwriter before going to jail in 1950 as one of the Hollywood Ten.

Hellman hated her job. It was a substantial comedown from the casual yet prestigious Liveright offices, and it lacked even the freedom of movement and independence of press-agentry. With the long hours and low pay, the degrading regimentation in a row of equally underpaid and probably equally bright readers, Hellman's political sense, theoretical until now, received a personal boost. According to Sam Marx, then head of MGM's story department, she attempted to organize her fellow readers.

Hellman's strongly political nature was thought by many to have been aroused by Dashiell Hammett. If she did make serious efforts to organize workers at that early date in the labor-phobic atmosphere of the film industry, it would indicate not just convictions, but a readiness to act on them. But with or without any unionizing efforts, Hellman's stint at MGM certainly hardened her hostility toward bosses in general and toward the studio bosses in particular. Her experience on this job helps explain the speed and energy with which Hellman later, when a highly paid and celebrated author, threw herself into the bitter battles to establish the Screen Writers' Guild.

Hellman says nothing in her memoirs about feelings of exploitation or indeed expresses any thoughts with political overtones from this period. Instead she points to the long automobile trip to and from the studio as the source of her unhappiness. The picture she creates of her young Hollywood self from a distance of many years is, in fact, a far different Lillian Hellman than the woman she would soon become. Yet, except for the activist hint at MGM, the dissimilarity is corroborated by friends of that time.

Helen Asbury, the wife of the writer Herbert Asbury, was a good friend in those early Hollywood days ("I never knew Lillian Hellman, but I knew Lillian Kober well"). She had not seen Hellman for forty years when she read *An Unfinished Woman,* and broke down in tears at the realization of how superficially she had known Hellman despite having seen her almost every day for several years. "Lillian never mentioned any ambitions. She didn't seem restless with the pleasant, pointless life we were all leading either. I never once heard Lillian discuss politics," Helen Asbury said, "but then, none of us discussed politics." She assumed, however, that the Hellman of the plays and memoirs was present just below the surface, needing only sympathetic encouragement to be brought forth.

Hellman's self-portrait of this time in her life exonerates Helen Asbury's guilt at not detecting the complex personality that would soon emerge. Looking back at herself, Hellman admits to being spoiled, frivolous and directionless. She indicates no torment of pent-up creativity, no irrepressible political stirrings, no concern for the victims of the Depression. Instead, she recalls being disgusted with herself for falling into such bad California habits as serving grapefruit with dinner. Such self-absorbed isolation from the wracked world around her would shortly be replaced by the hawk-eyed political awareness that would, for the rest of her life, remain a dominant aspect of her personality. It is a mistake to assume that in 1930 it was already a dominant aspect, merely invisible and mute.

Helen and Herbert Asbury were one of a number of Hollywood couples Lillian and Arthur Kober saw regularly. Like most others in their group, Asbury had come west from New York to write screenplays, but unlike the others, he was an established author, having received considerable acclaim for several nonfiction books about the New York underworld. So vivid and informed were these works, Asbury was acknowledged as a reigning authority on American crime and its practitioners. It was natural for Hollywood, with its new craze for gangster pictures, to make good use of him.

A few years before the Kobers arrived in Hollywood, Dashiell Hammett, also a practitioner in the crime genre, had moved from writing for pulp detective magazines to novels. He sent Asbury, whom he had never met, his first books, *Red Harvest* and *The Dain Curse*, both of which were published by Alfred Knopf. Asbury had responded as hoped and became an early champion of Hammett's tough, hard new approach to detective fiction.

Hammett's first two novels were reasonably well received by the critics and the public, but it wasn't until the publication in the spring of 1930 of his third novel, *The Maltese Falcon,* that Hammett established himself as an important new talent among American writers. Reviews of *The Maltese Falcon* went beyond mere praise for an expertly done thriller and commented on Hammett's having elevated the genre itself from entertainment to literature. When he met Lillian Hellman, Hammett was thirty-six years old and a writer the decision-makers in both publishing and films considered "hot"—his detective fiction was new, commercial and of high quality.

An odd background preceded Hammett's major and custom-tailored success. He had been born in Maryland to a genteel but somewhat threadbare family who, on both sides, could trace their presence in America to the pre-Revolutionary period. Family finances forced him to quit school when he was thirteen and go to work. He held a number of laborer's jobs and was employed briefly as a Pinkerton detective when he was only twenty. During World War I he served in the Army on the West Coast, but was disabled with tuberculosis, which led to his discharge and put him in and out of U.S. Public Health hospitals for a number of years. While convalescing in one of them, he fell in love with a pretty nurse, Josephine Dolan, whom he married.

Living in various West Coast cities, they had two daughters, while he held an assortment of jobs, including another stint with Pinkerton and later as an advertising copywriter. During this period he had two goals: to build up his health and become a writer. He started selling short stories to pulp detective-fiction magazines and became a regular contributor to the most prestigious of these, *Black Mask*. When his finances made it possible, he lived apart from his family, ostensibly from fear of infecting them with tuberculosis, but in greater part from the same kind of no-hard-feelings restlessness that marked the Hellman-Kober marriage.

After the warm reception his books received from New York critics, Hammett had moved to Manhattan, but in 1930, with the triumph of *The Maltese Falcon*, he returned to Los Angeles, where his wife and daughters were then living. A more likely inducement was that in 1930 Hollywood was the place for a "hot" writer, particularly if he had been immunized against hackdom by solid hardcover victories. Even with such victories, Hammett, always fascinated by crime, still looked up to Herbert Asbury and was pleased to be welcomed into the Asburys' Hollywood circle.

First meetings are often tricky moments to recapture, even for the most meticulous self-chroniclers. It is rare for anyone to know at the moment, or even within the next year or two, the life-shaping importance of a particular encounter. As a result dates that later become important are irretrievable. Hellman admits to a vagueness about her meeting Hammett, particularly regarding the date; in the years to come she and Hammett would arbitrarily settle on November 25, 1930, as their "anniversary"—which would make Hellman twenty-five and Hammett thirty-six when they met.

Hellman recalls that she and Hammett were introduced at a Hollywood restaurant, where their attraction, both mental and physical, was immediate and strong. They left the restaurant and the people they were with and sat in a parked car talking all night, mostly about books. Her version of their meeting, however, is contradicted by Helen Asbury, who remembers introducing Hellman to Hammett at one of her parties in the Asburys' house on Vine Street near Hollywood Boulevard. She recalls them conversing for an ample time, but without sending off the shock waves, or even slight tremors, of an epic literary or sexual encounter. It was not the sort of *tête-à-tête* to raise the eyebrow of even the most avid gossipmonger. After a time, according to Asbury, Hellman circulated through the party, later leaving, decorum intact, with her husband.

There is a scenario that perhaps validates both versions: Hellman met Hammett casually at a party, then met him later under more fertile circumstances (Hellman without Kober? Hammett on the make?) at a restaurant when, for the first time, the attraction between them was unleashed. If this was the case, it is understandable that the restaurant meeting is the one that stuck in Hellman's memory.

They started seeing each other, and one afternoon not much later, they made love. They were soon deep into an all-out affair, and when asked if Kober was aware of it, Helen Asbury replied, "It would have been hard for him not to have been. All the rest of us knew what was going on. Besides, it was not Lillian's nature to be secretive."

Quite apart from Hellman's candor, the relationship would have been hard to conceal given Hammett's drink-induced volatility. At a party early in their relationship, they got into a loud argument that ended with Hammett's punching Hellman in the jaw hard enough to knock her down. When the furor subsided, a friend of Hellman's, Eddie Mayer, commiserated with her, saying how horrible she must feel.

"You don't know the half of it," Hellman snorted. "I can't stand even to be *touched!*"

For Arthur Kober's part, his marriage to Hellman had not given him reason to expect much from her in terms of conjugal propriety. She had pursued the David Cort affair at a considerable geographic distance from her husband, but whether from the new affair's proximity or its intensity, Kober was dismayed. When Hellman left him to live with Hammett, he was crushed.

The devastation did not last long. Kober joked to a friend about being wakened in the middle of the night by Hellman's asking him for a glass of water. He brought the water back to an empty bed. Kober forgot he was now alone. The voice had come from the adjoining room in the Garden of Allah, where Kober had returned after Hellman left him. But he would remain close to Hellman throughout his life, and he became a friend of Hammett's as well. When he remarried, his wife was welcomed warmly by both Hellman and Hammett.

If one event can be singled out as the most important of a life, the meeting between Hellman and Hammett would rank as such a milestone. Until his death thirty-one years later, Hammett would remain the most important person for Hellman, as she was for him. Much has been made of Hammett's influence on Hellman's writing career. That influence was indeed enormous. But even more important was the emotional anchor he provided, the stability he gave to her personal life, which, even with him as a fixture in it, remained turbulent. Given Hellman's impulsiveness and quirkiness, as well as her romantic and sensual nature, the absence of even the degree of stability he provided conjures up a very different life and output.

Hammett's influence on Hellman was far greater than a mere ever-present love object who could be relied on for nurture and support—and editorial advice. With her wary acquiescence, Hammett set out to change Hellman, and he succeeded to a remarkable degree. Under his influence, Hellman realized herself as a creative artist; her political nature was unlocked; and a rebelliousness that threatened as much havoc in her emotional life as in her professional one was brought under control.

It wasn't a matter of Hammett's bending Hellman to his views, to his way of doing things. Such an attempt at wholesale overhaul would surely have reactivated the rebellion she now held in suspension. And it is unlikely that he would have taken her on if he felt she needed total renovation. It was more a matter of his encouraging what he saw as the good in her and ridiculing away the bad. As for which was which, they both had no doubt that Hammett "knew." It would be hard to imagine a personality more unfocused and aimless than the pre-Hammett Hellman. In her memoirs she writes of her need for a "cool teacher," but in her failed second play, *Days to Come*, a speech by the heroine, Julie, provides a more revealing description of Hellman's guru-craving at the time she met Hammett.

"When I was young, I guess I was looking for something I could do. Then for something I could be. Finally, just for something to want, or to think, or to believe in. I always wanted somebody to show me the way. . . . I decided a long time ago there were people who had to learn from other people. I'm one of them."

Nothing could more precisely describe Hellman's hunger for a person to provide direction at the point in her life when she met Hammett. She was a disciple without a teacher. That until now she had rejected all who tried out for the role did nothing to diminish her hope of finding such a mentor. An awareness of her propensity "to be taught" surely made her more critical of candidates. Kober's appeal was that he made no attempt along those lines; he was the ideal pro tem custodian until the right caretaker came along.

The Hellman who was so quick to bestow contempt had nothing but respect bordering on veneration for Hammett. To her he appeared a man almost unique for his lack of artifice, self-delusion, hypocrisy—all the things that disgusted her about most people and, to a degree, about herself. He was experienced in the world as few people are—and not in just one, but many worlds: movie-making, publishing, labor organizing, detective work, the underworld, heavy drinking, whoring. He was a celebrity, very handsome, a man with a good mind and intellectual curiosity. They shared a blunt, somewhat tough sense of humor. Perhaps most important of all, he was a superb writer.

And for Hellman, as with many who are disdainful of authority yet are eager to find one person to whom they can subjugate themselves, the desire was tied up with sexuality. Her requirements for the sought-after teacher were all but impossible to fulfill without including physical attraction as well. Lillian Hellman found them all in Dashiell Hammett.

Her eagerness for a teacher was almost matched by his desire to teach. So enthusiastically did Hammett throw himself into the coach-Svengali role, he appears to have reached a point when he preferred shaping someone else's life to living his own. Perhaps he had grown weary of "becoming" and "developing into" the adult Dashiell Hammett—and to judge from his drinking, perhaps he was weary of Hammett himself. He felt he had acquired all the knowledge and wisdom to win the game—professionally he was clearly winning it—but he had lost interest in the game itself. It was more amusing, less tiring (and perhaps less risky), to pass on to someone else what he knew and watch her win in his place. That Hellman had a real zest for the game and its rewards, a zest Hammett had lost, made it all the better.

Because he was a writer, and Hellman wanted to write, that was a major part of his counsel, and his influence cannot be overestimated. But he held up for review every aspect of her being—her politics, her intellectual life, her taste in books and in people, her social conscience. Lovers often attempt some reworking of their partners. What made the Hellman-Hammett relationship unusual was that both had a strong predilection for their complementary roles. Yet Hammett's efforts probably would not have succeeded if he had not embodied an array of attitudes and responses that were already partially formed and struggling for validation from within the welter of arrogance and timidity, knowledge and ignorance, cynicism and naiveté Hellman admits to having been.

Hammett took the raw Hellman material and, through a campaign that occasionally used patient counsel, but more often ridicule, sarcasm, bullying, sulking, and threats of abandonment, he managed to edit into existence the Lillian Hellman that would remain fixed throughout most of her adult life.

There are several chronological facts, stark and curious, that lend testimony to the nature of their relationship. Hammett's productivity as a writer ended in 1934, the year of Hellman's first success. The few major changes that occurred in Hellman's personality and style of living (by choice rather than circumstance) did not occur until after Hammett's death thirty years later. But the most telling evidence can be found throughout her work and throughout her life during the three decades they were together.

Not long after joining Hammett, Hellman, compared to her former self, became a model of purposefulness and decisiveness. Although the purposes and decisions were markedly colored by Hammett's own, they were still hers. Hammett was genuinely fascinated by the person he saw behind the confusions and contradictions of Hellman. Energized by his love for her, he set to work to bring that person into being. Hammett is frequently given credit for Hellman's emergence as a playwright—which is certainly true, but not in the collaborative way that is often implied; his contribution was far broader. He was a collaborator in the creation not so much of the plays as of Lillian Hellman herself.

5

A STRONG APPEAL of Hammett for Hellman was his lack of vanity and his disinterest in talking about himself—a personality aspect which has plagued the many writers who have attempted to explain him. He deplored the public posturing and image-building of his fellow authors. When asked in one early interview if it was true he had served in the army in World War I, he emphasized that he had served in the army *during* World War I but not *in* it. He had no patience with even the smallest distortion of truth. Hammett's disdain for the celebrity interview was strong enough to arouse suspicion that he deliberately falsified his public utterances about himself, perhaps on the grounds that they should not have been called forth in the first place, or perhaps from a bored mystery writer's impulse to leave false clues. He could be equally uncommunicative on a personal level. One of his biographers, Diane Johnson, wrote: "There was something impenetrable as much in the sweetness of his smile as in his blackest silences." In company his moods would careen unpredictably from shyness to cozy humor to acid-tongued cruelty to violence.

In social situations he rarely spoke about himself and, as

years went by, exposed himself less and less to outsiders, even avoiding guests of Hellman's who were staying under the same roof. Hellman herself encountered the psychological wall he built up and wrote of her difficulty in getting him to talk about himself. When she once asked him to tell her more about a San Francisco girl he had known, "the silly one who lived across the hall in Pine Street," Hammett replied, "She lived across the hall in Pine Street and was silly." Hammett knew too much of the world, was too repulsed by the phony posturing of most people's talk, to be caught doing it himself. Rather than run such a risk, he opted for silence. He was a man stifled by his own sophistication.

For her part, Hellman was committed to emotional outbursts and dramatic displays of temper—particularly about the steady stream of other women in Hammett's life. Her impulse was invariably to get things on the table, thrash them out. His response to the rages was to let them run themselves out, or, with efforts at argument, to cut off further discussion with a "Leave it alone" or "I don't want to talk about that now."

The few autobiographical allusions that crept into Hammett's writing would be recognized only by those who knew him very well, and were invariably included to enhance the story rather than as an exercise in self-revelation. Equally repugnant to Hammett was talk about his writing; perhaps because of this, he did not like the company of other writers (with a few noteworthy exceptions such as Faulkner).

He was a man of enormous pride and, when sober, dignity. He was bound by a code of honor and loyalty sufficient to land him in jail when he refused to answer a question to which he could have honestly replied, "I don't know," and gotten off. This code extended to such social niceties as a refusal to avail himself of the polite lie, the face-saving excuse or the mending apology. This was another aspect of Hammett that appealed enormously to Hellman, who was often disgusted by her own tongue-tied attempts at self-justification.

Still, certain larger questions raised by the life of Hammett resist explanation. Although he acted upon his radical politics, he never wrote about them and rarely discussed them, even with intimates like Hellman. After the publication of *The Thin Man* in 1934, he never completed another book in the twenty-seven years remaining to him. The desperation and suicidal nature of his drinking bouts has never been traced to any specific area of anguish or dislodgement in his history. His unshakable fascination with and dependence on Hellman defies several laws of natural selection and simply stands, like so much that was central to Hammett, as an unlikely, unencumbered fact.

In her memoirs, Hellman offered the world a spectacular love story that was not only lifelong but had more than its share of enhancements: fame, wealth, artistic distinction, shared persecution, dogged loyalty, steadfastness through an ugly terminal illness—enough poignant and dramatic elements for a packet of Tracy-Hepburn films. The much later evidence that she was guilty of myth-making in other aspects of her life made this particularly attractive story a prime target for disbelief.* It happens, in the greater part, to have been true.

There were thirty years of witnesses to the bond between them that proved more durable than most marriages—as well as thirty years of witnesses to epic fights, long stretches of estrangement and chronic infidelities which, on Hammett's part, began without so much as a nod to the most minimal "honeymoon" grace period, and on Hellman's part with love affairs that, at least twice, came close to marriage. Hammett's strayings, which definitely started before Hellman's, were rarely more than sexual pranks—adventures of the body pursued with a studied naughtiness. Yet they devastated Hellman, who admitted to a highly jealous nature. Writing about their affairs after his death, she referred to his having come close to "spoiling everything" between them, in a painful shudder at forty-year-old infidelities.

When Hellman eventually took advantage of his prying open their arrangement, she set out on a string of affairs of various durations. Unlike Hammett's quick flings, however, her affairs usually involved the heart and mind as well as the body. Yet for both, there would be little question of returning to the other at the end of these excursions; neither had ever left.

Some skeptics have suggested Hellman may have been for Hammett not a lover but a steadfast soulmate to whom he could return after his escapades, a spiritual haven where he was sure to

* For this the champion must be Gore Vidal, who, shortly before Hellman's death, purred, "Did anyone ever see them together?"

find comforting companionship, a drinking buddy and an intelligence receptive to discussions of his broad range of intellectual interests. Contrary evidence can be found, however, in the long periods they spent alone except for each other. In their first years together, they isolated themselves for months at a time in such romantic and removed places as the Florida keys and New England coastal islands. Fishing, reading and writing, they would see almost no one and would return to the world only when a demand on one of them could not be avoided. In later years they arranged their lives so that such isolation would be theirs as a matter of course—with both free to check in and out, but Hellman making far greater use of that freedom.

If the physical side of Hellman and Hammett's relationship eventually gave way to a more emotional bond, they would hardly be alone in that among lifelong couples. That the affair started out and continued for many years on a strongly erotic footing is borne out by the aggressively sensual nature of both— few men or women have thrown themselves into the heterosexual maelstrom with more enthusiasm than these two—or had less trouble or compunction about getting what they wanted.

The compellingly physical side of their affair is also borne out by letters from Hammett to Hellman. In March 1931 he wrote her a poem, the "beginning of a thousand stanza verse," in which he portrayed himself as the hero of a book he was then working on, a fictional detective named Elfinstone:

> *In San Francisco Elfinstone*
> *Fell in with a red-haired slut*
> *Whose eyes were bright as the devil's own*
> *With green-eyed greed, whose jaw was cut*
> *Wolfishly. Her body was lean and tough as a whip,*
> *With little of breast and little of hip,*
> *And her voice was thin and hard as her lip,*
> *And her lip was hard as a bone.*

On one occasion when it was necessary to leave Hellman in New York and travel to the West Coast by train, Hammett sent her telegrams from stops along the way: "AM MISSING OF YOU PLENTY" and then from five hundred miles farther west, "HAVE NOT GOT USED TO BEING WITHOUT YOU YET." In a letter recounting some name-dappled escapades in Hollywood, he suddenly broke off and blurted out: "BUT ALL THE WHILE I'M LOVING YOU VERY MUCH." This sentence would show up frequently in his letters, always written in capitals, sometimes abbreviated to its acronym, serving as a descant to his social notes.

When Hellman went on trips by herself, even after they had been together for as long as ten years, Hammett would sulk, grumble and send off whining letters about her staying away too long and not writing often enough. He ragged her about her fondness for travel, saying she would sell her country down the river for a free trip; the destination did not have to be anything as costly as Europe, Jersey City would do. Behind the paternal amusement at what he considered a frivolous quirk of hers, there was a childlike fear of being abandoned by Hellman, even for a few weeks.

From the beginning Hammett made it clear that although he adored her and intended to remain forever hers, he could not be hers *exclusively*. His womanizing, he pleaded, was an unalterable part of his nature. Hellman said she understood. Perhaps she did on an intellectual level, but when she would return from a trip to find a besotted floozy lolling in her bedroom, it was not Hellman's intellect that was called into clamorous action. Nor was her reaction that of a drinking-buddy roommate.

Part of Hammett's fidelity problem worked well with Hellman's own fear of romantic imprisonment, her dread of the claustrophobia brought on by feelings of obligation. The more Hammett misbehaved, the less she felt entrapped. While such a felicitous meshing of quirks did not eliminate the blowups—she never learned to accept his sexual excursions—it mitigated somewhat the pain she felt about them.

When Hellman began her affair with Hammett, he had emerged from a decade of desultory career-struggling into the light of recognition as one of the most talented and glamorous writers of his day. He was urbane, witty and even better-looking than William Powell, who would soon play Nick Charles, the Hammett character, in the film *The Thin Man*. His fascination with the underworld—as well as firsthand experience as a detective—gave a dimension to his sophistication that placed it well above the generally high level of worldliness of most New York authors or Hollywood screenwriters.

Hammett was also an alcoholic given to marathon and costly binges. He would check into a suite of rooms at the Beverly Wilshire in L.A. or the St. Francis in San Francisco and emerge four or five days later owing the management an amount many American families of the day would have welcomed as an annual income. He could be tender and loving to his wife and daughters. When an advance or royalty check appeared, he would lavish money, gifts and letters on them, only to ignore them ruthlessly when his funds ran low or his drinking was heavy. The year before *The Thin Man* came out, Hammett's wife was forced into a humiliating correspondence with Alfred Knopf, first asking the publisher if he knew her husband's whereabouts, and when Knopf pleaded ignorance, asking if there was some way she could cash Hammett's royalty checks that arrived at her address; their daughters did not have enough to eat.

With so much destructiveness aimed at himself, Hammett could also abuse others. In 1932 Elise De Viane, an actress he had seen off and on, sued Hammett for $35,000 for assault and battery. The suit made the papers and ended with an award to her of $2,500. The mayhem he sometimes created could take the form of gratuitous cruelty. Nathanael West, whose acclaimed novels never earned much money, was known to borrow frequently from his friends, most of whom were glad to oblige. At a party, West buttonholed his friend Hammett to ask for help in finding a screenwriting job. Although West said nothing about a loan, Hammett replied in a voice loud enough for everyone to hear, "I wish I could help you, old man, but I'm strapped myself. Maybe next week I could lend you a little . . ." West left in humiliation. Prior to this incident, West had provided Hammett and Hellman with cheap lodgings when *they* had been strapped, so ingratitude must be added to the list of Hammett's drunken sins. But he may have had a specific reason for hostility toward West; it was widely known that Hellman had gone to bed with him a few times.

At another party Hammett was seated next to a formerly well-known actress who had aged beyond the roles for which she was famous. During the meal, tomato sauce spilled on her beige dress and Hammett boomed, "Doesn't it remind you of when we were both still menstruating?" The party was aghast, not at the explicit physiological reference, but at the implication of advancing age, which in Hollywood is farther out of bounds for dinner-party banter with actresses than menstruation.

In addition to being hurtful, Hammett's impulses could be dangerous. Walking through the dining room of a popular speakeasy, he spotted a party of friends having dinner. As he passed the waiters' service table, he dug into the silverware, clutched handfuls of forks and knives and hurled them merrily at his friends' dinner table as they dived for cover. Everyone knew that liquor was behind such irrational spasms, but it was constant enough to make Hammett a menace on the Hollywood party circuit. "He's the hottest writer in town so we must invite him," the thinking went, "but a mean drunk, so steer clear." Of course the air of screw-it-all disdain that informed such displays was mightily impressive to craven, toe-the-mark Hollywood—thus the Hammett legend flourished.

While liquor and contempt for Hollywood surely prompted much of his recklessness, both were common among the town's writers. In Hammett's case, it was reinforced by his problematic health. He was convinced that the tuberculosis he had inherited from his mother, which had plagued him off and on since he served briefly in the army during World War I, would kill him sooner rather than later. Discussing his good friend Hammett in a letter, Nunnally Johnson said that Dash "had no expectation of being alive much beyond Thursday."

A man who feels he has but a short time to live is not given to budgeting his money or worrying overmuch about his good standing in the polite society for which he has little use. Capitalizing on the perquisites of the dying man, Hammett would, in fact, remain alive, and in reasonably good health, for another quarter century. The bronchial condition which was expected to deteriorate improved considerably. But drunk or sober, the overriding fact of his present would always be his belief that he had no future.

The cruelty and viciousness only surfaced when he drank. Sober, Hammett was quiet, almost shy, and generally kind and thoughtful of others. Sober he was uncommunicative, withdrawn and uneasy. With a few drinks he would become voluble and, to many, vastly amusing. After a certain point of intake, anything could happen.

Intellectually he had an insatiable curiosity; he was a voracious reader with a remarkable range of interests, not just fiction, but subjects ranging from eighteenth-century political philosophers to the cross-pollination of corn. He had a great respect for books, and despite the low estate of most detective fiction when Hammett set out to be a writer, he took writing very seriously, even in his pulp-magazine days. He once said that if a writer wasn't trying to make art, he shouldn't bother. He labored hard over each sentence and struggled for the precise word. When he was at work on a novel, he shut out everything else, even Hellman, to her chagrin—although she did the same thing.

Just in terms of his tough standards and unshakable sense of self, Hammett would have attracted Hellman. In addition to his other allurements such as looks, humor, talent and fame, Hammett had the one quality that made the aggregate irresistible to her: a fascination with and belief in Lillian Hellman. She had no doubts that she had found, not only the "cool teacher," but the central involvement of her life. She still had no idea of what she would do with that life, but on a deeper level she knew that the floundering was over.

6

LILLIAN HELLMAN made her entrance into the world of celebrity—the world she would inhabit for the rest of her life—as the girlfriend of a famous man. Her independent achievements would come later, yet at a remarkably youthful age. However, she passed a number of her adult years in the company of such eminent figures as William Faulkner, James Thurber and S. J. Perelman not because of anything she had accomplished, but merely because she was the love interest of a man whose highly regarded books had won him entree into these select circles.

Such a tag-along position has its problems even for the legitimately married or the very beautiful. For Hellman, who was neither, her paramour status surely rankled and intensified her resolve to make something of whatever talent or ability she had. Being nothing more than "Hammett's girl" was an increasingly unacceptable epithet that could only be escaped by achievement of her own. She had always intended to become a writer eventually, but now, finding herself with a distasteful label, she had a stronger motive than ever before to make this ambition a reality. Acquaintance with Hammett's friends, powerful publishing figures as well as successful writers, made such a goal feasible.

The process was gradual and did not move Hellman to concerted action until she had been with Hammett for over two
years. In the early part of their relationship, she continued to
work on short stories while he tried to push to completion his
novel *The Thin Man*. Mostly their time was taken up with each
other—diligent partying and pub-crawling followed by weeks of
isolation with bouts of intense reading, both periods marked by
heavy drinking.

Neither Hammett nor Hellman had ever been enthusiastic
about Hollywood; because of that and because of a lingering
stickiness concerning Kober, they moved to New York, stayed in
fancy hotels, traveled to Florida in the winter and rented a beach
house close by New York for the summer. Living for months at a
time in a good Manhattan hotel was more economically feasible
in those Depression days than it would be later on. Hammett,
who never worried much about fiscal matters even when he had
been poor, now had money coming in and ample prospects for
more, but he still managed to run up bills he couldn't pay,
prompting sudden, furtive moves from first- to third-class estab-
lishments.

In New York they lived for a time at the Hotel Elysée on
East Fifty-fourth Street, then at the Biltmore. Nick and Nora
Charles, the hero and heroine of *The Thin Man*, also lived in
New York hotels, and Hammett drew on his life with Hellman in
New York for the novel's mood and ambience. For Hammett and
Hellman, a suite of one bedroom and a sitting room would be the
setting for days dedicated to desultory amusement: pre-breakfast
martinis, visitors announced and asked up whose names neither
he nor she could place, meals sent in from neighborhood restaurants, constant comings and goings—writers, actors, underworld
figures—more than five drop-ins at one time constituting a party
with the ordering up of additional food and drink, hurried *tête-
à-têtes* in the bedroom for whatever intrigue was at hand, anything from ejecting a drunken guest to cooling an over-ardent
Hammett fan. It was the kind of unpredictable turmoil that
amused Hammett and that he made amusing for everyone else
in *The Thin Man*.

Their pub crawls might range from Small's in Harlem to
midtown newspapermen's hangouts like Tony's, where James

Thurber once capped an argument with Hellman by throwing a glass at her. (When asked about this years later, Hellman laughed heartily and said, "Yes, Thurber was a vicious drunk.") During the years she was married to Kober, Hellman had started relying on alcohol to dilute the fecklessness of her "little woman" existence. By her own account, however, she didn't know the meaning of serious drinking until she took up with Hammett. She says that during this early period with him she became an alcoholic. If the term is taken to mean one who drinks too much, Hellman certainly qualified. But if the word signifies physiological and psychological addiction requiring in most cases strenuous therapy and lifelong abstinence in order to break, Hellman did not fit. Self-dramatization can be pejorative as well as flattering, to be sure, but Hellman's exaggeration of her liquor problem probably stemmed from the same impulse that made her drink heavily: Hammett-worship—and an almost pathetic, somewhat tomboyish eagerness to be admitted to his one-man club. Few would deny that Hammett was an alcoholic, but he too could voluntarily stop from time to time. Late in his life a doctor warned that continued drinking would kill him; while such an admonition has failed to discourage legions of drinkers (most of whom are now dead), it was enough to move Hammett, on his own, to quit for good.

Liquor accounted for a large portion of the bills from hotels in which Hammett and Hellman stayed, and on one occasion when Hammett ran out of money, they took themselves to the Pierre, hardly an economy move, but symptomatic of Hammett's cavalier belief that a bill-paying windfall would probably turn up. The change also meant starting out with a blank tab; when the Pierre dunned him for the $1,000 bill that he quickly ran up there, he snuck out wearing as much of his wardrobe as he could stuff himself into, his cheeks puffed out to alter his appearance.

He and Hellman then moved into the last resort of strapped but well-connected writers, the Hotel Sutton at 330 East Fifty-sixth Street. The Sutton was owned by relatives of Nathanael West's who employed him as the night manager. Being himself a writer down on his luck, "Pep" West was sympathetic to fellow writers in similar straits; he made a practice of providing them with housing gratis or at greatly reduced rates.

The Sutton was an odd place with odd guests, whose mail

West would open to pass the long nights and to find inspiration for the novel he was then writing, *Miss Lonelyhearts*. West's brother-in-law, S. J. Perelman, wrote, "The food was terrible and the furniture sordid." Single men were assigned one floor, single women another, and married couples a third. Billeted with the marrieds, Hellman and Hammett were assigned one of the modest hotel's fancier suites and settled in for a long stay.

It was in the fall of 1931, shortly after they arrived in Manhattan, that Hellman and Hammett became friendly with William Faulkner, who just at that time was stunned to find himself lionized by the city's literary establishment as a result of the critical impact of *Sanctuary*. Before the two men became acquainted, Hammett had read *Sanctuary* and pronounced Faulkner overrated; part of his sour reaction was exasperation that Faulkner could repeatedly produce writing of this quality while drinking, word had it, as heavily as Hammett. Both Hammett and Hellman, however, took immediately to the quiet, unassuming Southerner who was as quick to like them. Hammett revised his verdict on Faulkner's writing, even to the point of objecting heatedly when Faulkner said that *Sanctuary* was a potboiler he had written only to make money.

On several occasions Faulkner spoke to the press of his dislike of "literary circles" and told one reporter he "never associated with other writers." It was not the only instance of Faulkner's striking a pose. The fact is, he spent many long evenings with Hellman and Hammett—just the three of them sitting up all night talking and drinking. Faulkner was intrigued by Hammett, recognizing at once his unaffected honesty. He also identified with Hammett's roustabout background and especially envied his years as a Pinkerton agent. One area of potential discord was politics. Hammett was then beginning his long involvement with Marxism. Although his opinions were unformulated and unorthodox, they were sufficiently communistic to upset Faulkner, who abhorred any form of radicalism.

Their mutual admiration was strong enough to withstand this disagreement. The two men shared many opinions, particularly a disdain for the smart celebrity salons that would have prized them both. They were voracious readers, as was Hellman, whom Faulkner warmed to as a fellow Southerner, and with whom he enjoyed discussing what they had read. Hellman was particularly impressed with Faulkner's ability to talk with great erudition and no affectation about American and European literature. And of course both Hammett and Faulkner were devout drinkers. It was not unusual for Hellman to arise late in the morning, blinded by a hangover, echoes of a nightlong discussion of Dostoyevski reverberating in her head, to find Faulkner asleep on the living-room sofa. It would have made a nice literary touch for *The Thin Man.*

She did not take part in all of their escapades. Once they were having lunch at "21" with Bennett Cerf, who bragged that he was dining that evening at the Alfred Knopfs'; Serge Koussevitzky, Willa Cather and H. L. Mencken would be among the guests. Hammett, pointing out that he was a Knopf author, said that he and Faulkner would also like to attend the party. Somewhat nonplussed, Cerf said he would phone Blanche Knopf to get them invited and asked where he should pick them up. They said they were not planning on going anywhere; they would still be at the "21" table.

When Cerf returned that evening, they were indeed still there, far worse for an afternoon of steady drinking. Cerf tried to dissuade them from going to the Knopfs', falling back on such ploys as their lack of black tie. They remained determined to attend the party. The Knopfs, who were noted for their hospitality, were at first delighted to add these distinguished names to their lineup and greeted the two men warmly. As they became aware of the condition of their two new guests, they tried to handle matters with as much graciousness as cold terror permitted. Faulkner and Hammett, unsteady but controlled, behaved with stiff decorum until, after dinner, Hammett suddenly keeled over unconscious on the living-room floor. Faulkner attempted a rescue, but in the struggle, collapsed in a heap on top of Hammett. Several guests tugged at Faulkner, until finally he and Hammett were disentangled and ushered out.

Thirty years later, Hellman ran into Faulkner at a literary luncheon. Although she was bitter at his not having responded to a plea for help during Hammett's political difficulties in the McCarthy period, she greeted him cordially and was pleased when he reminisced warmly about their all-night conversations and referred to their time together in New York as one of the best in his life.

Faulkner made another exception to his social ban on writers as company: Nathanael West. Both men were avid hunters and so spent happy hours exchanging hunting stories. When in 1933 West published *Miss Lonelyhearts,* Faulkner was back in Mississippi, but Hammett was one of the "name" writers who publicly hailed West's book as an important new work. West would write only one more book before his tragic death in an automobile accident in 1940; *The Thin Man* was Hammett's last work. Of these three major talents, only Faulkner would fulfill the promise of his early career.

Not long after Hellman and Hammett went to live at the Sutton, West pooled his small capital with that of his brother-in-law, S. J. Perelman, to buy a house in Erwinna, Pennsylvania, a village on the Delaware River a few miles north of the artists' colony of New Hope. Hellman and Hammett spent weekends there with West and Sid and Laura Perelman, often in the company of other literary guests such as Edmund Wilson and Robert Coates, and neighbors such as Josephine Herbst and John Herrmann. But eventually financial pressure drove Hammett back to purposeful work; he eased up on the drinking and settled down to finish *The Thin Man.*

Financial troubles were no rarity in those early years of the Depression, certainly no reason to avoid seeing people in New York. Because of Hammett's rising star, he and Hellman were invited to all the important parties. Hammett had not yet given in to his reclusive impulses, and they attended most of them. While on their celebrity rounds, Hellman met two people who were to have a strong and lasting significance in her life: Herman Shumlin and Dorothy Parker. With her 1926 book of light verse, *Enough Rope,* Parker had established herself as one of the brighter literary lights around New York and, as book reviewer for *The New Yorker,* a powerful one. Although none of Parker's few works has earned a solid place in American literature, she became one of a small handful who symbolize the period's literary brilliance. Hellman was never quick to warm to others of her own sex, and throughout her life had among her close friends many men but few women. Parker, whom Hellman met at a party at William Rose Benét's, would be a major exception.

Parker is best remembered for her wit, particularly her one-line variations on clichés ("One more drink and I'd have been under the host"), which could devastate others, particularly those who had just left the room (one reason why Hammett never liked her). Albert Hackett remembers a fine example of the Parker lines that delighted the aggressive side of Hellman and so many others. After her husband's death, Parker was seen around Hollywood with a good-looking young actor. A friend remarked on the boy's attractive suntan. "Ah, yes," said Parker, "the hue of availability."

Parker was a small, dark-haired woman, given to such girlish grooming flourishes as bangs and bows on her shoes. She was soft-spoken, quick to create a confidential intimacy with anyone with whom she was conversing, and while sweetly demolishing with her razor tongue whomever offended her—and often fame or importance was sufficient provocation—she never lost what Margaret Case Harriman called "an overpowering air of dulcet femininity."

Parker was a brilliant woman who used her brilliance to give grief to fools and stuffed shirts. Hellman liked that. Parker also made Hellman laugh. In Parker's review column, she had praised Hammett's writing, which made her an ally and less frightening to Hellman, and a great deal more likable. For her part, Parker warmed to the wry young woman from New Orleans who paraded no artifice, who relished strong drink, who laughed at the right places and who had won the heart of the glamorous Sam Spade prototype, Dashiell Hammett. In her review of *The Maltese Falcon*, Parker confessed to having fallen in love with Spade.

Not long after their meeting, Parker went to Hollywood, and the friendship would not be ratified until Hellman herself returned to Hollywood as a famous playwright. At that reunion they became lifelong friends despite Hammett's antipathy to Parker, which increased until eventually her appearance would send him running. He was once asked why. Although Parker was as radical politically as Hammett, they would often find themselves on opposite sides of a position. Hammett said he didn't want to be around Parker because he couldn't argue with her. "She cries," he explained.

Herman Shumlin would become even more important in Hellman's life than Parker. She had known Shumlin slightly through Kober before she ran into him again at a party given in New York by the Ira Gershwins in 1933. Shumlin had won himself a reputation as one of Broadway's most promising directors with his first play, Vicki Baum's Grand Hotel—the play Hellman had urged Anne Nichols to produce. It opened in 1930 and ran for two seasons. By 1933 Shumlin was considered not only one of Broadway's best directors but also one of the most prestigious. His plays, in addition to their box-office success, were known for their seriousness and high quality.

Shumlin had been born in Atwood, Colorado, but had grown up in Newark, New Jersey. After trying several fields, he fell into theatrical press agentry and before long won the job of company manager for Jed Harris, then the top producer of plays in New York. (Company manager was the job producer Kermit Bloomgarden would later hold with Shumlin before he too graduated to producing.) When working for Harris, Shumlin had for a time shared an office with Harris's press agent, Arthur Kober, and remembers encountering, but not really meeting, Hellman when she once dropped by to see Kober. When they did meet, Shumlin was looking for a reader and asked Hellman to work for him.

Hellman was tired of the financial crises that seemed chronic with Hammett and jumped at the chance to bring in some money. The arrangement with Shumlin was casual and did not prevent her leaving abruptly with Hammett for two months in Florida or a summer of reading and fishing on Long Island if an unexpected royalty check showed up. Hellman respected Shumlin, thought she could learn from him and was happy to be doing something constructive.

A case could be made that, after Hammett, Herman Shumlin was the most important person in Hellman's early adulthood. He served as her theatrical mentor, would produce and direct five of her plays, and, for a time, was her lover. He was six years older than Hellman—tall, stern, in the habit of shaving his head every day. His temper was legendary and more than a match for Hellman's own. Once again, a chance meeting at a party would alter the direction of Hellman's life.

After returning to New York from Hollywood with Hammett, Hellman had resumed her friendship with Louis Kronenberger, who had been laid off from the Boni and Liveright staff as part of a hard-times cutback. They decided to write a play together and set earnestly to work on a comedy they called *Dear Queen*. The effort did not mean that Hellman was beginning to think of herself as a playwright; rather, she still saw herself as talented with words, but unsure of what to be talented about. In that day, when a $15,000 Broadway production could be a passport to a fat screenwriter's contract, Hellman's stab at playwriting was done more in the spirit of the many newspapermen, publicity flacks and copywriters who were using their free time to bang out plays.

Dear Queen was completed late in 1932 and was read by every producer in New York, but elicited no interest. Eventually both Hellman and Kronenberger agreed the piece was pretty bad and laughed about it. But at the time the lesson Hellman learned from their failure was the wrong one. She seems to have concluded that playwriting was not her milieu, but that some other form of humorous writing was.

Hammett cited as one aspect of Hellman he particularly liked that she was "full of ambition." He also knew what a procrastinator she was. In one letter he chided her for being so critical of the writing of a former girlfriend of his, pointing out that at least the other woman was producing *something*. With a highly successful writer goading her on and with the assurance of a sympathetic reading by top-level editors because of the friendships she enjoyed through Hammett, she set to work. Abandoning the sensitive "ladylike" short stories she had tried before—it is not hard to imagine Hammett's reaction to these—she attempted satire. She wrote two short humor pieces and submitted them to a small but prestigious literary journal, *The American Spectator*, which had been launched in 1932 by Theodore Dreiser, Ernest Boyd and George Jean Nathan. Both pieces were accepted.

The first appeared in September 1933 under the title "I Call Her Mama Now" and is the lament of a student in a progressive high school who is being pressured to be more modern, more liberated. The student, on the other hand, is tradition-bound and just wishes to be left alone. The school is trying to interest her in sex, French food and other delights young people are tradition-ally expected to find on their own. The girl prefers reading Ma-caulay ("I like inhibited writers"), which she keeps hidden inside a copy of *Venus in Furs*.

When she hears her mother is coming for a visit, she says, "I haven't seen Mama since 1930, though I hear that was the year she took up dogs and Jews and has them in on Sunday!" Her mother, who has published a volume of poems entitled *Chaos in Taos*, insists on being called by her first name and tries to engage her daughter in a frank woman-to-woman chat. The girl says she would rather go back to reading Spengler. In light of Hellman's later reputation as a communist sympathizer, one satiric jibe is noteworthy. Speaking of her fondness for Spengler the girl re-marks, "Of course, I realized full well, even then, that in the Marxist sense, he hadn't the proper historical balance, but then it's quite nice stuff." At the end of the story the girl declares her intention to marry Morton, a man who likes plain food and is "ashamed of sex, which is swell."

The second story, "Perberty in Los Angeles," which was pub-lished four months later, is a prolongation of the same joke: A clutch of freewheeling bohemian adults try to liven up a bookish teenager who prefers classic literature to their brave new world. In this piece, a precocious young woman who is enrolled in a Jesuit school in Tacoma receives a sudden visit from her mother, an Auntie Mame precursor, plus an aunt and uncle. The three have rushed to the girl the minute they realized she must be ap-proaching puberty; their mission is to help her "adjust." As be-fore, the girl simply wants to be left alone, in this case so she can return to work on her translation of "the beautiful, severe prose" of Xenophon.

Both stories are funny and erudite, and they achieve their modest point of laughing at the day's faddish liberation. But they are remarkably similar; the second is like another draft of the first. It is possible Hellman was contemplating a series of stories on this theme, even a book; it is also possible that she had reached the limits of her satiric range. But with these stories it appears that Hellman, when contemplating how to make her mark, had decided that her long suit was humor.

She would, however, soon abandon not only short stories but humor, which is all but absent from her first play, *The Children's Hour*, and cannot be said to have contributed in any way to her emergence as an important writer. Her later plays, while certainly not devoid of humor, were, with one lamentable exception, resolutely serious. And in the overall tally of her work, both plays and books, humor occupies a minor place. In fact, her entire public persona—through interviews, lectures and articles as well as the major works—was that of a dead-serious, issue-oriented, let's-skip-the-frivolity woman, an image at considerable variance with the Hellman known to her friends. In private she was a woman who loved to laugh, who adored a joke and who took pride in her ability to make others laugh.

Hellman seemed reluctant to show this aspect of her personality to the public. In the early days of her celebrity, she may very well have thought displaying a light side would undermine her ambition to be taken seriously as a writer. When her confidence was bolstered by a number of serious successes, she may have found herself stuck with the grim-jawed demeanor that interviewers and the public had come to expect. In 1932 and 1933, however, Hellman sought recognition as a humorist. Having her efforts published in *The American Spectator* was in itself considerable endorsement, but there is no evidence that the review's readers or other editors clamored for more of the same from her—or that any publisher encouraged her to pursue this vein in a larger work. On the contrary, she was unable to sell the other stories she wrote in a light, satiric style.

It is ironic that Hellman, who would surpass by far Arthur Kober's success as a writer, made her debut in the world of professional writing using a form in which he would have great success and which she quickly abandoned. Four years later *The New Yorker* launched Kober's "Bella from the Bronx" stories, which ran for several years, were widely popular and were eventually published in book form. In 1937, Kober would also have a hit comedy on Broadway, *Having Wonderful Time*.

Thus, as her desire to make her mark as a writer continued to build, Hellman came to admit that humor and satire were not to be her vehicle. In 1933, nearing thirty, her life still had little direction. She and Kober had quietly obtained a divorce, and while her bond with Hammett was strengthening, marriage seemed an unlikely prospect. Both had misgivings about such a step, although they discussed it from time to time but never with enough concerted determination to bring it about. The play with Louis Kronenberger had come to nothing and had been an indulgence—like many collaborations, a writing project for people who dread writing. She now disliked her reading job for Shumlin. Her joyride as "Hammett's girl" was starting to pall. She had intelligence, talent and, above all, ambition, and she was growing sick of her own procrastinations. The time had come to stop fooling around.

7

IN AN INTERVIEW a quarter of a century after writing *The Children's Hour*, Hellman was unable to remember when the notion of becoming a playwright came over her, or indeed, if it ever had. The best she could recall was a strong admiration for the plays of Sidney Howard, who wrote *They Knew What They Wanted* and later the screenplay for *Gone With the Wind*. In another interview, also many years later, Hellman said she wrote a play for her first effort because "she didn't know anything else." Since she had been writing short stories for ten years, it is more likely that she arrived at playwriting not from an ignorance of other forms, but from frustration with them. She might also have pointed to a number of items on her pre-1934 resume that could have steered her toward writing for the theater: her work as a theatrical press agent, play reading for Anne Nichols and other producers, reading for MGM and, of course, reading for Shumlin. In addition, the plot that came to her—or, to be more precise, that was given to her by Hammett—may have had a lot to do with the choice of medium.

As Hammett was finishing *The Thin Man* in the spring of 1933, he cast about for a new idea and came across a collection of noteworthy British court cases in a book titled *Bad Companions* by an English writer named William Roughead. Hammett was particularly struck by one chapter, "Closed Doors, or The Great Drumsheugh Case." It concerned two headmistresses of a girls' school in Scotland who were accused by a student of having a lesbian relationship; the scandal forced the school to close. When the headmistresses sued for libel, the case became public. Hammett thought the story had the dramatic intensity for a good play and considered writing it himself. He then decided it would make a better project for Lilly. She would write it and he would coach from the sidelines. She was frantic to get working and this seemed ideal for her; the subject matter, with its calumny and monstrous injustice, could harness the anger and the contempt for self-righteousness that was so strong in Hellman's makeup.

There was another aspect to this particular story that would attract Hellman. Many years later, in her memoirs, she would reveal a fascination with malice, the human capacity to cause hurt to others for little or no reason. In her reminiscences about her childhood she alludes several times to the appearance of this quality in herself and in others. When she reports to her nurse that she has seen her father with another woman, Sophronia angrily tells her not to go through life making trouble for people. A striking story in the memoirs, about the lesbian Mrs. Smith, is a rumination on gratuitous malice. A central theme of Hellman's last work, the novella *Maybe,* is the malice lurking behind so many mysteries. The destructive effects of malice and unprovoked evil are very much the theme of "The Great Drumsheugh Case." Further, the malice in the case was implemented by a lie; the story hangs on a lie. With little provocation, the girl tells a deliberate, calculated falsehood that she imagines will destroy the lives of the headmistresses. In the work of both Hammett and Hellman there is a fascination with lies and the devastation they can cause.

In her choice of subject matter Hellman was attracted to a theme that had nothing whatever to do with the issues that were of increasing concern to liberals in those Depression years—the failure and corruption of capitalism, war profiteering, pacifism, economic and social injustices. The story concerned injustice, but of the sort that might occur in any society where an individual or a group of individuals have the power to destroy the lives and reputations of others.

Lesbianism was, of course, a social issue, and credit is often given Hellman for undertaking such a daring theme, particularly for her first play, braving barriers and forcing Broadway audiences to address an important but taboo subject. But she was not, in that regard, a pioneer; eight years earlier New York had seen a play about lesbianism, *The Captive,* which was a translation of a French success, *La Prisonnière,* by Edouard Bourdet. Despite good reviews, including a rave from Brooks Atkinson in *The New York Times,* the police closed down the play and arrested the leading ladies. As the scandal had been well covered in the newspapers, Hellman and Hammett were surely aware of *The Captive's* fate, but were undaunted by it. The accusation of active lesbianism in her story was, after all, untrue. In addition, the shocking theme could bring attention to an unknown playwright. Despite this sound justification, Hellman would later use her choice of such controversial subject matter as proof of her indifference to the box office when writing a play.

As the publication of *The Thin Man* approached, it was more and more apparent that the book would be a major success. Even before the release date of January 1934, Metro-Goldwyn-Mayer bought the film rights for $21,000, a substantial price for those Depression days; for Hammett and Hellman it was a major windfall. The book appeared in a condensed, cleaned-up form in the December 1933 issue of *Redbook.* The following month it was published in hardcover by Alfred Knopf and was an immediate hit, selling twenty thousand copies in the first three weeks. Hammett's financial woes appeared to be over.

Readers were fascinated by the fast-moving, intriguing plot, but equally fascinated by the glamorous and likable Nick and Nora Charles. There had never been a fictional couple like them, with their hard-boiled yet loving relationship, a thirst for fun and adventure (which seemed to drop constantly into their laps), a casual approach toward sex (with the unspoken subtext that they had a lot of it), and an offhand sophistication about everything, including danger. They had looks, money, brains and guts.

Hammett told Hellman and others that she had been his

model for Nora. Hellman later admitted with good-humored modesty that he subsequently told her he had also used her as the model for the book's villainess, Mimi Wynant, as well as the villainess's irritatingly dizzy daughter, Dorothy. The Nora comparison is puzzling, however. Nora was insatiably curious, loved excitement, had remarkable courage and was merrily unflappable whether in a barroom brawl or a shoot-out in her own bedroom. All of that might be Hellman. On the other hand, Nora was rich, a knockout beauty, chronically cheerful, more than a little daffy and flightily feminine. Hammett was clearly adding his own ingredients.

Regardless of how much Hellman there is in Nora, it is doubtful if, before or since *The Thin Man*, marriage has been presented so appealingly. Hellman later remarked on the rarity in fiction of portrayals of a husband and wife who like each other and enjoy each other's company, perhaps basking in the implicit tribute to her union to Hammett. It is clear, however, that the portrayal was prettified from the prototype to at least the same degree that Nora was. There is also a small irony in that the models for this legendary marriage, a glowing testimonial to the institution itself, should be the unmarried Hellman and Hammett.

The public grew curious about the handsome, tall and *thin* author who was pictured on the jacket of the book, looking mysterious and debonair, leaning rakishly on a cane, the other hand casually in the pocket of his natty tweed jacket, perhaps caressing a gun. The title, of course, refers to the villain, Clyde Wynant, not to Nick Charles, who was so obviously Hammett that it was rarely discussed.

In the early spring of 1934 Hellman and Hammett went back to their retreat in Homestead, Florida, to fish and write. He was working on a new book and she was working on *The Children's Hour*. (The finished play has a reference to "Homestead," Massachusetts, which is the first of many autobiographical allusions in Hellman's plays.) On the West Coast, meanwhile, MGM was rushing to produce a film of *The Thin Man*. A young husband-and-wife screenwriting team, Albert Hackett and Frances Goodrich, turned out a script in three weeks. William Powell and Myrna Loy were cast as Nick and Nora. The director, W. S.

Van Dyke, shot the film in eighteen days. As expected, it caused a sensation when it was released, and a sequel was planned immediately. When Hammett returned to New York in June, having just turned forty (Hellman was twenty-nine), he was more of a celebrity than ever. There would be five sequels to the film; the Hacketts, who would become close friends of Hellman and Hammett's, wrote two of them.

That summer Hellman and Hammett rented a beach house on Tavern Island in Long Island Sound off Norwalk, Connecticut, for more fishing, writing and, for Hellman, reading plays for Herman Shumlin while she worked on her own. The film *Julia*, made from one of Hellman's *Pentimento* reminiscences, opens in this beach house, with Hellman at work on *The Children's Hour* and Hammett accurately depicted as her mentor and demanding editor. While Hellman always emphasized the important help Hammett had given her on her first play—indeed she dedicated it to him "with thanks"—she also wrote much later in the story "Julia" that he was drinking so heavily while she was writing it that she found it necessary to get away from him. So he gave her the money to go to Europe for two and a half months.

Years later Hellman told a Harvard seminar in playwriting that in writing her first play she had been most fortunate to have Hammett give her the story. Starting with a ready-made plot, she said, freed her to concentrate her energies on dialogue, character development, pacing of scenes and all the other elements of a strong play. It was a more honest appraisal than that of the Hellman enthusiasts who belittle the Roughead book's contribution, apparently from fear that acknowledgment will diminish Hellman's achievement.

Whatever other virtues *The Children's Hour* may possess, it is a powerful and gripping story, as was "The Great Drumsheugh Case." Many plot elements are true of both: the two women started the school, they have invested all their assets in it, and are making a success of it; an aunt of one, a former actress, teaches at the school; the women are accused by a student of having sexual relations with each other; the girl tells her grandmother, a woman of sufficient influence to cause all the students to be withdrawn from the school within two days; the headmistresses sue for libel; testimony is given that the two women were seen embracing through a keyhole; at the trial, the door is shown to have no keyhole; even with such impeached testimony, the libel action fails; the school never reopens. All of this is true of both the play and the actual case.

There are, however, important differences. In Hellman's version, she gives one of the women a fiancé, and to make plausible young girls' knowing about adult lesbianism, the aunt, Mrs. Mortar, is overheard by some of the students alluding to it. Hellman gives a motive to the student, Mary Tilford, who makes the trouble: she feels picked on and disliked by the two teachers. To reinforce Mary's accusation, Hellman introduces a blackmailing hold that Mary has over another student, Rosalie, so that the girl falsely corroborates Mary's slander.

Perhaps the biggest difference between the drama and the actual tale (aside from moving it from the early nineteenth century to the present) is the suicide of one of the teachers at the play's end and the almost immediate arrival of the grandmother, who, having learned her granddaughter was lying, seeks to atone for her injustice. While the real grandmother never changed her attitude, the Scottish teachers finally succeeded in having the verdict overturned but many years later—too late to salvage their lives.

In an early draft Hellman introduced a fictional character, the judge who would try the libel case. Later deciding the character added little and cluttered the action, she eliminated him. Hellman also gives the story a surprise twist by having one of the teachers, Martha, admit that there is truth in the accusation, that she does harbor erotic feelings toward her friend Karen. The apparent reversal annoyed some critics, who felt Hellman, in Martha's confession speech, was trying to have it both ways: a play about two heterosexual women wrongly accused of lesbianism, and the altogether different story of a lesbian persecuted by a cruel and unjust society.

Hellman, who would often be accused of writing melodrama, was in this instance being penalized for subtlety. She goes to substantial pains to show that Martha is confessing to something about herself that she has only just then realized. The child's unfounded accusation has made her confront an aspect of her own nature that she has until that moment managed to suppress. Martha's unconscious attraction to Karen may also have prompted behavior on her part that was noticed by the students (as it appears to have been by the aunt, Mrs. Mortar), but that she herself did not understand. Hellman makes this intention clear in the play's text when Martha says, "I never knew it until all this happened." In addition, Hellman, in her notes for the play, describes Martha as "an unconscious lesbian." She later elaborated on the same idea by ruminating that Martha, if it hadn't been for the little girl's accusation, would have lived out her life unaware of her sexual nature.

To the Roughead outline Hellman also adds vivid characters that establish with remarkable speed and economy the qualities she wants us to recognize. Before we are very far into the first act, we know that Karen and Martha are intelligent, decent young women who are working hard to establish a business they believe in. They have humor, warmth, strength and patience. We like them and wish them well. We know, too, that Mrs. Mortar is a troublemaking, self-pitying hanger-on, delicately poised between being a laughable nuisance and a serious menace. Mary Tilford is pure menace. With great inventiveness, Hellman makes us acknowledge little Mary as a villain of breathtaking nastiness; she is drawn with originality and imagination, yet is at all times believable.

Despite her close adherence to an actual situation, Hellman, while writing *The Children's Hour,* was contemplating the material in the broadest artistic terms. In her notes she compares the troublemaking lie of Mary with that of Shakespeare's Iago, making the distinction that, while Iago had nothing to gain by his treachery, Mary did. Hellman appears to be pulling rank in her villain's nastiness when she terms Iago's actions "unconscious wrongdoing" as opposed to Mary's "perfect and complete villainy."

When in an interview Hellman was asked where the character of Mary had come from, she replied "from my head." Almost immediately a wag commented, "She should have said, 'from her Roughead.'" Funny as the remark was, it was unfair. The accusing schoolgirl in Roughead's text comes across with little clarity. Hellman's Mary is sharply etched; her style, her methods and her evil are portrayed vividly and precisely. She is as much a "creation" as any character in fiction.

In fact, there is an enormous difference between the real "Mary" and Hellman's character—one that is oddly not noted by the Hellman scholars who consulted the Roughead text. The girl in "The Drumsheugh Case" was a mulatto, an illegitimate daughter of the aristocratic old woman's deceased son. Roughead makes clear that the girl, whom he refers to as "black," felt odd and unwanted at the Scottish boarding school and hints that those feelings prompted her ruinous lie.

The real Mary's race might have provided a strong plot twist and possible motivation that would have translated interestingly to the period in which Hellman moved the action, a period when sexual deviance and racial antagonisms were problems looming in the public consciousness. But she gives little motive other than pure malice to Mary. She may have felt a black student in a New England boarding school would be hard to believe in 1934. Or she may have been afraid of overloading the plot. But it is most likely she changed the girl to white from a fear that a specific resentment would weaken Mary as a symbol of pristine evil.

The real events of "The Drumsheugh Case" occurred in 1810, another fact rarely noted, and it is hard to imagine what attitudes toward lesbianism might have been at that time, when, a half century later, Queen Victoria refused to believe such a practice could exist. To take a story so rooted in sexual morality and move it ahead more than a hundred years was, on the part of Hellman (and probably Hammett), an impressive feat of the imagination.

It is not clear when Hellman's affair with Herman Shumlin began. They had started out as social acquaintances, so were never on a formal employer-employee basis. Whether or not romance had already entered the friendship, they had a casual, familiar way with each other in the summer of 1934 when Hellman placed on his desk the unsigned script of *The Children's Hour* with a note saying that in the time she had been reading for him this was the best play she had come across and the most worth producing. After reading the first act Shumlin told her he agreed. When he had completed it, he said he would produce it.

A friend remarked to Hellman years later how fortunate she was to have been working for an important producer when she wrote her first play and was seeking to get it put on. "If Herman hadn't done *The Children's Hour*," Hellman snapped, "don't you think someone else would have?"

Shumlin was delighted to learn who the author was. He set out immediately to cast the play and put it into rehearsal. It was an anxious and exciting time in Hellman's life. Hammett, who had nursed her through the writing (she claimed fourteen re-writes), was proud and delighted; but then he abruptly left for California on October 26, as the play went into rehearsal. He had accepted an offer from MGM to write the script for a *Thin Man* sequel.

It is unlikely that Hammett felt himself an unwanted acces-sory to any Hellman-Shumlin romance at this point; he wrote some of his most loving and bereft messages to her during his absence, with no hint that he had been banished. Although 1934 had been one of his top earning years—the princely sum of $80,000 in the depth of the Depression—he was still not in a posi-tion to turn down the $2,000 a week MGM was offering. On the other hand, the *Thin Man* producer, Hunt Stromberg, could surely have waited a month to allow Hammett to stay in New York until the opening of *The Children's Hour*.

Given Hammett's propensity for cryptic nobility, he prob-ably went off to Hollywood when he did in order to give Lilly a clear field with the success he was sure she would have—and possibly to lessen the suspicion that he had anything to do with it. In later years, Hammett would show an avid interest in the production of Hellman's plays, regularly attending rehearsals, joining in on discussions with the actors, openly offering advice on every aspect. For her first foray into the professional theater, however, he took himself three thousand miles away.

If Herman Shumlin had any doubt that he had taken on a controversial theme, he was brought up short by the number of actresses who turned down the roles of Karen and Martha. It seemed that none of New York's leading ladies wanted to end up in a paddy wagon like Helen Mencken and the cast of *The Captive*. Shumlin finally cast Anne Revere as Martha, Katherine

Emery as Karen and Aline McDermott as Mrs. Mortar. In the pivotal part of Mary Tilford he cast Florence McGee, who was twenty-four but was convincing playing a fourteen-year-old. Aline Bernstein, the distinguished set designer, was recovering from a nervous collapse over her failed love affair with Thomas Wolfe. Her friend Shumlin had persuaded her to design the sets for *The Children's Hour* as recuperative therapy. This blue-chip production cost Shumlin $10,000.

Shumlin later said that between his first reading of *The Children's Hour* and the end of rehearsals, not more than a dozen lines were changed. The play that opened in New York was essentially the play Hellman presented to him. The one large disagreement between author and director concerned the title, which alluded to the Longfellow poem. Hellman loved the title, felt its heavy irony would be recognized by all. Shumlin hated it and was convinced people would be misled into thinking the play was for children. Since the work was later considered by certain authorities as too racy for adults, such a misconception was serious. Hammett liked the title as much as Hellman, although he had often been criticized for his wretched taste in titles—by, among others, Alfred Knopf (who disliked the titles of both *The Glass Key* and *The Dain Curse*) and Dorothy Parker (who came up with *The Little Foxes* as the title for Hellman's third play).

Pressure to make changes is a constant in playwriting. The producer, the director, the actors, the set designer—all continually trip over aspects of the script which they fervently believe render their jobs impossible. The excitement of their own creativity has produced a momentum they now find stopped short by an obstacle, these particular words, that only the playwright can remove. The momentum is turned full force on the playwright. But Hellman learned early to weigh each request for change on its merits, then accede or refuse on that basis only, not on the basis of the eminence of the director, the power of the producer or the volume of the star's tantrum. She considered Shumlin's impassioned arguments, then refused to change the title.

Eugenia Rawls, a young would-be actress, had just arrived in New York and was making the rounds of directors, attempting to start what would turn out to be a distinguished acting career. Still in her teens, she felt she would be ideal for one of the students in the new Herman Shumlin play. She went to his office and was told by an uninterested secretary to leave her name and number. On the way out she ran into Adrienne Morrison, an agent and the mother of Joan and Constance Bennett. Hearing of her quick dismissal from the Shumlin office, Morrison told Rawls to march right back—she was perfect for one of the students—and to insist on seeing Shumlin.

Rawls went back to the office, found the secretary away from her desk, and slipped into Shumlin's private office. At the sight of a young girl in front of his desk stammering something about playing one of the students, Shumlin released his famous temper and dressed her down for pushing her way past his secretary. Rawls's response was to burst into tears and flee. A few days later she received a call from the Shumlin office telling her she had been given the part of Peggy. "You haunted me for days," Shumlin told her later. "I couldn't figure out what I'd done to make you cry."

Eugenia Rawls has sharp recollections of *The Children's Hour.* "I'll never forget the tension and excitement of those rehearsals. We all knew it was going to be something special. None of us girls knew what the play was really about, except maybe Florence, who was married. I did not get to know Hellman too well. To all of us playing the students, she seemed so much older. Of course she wasn't. It was partly that we were playing children and partly that we were in awe of her. I remember her as a very quiet and reserved presence sitting in the theater at every rehearsal."

Once while rehearsing a scene in which Mary twists Peggy's arm, Hellman jumped up and said to Shumlin, "She's hurting that child."

"No, Lillian," he replied, "Eugenia is just *acting* pain."

"Miss Hellman was right," Rawls said years later. "It took weeks of treatment before my arm was all right."

Lee Shubert, who owned the Maxine Elliott Theater in which the play was to open, saw Hellman as an entirely different presence. In her memoirs, she tells how he came up to her during a rehearsal, demanded that she remove her dirty shoes from his chair and pushed her leg which was propped on the seat in front of her. Sharp words were exchanged, then Shubert went to Shumlin to ask the identity of "that girl."

"That girl, as you call her," Shumlin said, "is the author of the play."

Shubert still saw Hellman as a source of trouble. He later told her, "This play could land us all in jail."

When *The Children's Hour* opened on November 20, 1934, it was, from every standpoint, a triumph. The first-night audience was wildly enthusiastic, the police stayed away, and the critics rushed out to write excited praise. Recalling her first opening night almost forty years later, Hellman wrote that she was only dimly aware of her remarkable achievement and was wistful about not having comprehended "all the excited noise that comes only when the author is unknown and will never come again in quite so generous a fashion."

The critical approval for *The Children's Hour* was lavish. Brooks Atkinson in *The New York Times* led the praise, complaining only of the ending, which, he said, should have occurred fifteen minutes earlier (before the suicide of Martha). But he concluded that the play was "one of the most straightforward, driving dramas of the season, distinguished chiefly for its characterization of little Mary." Robert Benchley, writing in *The New Yorker*, picked up the theme of the overlong last act and said "the play has too many endings" but moved quickly into effusive approval, calling it "the season's dramatic high-water mark," and "finely and bravely written." (In her alcoholic haze on opening night, Hellman remembers Benchley pressing her arm and nodding affirmatively as he left the theater.)

Joseph Wood Krutch, writing in *The Nation*, also had reservations about the last act but called *The Children's Hour* the best play of recent seasons, adding that it was "unusually well written." There were many unqualified raves, the few cavils appearing more as demonstrations of critical caution than a lack of overall approbation. Clearly the consensus was that *The Children's Hour* was an excellent play and Hellman an excellent playwright.

George Jean Nathan in his monthly *Vanity Fair* column was as enthusiastic as the others. While he agreed that the last act contained a few melodramatic actions too many, he made an interesting comment to the effect that the critic must pounce on such flaws, but the playwright, to make plays succeed on the stage, must write them. "So we come," Nathan wrote, "once again to the reluctant conclusion and admission that the theater must woefully forgo fact and truth to make good plays better than they are and to satisfy even intelligent audiences."

Nathan may or may not have succeeded in detecting a fundamental incompatibility between successful theater and unblemished art, but he certainly was the only one to see two sides to the problem that would persist between Hellman and the critics throughout her long and highly successful playwriting career: her use of melodramatic devices.

Just about the only disparagement for Hellman's play came from Noël Coward. Skewering American puritanism rather than the play itself, he asked, "What's all the fuss about?" But it would take more than a quip—or quibbles about the last act—to diminish Hellman's brilliant victory. The response from theater professionals as well as the lines at the box office left no doubt that Hellman, with this one piece of work, had shed her persona as a celebrated writer's girlfriend and fringe contributor to literary journals and had leaped to the forefront of American dramatists.

By her own admission, Hellman spent her first opening night drinking heavily, and the day after, nursing a hangover. A few days later, after a number of pleasant congratulatory talks with Hammett in California, she suddenly remembered her opening-night call to him when a woman claiming to be his secretary had answered the phone. Belatedly realizing that it had been 3 A.M. in California at the time and that Hammett had no secretary, Hellman raced to the airport in a fury, boarded a plane for Los Angeles, went to Hammett's rented house in Pacific Palisades, smashed the basement soda fountain and took the next plane back to New York.

Considering 1934 flight schedules from coast to coast and the time required for the trip, her story is hard enough to believe. Adding mystery is the fact that Hammett *did* have a secretary at the time, a young woman named Mildred Lewis, who had been hired by his studio as an inducement to him to work. Because of Hammett's erratic life (and because he probably *was* sleeping with her), Lewis often stayed overnight. But it was not like Hammett to keep secrets from Hellman, even if he had had a reason.

If he had wanted to hide the secretary, he would not have allowed her to answer the phone—certainly not at three o'clock in the morning. As for Hellman's arrival at the house, Hammett had two black housemen, a homosexual couple, Jones and Winfield, who might have at least called Hammett when the demolition began.

Whatever the truth of the story, which was written twelve years after Hammett's death and almost forty years after it allegedly happened, it was more of a spasm of jealous anger at all the outrages and betrayals Hellman had been subjected to during their relationship, a wish-fulfillment fantasy made up of bits and pieces of jealous outbursts that had actually occurred. If she was guilty of melodrama in her plays, it would become a Hellman mechanism in her memoirs to distill a diffuse and unsatisfactory reality into a deft literary concentrate.

In an early interview Hellman snapped at a fawning writer for referring to her as one of the country's leading female playwrights. "I am a *playwright*," she said. "You wouldn't refer to Eugene O'Neill as one of America's foremost *male* playwrights." Hellman, who did not view the world in feminist terms, was speaking not so much from ideology as from her own sense of logic. The classifier seemed superfluous and, considering the level of some celebrated male playwrights of the day, an inappropriate condescension.

A few years later, a critic, commenting generally on the Broadway landscape, remarked how odd it was that the most masculine playwright on the scene was a woman, Hellman. In its way, his thinking would probably have been equally offensive to Hellman, who was perfectly happy to be a woman, still happier to have succeeded where many men of great talent had failed: to write a serious play that was enthusiastically received by both the critics and the public.

Still, the interviewer's remark revealed a state of mind as prevalent in the theater as it was in the rest of the world at the time of Hellman's emergence: women simply did not write serious plays. In light of that attitude, it was remarkable that very little mention was made of Hellman's gender in the reviews and other press comment about *The Children's Hour*. It was also remarkable considering that males dominated playwriting to an even greater degree than other forms of writing. English literature in the nineteenth and early twentieth centuries had many distinguished female novelists—Jane Austen, the Brontës, George Eliot, Edith Wharton—but no women playwrights of comparable importance. The reason was undoubtedly the moral stigma connected with the theater in both England and America. No "respectable" woman could become an actress. And for a woman to have the intellect and education to write a good play meant that she probably came from a social echelon where work in the theater was impermissible.

The prohibition was not only against working in the theater. Rachel Crothers, one of the few American women to make a mark as a playwright,* said that as a young woman she voluntarily forbade herself going to the theater because her minister had said it was the seat of evil. In her essay on American women playwrights, Judith Barlow makes the interesting additional point that the profession of playwriting involves not just the solitary act of writing, but the collaboration involved in getting a play onto the stage. A novel can be written and revised from the home; what collaboration is needed can be accomplished through correspondence. The playwright must leave the house for casting, rehearsals and meetings with directors. For many housebound women that would not be possible.

It seems odd to consider such mundane problems when discussing the creation of works of art. But moral strictures against women working outside the home—even in the theater—had relaxed by the time Hellman appeared. The early 1930s saw a number of successful women playwrights: Vicki Baum, Zoë Akins and, later, Clare Boothe Luce. All these women, however, wrote light comedies or romances. None undertook the tough, serious themes that, except for Hellman, were relinquished to men.

Hellman and Shumlin's relief that *The Children's Hour* had opened without controversy was premature. The first indication that not everyone in America was ready for candor about lesbianism came in the spring of 1935 when the members of the Pulitzer

* Other women who had written successful plays were Anna Cora Mowatt, Susan Glaspell, Zona Gale and Sophie Treadwell.

Prize Committee, in awarding their prize for the best drama of the 1934–35 season, passed it over. The prize went instead to *The Old Maid*, which, coincidentally, was also by a woman, Zoë Akins. The theater world was incensed. A few knowledgeable people felt the prize should have gone to Clifford Odets's *Awake and Sing;* others preferred Robert Sherwood's *The Petrified Forest;* but most observers, and particularly the theatrical press, had expected *The Children's Hour* to win.

Rumors circulated that one of the judges, the Reverend William Lyon Phelps, had refused to see Hellman's play. The Pulitzer committee had also provided its denigrators with additional ammunition: since *The Old Maid* was based on an Edith Wharton short story, the committee had violated its own rule against considering any but *original* stage works. Few people doubted that *The Children's Hour* had lost for one reason: its subject matter.

The drama critics of the major New York newspapers, indignant over the injustice to Hellman's play and to the implication of artistic censorship, banded together to form the Drama Critics Circle with the primary purpose of presenting its own annual prize for drama. Members of the circle made no secret that their motive was to protest the outdated standards of the Pulitzer judges and to establish awards based on more enlightened criteria.

Throughout the furor which went on in the newspapers for weeks, Hellman maintained a discreet silence. The episode would be the first, but by no means the last, example of her talent for landing in the center of controversy, in this case by no action other than writing her play. Sometimes she would provoke the controversy, other times simply abet it, but on several occasions the result, as in the formation of the Drama Critics Circle, was a lasting change.

In March 1935, Shumlin's plans to open a London production of *The Children's Hour* were stymied when the Lord Chamberlain, Earl Cromer, forbade the play's presentation "because of its theme." No one connected with the ban had seen the play; the decision was based on a reading of the text. Flamboyantly, Shumlin offered to fly his company to London for one performance for the Lord Chamberlain; the offer was declined. The play eventually circumvented the British ban by opening to critical acclaim at a private London theater "club" which was, and remained for many years, the standard ruse to evade censorship difficulties in England. With a logic Lewis Carroll would have admired, the English had figured out a way to have censorship and censored plays as well.

There was more in store for *The Children's Hour*. Toward the end of 1935, with the play still running to full houses in New York, Shumlin planned a national company that would, naturally, include Boston on its tour. After the Boston censor traveled to New York to see the play, his report back to the mayor of that city resulted in the play's being awarded the epithet so coveted by the publishers of trash novels: Banned in Boston. The considerable newspaper publicity from the ban spurred the box office in New York and the other cities of the tour, but it was in the natures of both Hellman and Shumlin to fight such bigotry, particularly since Shumlin believed and said many times the play was "so highly moral."

Shumlin, innocent of Massachusetts politics, tried to sneak past the mayor's injunction by booking the play into a suburban Boston theater. When that scheme failed, he took the issue to court and sued the city of Boston for $250,000, but this and other legal efforts eventually failed as well. Boston had to wait a quarter of a century for the Audrey Hepburn-Shirley MacLaine film before finding out what Mary Tilford had whispered to her grandmother.

Shumlin ran into more censorship trouble in Chicago, which was not prepared to take second place to Boston in forbidding slurs on American womanhood. Both Hellman and Shumlin relished an incident that occurred at the special performance set up for the Chicago censor. The censor, who was a woman, had brought with her a woman friend, and the two sat silent and expressionless until the scene toward the end in which Martha admits her love for Karen. The censor turned to whisper to her friend. Hellman and Shumlin, frantic for her reaction, leaned forward to hear the comment.

"I really like that suit she's wearing," the censor said.

Nevertheless, the play was banned in Chicago. But by now Shumlin had lost his zest for battle and the ban stood unchallenged.

In the chorus of kudos for *The Children's Hour*, after its original Broadway opening, a sour note had been struck by the eminent critic John Mason Brown. In a follow-up column to his laudatory *New York Post* review, Brown discussed a letter he received from a reader pointing out that "The Great Drumsheugh Case" in William Roughead's *Bad Companions* was the source for the play; in an accusatory tone, Brown reprimanded Hellman for not having mentioned it.

It is one of several ironies surrounding this contretemps that not only *had* Hellman mentioned it, she also had done so to an interviewer from Brown's own paper. The piece in which Hellman discussed the Roughead book as her inspiration appeared in the *Post* on November 23, three days after the opening but three days *before* Brown accused her of deceptively withholding the information.

It is true that nowhere in the play's program was there any indication of a source beyond the imagination of Lillian Hellman. While such acknowledgments are customary, they are not mandatory unless, of course, copyrights and contractual agreements are involved. That Hellman, in one of her first interviews, volunteered her source would seem to indicate she had no intention of passing the work off as totally original.

The flap was a small one, although it would continue to be mentioned by writers about Hellman off and on for the next fifty years. With her life over, however, it provides an irony of stunning symmetry. Hellman would begin her career as a public figure with the accusation that she had presented fact as fiction, and she would exit from it with the opposite accusation—that she presented fiction as fact.

8

A FEW PROMINENT writers in the thirties turned down the financial temptations of Hollywood—James T. Farrell, Josephine Herbst, for example—but they were a tiny band of holdouts compared to the platoons that trooped off into the Southern California sunset. Indeed, Hellman had been there, and from her low echelon and high ambition, watched them arrive with more than a little contempt. Now she was to be one of the arrivals. Three years earlier, she had quit her $50-a-week reader's job at MGM. Within a few months of the opening of *The Children's Hour*, she had accepted an offer from Samuel Goldwyn, whose Samuel Goldwyn Productions had been making films independently since 1922, to write screenplays for him at a salary of $2,500 a week. Even for Hollywood it was a newsworthy figure in that Depression year when only 10 percent of all screenwriters made over $10,000 a year.

Early in 1935 Hellman stepped off a plane at the Los Angeles airport, posed at the bottom of the steps for a newspaper photographer—fedora-style hat pulled over one eyebrow, clutching a new fur coat—and feeling uneasy about her fresh status as a celebrated New York writer, but not at all uneasy about her ability to handle Hollywood.

If a writer was of a mind to grab a share of the Hollywood riches, his or her integrity was in less jeopardy working for Sam Goldwyn than for almost any other producer. Despite Goldwyn's immortality through his inspired malapropisms (years after producing the distinguished film of Hellman's greatest play he would refer to it as *The Three Little Foxes*), he was a serious producer, determined to make films of the highest quality. To assure that the public thought of his films as *Goldwyn's,* he downplayed his directors in interviews and advertising, but that was a public-relations ploy. In artistic disputes, he often yielded to them. In fact, he saw his role as the writer and director's all-important go-between. Hellman was aware of Goldwyn's solid reputation and she did not share the snobbish beliefs of many of her fellow writers from the East that quality in films was precluded by the men running Hollywood, if not by the medium itself.

Underpinning Goldwyn's strategy for making distinguished pictures was his belief that the caliber of the writing was of paramount importance, a still somewhat revolutionary idea in an industry that considered electronically transmitted dialogue, that is, talking, a mere enhancement of the primary ingredient of films: action. While this belief never died out with some producers, in 1935 only a few gave a film's words the importance that Sam Goldwyn did. Even before the arrival of sound in motion pictures, Goldwyn was one of the first producers to seek writers of established literary reputations to script his films. In 1919 he had set up a producing subdivision called Eminent Writers.

With Goldwyn, it was not a matter of hiring prestigious names to dress up the credits on potboilers that Leo Tolstoy could not have salvaged. Goldwyn listened to his writers and, to a degree rare in Hollywood, left their work alone. Before Hellman arrived, Elmer Rice had written two films for Goldwyn (*Street Scene* in 1931 and *Counsellor-at-Law* in 1933), and Goldwyn would eventually lure Sidney Howard, Ben Hecht, Charles MacArthur and Robert Sherwood to his stable—all to work on serious film dramas few people would consider inappropriate to these particular talents.

Goldwyn never felt the same threat to his glory from writers that he did from directors. He lavished attention on his literary catches, crowing to the press about them as if they were rare Fragonards he had acquired by outbidding the Louvre. In three years, Hellman had leaped from anonymous reader at a rival studio to a prize of Goldwyn's collection.

For her return to Hollywood, Hellman moved into Hammett's rented house in Pacific Palisades—the same house in which she later claimed to have demolished the basement soda fountain—which was tended to by the black houseman, Jones, whom Hellman respected, and his older lover, Winfield, whom she did not. Hellman's arrival brought little change to Hammett's bachelor romps, not even to the extent of banishing the floozies from the premises. In her last book, *Maybe,* Hellman writes of returning to the house during this period to find one of Hammett's pickups in the living room playing the piano and refusing to leave. Hellman was not philosophical about such flagrant lapses in fidelity, and Pacific Palisades was the setting for some boisterous Hellman-Hammett battles. Perhaps to defuse her eruptions, or perhaps in the spirit of camaraderie, Hammett on occasion invited Hellman to join in the sport. She recounts his suggested threesomes in *Pentimento,* but does not indicate her response. Years later Hellman hinted to Hammett's biographer, Diane Johnson, that she had done the sporting thing.

Their reunion wasn't made up entirely of the turmoil caused by an interrupted bachelorhood. They saw friends like the Hacketts, went to the race track, dined frequently in high-visibility restaurants like the Brown Derby, gambled at the Clover Club and, on occasion, went on one of their Nick-and-Nora prowls of Los Angeles underlife.

Both of them were earning more money than any two people could dream of spending in 1935, but they had a good time in the attempt. Hellman had always loved expensive clothes and prided herself on her excellent taste. Even when she was married to Kober, she dressed expensively; whatever concessions she made toward her junior-wife budget were in the number of purchases, not the quality. Now with large sums arriving weekly from both the Goldwyn studios and the Maxine Elliott Theater, Hellman went on buying sprees, first in New York, then in Los Angeles, where Hammett, who also loved dressing expensively, would get into the pamper-Lillian spirit by nonchalantly buying her another designer dress or another fur coat (he bought her a mink and a broadtail).

That sort of grandee gesture had long marked Hammett's style, but with Hellman's massive contribution to their finances— a contribution Hammett, unlike Hellman, had no doubt would continue indefinitely—his profligacy with money escalated. He included his family in the largesse, buying his wife a new car and his daughters expensive gifts. In addition, he pressed loans on anyone, known to him or not, who possessed the temerity to approach him in a restaurant.

On occasion Hammett would pick up his daughters and bring them along for the shopping outings with Hellman. At first the girls thought she was just another one of the many women they had met with their father, but they soon came to accept her as a fixture. The younger daughter, Jo, who was then nine, remembers Hellman's stylish clothes and fancy getups. She also recalls being mortified by the way Hellman would snap at the sales clerks. She took her father's reaction, amusement, as proof that he loved Lillian.

Throughout her life Hellman had a quick temper and was not shy about turning it on strangers. She was also quick to respond when she felt she was confronting a correctable human failing, whether it was rudeness, ignorance, pomposity, inconsideration, meanness—or merely the incompetence of a salesgirl. She could bring to the most everyday human exchanges the same kind of moral anger that informed *The Children's Hour*. Later, she would often regret her outbursts of temper and sometimes apologize to whoever had been affronted, but her anger seemed to flare as spontaneously as her raucous laugh.

On the assumption that costly wardrobes are just one aspect of lives dedicated to the pursuit of partying and social status, a love of expensive clothes such as Hellman's is often taken as evidence of an across-the-board frivolity. Such extravagance in the days of mortgage foreclosures and breadlines cannot be brushed aside, but a status enhancement was not Hellman's motive. She saw the same friends she saw before she was rich and was as selective as ever about expanding her circle—in any direction. Her preoccupations remained her work and Hammett. She loved costly clothes, but not the life that generally went with them. That would change in time and, fifty years later, Hellman would be widely criticized for posing for a Blackglama mink ad. Other weaknesses contributed to that bizarre decision, but high among them was a lifelong passion for clothes.

As for guilt about spending freely on herself when others were hungry, Hellman never showed any sign of it. In the next few years, she would be generous to the causes she believed in—both with time and money—and quick to help out Max and Julia or friends in difficulties, but her altruism stopped short of stinting herself. Hellman was not the first radical with humanitarian concerns to live lavishly, but it would become a fact—a contradiction, to many—of her life. Neither did worries about her own future slow down her spending. By the time her next successful play opened in 1939, Hellman had gone through most of the considerable money she made from *The Children's Hour* and from Sam Goldwyn, with nothing permanent to show for it.

While it might not have been apparent except to a handful that Hammett's star was waning, it was obvious that Hellman's was rising spectacularly. Word of that shift in the Hammett-Hellman dynamic, however, had not yet reached as far as Paris. On a visit to Hollywood, Gertrude Stein was asked by her hostess whom she would like to meet. Without hesitation, Stein requested Charlie Chaplin, but after some reflection, added another name: Dashiell Hammett. On receiving the invitation to dine with Gertrude Stein, Hammett first thought it was an April Fool's joke (just the sort of thing Sid Perelman or Pep West would dream up), but eventually, convinced of its legitimacy, he accepted on the condition that he could bring Hellman. The hostess agreed. Gertrude Stein was indeed at the dinner, as were Alice B. Toklas, Charlie Chaplin, Paulette Goddard and Anita Loos.

In *Everybody's Autobiography* Stein writes at some length about her dinner with Hammett, showing a particular fascination with the logistics of how he came to be at the party. She even records his request that he might bring "someone." Despite Hellman's nameless appearance in the narrative, Stein makes no specific mention of having met her, writing instead about Hammett's views on the presentation of women in male-written fiction. To

Gertrude Stein, at least, Hammett was still the star. Hellman waited many years to repay Stein's snub. When in 1965 an interviewer from *Paris Review* asked her about the dinner, Hellman confirmed that Stein had paid no attention to her, but added that at one point during the meal, Charlie Chaplin had spilled a cup of coffee over an exquisite tablecloth. Stein, who was nowhere near the accident, calmed the group by saying, "Don't worry, none of it got on me."

Not everyone was as enthusiastic about Hammett's literary opinions as Gertrude Stein. In a letter written in 1934, John O'Hara bemoaned the indifference with which Scott Fitzgerald's latest novel, *Tender Is the Night,* had been received by the literary arbiters. After pointing out that Dorothy Parker told him she had only read a little and had been unable "to stay with it," O'Hara went on: "And I am proud to say I did not go along with the gutless thinking that all but destroyed *Tender Is the Night* and without a doubt broke Fitzgerald's heart. One group which I shall disguise under the heading of the Hammett-Hellman-Perelman-Kober group, had no time for Fitzgerald (or later, me) and I note with some sardonic pleasure that they are having trouble convincing the people that Pep West was better than Fitzgerald AND Jonathan Swift."

After a single hit play, Hellman, if only in O'Hara's eyes, was a key member of a literary faction capable of destroying an important novel. In fact, there is no evidence that Hellman was unenthusiastic about Fitzgerald's writing, which she praises in her memoirs; while they were never friends, she later wrote about him with solicitude and affection in describing a Hollywood encounter they had in 1937.

For her first job as a Hollywood writer, Goldwyn set Hellman to work on the screenplay of Guy Bolton's drama *Dark Angel.* She was to work in collaboration with the British playwright Mordaunt Shairp, who had also shocked Broadway in 1933 with a homosexual theme in his play *The Green Bay Tree,* thus giving his collaboration with Hellman an odd symmetry. The film, which starred Merle Oberon and Fredric March, was a sentimental love story with a strong overlay of British stiff-upper-lip nobility. A

British critic referred to it as "a three-hankie picture" and Hellman herself, years later, would dismiss the film as "an old silly." It was respectfully received at the time, however, and did well at the box office. Hellman's disdain for the film didn't prevent her from claiming that the screenplay was 90 percent hers, with only a few suggestions coming from her collaborator.

Hellman's contract was renewed with Goldwyn, who now gave her total freedom to select whatever project she wanted for her next film adaptation. She chose *The Children's Hour*. For $50,000, Goldwyn found himself owner of a drama whose theme had been audacious enough for a Broadway play but out of the question for a Hollywood film. A story went around at the time about Goldwyn's response when warned against buying the property because it concerned lesbians. "That's all right," he said, "we'll make them Americans."

Having outsmarted Goldwyn by getting him to buy her play, Hellman was magnanimous and pointed out a way the story could be filmed without bringing down the wrath of various censors. She insisted her play was not about lesbianism, but about the destructiveness of slander. She could write an adaptation that contained no hint of homosexuality.

While such a major change in a serious work raises the suspicion of artistic cynicism, Hellman was sincere in her belief and was not trashing her own play in order to extract movie dollars from it. Goldwyn surely could have wriggled out of his carte blanche promise had the play been impossible to film. When two decades later Hellman directed a Broadway revival of *The Children's Hour* she emphasized the same point to the cast. She had admired Shumlin's direction of the original, she told them, but felt he had overemphasized the homosexual theme at the expense of the real theme: the devastation caused by a lie.

In an interview at the time Hellman also said that, to her, the villain of the piece was not Mary Tilford, who told the lie, but her grandmother and all the others who believed and acted on it. In this offhand and somewhat indirect manner, Hellman seemed to be positing the play's strongest statement: evil as exemplified by Mary exists and will always exist. It is up to fundamentally decent people like Mrs. Tilford to recognize it, thwart it if possible, but certainly to avoid furthering it. The theme of the culpability of "decent" bystanders was one Hellman would return to on several occasions, both in her later plays and her memoirs.

Life with Hammett in Hollywood was providing more excitement than Hellman wanted, especially now that she was trying to work. After years of seeking an outlet for her talent, she was at the hard-won position of writing whatever she desired, and for high pay. Although that incentive unleashed stores of creative energy, Hellman realized that too much other energy, as well as too much of her time, was spent in getting drunk with Hammett, dealing with Hammett when he was drunk, or fighting with him about it afterward. The nastier fights would send her to a friend's house or for a long middle-of-the-night walk along the Santa Monica beach. When she had finished the screenplay for *The Children's Hour*, she packed up and returned to New York, convinced that she was finished with Hammett, too.

On the trip East, the DC-2 in which Hellman was flying ran into a dust storm during the night and was grounded in Albuquerque. As she was walking over the tarmac from the plane to the hangar, Hellman became aware of another passenger walking beside her and talking with her about the delay. He was a man in his thirties, tall, not bad-looking, who chatted at her with a preppie intensity that Hellman at first found annoying but later winning. His name, Ralph Ingersoll, meant nothing to Hellman, although it would have to many of her writer and publishing friends. Ingersoll had been the managing editor of *The New Yorker* under Harold Ross throughout its first years. Henry Luce then hired him away to oversee *Fortune*, which Ingersoll converted from a stuffy business journal into a dynamic and talked-about magazine. At the time he met Hellman, he was developing a new picture magazine that he had convinced a skeptical Luce would be the next great advance in journalism and a major money-maker for Time, Inc.

Hellman, talking in the hangar with this enthusiastic young man on the rise, found herself strongly drawn to him even though he was such a prime specimen of types about which she had mixed feelings—old family, Ivy League, a dabbler at writing, a power in mainstream culture. He and the whole Luce operation, to Hellman and to many like her, smacked of Yale boys playing at press lords. In the discomfort of the interrupted flight, Ingersoll's effusions might have been expected to evoke the antiestablishment part of the Hellman mix. When he confessed that he had not heard of *The Children's Hour,* she came close to responding as she did to dawdling salesgirls.

But now Hellman was relaxed, glad to be away from the house in Pacific Palisades and untroubled by the delay in her trip. An intelligence and sensitivity started to emerge through Ingersoll's chatter, an evaluation no doubt helped along as Hellman found Ingersoll increasingly attractive. It was obvious he returned the feeling. He had first noticed her as she got off the plane, a small, blond woman walking on the runway, her face illuminated by the flashing green-then-white marker lights. His first impression was that she was not particularly pretty, but *interesting.*

Ingersoll was in a mood to be bewitched; he was on his way home from a difficult yet triumphant interview with William Randolph Hearst for *Fortune.* To celebrate his journalistic coup, he had brought onto the plane some bottles of champagne, which he insisted on sharing with Hellman. Sitting on hangar crates, sipping champagne from paper cups, they told each other about themselves and got their friendship off to the kind of "meeting cute" start that typified the Frank Capra film comedies of the day.

When after a few hours their mutual attraction was obvious to both, they were informed by the airline that the plane would not leave until morning; rooms had been arranged for all passengers in an Albuquerque hotel. Ingersoll said later that he and Hellman were so eager to have at each other, they neglected to close the door to Hellman's room, then looked up from their love-making to see a face frozen in shock peering through the door.

Ingersoll was by nature an impetuous type and a womanizer, but, although married, he saw himself as a man of honor. The night with Hellman was for him such an epiphany that the next morning he resolved to tell his wife he was in love with another woman. Hellman was almost equally affected and did nothing to dissuade him. After a few meetings in New York, they were convinced their Albuquerque episode was not just an unscheduled romance at an unscheduled stopover but an important meeting for them both. They were soon deeply involved.

Because Hellman's arrangement with Goldwyn was casual, and because she disliked Southern California and felt she needed a place apart from Hammett, she rented a duplex apartment at 14 East Seventh Street in Greenwich Village, which she decorated with Picasso prints. She gave a number of parties that were well stocked with theater celebrities, and invariably had George Gershwin playing the piano. She dined frequently with old friends. The central fact of her life, however, was Ralph Ingersoll.

The ramifications of their love affair were considerable. Ingersoll was one of the top editorial powers at a company that was on its way to becoming the most influential media combine in the country. He would later leave the Luce empire to start his own New York City daily newspaper, the legendary *PM*, for which Hellman thought up the title. For all his drive and curiosity, to say nothing of his strategic position in a vast news-gathering empire, he was, when he met Hellman, politically unaligned, a cipher. He prided himself on having the kind of journalistic openness to all sides that angered liberals and conservatives alike.

To the guests at Hellman's parties, most of whom had liberal leanings, Ingersoll was considered a hired spokesman for the capitalist establishment. His Time, Inc., cronies took his involvement with Hellman as proof he had gone over to the pinkos. Hellman herself was then becoming entrenched in radical positions, and Ingersoll told friends that they argued so much they were their own "private debating society." Other influences were working on Ingersoll at the time, but his arguments with Hellman were surely one cause of his swing to the left. For a brief period he actually joined the Communist party. His continued sympathy for communist thinking dominated his newspaper, *PM*, and to many observers was the cause of its destruction.

The Hellman-Ingersoll romance lasted over a year with frequent separations. Ingersoll would return sporadically to his wife, who was a semi-invalid, and Hellman would return to Hollywood to work on screenplays. During these trips, she had cautious reconciliations with Hammett without any cooling of her heated involvement with Ingersoll. Hellman and Hammett made a religion of respecting each other's privacy, and Hellman was now putting this faith to good use.

When Goldwyn released his film version of *The Children's Hour*, retitled *These Three*, it proved Hellman's point about the play's underlying theme. Eliminating the lesbian aspect, she had still managed to weave an engrossing drama about the destruction of a number of lives by the false accusation of an evil child acting from no other motive than irritation and boredom. In the film, the little girl, Mary, instead of accusing Karen and Martha of a lesbian relationship, tells her aunt that Martha is having illicit sex with Joe, Karen's fiancé. While this lie is almost as destructive to the school—parents being sure to condemn a headmistress for pursuing love affairs of any sort under their children's noses—Hellman's heterosexual transcription of her play had the strong added ingredient of sewing suspicion and mistrust between the two close friends, who, in the original play, knew for a certainty that Mary was lying.

The screenplay removed the danger that the sensational element of sexual aberration would distract audience focus from Hellman's more universal theme of destructive evil. It also put more distance between Hellman and her real-life source, laying to rest the sour hints that in fashioning a play from a case history she was something less than a creative talent.

The film starred Merle Oberon as Karen, Miriam Hopkins as Martha, Joel McCrea as Joe and Bonita Granville as Mary. It was the first of three films Hellman would do with director William Wyler, who would later establish himself as one of the greatest directors in Hollywood history. The cameraman for the film, Gregg Toland, would also establish a place for himself in motion-picture history with his filming of *Citizen Kane*. *These Three* was his first film with Wyler, and they would go on to make together such masterpieces as *Wuthering Heights* and *The Best Years of Our Lives*, as well as two more films written by Hellman, *Dead End* and *The Little Foxes*.

The reviews of *These Three* were excellent. The *New York Times* critic, Frank Nugent, called it "one of the finest screen dramas in years." Richard Watts, Jr., said that Hellman had written "a stirring, mature and powerful motion picture that is in every way worthy of its celebrated original, and perhaps, in one or two ways, surpasses it." Emboldened by Watts's somewhat timorous jab at orthodox theater attitudes toward Hollywood, several other critics proclaimed the film better than the play. One of the most unrestrained raves came from Graham Greene, who reviewed the film for the London *Spectator:* "I have seldom been so moved by a fictional film as *These Three.* After ten minutes or so of the usual screen sentiment, quaintness and exaggeration, one began to watch with incredulous pleasure nothing less than life."

Twenty-seven years later, when homosexuality was a permissible motion-picture topic, Wyler would make another film of *The Children's Hour,* this time adhering to the original play, with Shirley MacLaine as Martha, Audrey Hepburn as Karen, James Garner as Joe, Fay Bainter as Mrs. Tilford and, once again, Miriam Hopkins, now playing Mrs. Mortar. Despite the greater authenticity and the strong cast, the 1962 version was far less successful than Hellman's self-bowdlerized screenplay for Goldwyn and was viewed by many to be heavy-handed and outdated—in both its attitudes and treatment. Hellman had undertaken the second screenplay but quit the project when Hammett died in 1961.

When *These Three* opened, however, it would be hard to imagine a writer professionally more triumphant. Hellman had vanquished Broadway with her first produced play—not a comedy or a romance, but a serious, haunting, thoughtful drama. And now, at the youthful age of thirty-one, she had more than justified her large Hollywood salary with a powerful screenplay that was both a critical and commercial success. While a number of major literary talents were floundering around Hollywood turning in second-rate work and drinking away their embarrassment, Hellman's script had enhanced her reputation as a serious writer.

Many years later, when Hellman had abandoned playwriting and had turned to writing books, more than one critic remarked how rare it was for a writer who has achieved eminence in one field to change mediums with no loss of distinction. If it can be allowed that writing for the stage and the screen are different crafts, Hellman had, in effect, made another remarkable transformation at a far earlier age.

Hellman spent a considerable amount of time in Hollywood in the latter half of the 1930s. It was a period of great political ferment in the nation at large, but with particularly dramatic manifestations in Southern California and the film industry. Upton Sinclair, a longtime socialist, had been persuaded to switch his political affiliation and run for governor of California on an extremely liberal Democratic ticket. The cornerstone of his platform was an End-Poverty-in-California plan that had studio heads so alarmed they faked newsreels showing armies of drifters and hoboes heading for California to get in on the gravy train. Even Hellman's boss, Sam Goldwyn, docked his employees a day's wages to help fight the Sinclair candidacy.

The unemployment and labor unrest across the country reopened an old wound of Hammett's, the self-disgust he felt as a Pinkerton man who had been part of the force used by owners to stand down strikers, including on occasion hungry wives and children. His firsthand knowledge of owners' methods against workers enabled him to read beyond the expurgated press accounts of labor-owner confrontations such as the 1934 general strike in San Francisco when Harry Bridges's longshoremen, joined by thousands of sympathetic workers, had been beaten by police, run down by horse patrols, and fired upon (two workers were killed). Hammett knew how viciously owners could fight. He had been one of their goons.

If Hammett, given the passivity of his character, was not ready to fight back, Hellman was. It is generally thought that Hammett was responsible for politicizing Hellman. A case could be made for the opposite. First there was Hellman's nature, a far more angry and combative one than Hammett's. Then there was the youthful Hellman's record of rebelliousness and defiance of authority, starting with Julia and Max Hellman and later the teachers at Wadleigh High School. But more significantly, there was the possibility that, while working at MGM, Hellman had tried to organize her fellow readers. Her FBI file says that she was a member of the Marxist John Reed Club in New York before ever coming to Hollywood or meeting Hammett. Both assertions contradict the testimony of Hollywood friends to Hellman's disinterest in politics.

So while Hellman had a more active political history than Hammett (he would never be particularly *active* at politics or at anything), his role as a mentor in other areas of her life and his emerging Marxism are the two factors in favor of the argument that he set her political direction. Hellman never suggests that he did. The truth may be that she arrived at radicalism on her own, but Hammett provided strong and perhaps essential reinforcement over the decades to come.

Both, in any case, were writers, and of all the day's many owner-worker struggles, one of the bitterest was between studio heads and film writers. Since 1933, when writers had been forced to take wage cuts to keep the studios from closing down, they had deplored their powerlessness. Like workers across the country, they were seeking to remedy their impotence by organizing. The group they were trying to form and the studios were trying to quash was the Screen Writers' Guild.

The central issue was the right to organize, but the writers sought that right, as the owners knew, to alter a number of longstanding grievances. If screenwriters have since come to be thought of as among the most cozened and highly paid professionals, in 1934 fully one third of them earned less than $2,000 a year, most had no security between assignments, no say about what was done with their work, no say about what screen credit they would receive, if any, and, for those on contract, no say about whom they worked for next or on what project. When the nationwide spirit of collective bargaining was caught by film writers, the studio heads reacted as though Marx and Lenin had launched a proxy battle for control of MGM.

Although the screenwriters' attempt at unionization had made remarkable progress in a short time, it was 1935, the year of Hellman's return to Hollywood, that the moguls closed ranks in an all-out push to destroy the union. The following summer, after Hellman's triumph with *These Three*, the Guild saw as its only chance for survival an amalgamation with the Dramatists Guild in New York to create a virtual monopoly on dramatic writing talent. The studio heads saw the ploy as a showdown over who would run Hollywood and hunkered down for a major fight.

Some of the most active battlers for the Guild were avowed communists, or those attracted to communism as the only remedy for a collapsing society. But many who were equally committed to the Guild struggle were not. As part of an intense drive for new members, Hellman and Hammett joined the Guild, in itself a defiant (and perilously selfless) act, along with such Eastern colleagues as Robert Benchley, George S. Kaufman and Theodore Dreiser. Hellman threw herself into the struggle and, together with friends like Albert and Frances Hackett, used their studio lunch periods to lobby unaligned writers to join too.

Maurice Rapf, whose father was one of Louis B. Mayer's top lieutenants at MGM, was on that studio's payroll as a junior writer, having only recently graduated from Dartmouth. Working one day in his tiny, airless office, he was dumbfounded by the sudden appearance of the famous Lillian Hellman, formidable in a large hat, chain-smoking, sitting on the edge of his desk and explaining that he was wrong to consider himself fortunate to be working for MGM; he was oppressed. Rapf, who by birth and ability was clearly marked for major power in Hollywood, was soon radicalized (not necessarily by Hellman), and he joined the Communist party along with his close college pal Budd Schulberg, another Hollywood heir apparent, whose father, B. P. Schulberg, ran the Paramount studio.

In the struggle with the studio heads, the majority of screenwriters were putting themselves in considerable jeopardy. Despite the contempt in which most were held by the moguls, these writers, unlike striking factory workers, had contracts and were known to their bosses as individuals. Thus there were genuine risks to aligning openly with the Guild. Regardless of the outcome, the ill will of the owners could be a serious and lingering career disadvantage to even the most successful writers. That was equally true of many other writers who, while in favor of the Guild, were terrified of agitating themselves out of dreamlike sinecures and so would not support it. Some with big reputations in the theater or book publishing, writers the Guild was most anxious to attract, had few complaints and many reasons to be delighted with the status quo. They were highly paid, they had control of their destinies and they could be assured of a fat and steady income through hits and flops for the rest of their working lives.

Hellman, who was among those not dependent on films for her livelihood, quickly became one of the most militant of the group working for a strong Guild. Albert Hackett, who was also a writer who had other possible markets besides the motion-

picture business, remembers her as one of the most fearless cru-
saders in the Guild strategy meetings. She would often take the
floor and inveigh against the others for cowardice and petty self-
interest in the face of intolerable injustice. "While the rest of us
considered various tactics against the studios and the dangers involved," Hackett recalled, "Lillian would contemptuously brush
such caution aside and say something like, 'They're bastards.
Let's clean them out!'"

It was Hellman's first public battle, and eager as she was to
hurl herself into the fray, her attitudes and responses, then and
in later political battles, appear more visceral than intellectual.
The remarkably few times she ever wrote about politics, her writing was dramatic or denunciatory, never polemical or dialectic.
When Nate Witt of the National Labor Relations Board came to
Hollywood to talk with various union representatives, he met
with Hammett, Hellman and Donald Ogden Stewart to discuss
the Screen Writers' Guild. Witt recalled that although Hellman
talked at length about politics, she was "immersed in the minutiae of it, but not really on top of it." Hellman's fierce political nature drew far more from her emotional side than her intellectual.

In the summer of 1936, the studio heads succeeded in quash-
ing the Guild's power play. Within a few years the Screen Writers' Guild would return and achieve its first goals, but the short-
term effect of this defeat was the embitterment and disaffection
of many writers, who felt their blackest visions about owner
treachery had been confirmed. They were stunned by the studio
heads' bare-fisted determination not to yield even the smallest
portion of their sovereignty. The battle left lifelong enmity between the writers who supported the Guild and their well-paid
colleagues who had sided with the studios. But the most important effect was the radicalization of large numbers of writers for
whom, until this fight, politics and the labor-management struggle had been abstractions.

Another event that same summer of 1936 forced disillusioned Americans deeper into disaffection with the democratic
system. In July there was a military revolt in Spanish Morocco
against the central Republican government in Madrid. With
Mussolini in Italy and Hitler in Germany firmly established in
power, observers of the international scene were growing in-

creasingly alarmed that fascism was spreading, with no resistance, throughout the world. Now two generals, Francisco Franco and Emilio Mola, were trying to replace a duly elected government by a military dictatorship. Most alarming of all to liberal Americans about developments in Spain was President Roosevelt's haste to make a hands-off statement of neutrality regarding the civil war there. The American economy had collapsed and the world seemed to be going fascist with no counterforce to stop it. To ever-increasing numbers of thoughtful and concerned Americans, it appeared that the only people who understood these catastrophes and offered forceful, lasting programs to confront and solve them were the communists.

9

THE FAME that descended on Hellman in November 1934 brought with it many demands: press interviews, social lionization, handling new wealth. She had all that to deal with, in addition to a lucrative film contract with an exacting producer, her crusade on behalf of the Screen Writers' Guild, and a captain's paradise with a lover on each coast. Yet none of these claims distracted her from her recently found purpose: she was a playwright and she would write plays. As soon as she finished her two screenplays for Goldwyn, she set to work on a new play, a drama about labor strife in a midwestern town which she titled *Days to Come.**

Hammett was undoubtedly aware of her romance with Ingersoll, given Hellman's candor and her frequent commutes between her Greenwich Village apartment and Pacific Palisades. Whether or not that was the trigger, he went into one of his worst declines when Hellman left for New York at the beginning of 1936, her work for Goldwyn completed for the time being. He gave up his house and moved into a grandiose suite in the Beverly Wilshire where he could enlist its staff in the service of a full-

* Nathanael West had wanted to use this title for *Day of the Locust* but Hellman beat him to it.

throttle, I'll-show-her debauch. He drank and whored with a suicidal determination that set records even for him, staying up for two days at a time, then passing out. His weight went down to 127 pounds.

Finally his friends, who had witnessed many similar bouts, grew seriously alarmed. Frances and Albert Hackett phoned Hellman in New York to tell her of the crisis: Hammett would surely die if he wasn't stopped. Although he was out of control, they felt they still had one lever over him: he respected Frances Hackett, and, in the clumsy struggles to get him to focus on his predicament, he had said he would do whatever she asked. Hellman told the Hacketts to use this power to get him on a plane and send him to her in New York.

When Albert Hackett went to the suite, he found Hammett sprawled on the bed, barely conscious. Frances Hackett, who had been conferring downstairs with the hotel management, appeared in the room and told her husband that their rescue operation had hit a snag: the hotel would not let Hammett leave until his bill was paid. More worried about the body on the bed, Hackett snapped at his wife to pay the bloody bill and they would settle with Hammett later.

"You don't understand, Albert," she said. "It's eight thousand dollars!"

In a few weeks Hammett, who only a short time before had written pleading letters to Alfred Knopf for a $1,000 advance for living expenses, had run up an amount most people did not earn in two years. Even the well-paid Hacketts were reluctant to advance such a sum, but they worked out an arrangement with the Beverly Wilshire, phoned Hellman, and got Hammett to the airport.

Hellman met the plane in New York with an ambulance and took Hammett directly to the hospital. There it was discovered that among the many problems that had brought him near death was a galloping case of gonorrhea. The infection required prolonged treatments, painful and humiliating, which kept Hammett in Manhattan for months after his release from the hospital. If his monumental debauch had been in protest against Hellman's affair with Ingersoll, he was too sick to make a stand to win her back.

After the brilliant New York opening of her film *These Three* in March, Hellman went off to Havana with Ingersoll, feeling that Hammett was at least grounded from dangerous action for the time being. When she returned, she again rented the house on Tavern Island off the coast of Connecticut, where she had written much of *The Children's Hour,* and settled down to work on *Days to Come.* It was the scene of her early days with Hammett, as much a honeymoon locale as any, and a significant choice in light of the quandary in her emotional life. As Hammett recovered his strength, Hellman was confronted with a crisis about her two lovers. Hammett, who was devoted to plain talk, cryptically warned her about "juggling oranges" and made it clear that if she didn't stop it, he wouldn't be around much longer. The showdown came at the Tavern Island beach house.

According to Ralph Ingersoll, Hellman invited him for a weekend, and he arrived to find Hammett there and, perhaps for comic relief, Arthur Kober. Hammett may have been in the house all along, or he may have showed up unannounced, but Ingersoll makes a point of saying Hellman had "invited" them both. If so, she also had a taste for drama in her private life. In the course of the weekend, Hellman and Hammett had an emotional reconciliation. When they broke the news to Ingersoll, he was devastated. He had arrived in a weakened state, since he was in the midst of a professional crisis as well. As Ingersoll's picture-magazine project, now named *Life,* was at the point of making its debut, the auguries were so auspicious that Henry Luce took the magazine back from Ingersoll and announced he would edit it himself. He removed Ingersoll from the scene by making him publisher of *Time,* a post in which he had no interest whatever. Such a high-handed confiscation of what he considered his brainchild shattered Ingersoll. Now he had been dismissed by Hellman.

Relating the calamity years later, Ingersoll says he left her house, went to the water's edge, got in a canoe and paddled "until the island was no more than a dot on the skyline." Ingersoll goes on: "It was there that I experienced an almost overwhelming crisis in which . . . I was again a small boy defeated by the woman I love, full of passions I did not understand. I saved my soul by my resolve. I would be a man. I would take no man's ideas. I would work for no other man, except as a means to acquire my own ends . . . I would prove my manhood by creating a publication of my own."

If *PM* was indeed born in a canoe off the dock of a heartless Hellman, Ingersoll would retain his friendship with both Hellman and Hammett and, in much later years, talk with ardor to his biographer about his affair with her. The compliment is not repaid. While Hellman doesn't banish him from her recollections completely, she presents him simply as a friend.

Hammett's flirtation with death and his victorious return calmed him considerably, and he and Hellman spent a relatively tranquil summer on Tavern Island. At one point they seriously considered collaborating on *Days to Come,* but thought better of the idea. Instead, he continued to fight his own literary demons and she got on with the play. As the summer ended, Hammett had no desire to return to either Manhattan or Hollywood. Picking a town near New York almost at random, he rented a large house with spacious grounds at 10 Cleveland Lane in Princeton. Hellman spent her time between that house and a new apartment she had rented on Seventy-fifth Street off Fifth Avenue.

Hammett stepped up his drinking, which angered Hellman; his debauches now had the added twist of including Princeton students who liked Hammett and were impressed by his reputation, but liked even more the free liquor that came with a visit. Hellman grew so disgusted with the drunken students draped around the house, she spent less and less time there and more time working alone. By the end of the fall, she was ready to show *Days to Come* to Shumlin. Only two years had passed since the opening of *The Children's Hour;* no one could accuse Hellman of lolling overlong in the warm tub of success. But reflecting on this period after many years, Hellman felt the shower of attention and flattery did indeed harm her, not by keeping her from her typewriter, but rather by sending her back to it with an excess of confidence.

Hellman had only dim recollections of the opening night of *Days to Come,* on December 15, 1936. During the first act she vomited from nerves, went home to change her dress and returned to the theater in the middle of the last act to see William Randolph Hearst and his party of six walking noisily up the aisle. Others recall that Hearst was not alone in his impatience for the final curtain. The bar next to the theater had been filling up gradually throughout the performance with first-nighters seeking a better way to pass the time before going on to the opening-night party.

The party, interestingly enough, was given by Ralph Ingersoll at his sumptuous Fifth Avenue apartment, which had spectacular views of midtown Manhattan and a barroom with cork walls and brass trim. Before Hellman arrived at the flashy gathering, it was clear the play was in for a trouncing from the critics. She entered the apartment, stormed past a few hundred of New York's most dazzling people and went straight to Ingersoll's bedroom, where she slammed and locked the door.

She said later that during the play she had given an usher five dollars to buy her a bottle of brandy to get her through the performance. After drinking most of it, she noticed the change the usher had handed her was still clenched in her fist: four dollars and six cents. The dash for the bedroom was blamed on the rotgut brandy, but the play's reception surely contributed. After about an hour, she emerged. Having recovered her truculence, Hellman went straight to Hammett and broke into an involved conversation he was having with James Farrell. "You son of a bitch!" she said. "Didn't you tell me just last week that *Days to Come* was the best play you'd ever read?"

"I did," he replied, "but I saw it tonight and I've changed my mind." With that, he put on his coat and left the party.

With one or two exceptions the New York critics agreed that *Days to Come* was a rambling and confused bit of pomposity, with too much plot, too much message and too many characters. There was little about the play that didn't smack of overreach. Many of the critics took the occasion to recall their admiration for Hellman's first play, often expanding on their praise and, while unwavering in their dismissal of the current effort, excused it as a misfire from a talented and promising playwright.

The story concerns a brother and sister, Arthur and Cora Rodman, who own a brush factory in a small Ohio town. Business is down, wages have been cut, and a union organizer, Leo

Whalen, arrives in town to supervise a strike. The Rodmans' lawyer, Henry Ellicott, persuades Rodman to hire strikebreakers led by a professional goon, Sam Wilkie.

Hellman sets up the union organizer as the hero, the lawyer and his strikebreakers as the villains—with the well-meaning Rodmans caught in the middle. Arthur Rodman's wife, Julie, is sympathetic to the strikers and falls in love with the organizer, Whalen. A murder of one of the strikebreakers then occurs and is used to frame Whalen by Wilkie, who places the murder victim outside the organizer's office. While incriminating evidence is being deposited on his doorstep, Whalen is in the midst of a visit from Julie, but he gets her out through a back door before she is compromised.

The next day, when it appears Wilkie's frameup of Whalen will succeed, Julie nobly confesses she was with him at the time he was supposed to have been murdering the goon. Although her husband believes her story, thereby destroying their marriage, the authorities don't, and Whalen is sent to jail. With Whalen no longer around to restrain the strikers, serious fighting breaks out with the goons.

The third act has as many plot twists and pent-up confessions as three or four normal plays. The child of a beloved worker is shot and killed, Rodman loses heart and orders the goons to leave, the workers lose heart and sheepishly return to work, Julie tells Arthur she has never loved him and, indeed, has had an affair with their lawyer, Ellicott. For his part, Ellicott reveals he has lent Arthur so much money to pay for Julie's extravagances that he all but owns the company. Not to be left out of the general breast-baring, Rodman's sister, Cora, announces that she has always hated Julie while living in the same house. There is more, although many in the opening-night audience did not stay long enough to see it.

In an interview shortly before the play opened, Hellman said she had been working on the idea for *Days to Come* for five or six years—which would mean she had contemplated writing about the labor struggle since around 1930, perhaps when she was reading for MGM and a part of "labor" herself. The plot she fashioned was not, she said, based on any one incident, but was a classic situation in which a local workers' struggle escalates to violence despite relatively decent people on both sides. In fact, the degree of sympathy she shows for the owners does not remove the play altogether from political bias. But it has the effect of giving more importance to the drama than to the ideology.

In the same interview, Hellman said she wanted to show what happens when someone sets into motion events that he cannot later control, rather "a parallel among adults to what I did with children in *The Children's Hour.*" Then, commenting on the difficulty while writing a play of adhering to whatever abstract idea inspired it, she added: "You have no idea of how hard it is to retain an editorial point of view or an idea that you want to put across all through the business of writing a play. You may have a clearly defined point of view and something vital on your mind when you sit down to that nice fresh copy paper, but when you get through and write 'Curtain' for the last time, where are those fine ideas?"

The play's failure, however, stems not from a lack of fine ideas, but an overabundance of them. Hellman later said that her greatest error in writing *Days to Come* was her attempt to squeeze into it everything that was on her mind at the moment, that she was gripped by a panicky sensation that she would not have another opportunity to speak out. It is a shrewd insight. Elements of most of Hellman's later plays can be traced in *Days to Come.* There is the ruthless infighting of the Hubbards; the well-intentioned befuddlement of the families of *Watch on the Rhine* and *The Searching Wind;* the jettisoning of lifelong lies of *Toys in the Attic* and *The Autumn Garden. Days to Come* simply collapses from overload and the unsuccessful attempt to integrate its many themes.

Another damaging flaw is the characterization of Julie. Hellman burdens her heroine with an attraction to the labor organizer which takes her out of the crisis of conscience the labor strife provokes and places her instead in a dither. Julie Rodman is one of Hellman's most self-revealing characters in that she speaks of her infatuation for the labor organizer in terms of her lifelong need for a teacher, someone she can look up to and follow (the speech quoted earlier). But while the parallel with Hammett is obvious, Julie, because of the hero-worship basis for her love, makes a hash of her life and those of the people around her. There is no suggestion that Hellman actually believed, then or ever, that such problems lurked in the master-disciple bond with Hammett or, indeed, that there was *any* flaw in the dynamics of their relationship. In spinning out her plot in *Days to Come,* however, Hellman acknowledged the danger in anyone's abdicating judgment to another at the time when she and Hammett were coming to recognize that their involvement was not going to be a mere episode.

Days to Come closed after six performances. The disaster produced a crisis for Hellman. Cocksure about so much, she was oddly insecure about her talent as a writer, particularly at this early stage in her career. She had been surprised, she said, by the fervent reception of *The Children's Hour.* Like so many sudden successes struggling to absorb what has happened to them, she was plagued by fears that her first play's success had been a fluke. The trouncing received by her second play went a long way toward confirming her fears.

Eventually her psychic system developed an antibody for her insecurity: defiance. Years later, discussing the play's failure in her memoirs, she talks of missed lighting cues, broken props and substandard performances. But in 1936 Hellman assumed full responsibility for the play's failure and was devastated. She felt she faced two choices: give up playwriting or try much harder on the next play. She gave it up for two years, then tried much harder and wrote *The Little Foxes.*

If *Days to Come* equivocated somewhat on its politics, it is still Hellman's most political play and was written at a time when she herself was becoming staunchly political. It was also a time when the many ideological forces that sprang from the economic turmoil of the 1930s were brought into rare harmony by an issue that all but the most conservative groups could agree on: the Spanish civil war. Not just the radicals and liberals were outraged by General Franco's attempt to take over Spain—almost everyone opposed to fascism regarded with alarm a military assault on a duly elected government of a major European nation. Many saw what was happening in Spain as a crucial advance in a fascist sweep of Europe, a belief that was strengthened when the two countries that were already fascist, Germany and Italy, rushed to Franco's assistance.

The communists, who long had said, "If you are not with us you are against us," now tried to co-opt the Spanish war by twisting the maxim around to "If you are not for us, you are for our enemies." In this case their enemies were the fascists, but that spurious bit of logic was a constant ploy of the American Communist party and was used again with great effectiveness during the McCarthy period when anticommunist sentiments brought accusations of profascist ones.

It would be hard to overestimate the role antifascism played during the mid-1930s in the radicalization of so many American writers and intellectuals, Hellman included. To be sure, in the confused wreckage caused by the Depression, the initial appeals of socialism and communism were the wide-ranging programs they offered for correcting the apparent failure of capitalism. But the communists had long linked capitalism with fascism, and Marx had predicted war as an inevitability of the profit system. With the outbreak of the Spanish civil war—which as moderate an observer as Ernest Hemingway considered a mere rehearsal for the inevitable war with Germany—Marx's apocalypse seemed to be at hand.

In addition to these harsh confirmations of Marxist theory was the culminating horror of Hitler's anti-Semitism. Since so many American writers and intellectuals were Jewish, especially in Hollywood, antifascism understandably became, as it did for Hellman, the guiding principle of their political lives. These well-situated liberals were reluctant to increase their physical involvement in a battle still being fought so far away. Some did, but many more showed their concern by turning to the group at hand that was the most vociferously antifascist—the communists.

The American Communist party responded to its broadening appeal by softening its posture; world revolution, the most extreme aspect of its program, was downplayed; emphasized instead was the most alluring—antifascism. When in 1937 Roosevelt formally denounced isolationism and insisted on the need for collective security against the Nazi menace, the Communist party found him palatable for the first time. And because of its approval of this popular President, many liberals found the Communist party more palatable. Now it was possible to support the New Deal *and* the communists.

Party recruitment reached its peak in 1937 with a particular effort made among writers, academics and other intellectuals. Looking back after many years at the writers drawn into the Party at this time, Daniel Bell makes an interesting distinction between the first wave who joined in the early 1930s and those who came in a few years later:

"The earliest converts were the literary individuals concerned with problems of self-expression and integrity—Dos Passos, James Farrell, Richard Wright, Sherwood Anderson and Edmund Wilson. As these became aware of the dishonesty of the Communist tactics, a new group appeared, the slick writers, the actors, the stage people—in short 'Hollywood'—for whom causes brought excitement, purpose and, equally important, answers to the world's problems."

A Hollywood communist who, two decades later, became a friendly witness to the House Committee on Un-American Activities, Martin Berkeley, testified that Lillian Hellman was one of the group that met at his house in Hollywood in June of 1937 to organize a Hollywood branch of the Communist party. Others at the meeting, he said, were Hammett, Dorothy Parker, Alan Campbell, Donald Ogden Stewart and the cultural head of the American Communist party, V. J. Jerome. Hellman denied being at the gathering or ever having met Berkeley, although she pleaded the Fifth Amendment to those questions at her own hearing before the House Committee. Of all the other hundreds of witnesses before that committee, no one else testified to Hellman's affiliation with the communists. (Her FBI files have three additional informants to Hellman's Party membership—which is by no means proof she was a member.)

Budd Schulberg says that even though he knew Hellman socially and was himself a Party member, he never knew her to be one as well. He added that he would not necessarily have known if she had been. In certain circumstances when the individual was well known and wanted anonymity, the Party granted it. And of course, as was learned during the Alger Hiss trial, if the individual was working underground for the Party, anonymity was required.

In her memoirs, Hellman again denies ever having become a communist. "I did not join the party, although mild overtures were made by Earl Browder and the party theorist, V. J. Jerome." She adds that she suspects Hammett joined the Party in 1937, but did not know for certain; the disarmingly simple reason she gives for her ignorance was that she never asked him. And the reason she never asked him was that she knew he would not answer.

There is stronger evidence that Hellman was not a Party member, at least not in 1936. Her play *Days to Come* poses Marxist problems, but, as the communist press testily pointed out, shunned Marxist solutions. The play was also far more sympathetic to the problems of the factory owners than any good communist writer would have been. When two years later Hellman wrote her strongly anti-Nazi play, *Watch on the Rhine,* it was during the period of the Russian-German alliance, when American communists were either mute about Hitler or actively seeking justifications for him. For this reason, the play was denounced by the communist press in the United States—but later praised, after Hitler invaded Russia thereby rendering anti-Nazism once again the Party line. If Hellman was a communist, she was remarkably free of its discipline.

In the late thirties Hellman did, however, join a number of political organizations, many of which were considered communist-front groups by the Attorney General's office. She would joke about her propensity for signing petitions and joining committees. One of the groups in which she was active was the Exiled Writers Committee for the League of American Writers, said by the FBI to be made up entirely of open or undercover communists. The FBI also had reports of Hellman's presence at the Tenth National Convention of the Communist party that took place in New York in June 1938, and the agency had been advised that she had "associated herself" with the communist wing of the American Labor Party.

Screenwriter Allen Rivkin tells of having been at the Bel Air home of Sidney Buchman, another writer, in June 1941, when word arrived of Hitler's invasion of Russia. Hellman burst in dressed completely in white and cried, "The Motherland has been invaded!" Rivkin admits to being unsure if she was joking. "Motherland" would seem to be too emotional a term for Hellman. But some such remark would have been consistent with Hellman's frequently proclaimed love for Russia, a sympathy that began in the mid 1930s and was reinforced by her firsthand experience of the country in 1937. It sprang from the belief, shared by many noncommunist liberals, that Russia was the crucible for change, the one nation that aspired to a more just world and that was making a historic effort to achieve it. One could applaud the effort without endorsing the specific means involved. It was not until after World War II, when America's relations with Russia had deteriorated sharply, that even such a degree of sympathy became impermissible to the appraisers of loyalty.

Later still, with the publication of *Scoundrel Time*, Hellman's account of her encounter with the House Committee on Un-American Activities, more than one of the writers who attacked both the book and its author said that whether or not Hellman had been a communist was moot in that she adhered to the Party line more than some communists did. That was an exaggeration in the late thirties and forties, when Hellman occasionally deviated from the Party line, but it became true in the postwar years when many American communists openly broke with the Party or denounced Russia's leadership of it, while Hellman was either defensive or silent.

Stefan Kanfer in his book *Journal of the Plague Years* has fun with Hellman as one of the famous names the red-baiters of this period used to establish the bona fides of a particular group's subversiveness, calling her and other stalwarts like Hammett and Dorothy Parker the "old money" of left-wing causes. During the unfunny 1950s, Hammett saw humor in a similar categorizing when the House Committee on Un-American Activities divided suspected radicals into categories: those who belonged to one or more left-wing organizations, those who belonged to five or more, twelve or more, and so on. Hammett said Hellman was sulking because she only belonged to the thirty-one-to-forty category while he belonged to the far more exclusive forty-one-to-fifty group. In fact, Hammett's claim for greater exclusivity was exaggerated. He shared his classification with eight other names, she with ten.

There is no doubt, however, that Hellman, regardless of whether or not she actually joined the Party, was strongly sympathetic to many, if not most, of the Party positions in the mid- and late 1930s. She would have been unusual among Hollywood-Broadway intellectuals if she hadn't been. What set Hellman very much apart was the tenacity with which she clung to those anticapitalist, procommunist views long after world events and a succession of shocking revelations about the Soviet system forced the majority of sympathizers to jump ship.

The most salient fact is that Hellman was, and remained, passionate about the world's ills and was an outspoken advocate for the actions, causes or organizations she felt were effectively combatting them. As for political parties, it seems clear that she felt the communists, more than any of the others, were on the right track. However right or wrong, she followed those convictions wherever they took her without fear of offending entrenched power or flouting ideological orthodoxy. Given her fundamental rebelliousness, such considerations were, in all likelihood, incitements.

While radicalism was commonplace during the late 1930s in the circles she frequented, her militancy did not endear her to everyone. Sitting at Tony's bar in New York with a group that included James Thurber, Hellman was urging them all to action in support of Loyalist Spain. Thurber, probably bored with yet another call to arms from one in no danger of being called, turned on her: she was a writer, he said, and should stick to writing.

In recounting the episode in a letter, Thurber was taken aback by Hellman's reply: she would give up writing immediately if she could improve the condition of the world or of one person in it. Such a pronouncement of altruism, here cited in a different time with different values, sounds ludicrously self-glorifying, but it was not so remarkable in the late 1930s, particularly among people of Hellman's nature, who often were guilt-ridden about their comfortable distance from such rampant evils as the Depression and fascism.

Hellman once said she did not believe in stupidity; she assumed everyone was reasoning with basically the same mental equipment. The day she met a truly stupid man, she would be delighted. Charming as this egalitarian outlook is, it has a dark side. Anyone disagreeing with Hellman's vision for an improved world, if disallowed stupidity, must be venal and base, probably a fascist.

Hellman, even from her very first political crusade on behalf of the Screen Writers' Guild, seemed to see the world as divided into two groups: those who cared about their fellow man and those who didn't. If you didn't share her passionate concerns or subscribe to her solutions, you were not stupid—you were a villain. Although she professes to have come to believe in the possibility of stupidity, it would be an excuse she granted few opponents; most were villains.

This same black-and-white view of the world was still much in force when she wrote *Scoundrel Time*. While there were indeed scoundrels central to that calamity, there were other issues involved as well, perhaps other points of view. But Hellman saw it as she invariably saw complex political situations—as simply good guys versus bad guys. The unspoken part of her democratic leveling of all intellects was: Everyone is as smart as I am, therefore everyone must agree with me. It was a form of intellectual totalitarianism that would cause her not just perplexity, but much frustration, bitterness and anger.

10

ELLMAN'S THIRD screenplay for Goldwyn, and her second with William Wyler as director, was an adaptation of Sidney Kingsley's 1935 Broadway success, *Dead End*. Hellman had thought highly of the play, with its theme of the social evils that result from the rich and poor living on top of each other in big cities. While she and Goldwyn wanted to remain as faithful as possible to Kingsley's play, the translation to the screen mandated a number of substantial changes. Here again Hellman showed great skill as a screenwriter. The film—which starred Sylvia Sidney, Joel McCrea, Humphrey Bogart and Claire Trevor—was praised by the critics and has become a classic of Depression realism.

Although the Hellman-Goldwyn collaboration was relatively trouble-free—primarily because he left her alone—they occasionally disagreed about her scripts. One such disagreement occurred during work on *Dead End* and produced a fine Goldwynism. To resolve his argument with Hellman, Goldwyn phoned the original author, Sidney Kingsley, in New York. But Kingsley refused to get involved, saying that he was a playwright, Goldwyn the filmmaker, and Goldwyn should decide the issue.

Goldwyn got furious. "If you don't disagree with me," he bellowed, "how will I know I'm right?"

Although the failure of *Days to Come* precipitated a creative crisis, the year following, 1937, was one of the most eventful of Hellman's life. She wrote *Dead End*, became involved in making a documentary about Spain, amused herself for several weeks in Paris with Dorothy Parker, the Gerald Murphys and Ernest Hemingway, visited Russia for the first time and dropped in on the Spanish civil war. It was also the year during which she claimed to have gone on a dangerous mission to Berlin for the Nazi resistance, or more specifically, for her friend Julia.

The account of her trip to Spain was related by Hellman in *An Unfinished Woman*, published thirty-two years later, in 1969; the story of Julia was told in *Pentimento*, published in 1973. The truth of both accounts was challenged. The events of Hellman's visit to Spain during the civil war were treated to a line-by-line refutation in *Paris Review* by Ernest Hemingway's third wife, Martha Gellhorn, who was also in Spain at the time. The story of Julia became the target of many refutations, most particularly and somewhat inadvertently by the publication in 1983 of the memoirs of a woman many feel was the real Julia.

Chronologically these two episodes occurred within a month of each other, and there may be no greater significance to this concentration of beleaguered self-anecdote than that, for the first time since acquiring the mobility and access of celebrity, Hellman was not consumed with her own work. She had the time and resources to travel, to make new friendships and to pursue her political interests. Characteristically, she sought out the scenes of the day's most dramatic events. And looking back on 1937 from the last years of her life, she may have seen it as a year in which she wished she had done more than she had.

Early in the year, Hellman was approached by her friend Archibald MacLeish about joining him, Ernest Hemingway and the talented Dutch film director Joris Ivens, to make a documentary film about the war in Spain with the aim of whipping up support for the Loyalist cause—not just from private individuals but from the U.S. Government and the governments of other democracies. Hellman, eager to get involved in a more tangible way than merely by writing checks, says she "jumped at the chance."

As it turned out, writing a check and getting others to do the same were her only contributions to the project. She went to Paris early in 1937 to join Ivens in Spain, but got pneumonia and was forced to return home. To finance the film, which would be called *The Spanish Earth,* she and MacLeish formed a corporation called Contemporary Historians. Putting up $500 apiece were Hellman, Hammett, Ralph Ingersoll, Dorothy Parker, Gerald Murphy, Herman Shumlin and Ward Cheney. The North American Committee for Spain put up $4,000 and Hemingway put up $2,750, and probably added more later, until the $13,000 cost of the film was reached.

Hellman had reason to believe in the need for a hard-hitting antifascist film on Spain. The director Walter Wanger, a friend of Hellman's, had commissioned a script on the Spanish war from John Howard Lawson, a prominent screenwriter and a leader of the Hollywood communist group. Knowing of Hellman's strong feelings about the war, Wanger invited her to a screening of the picture, which was titled *Blockade.* When it was over, he asked how she liked it.

"Fine," she said, "but one question. Which side was it on?"

Hellman had a point. About the strongest statement the film made was that it was wrong to bomb civilian populations. Still it was considered sufficiently partisan to be picketed in New York and other cities by Catholic groups.

Hammett and Hellman were as often apart as together that year. Hammett had remained in Princeton when Hellman left for Hollywood, and he wrote her constantly of his activities and on several occasions sent people for her to meet in Los Angeles. One was André Malraux, who had given a talk in Princeton while touring the country raising money for the Spanish Loyalists. He confused Hammett by telling him he was "the technical link between Dreiser and Hemingway." Hammett added, "I really like him, which is more than I can say for your friend MacLeish (or however you spell it) who is a stuffed shirt if ever I saw one."

Hammett had made no progress on his novel, and finally his Princeton idyll came to a messy end. One version has it that he did so much damage to the house that he was evicted, another that his neighbors banded together and asked him to find another town. Both could be true. In any case, he missed Hellman and was ready to return to Hollywood, where he had alluring prospects. William Randolph Hearst offered him $50,000 to write a film for his mistress, Marion Davies.

June 1937 was the month in which the organizational meeting of the Hollywood branch of the Communist party occurred at the house of Martin Berkeley, who later testified that Hellman and Hammett had been present—which Hellman denied. August found Hellman back in New York, where she attended the opening of *Dead End* at the Rivoli Theater and the next day, with a send-off of critical acclaim, sailed for Europe on the *Normandie*. She was on her way to Paris, then to Moscow to attend a theater festival and, on a last-minute impulse, to Spain. Hammett disapproved of the trip, as he did most of her trips. He said that Hellman had no business attending a theater festival because she really didn't like the theater. His grumbles about her absences became stronger and, for all their humor, more desperate.

By Hellman's account of this trip in *An Unfinished Woman*, Dorothy Parker and her husband, Alan Campbell, were with Hellman on the *Normandie*, as was Martha Gellhorn, who had only recently become Ernest Hemingway's mistress and would later be his third wife. Hellman spent three or four weeks in Paris amusing herself with the Campbells and the Gerald Murphys, whom she was meeting for the first time and who would remain good friends. This was also the first time Hellman met Ernest Hemingway, who had been waiting in Paris for the arrival of Martha Gellhorn.

Gerald and Sara Murphy had now established themselves at the center of a circle of artists and writers, many expatriate Americans like themselves, who convened in Paris. Although Gerald was a painter, the Murphys were essentially dilettantes, in the good sense of that word, offering friendship, help and hospitality at their Villa America at Cap d'Antibes to a varied collection of unpredictable and temperamental talents, including Hemingway, Picasso and Scott Fitzgerald, who used them (along with himself and his wife Zelda) as models for Dick and Nicole Diver in *Tender Is the Night*. The Murphys personified the world of fashionable celebrity that Hammett detested; in fact, he worked persistently to squelch Hellman's hankerings in that direction. But on her own in Paris, and now a celebrity herself, she established a friendship with the Murphys and joined their circle with relish.

The interval between Hellman's departure from Paris and her arrival in Moscow is the time of the climactic action of the "Julia" chapter of *Pentimento*. As for the Russian portion of her journey, Hellman's first visit to that country, it rates only one paragraph in *An Unfinished Woman* and just a quick reference in *Pentimento*. She says she did not enjoy the theater festival, but gives no indication of what she felt about Russia. That in itself is surprising, given her strong communist sympathies. Even more extraordinary is the statement that she didn't know that she "was there during the ugliest purge period. . . ."

The Moscow purge trials, which reached their peak in 1937, were, along with the Spanish civil war, perhaps the two most significant political events between the two world wars. They were covered extensively by the international press and discussed with passion by politically conscious people throughout the world. The first wave of trials, in August 1936, had resulted in the conviction and execution of sixteen of the top men in the Russian government. In January 1937 the celebrated Radek trial brought the conviction of seventeen more. In June a number of commanders of the Russian army, most of them heroes of the Revolution, were tried and shot. When Hellman arrived in October, she socialized regularly with the diplomats and journalists then in Moscow, for whom the trials were, to say the least, the subject of greatest interest. It would seem inconceivable that she was unaware the trials were in progress or unaware of their nature.

The trials had the world's attention, to be sure, but they were of particular significance to liberals. In their monstrous injustice, the legal proceedings, which also came to be called the Moscow show trials, were the first of a series of major blows to the faith of non-Russian progressives in the humanitarian aims of the Soviet government. Throughout the world, people who had been sympathetic to Russia's communist experiment, who believed its aim was a more just society and, eventually, a more just world, who had excused earlier transgressions as necessities of survival, now found themselves unable to rationalize Stalin's trumped-up charges against so many of his comrades of the Revolution. In revulsion at these judicial travesties, many communists and communist sympathizers became permanently disillusioned. Others who had always been less sympathetic felt that Stalin was finally proving what they had suspected all along—that he was a murderous, if not deranged, tyrant, and that his utopian system was in actuality another face of fascism.

Hellman says that she was confused about all this by the diplomats and journalists in Moscow who spoke "gobbledygook," except for two foreign correspondents. One of those who spoke sense for her was Walter Duranty of *The New York Times*, a correspondent well known for being among a meager handful* who at first believed Stalin was justified in liquidating a good portion of his government. Otherwise, Hellman was unable to distinguish "the true charges from the wild hatred," and "fact from invention when it is mixed with blind bitterness about a place and a people." So apparently she chose not to believe any of it.

Whether or not Hellman was unaware of the rights and wrongs of the 1937 trials or was confused by "gobbledygook," she was certain enough about their legitimacy to be one of a number of prominent American writers who, seven months later, put their names to an advertisement endorsing them in *The New Masses*. Despite such distinguished names as Nelson Algren, Malcolm Cowley, Langston Hughes, Irwin Shaw and Richard Wright, the *New Masses* letter was taken by critics of the Stalinists to be a high-water mark of their unhesitating endorsement of the most flagrant and heinous atrocities Stalin cared to perpetrate.

There is no question that Hellman displayed an unshakable fidelity to the Stalinist cause—that is to say, to a belief in the benevolent and humanitarian aims of the Soviet government under Stalin. And she was equally convinced that the Western press was misrepresenting him. In the next twenty years, there would be other blatant manifestations of Stalin's cynicism and inhumanity, reports of which Hellman was invariably able to dismiss as distortions and lies, products of the "wild hatred" of the capitalist press. The question remaining, then, is why Hellman would later

---

* The only other authoritative American to defend Stalin's purges was, ironically, the U.S. Ambassador, Joseph Davies, who was the plutocratic husband at the time of arch-capitalist Marjorie Merriweather Post.

write so sparingly, and often so obliquely, about her powerful political convictions.

After a two-week visit to Prague, Hellman arrived back in Paris, where she had dinner with Otto Simon, a Czech communist and a well-known journalist who was then serving as a director of press relations for the Spanish Loyalist government. Hellman said Simon persuaded her to go to Spain, overcoming her misgivings by promising she would be looked after by press-relations people on the scene.

By her own account, Hellman had no intention of going to Spain when she set out for Europe that year. She admits that the war frightened her—not only in the abstract political sense, but in the sense of getting hurt—a remarkably candid admission considering the many American noncombatants who had recently been there, some of them friends like Dorothy Parker, Alan Campbell, Josephine Herbst and Ernest Hemingway. Nevertheless, Hellman believed that going to Spain at that time was very dangerous, and wrote ten letters to her father, leaving them with her Paris maid with instructions to mail them at regular intervals.

By the time Hellman arrived in Spain in October 1937, Joris Ivens and Hemingway had finished their film. Hellman thought highly of it, particularly the narration by Hemingway. She had had no part in writing the script but was credited with the original story idea.

She went first to Valencia, which was relatively quiet, and settled into a hotel. The government press people showed her around a bit, but for the most part she had an untroubled, unhurried time reading and taking walks, although during one of her walks, she was caught in a bombing raid and was terrified. After a few days she was taken by car to Madrid, which she knew would be more dangerous than Valencia. There she had dinner with Hemingway and Martha Gellhorn, after which she made a radio broadcast back to America. Unlike Gellhorn and Hemingway and many other foreign observers, Hellman made no effort to get close to the front during her time in Spain and saw no fighting after Valencia except the bombardment of Madrid, which she said occurred nightly while she was there.

Her time in Spain, which lasted not more than two or three

weeks, had both drama and danger, but far more empty stretches to fill with reading, taking walks and worrying about the lack of food. In her descriptions of these weeks, Hellman vividly depicts the hard conditions in Spain, but presents them unabashedly from the point of view of a visiting VIP rather than from a person living or fighting there—or from a woman of her own passionate antifascism. If her account of the trip in *An Unfinished Woman* was, as Hellman said, based on diaries written at the time, oddly she either was not interested enough in the political issues to write about them while on the scene or chose to eliminate such writing in her 1969 memoirs.

Her strong antifascist sympathies did, however, emerge forcefully the following summer when she wrote a three-page attack, apparently never published, on William Carney, the correspondent covering the Spanish civil war for *The New York Times*, whom Hellman considered a fascist because of what she saw as his eagerness to believe Franco's propaganda. The manuscript of this piece, which has found its way into the Rutgers University Library, reveals how viciously Hellman could fight whomever she saw as her enemy. Not content with the nasty suggestion that Carney was writing his war coverage from the safety of a French Riviera resort town, Hellman said she recalled years earlier a group of newspapermen in Paris "telling strange stories" about a fellow journalist. Then she wrote: "I have gone back through memory's album and there was Mr. Carney who was the man the other men were telling the strange stories about." She offered no substantiation that Carney was the man being gossiped about except "memory's album," and there was no indication of the stories' nature other than that they were "strange."

Hellman was reacting violently to information that challenged her political convictions, and the bearer of that information was denounced as gullible, a malingerer, a coward and, to finish him off, the subject of "strange stories." The innuendo smacks of applying the *Children's Hour* strategy to the Loyalist cause. But Mary Tilford at least had the courage to be specific in her slander. Hellman, however, or perhaps an editor, had second thoughts about this particular slur against Carney; the "strange story" sentences are crossed out in pencil.

Regardless of whether or not Carney was a responsible journalist, Hellman had been back from Spain at least six months when she wrote her diatribe against him; her few weeks there gave her few grounds for refuting any report emanating from such a confusing and fast-changing war. Despite major difficulties for the perceptions of Spain watchers, which, if nothing else, her visit should have taught her, Hellman saw no difficulties. She had a clear vision of who was right, a murderous rage against those who disagreed, and no hesitation in applying this rage, even if it meant applying it unscrupulously and against *The New York Times*.

That rage is absent in her account of her trip to Spain in *An Unfinished Woman*. Hellman writes about Loyalist attempts to brief her shortly after her arrival in Spain: "I was told a great many things . . . atrocities on one side or the other . . . why what government fell when; the fights among the Anarchists and Communists and Socialists; who is on what side today and who wasn't yesterday—but this is not the way I learn things and so I only half listened . . ." Since the people talking to Hellman were all on the scene and all on the same side, it raises the question of how and from whom she did "learn things."

It is also possible she wasn't terribly interested. Except for this one reference, her memoirs do not discuss, either in later reflection or in her activities at the time, the political struggles going on within the ranks of those fighting Franco. She mentions going to "a political meeting," which she describes as a pointless farce but does not mention which party was holding it. (Because of the observers from Russia, it appears to have been communist.)

The communist fight for control of the anti-Franco effort, despite the failure of that effort, would have important ramifications in the political future of Europe. It would have another important long-range effect—the disillusionment with communism on the part of many American and European intellectuals, among them John Dos Passos and George Orwell. Hellman indicates only the mildest interest in this bitter internecine fighting. She brushes it aside with the suggestion that it was all too muddled to think about—like the Moscow purge trials.

11

The *Little Foxes* is generally considered Lillian Hellman's finest play, although that opinion is by no means unanimous. While it did not run as long as *The Children's Hour* (410 performances against *The Children's Hour*'s 691), it was nevertheless a major success, a landmark in the Broadway theater; it was made into an important film and has been revived more frequently than any of her other plays—twice in full-scale Broadway productions. The play presented a family, the Hubbards, who have become cultural familiars along with the Snopes and the Joads (who arrived the same year in *The Grapes of Wrath*). It also brought forth a performance from Tallulah Bankhead as Regina that many consider one of the most outstanding in Broadway history. All these factors have combined to place *The Little Foxes*, to a degree, beyond the reach of critics and have made it a classic of the American theater.

In an interview with *The New York Times* shortly after *The Little Foxes* opened, Hellman said that the idea for the play first came to her at the end of her visit to the Spanish civil war when she was flying out of Spain to Toulouse.* She said, too, that *The*

* In the long account of this trip in *An Unfinished Woman*, Hellman writes of making the journey out of Spain to France by train. Since there could

Little Foxes was the most difficult play she ever wrote and that she rewrote it nine times, sometimes by her own choice and sometimes because Hammett—and on one occasion Shumlin—came down hard on what she had written. Even before she began that laborious process, she spent months researching the post-bellum South, filling two notebooks with enough material for a prolix historical novel.

The play, which takes place in the American South in 1900, concerns the wealthy but unaristocratic Hubbards, a family rapaciously eager to parlay their modest mercantile success into one of the vast fortunes others are reaping from the free-enterprise firestorm sweeping America in the decades following the Civil War. The Hubbards feel their moment has arrived—in the form of a specific business opportunity—to make the leap from small-town financial success to great wealth. They want it desperately. Hellman was seeking to craft a play that demonstrated their money lust and its corrosive consequences.

When Hellman began to write the play, she had just returned from the Spanish war, from being honored in Moscow, from amusing herself in Paris with celebrated friends. The Screen Writers' Guild was now enjoying a resurgence, and Hellman had agreed to sit on the bargaining committee. The spread of fascism in Europe was a major concern. Yet it is hard to discern any of these yeasty influences in *The Little Foxes*. The play is an angry denunciation of greed, the ruthlessness it inspires and the havoc it spreads. While this was a fundamental theme of the left, it was not a theme being stressed at that particular time when the communists were downplaying such ideological differences as private ownership and the profit motive with their allies against fascism.

As with *The Children's Hour*, her new play had little connection with the topical issues that concerned Hellman or with the personal currents in her life at the moment. More than anything else, Hellman seems to have been motivated by a desire to write a good play. She was drawing on strong characters that she knew,

---

have been no motive for changing her transport from a plane to a train, it has to be taken as an example of Hellman's faulty memory for details, which is an explanation rarely allowed, even in part, by those who later attacked the truthfulness of her tales.

that she had in fact grown up with, and was drawing on the anger generated by her firsthand disgust.

To write a good play on a serious theme had been the unencumbered motivation behind *The Children's Hour,* which was as independent of specifics in the author's life as a work of the imagination can be. It was a great success. When she undertook *Days to Come,* a play that aired her immediate passions, it was a disaster. Of course, she felt passionately about the Hubbards, but she viewed them from a distance—they no longer touched her directly. Perhaps it was this remove that enabled Hellman to write about them with clarity and control.

Hellman readily acknowledged Hammett's role in the creation of *The Little Foxes.* She said he worked harder with her on this play than any of the others, an effort she ascribed to his chagrin over the disaster of *Days to Come.* He was most effective in preventing mistakes. One of the most overworked devices of the playwright is to fill missing plot strands with servants telling each other what has gone on before the curtain rises, describing the characters we are about to meet, indicating which ones we are to root for and which to beware of. Working on *The Little Foxes* in the Tavern Island house, Hellman fell into this familiar trap, and one night, after a long stretch at her typewriter, she left a new draft of the first act for Hammett to read, then went to bed. Among the play's characters were two Negro servants who commented at length about the household.

The next morning Hellman awoke to find Hammett had left for Manhattan, but had written a note that read:

> *"Missy write blackamoor chit-chat.*
> *Missy better stop writing blackamoor chit-chat."*

Since Hellman was not a woman who enjoyed being ridiculed, Hammett's technique for editing out the servant palaver was indeed effective and probably typified his methods of influencing her work. This time, however, he had cut almost too deep. On reading the note, Hellman went for a long swim, and mid-swim considered drowning herself, but decided instead to cut the servant dialogue. Years later, Hellman commented on "the toughness of his criticism, the coldness of his praise," but saw in it, and admired greatly, a refusal "to decorate or apologize or placate"—with her or anyone else, a refusal that "came from the most carefully guarded honesty I have ever known, as if one lie would muck up his world."

Although Hammett was still not producing any writing of his own, money was plentiful from royalties from his books and the various spinoffs of *The Thin Man*. He spoke to a psychiatrist about his inability to write and offered them his own explanation for his block: that he had nothing to write about, that his real life had ended when he became famous and was lifted out of the social class to which he belonged but in which he no longer fit. Also the extravagant praise for his work gave him an insupportable sense of fraudulence. But if he could not write, Hammett was becoming more politically active. He was on the editorial board of *Jewish Survey* and took a prominent part in launching a new magazine called *Equality*—a monthly aimed primarily at combatting anti-Semitism. Hellman was also on the editorial board of *Equality*.

In discussing her inspiration for *The Little Foxes* in her memoirs, Hellman acknowledged a "distant connection" between the Hubbards and her mother's rich relatives, the Marxes and the Newhouses, and pointed out that she had softened somewhat the character of her central figure, Regina. Because the husband of the real-life prototype had had syphilis, she had banished him to an outbuilding on the pretext that he might infect their children. In earlier drafts, Hellman incorporated the syphilis and the banishment, but later changed the husband's ailment to heart trouble and moved him into the main house.

When Shumlin read the play he was enthusiastic, but told Hellman she would have to wait; he was signed to direct another play. Hellman refused to wait, urged him to get out of the commitment and threatened to go to another producer. Shumlin succeeded in quitting the other play—which was *Life with Father*, one of the longest-running hits in Broadway history. Shumlin became wealthy as a director, but ran into trouble with the Internal Revenue Service and died a poor man. Still, there is no record that he ever regretted choosing *The Little Foxes* over *Life with Father.*

In casting the central part of Regina, Shumlin tried first to get Ina Claire, then Judith Anderson. Both turned him down. They cited other commitments, but the suspicion was strong that the actresses were reluctant to play a character as unsympathetic as Regina. Shumlin then asked Hellman how she would feel about Tallulah Bankhead. He considered her a good actress and she had the added advantage of being Southern. Generally Hellman had little use for performers, and she had a particular aversion to actresses like Bankhead whose offstage flamboyance she considered calculated entirely for effect. She also felt that Bankhead, then thirty-six, was too young to play Regina, a forty-year-old with a seventeen-year-old daughter.

Bankhead had started her career in New York in the 1920s but, having made little mark, had gone to London where she became the darling of the West End in a series of light comedies. In 1933 she had returned with the intention of conquering her native country in like fashion, but in six years on Broadway had managed only a dispiriting series of flops and near-misses. Sometimes she received good notices personally, but not always; her performance in *Antony and Cleopatra* had inspired John Mason Brown's famous line: "Tallulah Bankhead barged down the Nile as Cleopatra and sank." In 1939, when Shumlin approached her, Bankhead's career was at a low ebb: she was in debt, had just married an actor with equally bleak prospects and, in spite of being considered a front-runner to play Scarlett, had just lost out in the *Gone With the Wind* sweepstakes.

Hellman told Shumlin to go ahead and talk with Bankhead about playing the part but declined joining him, even though both women were then living at the same hotel, the Elysée. Shumlin stopped by Hellman's suite to announce his certainty that Tallulah would make a splendid Regina. He convinced Hellman as well, despite his still being shaken by his interview with the actress. It seems that Bankhead had received him in bed. Lying beside her under the covers was her new husband, John Emery. At the conclusion of the conversation about Bankhead's conception of Regina, when Shumlin got up to leave he was stopped by Bankhead, who said she wanted to show him something. She threw the covers from Emery and said, "Just tell me, darling, if you've ever seen a prick that big."

Hellman tells this story in *Pentimento* and uses it as one of her nastiest cuts at Bankhead in a feud that began with *The Little Foxes* and lasted, for Hellman, at least, long after Bankhead was dead. Ruminating on penis size as being an exclusively homosexual preoccupation, then expressing doubt that most women care about it, Hellman concludes: "Almost certainly Tallulah didn't care about the size or the function. . . ." The last three words must surely have surprised Bankhead's numerous lovers, including Jock Whitney and Edward R. Murrow.

Bankhead was cast in the part of Regina, and the play went into rehearsals. Hellman had cooled on her friend Aline Bernstein as a set designer and agreed only to her doing the costumes. To design the production, Shumlin hired the twenty-seven-year-old Howard Bay, who would design a number of Hellman's plays and become a lifelong friend of hers.

While everyone connected with *The Little Foxes* knew it was a powerful play, they were far from confident that it would be a hit, in contrast to the optimism of the cast of *The Children's Hour* with regard to that play. The setting was so remote from the concerns of 1939, the characters so rotten. The uncertainty was not helped by the play's out-of-town tryouts, which brought mixed reviews—and as the New York opening drew near, tensions mounted. Still, Hellman, Bankhead and Shumlin—all noted for their tempers—got along remarkably well. The famous feud between Hellman and Bankhead did not begin until after the play had been running many months in New York.

Although *The Little Foxes* got good notices when it opened in Baltimore, the first performance was not the sort to assure all the participants that they had a sure success. Shumlin and Bankhead felt that at least fifteen minutes had to be cut from the last act, and Hellman reluctantly agreed. Even with such problems, an effort was made for a festive opening-night party, largely because of the friends of the principals who had made the journey to Baltimore. Hammett had come down a week in advance. For the opening, he was joined in the Hellman cheering section by the Gerald Murphys, who were recently back from France, Dorothy Parker and Alan Campbell. Up from Washington to cheer his daughter on were the Speaker of the House of Representatives, William B. Bankhead, and his brother, the Senator from Alabama, John Bankhead. In her description of the opening-night party in *Pentimento,* Hellman added to her list of complaints against Bankhead her boozy relatives, her use of cocaine and a drunken pass she made at a black waiter.

The distinguished writer John Malcolm Brinnin for many years taught *The Little Foxes* in a course on American drama at the University of Connecticut. "Every year I taught that play, my admiration increased for its brilliant construction," he said. "It was like a Chinese box, each piece fitting precisely with the next."

Few would argue with the deftness of Hellman's plot: Regina and her two brothers, Oscar and Ben, have a chance at an investment that is certain to make them rich. Each must put up $75,000 for a one-third interest. Regina will get her third from her husband, Horace, who has $83,000 in Union Pacific bonds in a strongbox at the bank where their nephew, Ben's son, Leo, works. Because of a heart condition, Horace has been at a hospital in Baltimore, as much to stay away from Regina as for his health. Now that Regina needs Horace for her deal, she has sent her daughter, Alexandra, to bring him home. Once home, Horace flummoxes Regina by refusing to advance the money. Her brothers tell her they will go elsewhere for the third, but would prefer not bringing in an outsider. When the brothers learn from Leo that Horace's bonds are available and could be "borrowed" with no fear of discovery, they take the bonds and tell Regina she is out of the deal.

Learning of the theft, Regina uses the information to blackmail her brothers into giving her a 75 percent interest for her unauthorized "investment." When she makes it clear that their alternative is jail, they are forced to comply. When Horace discovers the bonds are missing and learns of his wife's greedy trickery, he overturns her triumph by saying he will claim he loaned the bonds to his brothers-in-law. Regina is incited to a scathing attack on Horace, which brings on a heart attack. Since his death will eliminate her problems and make her rich, she stands immobile while he pleads with her for his medicine. She coldly watches his desperate struggle up the stairs that will end in death. Since the bonds now belong to her, Regina is once again victorious. The only cloud comes from her daughter, Alexandra, who suspects her mother's complicity in her father's death, voices her disgust and leaves home. At the play's end, the disaffection bothers Regina some, but not a lot.

To capsulize an already dense plot intensifies its melodramatic aspects. In the theater, however, the events seem to unfold with a believable logic, a logic on which Hellman worked assiduously. For instance, Leo has tempted his father and uncle into the theft of the bonds by assuring them that Horace never checks his strongbox. But when the bonds kept there become an issue between Regina and Horace, he has reason to break his custom and ask to see them, thus discovering the theft very soon after it occurs. In like fashion, Hellman has nailed down all the loose boards in her construction, and the result is action that moves forward swiftly, yet makes frequent turns, sudden and unexpected, that result in major shifts in the power balance between the contenders. Not only is it a virtuoso display of plotting on the part of the author, but the "plotting" of her characters turns the three hours spent with them into a virtuoso display of human cunning.

The Little Foxes, which Hellman dedicated to Arthur Kober and Louis Kronenberger, opened at the National Theater on West Forty-first Street on February 2, 1939. Max Hellman was in the audience along with many of her other relatives and most of her close friends. During the first-act intermission, Hellman went up to Florence Newhouse, one of her mother's two unmarried sisters and said, "Well, do you recognize your relatives?" Julia Hellman had died of cancer a few years before, so never saw her likeness in Birdie, Ben Hubbard's genteel and utterly defeated wife. The opening-night party was given by Clare and Henry Luce, who had become friendly with Hellman through Ralph Ingersoll.

It was a rich season for the Broadway theater. Running at the same time as *The Little Foxes* were Saroyan's *The Time of Your Life*, Philip Barry's *The Philadelphia Story*, with Katharine Hepburn, Kaufman and Hart's *The Man Who Came to Dinner*, Maxwell Anderson's *Key Largo*, with Paul Muni, Emlyn Williams's *The Corn Is Green*, with Ethel Barrymore, *No Time for Comedy*, with Katharine Cornell and Laurence Olivier, and the record-breaking *Life with Father*. Among the musicals were Cole Porter's *Leave It to Me* in which Mary Martin established herself as a star singing "My Heart Belongs to Daddy" and two by Rodgers and Hart: *The Boys from Syracuse* and *I Married an Angel*, the latter with Vera Zorina.

Hellman rose above this formidable competition. The New York critics heaped praise on both the play and Tallulah Bankhead's performance. Brooks Atkinson in *The Times* had some complaints about the contrivance, but called the play "excoriating" and "a vibrant play that works." Robert Benchley pronounced the play "awfully, awfully good." *Time* said that Hellman's play "brilliantly succeeds" and that she makes "her plot crouch, coil, dart like a snake. . . ." *Life* called it "the year's strongest play." These were the critics who decided whether or not *The Little Foxes* would be a hit, which it certainly was.

The scholarly and intellectual commentators who decide whether or not a play will endure have had a more difficult time determining whether or not they like it. Frequently the more reflective essays on *The Little Foxes*, rather than clarifying where it should rank among twentieth-century American plays, succeed only in conveying their writers' uncertainty about what to make of it. In many instances those who like it are no more convincing in their rationales than those who dismiss it. Both supporters and detractors grant the play seriousness and an unflinching directness in making its points. They also acknowledge the power it has over audiences. But many are bothered by its plot heaviness: so much happens in so short a time, the action takes so many surprise turns, the characters are so unrelentingly vicious. Such complaints invariably lead up to the same conclusion: melodrama.

One problem with a term like "melodrama" is that no two of the critics using it could agree on a mutually satisfying definition. Many tried, but their verbal contortions drove one wag to say that melodrama is when you care what happens next. With that criterion *The Little Foxes* certainly qualifies—as do most of Hellman's plays. One group dubs as melodramas plays that are marked by excessive use of action, particularly violent action. Again *The Little Foxes* qualifies; it is full of action and a sort of drawing-room brutality that could be called violence. Others reject that test, Hellman among them, by pointing out that the literature of great theater rocks with violence. Another indicator for some is the *random* use of violence and all plot developments; that is, when events on the stage merely *happen*, to no overall purpose on the author's part. With that as the determinant, *The Little Foxes* beats the charge handily; few characters can match the Hubbards' single-mindedness in pushing their author's point.

A more interesting distinction is made between serious theater and melodrama when the term "serious" is reserved for plays in which the events lead the characters, and by extension the audience, into deeper understanding of the world or of themselves. In this, *The Little Foxes* falls down. There is almost no introspection on the Hubbards' part, nor does the author reveal much dimension in them other than the depth of their corruption.

Here, however, the play could make an alternative claim for this sort of seriousness. While we are not led by the action into a larger perception of the characters at hand, and by extension of human nature, we are given an alternative broadening of vision by the characters' throwing light on the culture from which they have sprung. We come away not necessarily with a deeper understanding of the human condition but with a deeper understanding of American society as a molder of individuals. And this society, after nearly a decade of the Depression, was subjecting itself to an excoriating reexamination of its values.

There are two problems with this analysis. Foremost is that Hellman herself denies that her play aims at making a broad statement on capitalism or the industrialization of the South. Second, and surely an outgrowth of the first, there is no question that we care far more about her characters' relationships with each other than their relationship to society—or, indeed, whether or not they function well as exemplars of their society's values. They are too forcefully drawn as individuals.

If *The Little Foxes* is melodrama, the question then becomes: Is melodrama such a bad thing? A compromise might be found by calling melodrama a classification inferior to plays that achieve art, and by calling *The Little Foxes* a highly superior melodrama—which is what many of the play's more perplexed critics end up doing. Even with the play finally forced into a category, the question remains whether anything has been accomplished.

Another problem the play presents for serious critics of a moralistic bent is the audience's fascination with characters of such unmitigated venality. In most of the great classic dramas, heroes or heroines do battle with evil. They are characters with whom the audience can align its righteous impulses. In *The Little Foxes,* only the incapacitated Horace tries to thwart the evil, and he is destroyed. Hellman's conflict is evil versus evil, and evil triumphs, with the decent characters merely impotent onlookers. Of course, that is one of Hellman's primary points as borne out in the maid Addie's speech: "Well, there are people who eat the earth and eat all the people on it . . . and other people who stand around and watch them do it." If that is the way Hellman viewed the world, it would be a serious compromise for her to alter her vision to accommodate a rule of dramaturgical construction. Addie goes on to say, "Sometimes I think it ain't right to stand and watch them do it." But that is about as moralistic as the play gets.

The Little Foxes presents another problem for serious critics, one that shows why its audiences have far greater freedom than its critics in bestowing their accolades. It lies in the character of Regina. She is the "heroine" of the play, yet allows her husband to die, so she is, in effect, a murderess. And we cannot applaud murderesses, at least not from the clearheaded distance of the scholarly study. But Regina's hold over audiences raises the suggestion that we *can* applaud them from a theater seat. Hellman has created perhaps her most vivid character in Regina. She is smart, good-looking and funny—all winning attributes in a heroine. She is strong, allows no one to push her around and is cannily resourceful in getting what she wants. Those, too, are qualities to be admired. Regina is trapped in a hate-filled marriage and stifled in a small town that offers her nothing. She desperately wants romance and the stimulations of a large city while she is still young enough to enjoy them. A Broadway theater audience is not likely to scorn her for that.

The fact is, we root for her, and if Hellman didn't want us to, she is a very clumsy playwright indeed. We are well into the first act and well charmed by Regina before Hellman allows some of her unscrupulousness to show, but even that is in response to her brother's threat to cut her out of the deal. We see it as pluck, giving as good as she gets. When for selfish reasons she abets the death of another human, however, a moral siren goes off for the serious-minded, and she is without ceremony dismissed as a villainess. Case closed.

Audiences, it appears, are less quick to condemn. The character, who has intrigued us and made us want to see her win, is at the point of victory, when she has it snatched from her by a husband acting, at least to some degree, from spite. Seeing herself cornered, about to lose her last chance at getting what she wants from the world, Regina does something desperate. Audiences can also identify with that. Regina does not *plan* her husband's death. She merely permits it to happen. And Hellman further softens the crime by portraying Horace as tired of life and already close to death.

It is this ability on Hellman's part to make us follow with fascination the play's central character up to and into murder that is the hidden strength of *The Little Foxes*. Hellman professed a repugnance for the rich, yet she would be delighted to become one of them. That same ambivalence is revealed in her portrait of Regina. It is doubtful that Hellman would ever admit to admiring her, yet something akin to admiration, perhaps unconscious, seems to have been present to energize the creation of a character who holds our attention so completely.

Hellman was surprised by the reaction to the play on the part of the critics and the public. She was gratified that they liked it but dismayed that they saw the Hubbards as curious case histories. She had wanted them to see themselves. She also saw the play more as a comedy, albeit a black comedy, not to be taken so seriously. She later wrote that she saw humor in the greedy sparring of the Hubbards in the same way she had seen humor mixed with disgust in her mother's money-obsessed relatives.

Since Hellman made so many remarks contradicting the general perception of her work, especially *The Little Foxes*, the suspicion arises that she did it to confound, perhaps from a fear of being interpreted too easily. A friend once paid her an extravagant compliment by saying that she doubted Tennessee Williams could have written the character of Amanda in *The Glass Menagerie* if Hellman hadn't first created the character of Birdie, Oscar Hubbard's pathetic wife. Hellman said she never understood why audiences were so touched by Birdie; she, Hellman, didn't like her. She had expected audiences to feel contempt for Birdie's weakness and genteel passivity.

Just as it is difficult to believe Hellman wanted us to despise Regina, it is hard to believe she wanted us to feel contempt for Birdie as well. The ability to create ambiguous characters, neither saints nor villains, was one of Hellman's great strengths as a dramatist. While she is writing her characters, she inhabits them to a degree that renders irrelevant questions of like or dislike. Whether a good or bad character, Hellman becomes that character and argues his or her position as persuasively as she herself would. It is a schizophrenic legerdemain suggesting that if Hellman had been a weak, silly aristocrat, she would have been as appealing and touching as Birdie, and that if she had been an avaricious husband-killer, she would have been as awesome and unforgettable as Regina.

Perhaps the best example of her deftness at making bad characters persuasive is Mrs. Tilford in *The Children's Hour*. By the conclusion of the story, it is clear Hellman loathes Mrs. Tilford; at the same time she has given her dignity, intelligence and a degree of eloquence. Hellman's primary motive seems to be to make her evil characters vivid and engaging, as well as plausible and dimensional—perhaps so that they will be worthy adversaries to whatever force she has set in opposition to them. In her striving for that balance, she loses a degree of control over whether or not the audience will like or dislike them. And for Hellman, it appears, the loss was not important.

12

AFTER THE RECEPTION of *The Little Foxes,* Hellman had to grapple with an alarming fact: at the age of thirty-four she was a major American playwright. She would not be the first to find recognition of such magnitude profoundly unsettling. Prominent among her anxieties was a fear of being seduced by the rewards of theater. Speaking in later years about the period after the opening of *The Little Foxes,* she said, "When success came, I gave it four days of fun, then ran away fast, frightened that it would become a way of life." In addition, she had good reason to fear the praise itself. Close at hand, she had the sorry spectacle of a writer who had been praised into inertia. Hammett's writer's block, which had gone on for three years and would be permanent, began when important critics and writers started calling him great.

Now Hellman felt the same sort of vertigo. She could view *The Children's Hour* as a fluke, or her screenplays as distinguished only when compared to the usual Hollywood product. She was not so many years away from her first college-girl encounters with truly great writers, which in her case were marked by more than the usual infatuations and intolerance of lesser talents. With another of her plays being vaunted as a landmark in the American theater, she was being pushed dangerously close to her literary gods and it made her acutely anxious. Hellman started drinking heavily and sailed off to Havana "for a rest." What should have been one of the best years of her life became one of the worst.

Hellman's uncertainty about her ability to write another hit play had a practical by-product: fears about money. She had saved almost nothing from the lavish proceeds from her first play and had made no investments of any significance. Now with *The Little Foxes* settling down for a long run, she resolved not to fritter away the winnings a second time; she might not have another chance at a windfall. She would make a solid investment, buy a property. Not only did that prove to be a smart course from a financial point of view, it was a sound emotional investment as well. By acting on her decision, she was diverted from the corrosive psychic ramifications of success, and in all likelihood saved herself from a crack-up.

Taking most of the money she had, she bought a farm about an hour and a half's drive north of the city on the Saw Mill River Parkway, just outside the village of Pleasantville in Westchester County. It was a sprawling acreage, only a portion of it under cultivation, the rest raw woods surrounding a swampy lake. The main house was an enlarged farmhouse—part white frame, part stone. There were also a number of outbuildings including two guesthouses and a springhouse. The stone barn was converted by Hellman into a party house complete with a carved wood bar, a relic from a local taproom.

An idiosyncrasy that drew Hellman to the property was the incongruity between the house and the grounds. Formal gardens, bridle paths, exotic trees suggested an estate, but the house itself, while not small, was simple, almost folksy. Another unusual feature of the place, which was known as (and would remain) Hardscrabble Farm, was the situation of the house. It seemed to sit in a depression—too small for a valley, too big for a gully— with land rising behind it and, to the front and sides, after a modest sweep of lawn, a border of tall trees that had the effect of completing the encirclement. In a region of rolling hills and sweeping vistas, Hellman, for all her 130 acres, chose a house that was closed in, offering not just privacy but a sense of protection, fortification by nature. From the main house the small amount of the world that was visible belonged to Lillian Hellman—and you couldn't see very much of that.

Hellman loved the farm and so did Hammett. She spent what little money she had left on the addition of a sunny ground-floor workroom, opening onto the lawn, which she painted white and lined with bookshelves. The second floor of the main house was a confusion of rooms, most of them small, that added up to only two bedroom suites. Hellman took one, Hammett the other; guests were put in the outbuildings.

Once settled in the house, Hellman threw herself into gardening, flowers and vegetables both, and became serious about raising things to sell, from ducks to Belgian asparagus. To oversee these projects she hired a young German farmer who lived in the area. Hellman had always had strong homemaking instincts—perhaps a throwback to her aunts' well-run boardinghouse—and even with servants at hand, would pitch in on the domestic chores. She enjoyed cooking in particular and now took it up in a serious way, often the Creole and Cajun dishes of her New Orleans childhood, but also improvisations concocted from the local bounty. Some of these dishes, Hellman inspirations like boiled skunkweed, had never been considered edible by the local people, nor were they by Hellman's guests.

Except for the apartment on West Ninety-fifth Street, Hellman had never had a real home. In New Orleans it had been a boardinghouse, rented houses with Kober and Hammett, hotels and apartments. Even after the success of her first play, she continued to rent temporary quarters. It is not surprising that, finally settled, she formed a deep bond with her farm, spent as much time there as she could, and was fascinated by every aspect of its management from laying paving stones to planting acorn squash. The thirteen years she owned Hardscrabble Farm would be the happiest of her life. They were the happiest of Hammett's as well.

The farm saw a constant parade of guests: mostly good friends such as Dorothy Parker, Louis Kronenberger, Arthur Kober and his new wife, and an occasional new enthusiasm of Hellman's, usually political or intellectual, but occasionally amatory. She shied away from theater people, an aversion she frequently passed off as snobbery, but for which she once gave a quite different explanation. "I didn't think it out," she said, "but I stayed away from them. I was afraid of competing." Theater people might also be anxiety-inducing reminders of the uncomfortably weighty position she now held in the American theater. The farm was to be an escape from that.

Hellman admitted to having a jealous nature and hypothesized that it was the root cause of her frequent extra-Hammett involvements: she was repaying him for his many "casual ladies." While no one, including Hellman, would deny that she had a vindictive streak, she also had a sexually greedy one, so if her rationale was valid, she could appease both impulses with each lover.

At some point during the run of *The Little Foxes,* Hellman's relationship with Shumlin turned romantic, but it would be hard to pin down an exact time, since Hellman, Hammett and Shumlin had come to be close friends and spent considerable time together; on at least one occasion Hellman and Hammett stayed with Shumlin while waiting to move into Hardscrabble Farm. Shumlin was also a frequent guest at the farm, and since their evenings often ended up in a haze of alcohol, they may have grown lax about who belonged in which bed. Rumors soon began circulating around New York that Hellman had become a Westchester County Catherine the Great, keeping a stable of lovers in assorted guesthouses on her estate and of an evening paying them each a call. True or not, the billeting of each guest in a separate building made possible such after-lights-out bed-hopping.

Whatever the arrangement, it seemed to work well for both Hellman and Hammett. A photograph of them shortly after moving to Hardscrabble Farm shows her in tennis whites and him in a suit, sitting at a table set up on the lawn with the house behind them, a tea tray on the table in front of them. To look at the photograph, World War II would seem to be very far away. As it turned out, it wasn't, at least in that part of Westchester County; soon after moving to the farm Hellman started work on a new play, *Watch on the Rhine,* that would be an attack on this very picture of insular comfort while "the earth was being eaten" by the fascists.

According to Tallulah Bankhead, her relations with Hellman were cordial until *The Little Foxes* had been running for almost a year. Presumably the two women held many liberal views in common. Bankhead was not only a passionate and lifelong Democrat, she would also throw her support behind causes that were too far left for many Democrats. She was one of a group of actors who went to Washington and worked strenuously to save the Federal Theater Project when many supporters had abandoned it, believing the group had fallen hostage to the communists. During the run of *The Little Foxes*, Bankhead even persuaded the police around the theater to help out. Howard Bay recalls theatergoers startled to be greeted on arrival at the National by a hulking cop handing them a pamphlet and saying, "We gotta save duh theatah."

The American left was stunned on August 23, 1939, by the announcement of a nonaggression pact between Russia and Germany. Only nine days earlier an advertisement had appeared, signed by Hellman, Hammett and 400 other American intellectuals, denouncing the recently formed Committee for Cultural Freedom and its "fantastic falsehood" that the USSR was no different from the other totalitarian states. Such slanders, the open letter said, were calculated to damage relations between Russia and other peace-loving nations.

The intellectuals' insistence that Russia was Nazi Germany's number one enemy was made to look absurd by the Hitler-Stalin pact. A week later (September 1), the Germans and the Russians invaded Poland, signaling the beginning of World War II. While the world was still trying to digest this development, the Russians invaded Finland. In a very short time the Soviet-German agreement was converted from an abstract accord (surely a time-buying ploy, the loyal insisted) into a concrete collaboration.

The Russian invasion of Finland was one of those alarming international developments that united a wide range of political opinion into a united cry of outrage. Sympathy was enormous for the tiny country being overrun by its gigantic neighbor, and supportive responses sprang up from diverse quarters. Bankhead and several of the cast of *The Little Foxes* announced to the press their intention of doing a benefit performance for Finland and

Lillian Hellman, three years old, photographed in New
Orleans with her nurse, Sophronia, who scolded her, "Don't
go through life making trouble for people."

ABOVE: Hellman's only marriage, to humorist and playwright Arthur Kober, ended amicably in 1930 when she met Dashiell Hammett in Hollywood.

LEFT: Brilliant creator of detective fiction, alcoholic, relentless womanizer, Hammett was the dominant figure in Hellman's life for more than thirty years.

BELOW: Guided by Hammett in both playwriting and leftist politics, Hellman was twenty-nine when the success of her first play, *The Children's Hour*, established her as an important new dramatist.

ABOVE: Just 3 years after quitting a $50-a-week reader's job at MGM, Hellman stepped off a plane in Los Angeles to start work as a $2,500-a-week scriptwriter for Samuel Goldwyn.

LEFT: Leaving an unruly Hammett in Hollywood, Hellman for a time enjoyed a captain's paradise in New York with Time-Life dynamo Ralph Ingersoll.

LEFT: Dorothy Parker, one of Hellman's few close women friends, once remarked, "When Lillian gets angry, I regret to say she screams."

BELOW: During rehearsals for *The Little Foxes* in 1939, relations between Hellman and its temperamental star, Tallulah Bankhead, were not yet stormy, and between Hellman and director Herman Shumlin, not yet amorous.

OPPOSITE TOP: The Hellman screenplay for the highly acclaimed film version of *The Little Foxes* starred Bette Davis and Herbert Marshall, shown here with director William Wyler and cameraman Gregg Toland. Hellman and Wyler had scored other film triumphs with *These Three* and *Dead End.*

OPPOSITE BOTTOM: During the thirteen years Hellman and Hammett spent together at her Westchester County farm, her reputation as a dramatist burgeoned while he suffered a writer's block that would become permanent.

ABOVE: Hellman and Hammett at "21" in 1941, shortly before the forty-eight-year-old Hammett enlisted in the army as a private, "the happiest day of his life."

LEFT: Well known for her communist sympathies, Hellman embarked on a perilous trip across Siberia to Moscow in 1944 at the invitation of the Soviet government.

RIGHT: Hellman and John Melby, an under secretary at the U.S. Embassy, fell in love in Moscow and had an affair, a relationship that would contribute to Melby's downfall in the State Department during the communist witch hunts of the early 1950s.

BELOW: Hellman, shown here with Dmitri Shostakovich, was a guiding force behind the 1949 "Waldorf Conference" of the National Council of the Arts, Sciences and Professions, which, for the American left, was a last hurrah before the ascendancy of McCarthyism.

OPPOSITE TOP: Cited for contempt of a Federal court, Hammett was sent to jail in 1951 for refusing to respond to a question he could honestly have answered by saying "I don't know."

OPPOSITE BOTTOM: Her fame and fortune at low ebb after her appearance before the House Un-American Activities Committee in 1952, Hellman divided her time between New York and a house on Martha's Vineyard. Here, her housekeeper of many years, Helen Jackson, serves lunch to Hellman and a friend.

ABOVE: In deteriorating health and totally dependent on Hellman financially until his death in 1961, Hammett saw only a few close friends in his last years, among them poet Richard Wilbur and his wife Charlee, shown here with Hammett.

BELOW: In spite of such stars as Ruth Gordon (to her right), Walter Matthau and Lili Darvas (to her left), Hellman's 1963 absurdist farce, *My Mother, My Father and Me,* was a resounding failure. Producer Kermit Bloomgarden is standing to her right and the play's director, Gower Champion, to her left.

BELOW: Although Hellman and Champion clowned during a rehearsal, she was unhappy about his direction and remarked to a friend that she suspected he had never read the play.

TWO PHOTOS: NEW YORK PUBLIC LIBRARY AT LINCOLN CENTER

BELOW: Hellman gave up playwriting and turned to auto-biography in the 1960s. Her memoirs, *An Unfinished Woman* and *Pentimento*, written in part at her new beach house in Vineyard Haven, were best-sellers, transforming Hellman from dramatist to literary celebrity.

AP
UPI/BETTMANN ARCHIVE

OPPOSITE TOP: Hellman marshaled her many powerful friends to launch the Committee for Public Justice, among them Mike Nichols, who attended the 1975 Circle-in-the-Square benefit honoring Hellman's literary and political achievements.

OPPOSITE BOTTOM: After Warren Beatty greeted her at the Circle-in-the-Square tribute with a hug, Hellman said, "If you only knew how wonderful it is to be held in your arms."

BELOW: Cooking and clothes were passions throughout Hellman's lifetime. She sometimes changed her dress three times before receiving her friend, writer and photographer Richard de Combray, for dinner in her Park Avenue apartment.

LEFT: The 1977 film *Julia*, based on a chapter in *Pentimento* and starring Jason Robards, Jr., as Hammett and Jane Fonda as Hellman, added to Hellman's renown as a woman of courage and strong political convictions.

BELOW: Greeting Leonard Bernstein with an affectionate pinch at the New York premiere party for *Julia*, Hellman was seventy-two and at the peak of her fame. But critics of her memoir of the McCarthy years, *Scoundrel Time*, had begun to question her political past and her versions of the truth.

PHOTOTEQUE

RIGHT: The most serious challenge to Hellman's veracity came with the publication in 1983 of the memoirs of Muriel Gardiner Buttinger, shown here as a young woman, whose early life almost exactly paralleled the life of Hellman's friend Julia. Gardiner said she had never met Hellman.

BELOW: Fishing off the Vineyard, Hellman often swore and hoisted a finger at motorboats that came too close—the same attitude she adopted toward the crescendo of charges that she had been less than truthful in all her memoirs.

Nearly blind, severely crippled and suffering with emphysema from years of heavy smoking, Hellman died in 1984, feisty and combative until the end. "If you don't give me a cigarette this minute," she told a nurse, "I'm going to start screaming."

were dumbfounded when Hellman and Shumlin turned them down on the grounds that it wasn't America's fight and that outcries for Finland were warmongering. Bankhead was incensed and took her wrath to the newspapers, charging Hellman and Shumlin with hiding their real reasons for refusing the benefit—their pro-Russian sympathies. ("I've adopted Spanish Loyalist orphans and sent money to China, causes for which both Mr. Shumlin and Miss Hellman were strenuous proponents. . . . Why should [they] suddenly become so insular?")

Hellman countered with a statement explaining her position. "I don't believe in that fine, lovable little Republic of Finland that everyone gets so weepy about. I've been there and it looks like a pro-Nazi little Republic to me." She also felt that playing a benefit for Finland would give a dangerous impetus to the war spirit in America.

Hellman's political involvements up to now had been relatively inconspicuous to the public at large: working for the Screen Writers' Guild, lending her name, along with hundreds of other celebrities, to numerous left-wing groups, writing a mildly liberal pro-labor play. But now with a widely publicized scrap with a famous actress and taking the unpopular side on the moment's most emotional political issue, Hellman's dogged pro-Sovietism became widely known and won her many enemies.

First the Moscow purge trials and now the nonaggression pact with Hitler had caused large numbers of American liberals to lose faith in Russia. Progressives who had clung to a belief in the Soviet government as humanity's brightest hope had been forced to recognize it a brutal totalitarian regime and a suitable ally for Hitler. A few years earlier, Hellman's siding with Moscow would have brought little notice; now it earned her the enmity of vast new reaches of the public. But as Hellman's friends already knew, the more the current tide forbade her a position, the more likely she was to cling to it, often defending her stance ferociously and with diminishing logic or honor.

The furor over the Finnish benefit had barely died down when Hellman re-ignited it, this time adding a twist. In a lengthy newspaper interview covering many subjects, she offered an additional reason why she had refused Bankhead her Finnish benefit: when the Spanish government fell, she and Shumlin had asked

Bankhead and the *Little Foxes* company to do a benefit for the Loyalists fleeing across the border into France. They had refused. Bankhead once again was outraged. "The charge that I had refused to play a benefit for Loyalist Spain was a brazen invention," she wrote in her memoirs. "Neither Shumlin nor Miss Hellman ever asked me to do any such thing. Nor did anyone else. Both were champions of Loyalist Spain, both were desolated when Barcelona fell. *The Little Foxes* was rehearsing on that black day. I remember taking Lillian to my dressing room to give her a shot of brandy to ease her anguish."

The truth seemed to favor Bankhead's side of the dispute. If Hellman had asked Bankhead and the cast of *The Little Foxes* to do a Loyalist benefit, it is hard to understand why she did not mention the request in any of the statements she made to the press at the time of the Finnish-benefit scandal. Also, a refusal would seem to be a petty and illogical defense on Hellman's part for denying the Finns her assistance.

The two women would not speak for the next thirty years; then Hellman initiated a reconciliation. But in her memoirs, written after Bankhead's death, she had the last word in the argument. Her portrait of Bankhead was scathing. And in corroboration of her earlier statement that she had refused to participate in the Finnish benefit because on a trip to Finland it looked like a "pro-Nazi little Republic to me," she said she had been in Finland in 1937 and had had to turn her head from "the giant posters of Hitler pasted to the side wall of my hotel." She also told of having been taken by a Finnish friend to a pro-Hitler rally—certainly an odd outing to relate just after positing a sensibility that recoiled from Hitler's likeness.

Aside from questions of whether or not Hellman's journalistic curiosity would motivate her to attend a Nazi pep rally, or if even in Germany at that time (or ever) buildings were festooned with Hitler's picture, it is doubtful that Hellman went to Finland in 1937. There was not sufficient time during her August visit to Paris, Moscow, Prague and Spain. She mentions having gone to Paris earlier that year to work on *The Spanish Earth* with Joris Ivens, but had come down with pneumonia and had to return home. And if she was there, even briefly, to help a desperate war situation with a propaganda film, it strains belief that she would have taken a leisurely two-week detour to Finland, a country which, at that time, had nothing to do with the Loyalist cause Hellman cared about so deeply.

Hellman's later version of the dispute with Bankhead would lengthen the list of stories in her memoirs that were challenged for their accuracy. But at the time, because of Bankhead's flamboyance, her complaints against Hellman were written off by many as, at best, political differences, and, at worst, so much theatrics, perhaps publicity-getting theatrics. Yet none of those who disliked Bankhead, including Hellman, ever accused her of lying. (The two women's favorite insult to hurl at each other was "boring.") It would seem, then, to be another example of the way in which Hellman, when convinced she was on the side of right and her enemies on the side of wrong, felt no compunction about using whatever weapons were at hand, including her creative imagination.

13

IN THE MIDDLE of November 1939, when Hellman and Bankhead were trading insults in the New York newspapers, an American woman, a slim, striking brunette, boarded the *Manhattan* in Bordeaux to bring her husband, a leader of the Austrian resistance to the Nazis, and her eight-year-old daughter out of Europe to the safety of America. Although the dark-haired woman did not know it for forty-three years, her life would soon make a deep and lasting impression on Lillian Hellman.

The woman, who celebrated her thirty-eighth birthday during the voyage, had been born in Chicago as Muriel Morris. Her paternal grandfather, Nelson Beisinger, was a Jew who had emigrated from southern Germany, like Hellman's Marx and Newhouse forebears, among the hordes who left for America following the Revolution of 1848. Beisinger changed his name to Morris and worked his way up from impoverished immigrant to become the founder of a prosperous meat-packing firm on Chicago's South Side. His oldest son, Edward, married the daughter of another self-made meat packer, Gustavus Swift, who was of a non-Jewish family from New England and, before that, England. The Morris firm was merged into the Armour Company. As a daughter of this Swift-Morris marriage, Muriel had two very rich grandfathers.

She got her B.A. from Wellesley in 1922, then spent the following two years at Oxford doing graduate work in English literature. In 1926 Muriel went to Vienna in the hope of studying psychiatry with Sigmund Freud. When she learned Freud was not then accepting additional students, she enrolled in the University of Vienna to become a psychiatrist.

She was married briefly to an Englishman, Julian Gardiner, by whom she had a daughter. After separation from her husband, she had an affair with the poet Stephen Spender—his first with a woman, he told her disarmingly. Muriel was a socialist by conviction, and she became involved with the antifascist movement; as the Nazis spread their power in Austria, her involvement increased and her group went underground. Using the operational cover name "Mary," Muriel Gardiner ran dangerous errands for the underground, permitted the use of her two Vienna apartments for meetings, and put her considerable wealth at the service of the underground efforts. All of Gardiner's resistance activities were well known to many colleagues in Vienna and are well documented by the archives of the Austrian resistance. Her affair with Spender ended when, in the course of her work with the underground, she met and fell in love with Joe Buttinger, a fellow socialist who was in effect the leader of the Austrian resistance. They lived together for a while and eventually got married.

As the political situation worsened, the Buttingers' efforts increasingly involved helping Jews and others in danger to leave Austria. Both Joe and Muriel stayed in Europe until the last possible minute; then, when war broke out with Hitler's invasion of Poland, they managed to obtain passage on the *Manhattan,* which was the last American ship to leave France.

Once safely in America, Muriel needed a home for herself and her family. Her lawyer in New York, a man named Wolf Schwabacher, was at the time frantic to find someone to buy his brother's half of a double house the two men shared on a large farm in Pennington, New Jersey. The brother needed money and was in a hurry to sell, forcing on Schwabacher the prospect of sharing his house with strangers. On an impulse, Muriel offered to buy the brother's half, and was quickly settled into her lawyer's house.

Schwabacher had many friends in the theater, among them Lillian Hellman, for whom he had tried to lift the Boston ban of *The Children's Hour*. Years later Muriel Gardiner Buttinger said that in those first days back in America, still numb from the grimness of Europe on the brink of war, she was cheered by the stories her friend Wolf told about his glamorous friends in the New York theater. Since Muriel was now herself a figure of considerable glamour, an American heiress who had risked her life defying the Nazis, her story would surely have been of interest to some of Schwabacher's American friends, especially those most concerned about Nazism.

Muriel and Joe Buttinger had been settled in New Jersey for about five months when Hellman started writing *Watch on the Rhine*, a play about a wealthy young American woman who returns to America with her three children, all of whom had been born in Europe, and her German husband, a leader of the Nazi resistance.

At the completion of *Watch on the Rhine*, Hellman said that she had been working the idea over in her mind for several years. Her original plan had been to write a drama about a European couple, worldly and aristocratic, settling into an Ohio town. It was to have been an examination of European versus American values, rather along the lines of Henry James's *The Europeans*. While that may have been how the idea for the play first formed in her mind, the finished product was very different. The aristocratic European couple was demoted to secondary roles, giving way to new central figures: an American heiress and her Resistance-leader husband. The basic conflict in *Watch on the Rhine* is not between new and old world values, but between a firsthand awareness of the Nazi horror and the it's-all-so-far-away comfort of a Washington, D.C., drawing room.

In all the later discussion about whether Muriel Buttinger was Hellman's Julia, no one ever suggested she was also the inspiration for Sara Muller in *Watch on the Rhine*. In view of the timing and similarities, however, that conclusion is all but inevitable. If so, Hellman can only be applauded for seeing the dramatic possibilities in this woman's life and its current relevance for all Americans. In writing the play, Hellman drew, as she always did, on other elements from her experience. The villain in the play, the Rumanian Count Teck, was based on someone she knew firsthand, an English aristocrat to whom she lost a considerable sum in a crooked poker game in London.

None of that diminishes Hellman's creativity in writing *Watch on the Rhine*. The strong plot in which she involved her characters had no connection with the events in the Buttingers' history—or, as far as is known, that of the aristocratic English poker player. Hellman was following no real-life story line as she did in *The Children's Hour;* she was saying, in effect, What if this couple who were fighting the brutality of Nazism in Europe were to bring their fight into the comfortable home of Americans as yet uninvolved but equally threatened by Nazism's spread? If the couple encountered serious opposition, how would they react? How would the American bystanders react?

Making Muriel Gardiner a principal character in *Watch on the Rhine* did not conclude Hellman's fascination with her. On the contrary, she included her several more times in her writings, but with a gradual erosion between the woman as an inspiration for fiction and an actual person in Hellman's life.

Even before she began work on *Watch on the Rhine*, Hellman became actively involved in the organization of Ralph Ingersoll's new newspaper, *PM;* Hammett did, as well. The project excited many leftist intellectuals who were convinced they were not getting the true state of the world from the existing media outlets with their procapitalist, anti-Russian bias. Hammett and Hellman had other reasons to be excited. In addition to their friendship with Ingersoll, they had become to a large extent his political mentors. Hellman wrote letters to writer friends asking them to get involved with the new paper. Some, like Louis Kronenberger, took positions on the staff. Others such as Richard Wright and Hellman herself undertook specific writing assignments. Hammett was then staying at the Plaza Hotel when not at Hardscrabble Farm; from his room there, he interviewed applicants for editorial positions. And when the paper finally emerged on June 18, 1940, Hammett read every word of each issue before it was set in type.

Hellman's involvement with *PM* was a clear indication that her long preoccupation with the fascist menace in Europe was being overtaken by an even greater concern about what she and many others felt was an echoing response to fascism in America. At a luncheon of the American Booksellers Association early in 1940, Hellman, sharing the dais with Edna Ferber and Dr. Lin Yutang, spoke forcibly on the totalitarian menace close at hand.

"I am a writer and I am also a Jew. I want to be quite sure that I can continue to be a writer and that if I want to say that greed is bad or persecution is worse, I can do so without being branded by the malice of people who make a living by that malice. I also want to be able to go on saying that I am a Jew without being afraid of being called names or end in a prison camp or be forbidden to walk down the street at night."

She told the audience she was aware that only a short time ago such fears would be laughed at as melodramatic but that after visiting Europe, she had returned to recognize the signs of propaganda and censorship. "Unless we are very careful and very smart," she said, "and very protective of our liberties, a writer will be taking his chances if he tells the truth, for as the lights dim out over Europe, they seem to flicker a little here too."

The same precautionary spirit motivated her work on *Watch on the Rhine,* and when she took time off to write a piece on the 1940 Republican Convention, her anxieties propelled her into what appears to be a remarkable misperception about political repression in Philadelphia. The assignment was for *PM,* and the article is one of the few instances when Hellman's writing is purely political and undertaken with no concurrent motive such as constructing a drama or fashioning a memoir. (An FBI informant claimed that Hellman was under assignment to *PM* to write a series of articles smearing the FBI. If she did, they were unsigned.)

Hellman went to Philadelphia and wrote that she took leave of the political blather going on at the convention to wander out into the streets to test the political waters by speaking with "the little men." First her cabdriver tells her his company has instructed him and his fellow drivers not to discuss politics with passengers, then two men in a South Street store say they don't think much about politics, adding darkly that it is not healthy to think about such things. And when she asks two black kids who they think the Republicans will pick as their candidate, they stammer that they have no ideas on the subject, adding, "Sometimes it isn't smart to have ideas." With this rare and brief (one column) foray into political survey and analysis, Hellman reached a conclusion that is perhaps as strong an indictment of the United States as has ever been made by one of its citizens: police-state fear hangs so heavily over America that cabdrivers, shopkeepers and shoeshine boys are afraid to voice political opinions of any sort.

Hellman had some basis for her fear; alarming instances of intolerance of heresy were cropping up. About this time, Harvard rescinded a lecture invitation to Earl Browder, the leader of the American Communist party, the first time such a step had been taken in the university's history. Throughout the country in the years just prior to World War II, communist meetings were broken up while the police looked the other way. But such infringements of free speech were still a considerable distance from the Animal Farm terror that Hellman described in Philadelphia: two shoeshine boys afraid to speculate on who might win the Republican nomination.

It is possible that Hellman's "little men" were too busy or too uninterested to talk politics with her; it is also possible that she made them up. Either way, she was guilty of the same kind of exaggeration that colored many of her less credible observations. She gets hold of an alarming fact about which she feels strongly—in this case the undeniable one that civil liberties were threatened in the prewar hysteria then rampant in the United States—and puts her creative imagination to work to bring this fact vividly and menacingly to the public. If that is what she was doing in the Philadelphia piece—and the fabrication may have been little more than adding a few lines of "I-don't-know-nothing dialogue" from Philadelphians she encountered—it is of highly questionable journalistic integrity. More glaring than the apparent distortions in her reporting is the wild conclusion she leaps to in explaining what she has observed. If the exaggeration was deliberate, the probable excuse—the rightness of her cause—

seems to have overridden all scruples. The other possibility is equally worrying: that Hellman actually believed Philadelphians were afraid to discuss the Presidential campaign.

In January 1940, Hellman began seeing a psychiatrist, the eminent Freudian Gregory Zilboorg. She was still troubled by her success, was drinking too heavily and was concerned about the anger which she always had difficulty controlling. She heard about Zilboorg through Ralph Ingersoll, who had felt the need to see a psychiatrist when his affair with Hellman ended, and had picked Zilboorg as the most conveniently located of three psychiatrists recommended to him. Hellman grew to have great esteem for Zilboorg and they became personal friends.

Zilboorg was an extraordinary man who had been born in Russia and in 1917 had served in the socialist Kerensky government as a secretary to the Minister of Labor. When the Kerensky government was overthrown by Lenin and Trotsky, Zilboorg fled Russia and came to New York, where he worked as a translator (he did an English translation of Leonid Andreyev's *He Who Gets Slapped*) to finance his way through Columbia University Medical School.

In spite of a short, stocky stature, Zilboorg was an imposing presence, with a black handlebar moustache and an incisive mind that bristled with a broad range of unyielding opinions. He had written a number of books, among them a history of psychiatric medicine that was considered definitive by many in the field. As a practitioner, he was not so highly regarded by his colleagues, numbers of whom considered him a complete phony who ignored the rigid rules governing the conduct of his profession, particularly those that concerned personal relations with patients.

Undoubtedly his enormous success contributed to the denigrations. Zilboorg was the prototype of the glamorous Park Avenue psychiatrist who was then fascinating the public and turning up frequently in plays and films. He was also the subject of much legend-building gossip, such as his alleged fee of $100 an hour, which in those prewar days was an adequate monthly salary for many people. Among his numerous prominent patients was Marshall Field, the heir to the Chicago department-store fortune, who became known as an energetic supporter of leftist causes.

Whatever Zilboorg did for Field's mental health, he was said to have played a major part in politicizing him. When word got around about his influence over men like Field and, later, Ingersoll, Zilboorg was portrayed in the press as a communist *éminence grise*, manipulating a number of wealthy dilettantes. Stories of this sort were based largely on Field's substantial financial support for the radical *PM*, which he eventually bought out. That owner and editor shared a psychiatrist seems to have been a co-incidence—Field and Ingersoll met under other circumstances—but that did not necessarily diminish Zilboorg's importance in their friendship.

There is no doubt that Zilboorg had a strong effect on the prominent figures he treated, and Lillian Hellman was no exception. She said of his politics, "He was an old-fashioned socialist who hated inherited wealth as undeserved and many of his patients were like that." Hellman had established a pattern of dismissing as knaves or nonentities most people she encountered, but when an individual was able to break through her wall of contempt and win approval, the approval was unrestrained. Zilboorg fell into the camp of the heavily approved.

During her analysis, Dr. Zilboorg recommended that Hellman buy a pet, preferably a dog; he predicted therapeutic benefits if she had custody of another living creature, one who would be totally dependent on her. She bought a large poodle and named him Gregory, but could muster no real interest in the animal, eventually turning him over to her houseman, who not only took care of the dog but kept him in his quarters, which were in another part of Hellman's apartment building.

In 1942, while Hellman was still under his care, Zilboorg ran into serious trouble from within his profession. Word got to a prominent Chicago colleague, Franz Alexander, that Zilboorg was accepting expensive gifts from patients, and because that was a serious breach of analytic standards, charges were brought against him in the American Psychoanalytic Association. A twelve-member panel investigated the charges and came up with a number of new ones concerning social contacts and involvements with his patients' private and professional affairs (finding backers for Ingersoll's newspaper fell in that category). The panel presented its verdict to a meeting of the Association's entire membership, nine to three for censure. When he addressed the group, Zilboorg ignored the charges and simply said that if the board vote went against him, he would sue the Association and each member as well. They voted to drop the charges.

After that episode, Zilboorg's calculated eccentricity slid into the more involuntary kind. He was rumored to have converted to Catholicism, which for many psychiatrists would be like hanging an astrological chart over the couch. Rather than alarming Hellman, however, Zilboorg's swing to religion may have heightened her fascination with him. Usually so intolerant of beliefs and systems not her own, Hellman, though not a believer, had always shown a wistful sympathy for those who were—an echo, perhaps, of her love for her mother, who had a strong spiritual side. A few years later, Arthur Kober brought a family crisis to Hardscrabble Farm: his daughter by his second marriage, Catherine, was considering turning against the religion of both her parents and becoming a Catholic. Catherine Kober recalls that of all the frenzied adults badgering her, the only one who listened to her with sympathy and understanding was Hellman.

In her memoirs Hellman gives only an occasional glimpse of the influence Zilboorg had in her personal life, and none of the political side of their relationship, although it says much about Hellman that she would choose a psychiatrist who was as radical in his political views as she was. Hellman was a patient of Zilboorg's for seven years and they remained friends until his death in 1959. In her memoirs, Hellman gives him a cryptic epitaph in a remark to a Russian friend: "Zilboorg ended odd, but the story is too long, too complicated and too American." After his death, Hellman continued to feel the need for counsel and started seeing another Manhattan psychiatrist, Dr. George Gero. She also had a psychiatrist in Los Angeles. But neither assumed the place Zilboorg had held in her life.

Hellman did most of the writing of *Watch on the Rhine* at Hardscrabble Farm, where she barricaded herself for long hours in her workroom. On a normal day she would write for three hours in the morning, another three in the afternoon, then return to her typewriter around ten in the evening and work until 1 or 2 A.M. Her schedule remained fixed regardless of the presence of guests, but Hellman relished leaving her workroom for lunch or dinner and finding two or three of her close friends at the table. These friends visited on the understanding that they would see her at meals; the rest of the time they were left to amuse themselves.

Catherine Kober recalls visiting Hardscrabble Farm as a small child and being in constant fear of doing something to upset Hellman. "She screamed at me one time for getting two different breeds of chickens mixed up. I was ten. When she got scratched by one of the chickens while she was sorting them out, she complained to everyone about it. Hammett was the only one around there who knew what it was to be a child. He would take me around and show me where all the bird nests were. Lillian and the others would order me to stay away from the lake, but never explained why. Hammett took me aside and told me that the lake had water moccasins."

Hellman had a housekeeper, a butler and a secretary whose primary job was retyping manuscripts. Once when away for a period she left a note on her desk to her secretary and her maid:

"To Miss Nancy and Miss Irene: Anyone caught rearranging these papers will find poison in their coffee." Hellman was fond of such whimsical instructions to the people in her house. Guests once found a note on her door which read:

THIS ROOM IS USED FOR WORKING. DO NOT ENTER WITHOUT KNOCKING. AFTER YOU KNOCK, WAIT FOR AN ANSWER. IF YOU GET NO ANSWER, GO AWAY AND DON'T COME BACK.
THIS MEANS EVERYBODY.
THIS MEANS YOU.
THIS MEANS NIGHT OR DAY.
> By order of the Hellman Military Commission for Playwrights. Court martialling [sic] will take place in the barn and your trial will not be a fair one.

She later added a notice saying that the Christmas court martialing had occurred and that the following people had been convicted: "Herman Shumlin, former *régisseur;* Samuel Dashiell Hammett, former eccentric; Mr. Arthur Kober, former itinerant street singer; Miss Sylvia Hermann, aged three, former daughter of a farmer (Hellman's overseer); Miss Nora, former dog; Mr. Max Bernard Hellman, father, a most constant offender. His age has saved him. This sentimentality may not continue."

The owner of Hardscrabble Farm in 1986, thirty-four years after Hellman sold the place, is a dentist who practices in the area. In a second-floor linen closet a paper label, yellowed and desiccated, is still glued to a shelf. On it in Hellman's hand is written: "Pink sheets go on Miss Hellman and Mr. Hammett's bed. Blue sheets go on the guest beds."

Presumably, Hellman and Hammett were sleeping together, but for all their fondness for each other, and for Hardscrabble Farm, both liked to keep separate retreats in Manhattan. Hellman retained the two-room apartment on the third floor of the Henry Clews mansion in the Seventies off Fifth Avenue. Hammett stayed at the Plaza and eventually took an apartment at 14 West Ninth Street, which was convenient to the Marxist-oriented Jefferson School, where he taught occasional classes.

In good weather, both spent most of their time at the farm. In the city they socialized, separately or together, often at dinner parties of various literary-intellectual groups, the leftist publishers, and the writers and editors of little magazines like *Partisan Review*. It was a period of enormous turmoil for the radical left; the Soviet-Nazi pact, the new appeal of Trotskyism, the stepped-up harassment of communists were just some of the issues that had the liberals fighting among themselves, frequently causing these dinners to erupt in verbal, even physical, violence, and frequently between two people who the week before had been devoted comrades-in-arms.

Hellman thrived on all this and threw her support to a number of causes. She gave a passionate radio appeal for funds for the refugees from the Spanish civil war in which she decried the inhumane rejection by so-called democracies of many of these brave fighters, and extolled Mexico for being one of the few countries in the Western Hemisphere to welcome them. She urged listeners to send money for an American rescue ship. With Ernest Hemingway, she co-chaired a dinner to raise funds for the same cause.

Hellman and Hammett's off-the-farm activities were not all political and intellectual. Hammett continued to disappear on benders, most often in Harlem whorehouses. Hellman had her own brand of wild good times, pub crawls that ended up in her or someone else's apartment with strangers. Rumors circulated of poker parties at the home of Frederick Vanderbilt Field, all male except for Hellman, at which the winner got to take Hellman into a bedroom.

While her previous play, *The Little Foxes*, proved harder to write than any of her other plays, *Watch on the Rhine* was the easiest and the quickest. The entire project took Hellman only eight months to complete, even though here again her research was considerable. She claimed to have read some twenty-five books on modern European history, but eventually drew on that information for only two speeches in the play.

When Hellman finished *Watch on the Rhine* early in 1941, Herman Shumlin was in Baltimore working on a new S. N. Behrman play, *The Talley Method*. With her script under her arm, Hellman took herself to Baltimore, where she paced the lobby of Shumlin's hotel, lighting and putting out cigarettes, while he read the play in his room. Shumlin was so excited by *Watch on the Rhine* that he spared Hellman from threatening to take it elsewhere in order to get him to mount it immediately. This time Shumlin announced he would get out of his current commitment, which was not going well, and put her new play into production immediately.

Watch on the Rhine, which Hellman dedicated to Shumlin, opened at the Martin Beck Theater on April 1, 1941, eight months before the United States entered the war in Europe. The consensus among the critics was highly favorable, with Brooks Atkinson of *The New York Times*, who had enthused over both *The Children's Hour* and *The Little Foxes*, calling it Hellman's finest play. It ran for 378 performances.

For once there could be no doubt that this play was written out of Hellman's overriding concern of the moment—the fascist threat and the need for everyone, including Broadway theatergoers, to take action against it. The events unfold in the drawing room of Fanny Farrelly, a wealthy and cosmopolitan widow. Her daughter, Sara, returns after many years in Europe, where she and her husband have been active in the anti-Nazi underground. Also staying in the house is a conniving and broke Rumanian count.

By snooping, the count learns that Sara's husband, Kurt, is about to return to Europe on a fake passport with $23,000 that has been collected for the resistance. Demanding nearly half the money, the count threatens Kurt with exposure. Kurt kills him, leaving Fanny and the rest of the family accessories to a murder committed in the cause of anti-Nazism.

The play has an important difference from Hellman's previous ones in that it has a clear hero in Kurt Muller. Both *The Children's Hour* and *The Little Foxes* were plays with no heroes, only villains and victims; *Days to Come* had a noble, forceful character in Leo Whalen, but he is a catalyst to the action rather than the center of it. In the earlier plays, Hellman provides no effective counterforce to the evil that abounds and, to a large degree, triumphs. In *Watch on the Rhine*, Kurt not only opposes the evil, he destroys it. He is also a character of understated yet clearly towering nobility. For the first time Hellman has produced a character she admires without reservation, and she has allowed the goodness he embodies to win out at the drama's end. In addition, the people of *Watch on the Rhine*, with the exception of Count Teck, are as full of love and decency as those of *The Little Foxes* are full of hate and greed.

There is another new element: humor. A strength of *Watch on the Rhine* that is often obscured by the serious theme and the exciting action is the witty interplay between the matron, Fanny, and the rest of the characters, particularly her youngest grandchild, the precocious and very European Bodo, whom she meets for the first time during the course of the play. With these two, Hellman has created a memorable comedic pairing. Much about the play's setting and early exposition draws so heavily on the stock drawing-room comedy implements that it flirts dangerously with becoming a parody of the form. Hellman rescues it with bright distractions like Fanny's sharp and funny tongue and the skill with which she has drawn all the characters and relationships.

In later years, *Watch on the Rhine* came to be regarded as one of Hellman's most overrated plays; out of the context of the period, it seemed breathlessly jingoistic and too elementary in its good-guys-bad-guys delineations. If it now appears a heavy-handed morality play, it was a lucid dramatization of the heavy-handed moral dilemma facing America at that time: Was a confrontation with fascism inevitable and at what point? By comparison to the other anti-Nazi plays of that time—principally Elmer Rice's *Flight to the West* and Robert Sherwood's *There Shall Be No Night*—*Watch on the Rhine* seems restrained. It builds with calm logic to its climactic violence, the killing of Teck, that renders that violence less melodramatically gratuitous than either the suicide of Martha in *The Children's Hour* or the heart attack of Horace in *The Little Foxes*. Hellman cloaks her message in an interesting drama of unwanted confrontation, imposing her plot, with unstrained logic, on characters who would probably act honorably if faced with a difficult moral situation, but who are comfortable in the knowledge they will never encounter one. Fanny's line after the murder on her terrace, "We've been shaken out of the magnolias," is a succinct summary of Hellman's theme: the mortal danger fascism represents to even the most insular and privileged.

Hellman had been the cause of the Drama Critics Circle Awards coming into existence, and now she finally won the award herself for *Watch on the Rhine*. It was an impressive victory, since most of the day's leading playwrights also had plays running on Broadway that 1941 season: Maxwell Anderson was represented with *Key Largo*; Robert Sherwood, *There Shall Be No Night*; Elmer Rice, *Flight to the West*; Philip Barry, *Liberty Jones*; and S. N. Behrman, *The Talley Method*. Even Ernest Hemingway had a play: *The Fifth Column*.

While there is occasional humor in Hellman's plays, and more in the memoirs, the face she turned to the public in interviews and other public utterances was increasingly serious, particularly concerning herself. Not long after the opening of *Watch on the Rhine*, she gave herself a birthday party; the telegrams of invitation show that she still retained the ability to laugh at herself, even about her most deep-felt concerns. A postscript to the invitation read, "A present for Lillian Hellman is a blow against fascism."

Even if the world seemed to Hellman to be sliding down a fascist hole, in terms of her own life at the age of thirty-six she could afford to laugh. Aside from winning the Drama Critics Circle Award with a play that was settling in for a long run, *The Lit-*

tle Foxes was still running on its national tour, Hammett was behaving reasonably well, and she had plenty of money to entertain, enhance the farm, buy expensive clothes and furniture and sail off to Cuba for a week with whomever she chose whenever she needed a break from work, Manhattan party-going or unratified monogamy.

The triumphs continued. In August, Sam Goldwyn released his film version of *The Little Foxes*, directed by William Wyler, with a screenplay by Hellman and photographed by Gregg Toland, who had recently made film history with his camera work on *Citizen Kane*. For Regina, Goldwyn was able to snag Bette Davis; Warner Brothers was willing to trade her to Goldwyn in exchange for Gary Cooper whom they were anxious to get to play Sergeant York. Because the screen credits for *The Little Foxes* list "Additional Scenes and Dialogue: Arthur Kober, Dorothy Parker, Alan Campbell," the rumor circulated that Hellman's three friends needed the money and she used her leverage with Goldwyn to cut them in on the Hollywood spoils. Kober said it was to give a boost to Alan Campbell's career. Both reasons may have been true, but Hellman definitely wanted help. She was convinced she could not write love scenes, and Goldwyn insisted that Regina's daughter, Alexandra (Teresa Wright), be given a love interest.

Hellman on several occasions during the run of the Broadway play had mentioned her distress that audiences failed to see themselves in the Hubbards, but simply watched them as remote curiosities. For the film she nudged them slightly with a statement that appeared on the screen after the credits: "Little Foxes have lived in all times and in all places. This family happened to live in the deep South in 1900." Otherwise the film follows the play faithfully for the most part. It made full use of Toland's new deep-focus technique, which permitted filming one character close up and, in the same frame, showing another character reacting in the background. The technique avoids the necessity of cutting back and forth, which can interrupt mounting intensity. Toland and Wyler had been experimenting with this innovation and Toland had used it to great effect in *Citizen Kane*. It is doubtful that it has ever been used more effectively than in the climactic scene of *The Little Foxes*. The camera remains on Bette Davis, who sits immobile in the foreground, while some distance behind her Horace can be seen struggling up the stairs, dying because she has refused to get his medicine.

An argument developed between Bette Davis and Wyler on how Regina should be played. While Davis did not relish copying Tallulah Bankhead, she felt Bankhead had played the part the only way it could be played: as a straight-out villainess. Wyler wanted to inject more subtlety, to make Regina more sympathetic at first and have her gradually become evil.

The same argument would reverberate for years as various directors of subsequent productions sought to impose onstage character development onto Regina and her brothers. After Wyler, the idea had perhaps its most impressive proponent in Mike Nichols who, in his 1967 production, wanted the Hubbards to be relatively decent people when the curtain rises, then to have events bring out the monsters in them.

Wyler brought Davis partially to heel and drew from her a Regina who was more modulated than Bankhead's, but instantly recognizable as no one to cross. The film was a great success with both the critics and the public, but it always left Bette Davis dissatisfied; years later she would name Regina as her least favorite performance. In addition, the constant fights with Wyler over her characterization of Regina resulted in their never working together again, despite her belief that he was a great director (he had directed her in two of her finest films, *The Letter* and *Jezebel*). While theirs was a private and artistic battle and not the sort of public controversy that surrounded *The Children's Hour*'s failure to win the Pulitzer, it was in effect another upheaval with lasting consequences caused by Hellman, once again from the disinterested act of writing a play.

As for Hellman's position in the Wyler-Davis controversy, she was silent at the time, but years later indicated which interpretation of the role she favored. When in 1980 *The Little Foxes* was being remounted in New York for Elizabeth Taylor, Hellman was discussing the various versions of the play with its current director, Austin Pendleton. "The one that came closest to what I intended," she said, "was Willie Wyler's film."

Pendleton agreed the film was superb, but said he personally had preferred the more subtle Mike Nichols version at the Vivian Beaumont Theater (in which Anne Bancroft had played Regina and Pendleton himself had played Leo).

"If I'd known that," she snorted, "I never would have let you get your hands on my play."

The remark was curiously inconsistent with the belief of many of Hellman's friends who felt she had admitted Nichols into the small fraternity of all-knowing teachers founded by Hammett. She may have meant only that she liked the way Wyler had softened Regina as opposed to the way Nichols had her evolve from decent to evil in one and a half acts; or extolling the Bette Davis version may have been nothing more than another slap at Bankhead, who most theater people considered the definitive Regina.

In November 1941, Hellman was profiled in *The New Yorker*. Then, as now, to be the subject of a *New Yorker* profile is often the culmination of a noteworthy career. Far from culminating her career, Hellman would write eight more plays and three more films, and twenty-eight years later would begin an entirely new career as an author of best-selling books. She would spend a good part of her final years receiving degrees and honors and she would be a distinguished guest-faculty member at Yale, Harvard and M.I.T. But for all the glory on her horizon, she would never be at a more exhilarating peak of recognition or accomplishment than on those first days of December 1941, when the United States entered World War II.

14

ITLER'S INVASION of Russia on June 22, 1941, ended an alliance that for most liberals and progressives had been at best confusing and embarrassing, and at worst shattering to their illusions about the humanitarian aims of the Soviet state. Falling into the first group, Hammett and Hellman could once again wish wholeheartedly for the destruction of Hitler without fear of violating Russian interests.

Much has been made of Hellman's pro-Russian sympathies—by herself as well as by others—but she had not joined other communist sympathizers in muting their denunciations of Nazi Germany or, even more remarkably, constructing tortured apologies for the Nazi-Soviet pact. On the contrary, she had chosen this particular moment to write and present *Watch on the Rhine*, a play which squarely posits as the greatest evil facing the world, not capitalism, imperialism or the profit motive, but fascism as championed by Russia's ally, Germany. It is strong evidence that she was, as she later claimed, acting on her own convictions and was "nobody's girl." Had she been under Party discipline, it is unlikely she would have defied so flagrantly the Party's policy of the moment. She could have taken the path of many other com-

181

munist sympathizers and remained silent. But writing the play when she did establishes that however strong Hellman's allegiance to Moscow, her allegiance to anti-Nazism was stronger.

With the German invasion of Russia and then the Japanese attack on Pearl Harbor, the lines were drawn for global conflict; capitalism and communism were fused into an unlikely alliance and no anti-Nazi message could be too strong. *Watch on the Rhine* was sold to Warner Brothers. Even though the part of Sara Muller was not a starring role, Bette Davis was so eager to play her that she was willing to waive her sovereignty because she so fervently approved the play's anti-Nazi message. Since Hellman was under contract to Goldwyn, she could not write the screenplay, but the producer, Hal Wallis, signed Hammett for the job in a Solomon-like stroke that assured Hellman's input and made everyone happy. The screenplay adhered loyally to Hellman's original script.

Hellman stayed tactfully in the background on this project until it was menaced by the Hays office, which balked at the unpunished killing at the play's conclusion. They insisted that the script include some sort of "punishment" for the killer, Kurt Muller. Hellman struck hard. In a scathing letter to Joseph Breen she asked if he was aware that killing Nazis was at the moment the national policy of the United States? To insist on punishing a character for doing just that was "to say the least, incongruous." The letter, which must be a high point of Hellman's outrage-powered sarcasm, had its effect, and the film ended like the play: Muller kills Teck—who was actually apolitical but who had sought to be useful to the Nazis—and he gets away with it.

Perhaps because of his basic mistrust of communists, even as allies, President Roosevelt spotted another incongruity—not in the prophetic message of *Watch on the Rhine* but in the playwright who delivered it. It was a tradition of the Roosevelt Administration to select an outstanding play of each Broadway season and present it in Washington before the President as a benefit for infantile paralysis. *Watch on the Rhine* was selected for 1942. Greatly honored, Hellman joined Shumlin and the cast for the expedition to Washington early in the year. The event received more press attention than usual because it was the President's first public appearance since the nation's entry into the war.

At dinner in the White House afterward, Roosevelt asked Hellman how long she had worked on the play. When she replied she had begun it a year and a half earlier, Roosevelt asked how it could be that the author of such a militantly anti-Nazi play had helped finance the antiwar pickets of a group called the American Peace Mobilization, who had plagued the White House in the months prior to Pearl Harbor. They had been a considerable embarrassment to the Administration and were widely believed to be communists. Hellman assured the President that he had been misinformed; she had never contributed to the pickets.

It is doubtful that Roosevelt was aware of it, but the FBI had already made a futile search of Hellman's bank records for evidence that she supported the group. The President appeared to believe her denial, but with many others the story of her support for the pickets persisted, causing Hellman to deny it again forty years later in *Pentimento*.

As the United States was launched into an all-out war, Hellman worked at a number of projects in aid of the European struggle—fund-raising, speechwriting and ambitious victory gardening at Hardscrabble Farm. She was, however, stunningly topped in patriotic gestures by Hammett, who slipped off in September 1942 and enlisted in the army as a private. He would have joined up sooner had he been within the age limit; the minute it was raised to include him, he was off.

Hellman was aghast. First came her fear of physical danger, which had always been exaggerated, and which was easily transferred to Hammett. But added to that fear were concerns about Hammett's frail constitution, which had been further weakened by years of strenuous dissipation. He was also forty-eight, looked older, and would be required to undergo basic training with eighteen-year-olds.

For his part, Hammett was more delighted than if he had just delivered a new novel. His failure to produce new works had not lessened his fame. John Huston's classic remake of *The Maltese Falcon* with Humphrey Bogart and Mary Astor had been released the previous October and had made Hammett more celebrated than ever. But he had not done much in the last eight years except read and get drunk, and now was exhilarated to have at last done not just *something*, but something brave, patriotic and, because of his age and celebrity, more than a little eccentric. The day he was accepted into the army was, he told Hellman, "the happiest day of my life."

For a time Hammett was stationed at Fort Monmouth, New Jersey, and used his weekend leaves to meet Hellman in Manhattan for show-off dinners in his private's uniform at favorite haunts like "21." Sometimes he did not contact Hellman at all but spent his two days at one of the Harlem whorehouses he had been frequenting in recent years. He was eventually stationed in the Aleutians, where he would remain until his discharge in the summer of 1945. From the political history of other GIs sent to this base, there was reason to suspect the army had a policy of isolating at such remote posts enlistees suspected of subversion. Whatever the reason, Hammett accepted the transfer with good cheer and fell enthusiastically into his assignment of editing a base newspaper.

Hellman had always maintained somewhat of a life apart from Hammett and now, with his absence, she made additional moves in that direction. She had money coming in from a number of sources. *Watch on the Rhine* was playing to capacity audiences. There was revenue from the stage version as well as the film of *The Little Foxes*. *Watch on the Rhine* was staged in London and was such a success that a production of *The Little Foxes* was mounted to open there the same year; but the latter was poorly received, a casualty, many felt, of opening *after* Londoners had seen the Bette Davis version. Hellman celebrated the ever-broadening appetite for her work by buying a Manhattan town house at 63 East Eighty-second Street, keeping two floors for her own use and renting out the rest. It would remain her New York base until 1969, when she sold the house and moved into a Park Avenue apartment.

With Hammett gone, Hellman's social life expanded considerably. Her devotion to him had always been strong enough to restrain her gregariousness and bend her to his preference for quiet seclusion. She now spent a greater amount of time in the city, seeing more of those friends whose fame and glamour had made them suspect in Hammett's eyes, and in the pursuit of fun. Howard Teichmann evokes this aspect of Hellman's wartime life with a funny incident that occurred when Hellman and Dorothy Parker were spending the weekend with the George S. Kaufmans in Bucks County, Pennsylvania.

During the weekend, a friend phoned Parker at Kaufman's house to warn her that a snide remark she had made about Kaufman and his collaborator, Moss Hart ("So much kudos for so little talent"), was quoted in a Sunday *New York Times* book review that would appear the next day. Fearing the demolition of the house party if the item was noticed, Parker and Hellman developed a strategy: they would rise early Sunday morning, seize the *Times* before anyone else got to it and remove the book-review section. Their hope was that the missing section would be thought an innocent error and overlooked by the Kaufmans.

Sunday morning came and the two women carried out their plan. Then, to avoid questions, they left a note saying they had gone for a long walk. When they returned, they found Kaufman engrossed in a bridge game. They went upstairs, packed their bags and returned to make their farewells to Beatrice Kaufman. They asked her to thank George for them, since they did not wish to disturb the game that was still in progress at the far end of the living room. They were at the point of a clean escape when Kaufman, who had received a phone call from Hart, looked over his glasses and said, "Dottie, did you take the real estate section?"

It is an index of how unanimously America stood behind the war effort that the White House would unabashedly solicit a prominent writer to undertake a tangential propaganda work and that no one thought it improper. The pragmatic Roosevelt recognized the military advantages of the new alliance with the Soviet Union and felt it in the nation's interest to bolster Russia's popularity. Not too long after her conversation with the President, Hellman was approached to write a film which the White House would persuade one of the film companies to produce. Its aim would be to make Americans like Russia better. She was happy to oblige.

Hellman again joined forces with William Wyler, this time to fashion a feature film in documentary style that would dramatize the bravery and valor of the Russian people in the face of the Nazi onslaught. Sam Goldwyn went along with the idea. Although he did not share Hellman and Wyler's enthusiasm for Russia, he was disposed to indulge the two *wunderkinder* who had made such good and profitable films for him. In addition, pro-Russia attitudes, which were considered disloyal a few months before, were now considered patriotic, perhaps even commercial.

Once the project became a Sam Goldwyn film, however, box-office considerations subsumed the production at the expense of documentary plausibility. The picture, titled *North Star*, came to look more and more like a Hollywood movie, and eventually, a musical. Work was not far along when Wyler suddenly left to enter the army. Goldwyn replaced him, at Hellman's request, with Lewis Milestone, who was a logical choice since he had been born in Russia and had recently directed the antiwar classic *All Quiet on the Western Front*.

North Star's story concerned a Russian village that was overrun by the Nazis, and to write it Hellman had done her usual exhaustive research, filling 250 pages with single-spaced typed notes on everything from Russian school curricula to medical practices. Milestone overlooked his misgivings about working for Goldwyn because of his admiration for Hellman's writing. It was, therefore, a bitter surprise that his troubles with the film came not from Goldwyn but from Hellman. "As it turned out," he said later, "Lillian knew *nothing* about Russia—especially the villages."

The collaboration was a disaster. To Hellman, Milestone appeared the sort of egomaniacal director who regarded the writer as a mere vehicle for his ideas. She was outraged when he sent her detailed pages of requests for script changes, an affront she had never experienced as a writer. It is doubtful that she would have tolerated such meddling even as a beginner; she had no intention of doing so now.

Milestone's version of the collaboration's breakdown places more blame on what he saw as Hellman's personal treachery than on her ignorance of Russia. He says that in the course of working together, she told him it would be pointless for him to go to Goldwyn about any changes he wanted in the script; Goldwyn would side with the writer. If he wanted any changes, he should present his requests to her. Milestone took that as an invitation to give Hellman his thoughts and sent her the fifty pages of requested changes that so infuriated Hellman, she herself went to Goldwyn.

Milestone was abruptly summoned to Goldwyn's office to be told that he had made the writer very unhappy by his attempts to change her script. Milestone felt he had been set up and wanted nothing further to do with Hellman. Trying to make peace, Goldwyn asked Milestone to join him and Hellman for dinner at his estate, after which they would work out the disagreements about the script. Milestone refused. Goldwyn reminded him he had a contract.

"Nothing in my contract says I have to have dinner," Milestone said.

He did, however, agree to join Hellman and Goldwyn after dinner, and at the meeting the three set to work with chilly professionalism on the writer-director conflicts. To Hellman's fury, Goldwyn repeatedly sided with Milestone, and eventually the arguments between writer and producer grew so heated that Milestone, having obtained his changes, excused himself and went home. The result of the evening was that Hellman bought her way out of her contract for $30,000. But more important, it brought to an end an association with Sam Goldwyn that had lasted eight years and produced four films, three of very high quality.

In spite of her temperament and her speed at bestowing contempt on others, Hellman had progressed far in the highly collaborative theater world without a major blowup, which may speak as much about her good fortune at falling in with men of the caliber of Shumlin and Wyler as it does about any beginner's malleability on Hellman's part. Throughout her career, she would try to avoid conflict by picking collaborators for whom her admiration was unrestrained (Wyler, Tyrone Guthrie, Mike Nichols), or newcomers she outranked and could bully. But once she had loaded the equation as much as possible in her favor, she was, from the testimony of many who worked with her, no more difficult than any other theatrical "star"—and a lot more reasonable than many.

North Star is a curiosity both in the career of Lillian Hellman and in the history of American films. It was one of three Hollywood pictures made that year that would later be accused of fostering communist propaganda (the other two were *Mission to Moscow* and *Song of Russia*). As usual with Goldwyn films, it had a blue-chip cast: Anne Baxter, Dana Andrews, Walter Huston,

Ann Harding, Jane Withers, Farley Granger, Walter Brennan and Erich von Stroheim. The music was by Aaron Copland with lyrics by Ira Gershwin.

Even though Hellman would later disavow the picture, calling it "a sentimental mess," she was proud enough of her part in it to arrange for the publication of her screenplay, which was not drastically different from the Milestone-doctored version Goldwyn released. The primary difference—and Hellman stressed this point in discussing *North Star*—was in the visual aspects of the film, which were far from what she had envisioned: the dirt-farmer realism she felt the subject matter demanded. The unwillingness to recreate meticulously a poor Russian village was not surprising from a producer who once complained to Wyler that his slum sets for *Dead End* "looked dirty." The prettified version of a Russian collective farm was perhaps the most ludicrous aspect of the film and was best summed up by the writer Irving Drutman, who was the film's publicist; in a post-screening discussion of *North Star*'s credits he snapped, "And patches by Irene."

Hellman's script is predictable in its heavy-handed determination to portray the Russians as history's bravest, noblest, most selfless people and the Germans as history's most vicious. But the mixed sentiments of others involved in making the picture are apparent in a strange vagueness about the finished product: the inhabitants of the village are never clearly designated as communists, nor is it ever stated explicitly that the village is in Russia, although it is obvious from the costumes and sets—even with Goldwyn's beautifications.

Although *North Star*, if remembered at all, is dismissed as either subversive or ridiculous, it was praised by the critics, particularly in New York. Bosley Crowther in *The New York Times* complained of the film's operetta look but commended Hellman's story for its "honest dignity" and its "tense, exciting action." Others such as the critics for the *World Telegram* and the *Herald Tribune* were even more laudatory; the few who disapproved of the picture did so on political grounds rather than artistic ones.

The film's career followed the course of America's shifting relations with Russia. When *North Star* was released for television in 1957 (renamed *Armored Attack*, not *Armored Train* as Hellman says in *An Unfinished Woman*), a voice-over prologue apologizes for any apparent pro-Russian sentiments. With the help of additional comments inserted throughout the story, the film is converted from being flagrantly pro-Russian to flagrantly anti-Russian.

Hellman began a new play in the summer of 1942 and delivered the script of *The Searching Wind* to Shumlin a year later, in August 1943. Her impetus was similar to that of *Watch on the Rhine:* to examine the interaction between spreading fascism and decent people who, in this play, might have done more to stop it. Hellman said the play gave her more trouble than any previous one, which is not surprising considering the large cast of characters and the erratic time shifts.

As with the earlier plays, Shumlin took on the new piece as producer and director, but this time with markedly less enthusiasm. Not only, for the first time, did he have serious misgivings about the script, but he hated the expense of Hellman's many settings, having just lost considerable money on another multi-set production. Also for the first time, Hellman was critical of Shumlin's direction. It would be the last play they would do together.

The Searching Wind is a rambling, talky three acts that set out to show the culpability of well-meaning people of privilege who do not use that privilege to stop an evil like fascism before it becomes too strong to stop. In *Watch on the Rhine*, Hellman had events drag her characters into the battle; in this play she has her characters positioned close to historic developments, but they deftly sidestep involvement. The confusing, undramatic result was a remarkable lapse for Hellman, who had come to be criticized by some and applauded by others as a fashioner of "well-made plays." In its unwieldy diffusiveness, *The Searching Wind* seems to have been written to refute the charge.

As in *Watch on the Rhine*, the action starts in the present in a Washington drawing room of wealth and influence but skips backward to Rome in 1922, Berlin in 1923, Paris in 1938, then returns to mid-1940s Washington. The fourteen characters—who are supplemented by assorted waiters, restaurant diners and pedestrians—have among them no discernible heroes, but this time neither are there any discernible villains. Hellman tried to interweave a complex political parable about bystanders' guilt with a fuzzy love triangle that threatens a symbolic application to the larger historical theme, but never succeeds in establishing one.

On several occasions when discussing her playwriting methods, Hellman allowed herself the frequent conceit of fiction writers: that she created characters, then set them loose to fashion their own plot. If this was her method, the people of *The Searching Wind* played her false and led her on a feckless chase that culminated in a denunciation of them all by the son of the principal family.

The play opened at the Fulton Theater in April 1944, with Dennis King, Cornelia Otis Skinner and Dudley Digges in the principal roles and settings by Howard Bay. Some critics found things to praise in the play (enough to have it miss the Drama Critics Circle Award for 1944 by one vote), but others could not even maintain a respectful tone in their dismissal of it. Two could not resist saying the play was more windy than searching.

Some of Hellman's collaborative efforts, films like *Dead End* and *North Star,* for instance, came to be remembered mainly because of her involvement. It is ironic then that *The Searching Wind*'s primary claim to a niche in theater history was that it introduced for the first time in a major role (that of the denouncing son) a young actor who would become one of the legends of his profession—Montgomery Clift. Four years later, Clift would star in a low-budget film called *The Search* that would launch him on his brilliant film career.

Those denigrators of Lillian Hellman's talent who stress the importance of Hammett's assistance in her playwriting have strong support for their theory in that two of her three weakest plays were written in his absence. *The Searching Wind* which opened in April of 1944 was written while Hammett was stationed in Alaska (*My Mother, My Father and Me* was written after his death). But any suggestion of Hammett's editorial infallibility is denied by the failure of *Days to Come,* with which he was closely involved and which was even less successful than *The Searching Wind.*

But even off in Alaska, Hammett bore some responsibility for the new play. Hellman sent him drafts and he would reply with suggestions. More often he would address himself to her morale, as in the following scolding he gave her for implying this was the first play to give her trouble: "If you'd had any memory, you'd know that the present dithers over the play are only the normal bellyaching of La Hellman at work. You still think you dashed off those other plays without a fear, a groan, or a sigh; but you didn't, sister: I haven't had a dry shoulder since your career began. . . ."

15

ELLMAN ASSUMED the Russians invited her to Moscow on a cultural mission because she had written *North Star;* she was chagrined to learn on her arrival that they thought the film a great joke. It is likely they considered the author's pro-Russian sympathies more significant than the film's quality. In addition, her plays had received the Kremlin's approval. At the time of her visit, the Russians were starting to give more thought to future relations with their wartime allies. The horrors of the Nazi invasion and the siege of Leningrad were now behind them; the Red armies were sweeping south through Russia on their triumphant push to Berlin. The end of the war in Europe was in sight.

Hellman's trip could not have occurred without the approval of the U.S. Government. Wartime travel restrictions, Hellman's prominence and the invitation's source from a foreign government all necessitated White House support for the trip. The U.S. Government obviously considered Hellman's pro-Russian attitudes useful to American interests at the time; eight years later the same sympathies would be considered a sufficient threat to warrant governmental action against her.

In September 1944 Hellman flew to Fairbanks, Alaska, where she was picked up by the Russians for the journey to Moscow. The war in Europe made it impossible to fly there the usual way, but other avenues were open that were more direct than crossing North America and Siberia. The route might have been chosen from a desire to visit Hammett, but that does not seem to be the case. Hellman makes no mention of a meeting in the Aleutians, nor do Hammett's biographers. Not visiting him would seem odd— letters between them during his military tour were as loving as they had ever been*—but it is probably explained by the distances involved. Fairbanks was some 1,300 miles from Hammett's post on Adak, one of the most westerly of the Aleutian chain.

While Hellman's trip had the endorsement of Roosevelt and his close adviser Harry Hopkins (with whom Hellman was rumored to have had an affair), other branches of the U.S. Government were less comfortable with a wartime trip to Russia by a well-known communist sympathizer. The FBI dogged her steps while she remained under its jurisdiction, and even after. Her FBI file contains a monitored radio conversation between two Russians, one (Kisilev) at Ladd Field in Alaska, the other (Rudenko) at the Embassy in Washington, who seem as perplexed and wary as the FBI about Hellman's trip.

> KISILEV: Comrade General, I have called you today because this writer, Lillian Hellman, arrived here. She is going to the USSR but I don't have any information or orders about it.
> RUDENKO: Hellman?
> KISILEV: Yes, Hellman.
> RUDENKO: I don't know anything either so you better wait until you send her over. I will call you about it.
> KISILEV: Okay, she is going from New York. The consul out there sent her through. She was showing me the telegram of who had invited her. It was Poudovkin and Moskvin and some other of our artists.

---

* All through his tour of duty, Hammett's emotional link to Hardscrabble Farm as "home" remained strong. While Hellman was in Moscow and unable to write to him, he corresponded with Nancy Bragdon, Hellman's secretary.

RUDENKO: Well, I don't know anything about it yet, so don't send her through.
KISILEV: All right, I won't.

Then, two days later, on October 18, 1944, the ever vigilant U.S. intelligence operation recorded another conversation, this time with a higher-ranking diplomat at the Russian Embassy in Washington.

KISILEV: Lillian Hellman—I don't have any information about her. You sent her here. Better find out right away. It is very hard to call you. I don't understand anything of what you say.
FEDOSEEV: Colonel Kisilev, she is an American citizen?
KISILEV: Yes, she is an American citizen.
FEDOSEEV: She has a passport?
KISILEV: Yes, she has a passport.
FEDOSEEV: And on the passport there should be our visa. If she's got a visa, you let her through.
KISILEV: Listen. Next time I would like you to give me advance notice.
FEDOSEEV: She might have received that visa from the Consulate in San Francisco.
KISILEV: Well, this one she received in New York. It is received from Kisilev [sic]. Why don't he notify me?
FEDOSEEV: Kisilev has signed it?
KISILEV: Yes.
FEDOSEEV: Well, so it is we that have issued the visa. We are going to have to let her through. One should notify you next time.

Hellman later wrote that the flight across Russia was, physically, the hardest time of her life. The trip was made in a two-engine C-47 with a maximum speed of 240 miles per hour. Its rudimentary instruments permitted flying only in good weather; storms were waited out in Siberian shacks. After a few days, when the heater broke down in the passengers' cabin, additional stops were made for no other reason than to allow Hellman to get warm. Even with such solicitousness for their distinguished passenger, she arrived in Moscow with a serious case of pneumonia.

Hellman's Russian hosts had lodged her at the National Hotel, but the American Embassy official who had been delegated to look after her considered her condition so serious that he cabled the U.S. Ambassador, Averell Harriman, who was then in New York, for permission to move Hellman into the Ambassador's residence, Spasso House. Harriman, who knew Hellman from the New York celebrity circuit, gave prompt consent. She was brought to the Embassy by George Kennan, then a minister-counselor but later an ambassador, and one of the top U.S. experts on Russia.

Harriman's wife, Marie, would not come to Moscow, ostensibly for health reasons. To serve as his hostess, Harriman brought to Russia a daughter by an earlier marriage, Kathleen Harriman, then a woman in her twenties, who was proud to be one of seven female American war correspondents in London. She was also in New York when Hellman arrived in Moscow. Now Mrs. Stanley Mortimer, she remembers with amusement the Harrimans' return to Russia for Christmas of 1944.

"My father and I were pleased that we would be having Lillian staying with us at Spasso House. We both knew her from New York and liked her. But we had some trepidations; we knew how difficult she could be. We didn't have to worry. By the time we got to Moscow some two weeks later, Lillian was already involved in an affair with the Embassy's third secretary. Our reaction was 'Thank God! She'll be a happy woman.'"

Contrary to any suggestion that Hellman was prompt to set herself up with an under secretary in every port of call as though it were a requisite amenity of travel, the affair Kathleen Mortimer alluded to was serious and long-lasting. The third secretary was a handsome, intelligent foreign-service career officer named John Melby, who was then thirty-one to Hellman's thirty-nine. Melby had been born in Portland, Oregon, but had spent much of his childhood in Brazil, where his father was an official for the International YMCA. When the senior Melby was transferred to Bloomington, Illinois, Melby attended Illinois Wesleyan ("It was the depth of the Depression and I could live at home"), then obtained a Ph.D. from the University of Chicago. He entered the Foreign Service and was stationed in Juarez, Mexico, where he married and had two children. He was then transferred to Russia, but wartime restrictions forced him to leave his family in El Paso.

When Hellman arrived at Spasso House, Melby was away for

a few days on an Embassy errand elsewhere in Russia. When he returned, she was already part of the Embassy "family." Visiting dignitaries are a constant of embassy life, but Melby remembers a small incident that first aroused his interest in the famous playwright from New York. During pre-dinner cocktails, the Embassy's first secretary was congratulating himself for having snatched up a jar of peanut butter which had miraculously appeared at the commissary and which he was now magnanimously about to share with the others for patriotic hors d'oeuvres. Instead of joining in the general congratulations, Hellman launched into a diatribe on the fecklessness of anyone lucky enough to be in the land of beluga caviar making a fuss about peanut butter. Her spiel was serious and energetic—she felt the man's homesick impulse exemplified the insular, chauvinistic failings of America's Foreign Service officers. Melby found himself attracted to this short, blond woman who didn't hesitate to demolish a convivial mood if she felt foolishness was afoot.

The attraction between Melby and Hellman was strong and mutual and by the time Ambassador Harriman returned to Moscow, everyone at the Embassy knew that they were in love and engrossed in an unrestrained affair. Hellman had kept her room at the National Hotel but was delighted when Harriman told her to stay on at Spasso House, where Melby was also living, as long as she wished. From the start of the affair, Hellman enjoyed the same kind of two-residence freedom it had taken years to establish with Hammett. Hellman also occasionally took a room at Moscow's Hotel Metropole, which fascinated her, but which Melby described as "a dump." Her marvelous description of the Metropole in *An Unfinished Woman* presents it as a cross between Vicki Baum's *Grand Hotel* and the hotel in the Marx Brothers' *Room Service*. To have three residences simultaneously in a city where more than one family often had to share a one-room apartment was evidence that Hellman kept her interest in communism and the Russian way of life on the theoretical level.

Hellman says she stayed in Moscow for five months. Melby remembers it as closer to three and a half months. Either way, it was a long time for a cultural mission of no specific purpose. Melby does not think he was the reason Hellman prolonged her stay; he was scheduled for rotation at the war's end, which then looked imminent. He and Hellman had every intention of continuing their relationship outside of Russia. He thinks, rather, she was lingering in Moscow to see the productions of *The Little Foxes* and *Watch on the Rhine*, which the Russians were mounting. But from Hellman's memoirs it appears she was not particularly interested in these efforts or optimistic about them. She says that both plays had been in rehearsal for six months before she arrived and were still in rehearsal when she left.

Others in Russia that winter agree that there was little for foreigners to do in Moscow, especially at night. During the day Hellman would do some sightseeing (compared to Leningrad, Moscow offered little in that line), attend rehearsals of her plays and have tea with Sergei Eisenstein, the famous filmmaker, whom she came to like enormously. The evenings would occasionally offer a party at another embassy or dinner with American and British journalists. John Hersey, who was then *Time* magazine's correspondent in Moscow, became a friend of Hellman's, a relationship that would grow over the years so that at the time of her death, Hersey was not just one of Hellman's two or three closest friends but as much a part of her family as anyone. When Hellman was not seeing Melby, Hersey would take her to the opera or theater, naturally limited in those war years, so most often the Moscow nights would be spent at dinner at Spasso House with Harriman and his staff, with much drinking on everybody's part.

Kathleen Mortimer recalls that the American Embassy made a great fuss over Hellman; she was the first dignitary "of that type," that is, from the arts, to come through Moscow. There had been military advisers and politicians but no cultural emissaries. And she was the first American to be invited by the Russians. At the American Embassy she was given a suite of rooms with her own sitting room; the Russians had provided her with a car and a driver.

"It was great fun having Lillian there," Kathleen Mortimer recalls. "She was a good guest, never difficult, and of course she was very enthusiastic about Russia. I remember her at the time being blondish—what the French call *une belle laide*—there is no doubt she was attractive, vibrant. She could really get herself up, at other times she could be terribly messy. In Moscow at that time, there was nothing to do at night. We would usually be about ten for dinner. After dinner the men would go back to work and Lillian and I would stay up and talk for hours. She and I became friends, in later years we would phone and get together."

Averell Harriman once remarked to his friend Arthur Schlesinger that during those dinners with Hellman in Moscow in 1944 he had tried repeatedly to engage her in discussions of the vast political and governmental issues then facing Russia and the Western democracies, but never succeeded in interesting her in such talk. Melby, however, suspects that Hellman did not have enough respect for Harriman's views to risk abusing his hospitality with arguments she knew would grow heated. Kathleen Mortimer thinks her father was too pragmatic in his views of world events to respond to the more theoretical and philosophical approach she feels would have been Hellman's interest.

Even with these explanations, Harriman's charge of a lack of interest on Hellman's part in serious discussions about Russia at a table that included several of the world's leading experts, men who were sympathetic to what the communists were trying to do and who had long years of firsthand experience behind them, hangs disturbingly over the picture of Hellman as an unprejudiced traveler and a woman of intellectual curiosity. It suggests a mind that, on the issue of Russia at least, was no longer open for business.

Hellman indicated the same sort of disinterest to her Russian hosts. When they asked her where she wanted to go and whom she wished to speak to, they were annoyed when she was unable to come up with specific requests. They apparently were more determined than she that her visit be instructive. Word arrived at Spasso House that Hellman was to be permitted to visit the Russian front lines. According to both John Melby and Kathleen Mortimer, the news rocked the international community, especially the U.S. military attaché and the newspapermen, all of whom had had requests for the same permission sitting on Kremlin desks for many months. While the others fumed, Hellman and her translator, Raya, whom she liked immediately and who would become a lifelong friend, left Moscow by train two days after Christmas, traveling south to Kiev, then west to the Polish city of Lublin, a hundred miles southeast of Warsaw.

Hellman wrote two accounts of this adventure, one for

Collier's magazine shortly after her return to New York in 1945, and another in her first memoir, *An Unfinished Woman,* in 1969. The two accounts, so revealing about Hellman's special approach to biographical facts, invited comparison. In both, the trip was exciting, historic, heartwarming and with moments of great beauty. The Russians and the events they are part of remained the same. What would be changed drastically in the account twenty-four years later was Hellman's role in those events.

16

IN *An Unfinished Woman* Hellman concludes a chapter with her return from Moscow in 1945 and picks up her story next in 1967, creating a gap of twenty-two years, easily one third of her adult life. During the missing years she would undergo her most grueling ordeal, her harassment during the McCarthy period. She would write three more original plays, four adaptations, and a film. She would have other affairs and nurse Hammett through his final days. She would become a distinguished presence on university faculties and move slowly but unstoppably into the pantheon of venerated cultural icons. In subsequent books she would treat some of these events, but writing in 1968, it seemed as though, in recounting her Russian trip, she had exhausted her capacity for self-narration. Instead she jumped over nearly a quarter of a century to the present, then concluded the book with portraits of Dorothy Parker, her housekeeper, Helen Jackson, and Dashiell Hammett. Two of the portraits were based on earlier writings. From the lost decades, there is much to relate.

After leaving Moscow early in 1945, Hellman spent a month in London before returning to New York. The total victory of the

Allied armies over Hitler was clearly at hand and the mood in both London and New York was euphoric. Hellman had not been home long when she was joined by John Melby, who had concluded his Moscow duty. Instead of returning to his wife in El Paso, he chose to remain in the East with Hellman. He eventually got a divorce and admits that Hellman was a major element in the termination of his marriage. Melby and Hellman decided to rent a house together for the summer while he awaited his next assignment. They chose East Hampton.

Apparently they did not consider spending the summer at Hardscrabble Farm. According to Melby the possibility was never discussed; in fact, he didn't think she owned the farm at that time. Of course Hellman *did* own Hardscrabble in 1945. The choice of East Hampton may have been an elaborate bit of deception on Hellman's part—or perhaps she considered the farm as much Hammett's home as her own.

Melby remains devoted to Hellman and loyally defends her against all denigrations. He does feel, however, that in her memoirs she exaggerated the importance of the Hammett relationship in her life. (She mentions Melby, but only as a friend she met in Moscow.) He barely remembers Hellman ever talking about Hammett; neither did she show the slightest feeling of guilt about betraying him in her involvement with Melby. He recalls meeting Hammett at Hellman's house on East Eighty-second Street on one occasion that summer, but does not recall seeing or hearing about him again. By the time Hammett was discharged from the army in August 1945, a week before V-J Day, Hellman and Melby were settled in their house on Long Island. Hellman apparently greeted Hammett in New York, took him up to Hardscrabble Farm, then returned to Melby and her East Hampton idyll. For his part, Melby has no idea what became of Hammett that summer.

If Hellman left Melby in the dark about the other man in her life, two things indicate that she was frank with Hammett about Melby. The first is that she allowed Hammett to meet him, which in itself was provocative, since Melby was an attractive young man—now clearly an intimate friend of Hellman's—who was unknown to her when Hammett left for the service. The second indication is the high visibility of East Hampton, which even then was on its way to preeminence as a café-society and theatrical display tank. Both Melby and Hellman had many friends there and socialized energetically among people who undoubtedly knew Hammett and knew Hellman's relationship to him. Coincidentally, Marie Harriman, the truant wife of Ambassador Averell Harriman, had also taken a house in East Hampton that summer, with a Polish count as her constant companion. Melby remembers encountering other friends of Hellman's—Marya Mannes and Mrs. Christian Herter—who greeted him at a party with "So you're the mysterious young man from Moscow!"

Had Hellman and Melby been trying for discretion, almost any place would have been better than East Hampton. It seems the only one being fooled about Hellman's ambidexterity was Melby, and in all likelihood the deception was possible because he was receiving most of her attention. Hellman seems to have wanted to maintain the Hammett bond, but was reluctant to allow Melby to learn of her divided affection. She also seems to have finally succeeded in bending Hammett to her conjugal rules. The victim was now culprit.

Melby and Hellman discussed marriage. They decided, however, to wait until his next career move was fixed before proceeding with plans. The State Department wanted Melby for a special diplomatic mission in Europe, but would not need him for the number of months needed to set it up. He was asked to fill in the wait with a temporary assignment in China. He agreed, and the marriage plans were postponed until after the China stint. The diplomatic mission in Europe fell through and Melby remained in China for three years.

Recalling the events of forty years ago, Melby does not feel the prolonged separation brought about the end of his affair with Hellman. They corresponded constantly. When he returned to America in 1949, they resumed where they had left off, but under a particularly ominous cloud. Both Hellman and Melby were about to be victims of the McCarthyism firestorms, and both knew it. In his own words: "I don't think it is correct to say that the relationship changed when I came back from China. But the times by 1949 had and the build-up for McCarthyism was well under way. All this was both distressing and paralyzing . . . it is being caught up in a Greek tragedy that destroys everything and everyone. I think neither of us wanted any change, but did not quite know what to do about it. Time is the mischief."

When Melby left for his China assignment in the fall of 1945, Hellman's life returned to its prewar pattern. She moved between Manhattan and Pleasantville; Hammett, who had again rented a Greenwich Village apartment, was a rather constant fixture at the farm, although it was during this period that the sexual side of their relationship ended. In her memoirs, Hellman tells of returning from a party with Hammett, who indicated his desire to make love. Because he was drunk, Hellman refused. He never tried again and the subject was never mentioned. The change seems to have had little effect on the paramount strength of their bond.

At the end of the summer at East Hampton with Melby, Hellman set to work on the screenplay of *The Searching Wind* that she had been commissioned to write for Hal Wallis at Paramount, which would be directed by the eminent William Dieterle. When it was released, the film was even less successful than the play, but before finishing the script that autumn, Hellman started work on a new play, *Another Part of the Forest*, which also concerned the Hubbard family, this time twenty years prior to the action of *The Little Foxes*, when Regina would have been twenty. In an interview at the time Hellman said she had vague plans to write a trilogy about the Hubbards; a third play, never started, would bring the family close to the present with Alexandra an embittered spinster living in Paris. Her motivation to write a play about the earlier period, the 1880s, was to show how the Hubbards of *The Little Foxes* came to be as nasty as they were. Of course, the Hubbards were also Hellman's most successful theatrical creations, and in casting about for the subjects of a new play after the failure of *The Searching Wind*, they were perhaps an obvious choice. With her Marx relations again as her models, and with Hammett again at hand to offer advice, work on the play went swiftly and it was soon ready for production.

Another Part of the Forest would be Hellman's first play without Shumlin, and she decided to direct it herself. In some ways it is remarkable that Shumlin and Hellman survived five plays and a romance. Both had legendary tempers and were dedicated to getting their own way. Despite the bad feeling underlying the split, Hellman was loyal to Shumlin publicly. When asked by an interviewer why she had decided on directing her new play herself, she replied that there were only a handful of firstrate directors of which Shumlin was one, and none were available at the moment. She didn't mention that Shumlin's unavailability on earlier occasions proved no obstacle; she had made him available. Privately she told friends she was tired of fighting with him.

Since Shumlin had served as both director and producer, Hellman needed someone to oversee the production and elected a young man named Kermit Bloomgarden, who had been Shumlin's general manager since 1935. Her maneuver launched one of Broadway's most distinguished producing careers. Bloomgarden would introduce all of Hellman's future plays to Broadway (except for *Candide*) as well as many landmark plays and musicals by other writers—such as *Death of a Salesman, The Diary of Anne Frank* and *The Music Man.* But at the time Hellman asked Bloomgarden to produce *Another Part of the Forest*, he was an untested beginner and no match for Hellman in terms of experience and clout.

From similar moves in the future, it appears this is what Hellman wanted. She was at a stage in her career where she had grown tired of compromising with other large egos that were reinforced by large reputations. With Bloomgarden she started a pattern of selecting tyros for her collaborators, young men (no women) who lacked the muscle that builds from a string of impressive credits. Her primary motive was, of course, to control her own work, but in the process Hellman launched a number of impressive careers.

In other interviews at the time, Hellman belittled the director's role, saying that it required no great skill, especially if the playwright provided, as she did, detailed stage directions. "The only directors who count," she said, "are those who make creative contributions and there are very few of those. Elia Kazan, Jed Harris, Herman Shumlin and maybe one or two others. And even for those creative directors, the play must be there to begin with." Perhaps she made a more specific reference to the cause of trouble with Shumlin when she said on another occasion that few plays are strong enough to stand up to the momentum of two creative energies. Hellman no longer wanted a collaborator on her plays.

Given the natures of Hellman and Shumlin, a professional split was probably inevitable as her stature came to equal, perhaps surpass, his. But in actual fact, the breakup's permanence stemmed as much from an altogether different matter—money. Hellman was forced to pay taxes which she felt were Shumlin's obligation. The matter went to court and Hellman lost. He sought a reconciliation, but Hellman did not forgive him for many years. When a short time after the break, Shumlin had a hernia operation, he told a mutual friend that he would recover faster if Lillian came to see him. Informed of this, Hellman went to the hospital, was friendly, but after his recovery, resumed the feud with full force.

Hellman was now forty, and if the Shumlin breakup suggests a growing arrogance, she had not forgotten entirely her own footless beginnings. Bloomgarden had hired as his secretary a young woman, Flora Roberts, who had aspirations to be an agent, and indeed would later become one of the top brokers of plays and films in New York. He asked her to read Hellman's new play and give an opinion. Roberts liked the play, but felt there was a serious flaw in the plot's resolution. When Hellman came to the office, Bloomgarden asked Roberts to tell her what she had told him. Terrified, Roberts recited her criticism. When she finished, Hellman glowered silently and Roberts considered gathering up her belongings.

"I think you're right," Hellman said slowly, "but it's too late for me to do anything about it now." And when she left the office that day, she called out to Bloomgarden, "Hey, Kermit, you should give this girl a raise."

On another occasion Hellman arrived at Bloomgarden's office wearing a stylish mink coat. From her desk Roberts watched in dismay as the coat was tossed onto a chair and slid to the floor. She chided Hellman about treating such a beautiful coat with so little care. "Easy come, easy go," Hellman said airily as she swept into the inner office.

Bloomgarden cast *Another Part of the Forest* in his usual blue-chip manner—Mildred Dunnock, Percy Waram, Leo Genn, Scott McKay and, as Regina, an unknown: Patricia Neal. Although Hellman worked earnestly at directing her play, it had not been in rehearsal long before members of the company grew worried. According to her good friend Howard Bay, "Lillian wasn't interested in the technical side of the theater and knew nothing about it." She made little effort to hide her ignorance. While she was directing a scene that involved Neal, a friend who was an experienced theater hand arrived for a visit and slipped into the seat beside Hellman. "Thank God you're here," Hellman said. "How do I tell Pat to come from the back of the stage to the front?"

Later, staging a scene with the entire company, she thought for a minute and said, "Why don't you walk over there and have your exchange? We haven't used that part of the set yet." The actors were nonplussed by her interior-decorating approach to staging. As for Hellman herself, she would later write that she thought she had done "a good job—so good that I fooled myself into thinking I was a director, a mistake that I was to discover a few years later."

As in the earlier Hubbard play, *Another Part of the Forest* concerns the nasty struggles of the Hubbards to gain supremacy over each other. Money is still the weapon. (More than one critic remarked that the enormous importance of money in Hellman's plots makes it a separate character.) The play's dominant figure is Marcus Hubbard, the father of Regina, Ben and Oscar of *The Little Foxes*. But for sheer villainy, Marcus far surpasses his progeny, bringing to the Hubbard saga a sadistic cruelty toward his wife and sons that goes beyond the ruthless conniving in the earlier play. In fact, Marcus as the ogre pater familias is a walking anthology of Freudian flaws: son castrater, wife enslaver, daughter coveter.

Like Hellman's maternal great-grandfather, Isaac Marx, Marcus's money comes from a dry-goods store and, like his Marx counterpart, he emerges from the Civil War a rich man, while the town's landed gentry has been impoverished by it. The play's fundamental struggle is between Marcus and his oldest son, Ben. Marcus holds Ben in humiliating subjugation throughout most of the action, but Ben is ultimately given the ammunition to overthrow and supplant his father by the weakling mother who harbors a secret about her husband—his betrayal of his Southern neighbors during the Civil War, which, if known, would bring about a prompt lynching.

If Hellman was troubled by the grumbles about her earlier plays' reliance on melodrama, she did not let it influence her in writing *Another Part of the Forest*. When the play opened in New York on November 20, 1947, even the critics who liked it, and many did, often couched their praise in acknowledgment of its melodramatic nature. Brooks Atkinson of *The Times*, apparently out of patience with Hellman's theatrical excesses, wrote that the play was "a witches' brew of blackmail, insanity, cruelty, theft, torture, insult, drunkenness, with a trace of incest thrown in for good measure." He wondered how the author of some of the electrifying yet spare scenes of *Another Part of the Forest* could also have ladled such ponderously clumsy plot developments into the same play. In his implication that two different artistic tastes were at work, Atkinson, whether intentionally or not, may have stumbled onto a truth of Hellman's playwriting.

For her dialogue, Hellman always had Hammett looking over her shoulder to keep her scenes from becoming mired in verbosity. But Hammett's plotting sense was less reliable. On several occasions he pointed to his inability to come up with a good story line as the reason he was unable to produce a new novel—and the ones already written frequently threatened to bog down in tortured plot complexities but were rescued handily by intriguing characters and startling realism, and more than anything else by the hard dialogue that sliced to a point with wit and economy. Few plays have a more deftly constructed plot than *The Little Foxes* and few plays have a clumsier one than *Days to Come*. Both had Hammett's full services—as did *Another Part of the Forest*.

Some critics liked the new play enormously. Richard Watts, writing for the *New York Post*, thought it superior to all Hellman's earlier efforts. The more lasting judgment of theater historians, however, was anticipated by Wolcott Gibbs, who wrote in *The New Yorker* that *Another Part of the Forest* was "merely an untidy sequel to an infinitely superior play."

Although Hellman had been hearing the melodrama charge for years, the Atkinson attack rankled to a degree that prompted a response. Brushing aside the basic theater law that forbids responding to critics, Hellman argued Atkinson's points in a piece for *The New York Times* theater section entitled "An Author Jabs Her Critics." It is a succinct summary of Hellman's basic thoughts about playwriting. To the charge of contrivance she said that all writing is contrivance; there is merely good or bad contrivance. As for Atkinson's objection to her excessive use of violence, she characterized it as a total revulsion at violence, then defended its use as a basic tool of the dramatist. Having implied that Atkinson was lily-livered in his approach to art, Hellman sportingly said that his view on the subject was so opposite to hers that they would never agree.

Another Part of the Forest remained at the Fulton Theater for 191 performances, a respectable run, but considerably shorter than those of four of Hellman's five earlier plays. Even the critics who disliked the play admitted that it was potent theater, and in terms of Hellman's overall reputation it seems to have validated her position as the country's preeminent crafter of excoriating drama. The play offered indications that Hellman, too, was starting to consider herself an "important writer," not just in the plethora of Freudian and mythic reverberations but in such high-flown literary allusions as the title, a common stage direction of Renaissance drama including Shakespeare, and in the parents' names, Marcus and Lavinia, which seem to be a reference to *Titus Andronicus*. The names also evoke Eugene O'Neill's *Mourning Becomes Electra*, as do the dark family tangles of the plot. Whatever literary ambition the play reveals, the tortured family relationships also reflected an aspect of Hellman's private life at the time; she was still undergoing analysis while she was writing the play, and she dedicated it to her analyst, Gregory Zilboorg.

Given the large amount of Oedipal-Electra vibrato in *Another Part of the Forest*—as well as the ever-present Hellman theme of money—an occurrence at the opening night carried a bizarre irony. Max Hellman sat through the first act of his daughter's sixth play crackling crisp currency bills as he counted them over and over, making a racket that bothered not only the people sitting near him but the actors as well. Then as the house lights went up at the end of Act One, Max stood and said to everyone around him, "My daughter wrote this play. It gets better."

When Hellman later expressed concern about her father to Gregory Zilboorg, the analyst did not mince words. "Your father has senile dementia," he said. "You must face it and do something about it very soon."

Hellman put off any action until six months later, when Max, to use her words, "cracked up" completely and she had him committed to a hospital in White Plains, not far from Hardscrabble Farm. Because Max could never forgive her for that, she says that she "lost" her father two years before his death in 1948.

The Marx-Newhouse clan had gradually disappeared from Hellman's life. Her mother had died of cancer. Her grandmother Newhouse and her great-uncles were all gone. The only family member Hellman had left in the New York area was her mother's wealthy sister, Florence, who became totally senile ten years before her death in 1970. While no one would have criticized Hellman for putting her aunt in a nursing home, she insisted the old woman should remain in the apartment she had always lived in, overseeing, if not paying for, her care. The Marxes and New-houses were also losing their hold on Hellman's imagination. She would not write another play about them after *Another Part of the Forest* but would turn her attention to her father's family.

In February 1946 an article appeared in *The New Masses* that shook the American Communist party and its sympathizers and had repercussions among writers and intellectuals throughout the country. Screenwriter Albert Maltz, a communist, wrote an essay suggesting that the party was wrong to judge creative works on purely political grounds, wrong to insist that literature, theater, painting, music should serve only as weapons to further revolutionary aims. While he allowed that it was a noble purpose to which art could be put, it should not be the only purpose. Maltz pleaded that room be made for works of art that succeeded on esthetic grounds, if not on political ones. To illustrate the spuriousness of the party's rigid critical approach, Maltz cited the attack made by *The New Masses* on Hellman's play *Watch on the Rhine* when it first opened on Broadway during the period in which Russia was allied with Hitler. When it "appeared unaltered as a film in 1942 (with Russia and Germany at war), *The New Masses* critic praised it."

While Maltz's plea seemed modest enough, it brought down upon him the full wrath of the Party. Meetings were called, Party officials flew to Hollywood, the next issue of *The New Masses* ran a number of denunciations of Maltz's heresy. The furor did not die down until Maltz was persuaded publicly to recant his error and admit in print he had been a bad communist to think in such a reactionary way.

Hellman was silent throughout the Maltz furor—about the only prominent radical who was. If she felt the Party had been wrong to condemn her own antifascist play for no other reason than Russia's momentary alliance with Hitler, she did not say so publicly. And if she felt the Party was right to dismiss any creative work that did not advance the people's struggle—*The Children's Hour* for example—she was also silent.

Communism's wartime alliance with capitalism had also proved to be momentary, and with the defeat of fascism and the postwar confusion and instability of many nations, communists saw an opportunity to seize power, by force if necessary, in the governments of its former allies. Eastern Europe was rapidly being communized, Greece and Turkey appeared to be ripe for similar takeovers and, for a time, France was in danger of falling to the communists. Putting a stop to the rapid expansion of communism became the number one priority of Western leaders, generating, in part, the anticommunist anxiety that soon gripped America.

Although Hellman was not to have her confrontation with the House Committee on Un-American Activities until 1952, she felt the chill of Cold War vigilantism in her own life far earlier. Ever since his return from the service, Hammett had been the focus of increasing interest to the FBI and at times was actually followed by agents. Typically, the police-state shadow that fell across her path did nothing to inhibit Hellman's political activities. In the period from 1945 to 1950 she was perhaps more active in leftist causes than she had ever been.

She was unshaken in her belief that Russia, far from being an enemy, was an example to emulate and no threat to anyone but war-prone governments and venal corporations. Her position is never easy to pin down with absolute clarity, but it seems to have remained strongly supportive of Russia as a country that was undertaking something vast and noble in its dedication to peace and social justice and in its unrelenting opposition to fascism.

Much later in *Scoundrel Time* when she quietly confesses to errors in judgment on these matters, Hellman acknowledges having been aware of violations of human rights within the Soviet Union but believed them to be temporary measures that would be abandoned when the revolution was secured. Sadly, she admits, fifty years after the Bolshevik Revolution, the suspension of individual rights did not turn out to be temporary.

In the late 1940s, however, her enthusiasm for Russia and her skepticism toward the U.S. Government remained as strong as in the late 1930s. Whatever doubts she had entertained about the Soviet custodians of Marxism as a result of the Moscow purge trials and the Stalin-Hitler pact of 1939 had been explained away to her satisfaction, and she was still able to justify any action emanating from the Kremlin, while subjecting her own government's actions to the harshest scrutiny. Even more of a target for her vigilance than Washington were the fascist elements that she had discovered, with Hammett's help, at work throughout American society.

In 1947 the U.S. Government gave Hellman and all other leftists plenty to be vigilant about. The House Committee on Un-American Activities, the infamous HUAC, held hearings in Washington to investigate communist infiltration into the film industry. The Congressmen had no trouble finding witnesses to testify that there was much cause for alarm: Jack Warner, Adolphe Menjou, Robert Taylor and Louis B. Mayer were some of the newsworthy names that propelled the entertainment-industry witch-hunt into headlines and ignited a nationwide brushfire that burned for ten years, inflicting many casualties and putting the country through one of its greatest agonies of identity.

Looking back on this period after many years, a number of observers feel that much havoc could have been avoided, in Hollywood at least, if the movie producers had stood together and defied the committee, challenging its right to pry into the political convictions of film industry personnel. Others feel that the public mood was too exercised about the alleged danger to accept such an arrogant brush-off from the movie producers. And, from their point of view, the public had long been the master their industry was dedicated to pleasing.

In any case, the producers capitulated. They held a meeting at New York's Waldorf-Astoria on November 24, 1947, that resulted in a joint statement to the effect that they would fire any of the writers and directors in their employ who had refused to answer the committee's questions. (The Hollywood Ten, the writers and directors who defied the committee, had just been cited for contempt of Congress.) They would also not hire anyone who was a communist "or a member of any group that advocates the overthrow of the Government of the United States by force, or by illegal or unconstitutional method." Thus the Hollywood "blacklist" became official.

The Hollywood Ten's raucous defiance of the committee had won them jail sentences, and now the top powers of Hollywood had sanctioned the committee's right to push ahead with its inquisitions. Shock waves of fear flashed through the film industry, as well as through the nation's intellectual community. One of the strongest denunciations from among those who did speak out was Lillian Hellman's. She wrote an editorial for the Screen Writers' Guild magazine which she titled "The Judas Goats." It was a sardonic condemnation of the Hollywood hearings and a clarion call to arms against the craven lack of opposition to the burgeoning persecutions:

> It was a week of turning the head in shame; of the horror of seeing politicians make the honorable institution of Congress into a honky tonk show; of listening to craven men lie and tattle, pushing each other in their efforts to lick the boots of their vilifiers; publicly trying to wreck the lives, not of strangers, mind you, but of men with whom they have worked and eaten and played, and made millions.
>
> No less the week of shame because of its awful comedy; the sight of the Congress of the United States of America being advised and lectured by a Mr. Adolphe Menjou, a haberdashers' gentleman; ladies screaming in elderly pleasure at the news that Mr. Robert Taylor was

forced to act in a movie—act in a movie. Act. Act is not the correct word for what Mr. Taylor does in pictures; the professionally awkward stammering of Mr. Gary Cooper who knew that Communist scripts had been submitted to him, but couldn't remember their names or their authors. And why couldn't he remember? Because he reads at night. That's sensible enough; naturally one cannot remember what one reads in the dark. Why not turn on the light, you might ask yourself.

But one character only out-did the other. To me, even Mrs. Rogers, mother of the middleaged queen, was put in the shade by the most blasphemous and irreligious remark I have ever heard in public; Mr. Leo McCarey spoke of God as a "character" in one of his pictures.

A sickening, sickening, immoral and degraded week. And why did it take place? It took place because those who wish war have not the common touch. Highly placed gentlemen are often really gentlemen, and don't know how to go about these things. Remember that when it was needed, in Europe, they had to find the house painter and gangster to make fear work and terror acceptable to the ignorant. Circuses will do it, and this was just such a circus; hide the invasion of the American Constitution with the faces of movie actors; pander to ignorance by telling people that ignorance is good, and lies even better; bring on the millionaire movie producer and show that he too is human, he too is frightened and cowardly. Take him away from his golden house and make him a betrayer and a fool for those who like such shows, and enjoy such moral degradation.

But why this particular industry, these particular people? Has it anything to do with Communism? Of course not. There has never been a single line or word of Communism in any American picture at any time. There has never or seldom been ideas of any kind. Naturally, men scared to make pictures about the American Negro, men who have only in the last year allowed the word Jew to be spoken in a picture, men who took more than ten years to make an anti-Fascist picture, those are frightened men and you pick frightened men to frighten first. Judas goats; they'll lead the others, maybe, to the slaughter for you. The others will be the radio, the press, the publishers, the trade unions, the colleges, the scientists, the churches—all of us. All of us who believe in this lovely land and its freedoms and rights, and who wish to keep it good and make it better.

They frighten mighty easy, and they talk mighty bad. For one week they made us, of course, the laughing stock of the educated and decent world. I suggest the rest of us don't frighten so easy. It's still not un-American to fight the enemies of one's country. Let's fight.

One could argue that the article was counterproductive in that the only people who could intercede between the Hollywood imperiled and the witch-hunters were the producers whom Hellman insulted so harshly. Still, it was a ringing and courageous rallying cry—but no one rallied. Purges progressed apace, and the blacklist remained a grim film industry reality.

Hellman was by no means indifferent to the possibility of being barred from film work. Although she had severed her arrangement with Sam Goldwyn and had turned down several recent offers, she liked working in films and considered Hollywood as an always available money source. It was her financial security to counterbalance the unreliable Broadway critics and box office. An irresistible offer came to her in 1948. William Wyler was planning a film version of Theodore Dreiser's *Sister Carrie* and wanted Hellman to write the screenplay. She was enthusiastic about the idea, and the project seemed to be going ahead. But soon Hellman was stunned to be told by Wyler that the producer, Barney Balaban, had vetoed her. She was blacklisted.

17

WITH ANTI-LEFT repression on the rise in the United States, Hellman felt no inclination to diminish her own political activities or limit herself to less conspicuous ones. The opposite was true. In the two years following the initiation of the blacklist, she escalated her efforts, engaging in her two most public involvements in radical activism. In 1948 she took an official position in the Presidential campaign of former Vice-President Henry Wallace on the ultraliberal Progressive party ticket. The following year, 1949, she was one of the principal sponsors of the Cultural and Scientific Conference for World Peace at the Waldorf-Astoria, the notorious "Waldorf Conference" that was denounced by the State Department and by most of the country's press as being pro-communist to a near-seditious level.

In 1946 Henry Wallace had given a speech at Madison Square Garden in which he inveighed against the U.S. Government's new get-tough-with-Russia policy. The speech had made him the hero to many of the left and a pariah to President Truman, who demanded that because of such opposition to his administration's foreign policy, Wallace should resign as Secretary of Commerce. Wallace left the Democratic party and formed the Progressive party, rallying all those who felt the Cold War an unnecessary and dangerous fabrication. When he ran for the Presidency, Hellman headed up the Progressives' women's committee, Women for Wallace, and took part in drafting the party platform, which asked for greater cooperation with the USSR, arms reductions, no universal military training and U.N. administration of U.S. foreign aid.

As the 1948 Presidential race got underway, accusations were made that Wallace and his Progressive party, perhaps inadvertently, had fallen under communist control. Budd Schulberg, himself a former communist and a Wallace enthusiast, was one of many to recognize the symptoms. Schulberg recalls his alarm when he lent his Bucks County farm for a Wallace rally. "The advance men were billed as Progressives," he said, "but the jargon they spoke was pure Communist Party."

Several of the key Progressive party figures were indeed communists, but as for their exercising control, this was denied by everyone in the Wallace camp, including Hellman, who said that if she learned it to be true she would resign from the campaign. For Hellman, this was an anticommunist statement of rare force. On the occasions when she had separated herself from Communist party positions, she invariably strained to avoid any hint of criticism in her polite disagreements. Now she was saying she wanted no part of a communist-controlled party.

In *Scoundrel Time* Hellman writes only briefly of her participation in the Wallace campaign. She relates that Wallace pulled her aside after a meeting to ask if the rumors were true that communists sat on his governing committee. Hellman laughed and said of course they did, but that they were obvious and harmless. Wallace made no comment.

A short time after this exchange, Hellman says she arranged a meeting with several of the men she thought to be among the more important communists working with the Progressives. According to her *Scoundrel Time* account, she warned them to back off, be more flexible or return to their own party. Her fear seems to have been that if they persisted in their attempts to dominate, they would fail, and when Wallace lost the election he would turn against them. She was thanked for her concern but told she was acting on a common delusion about communists: that they all operated under a centralized command. Her message would be passed along, she was told, but it would have little effect.

Writing about the incident twenty-five years later, Hellman takes credit for foreseeing the hopelessness of the situation. But the image she creates of the American Communist party as a loose network of independent and uncontrollable free spirits seems somewhat fanciful and in rather flagrant contradiction to the experience of others—Albert Maltz and Budd Schulberg, for instance—and may have been more a reflection of her own unique link with the Party, which she presents as that of a valued but independent friend. While there is no evidence the Party ever tried to exercise control over or even influence Hellman, she had too many friends who were communists—one in her own house—not to have been aware of the rigors of Party discipline. To suggest that communist officials, having won a footing in a national Presidential campaign, were acting at random to improvise a strategy is disingenuous and probably calculated to make communists appear less insidious than she knew them to be.

Having made this suspect assertion in *Scoundrel Time*, Hellman went on to accuse Henry Wallace of a similar dishonesty. She was perplexed, she wrote, when a short time after the election Wallace denied knowledge of communist participation in his campaign; she knew he was lying, she said, because she had told him of it. Perhaps to rule out the possibility that Wallace had not believed her, she adds that Wallace had been quoted to her as saying Hellman was the only one of his cadre he trusted completely.

Hellman had always been lukewarm about Wallace (Hammett had no use for him at all, calling him "the Iowa yogi"), but she was very enthusiastic about the Progressives, believing the nation desperately needed a third, more liberal, political party. Because of her dedication to the party rather than the man, she was constantly at odds with the other Progressive policymakers, who wanted to place all resources behind the Presidential campaign, as did, understandably, Henry Wallace. Convinced that Wallace's Presidential chances were hopeless, Hellman wanted the Progressives to shift their energies toward building a political organization on the local level, with a more practical eye to the future. When Harry Truman won the election with 24 million votes to Thomas Dewey's 21 million, Wallace came away with little over 1 million. The Progressives had no further influence.

In the spring of 1948, before becoming deeply involved in the Wallace campaign, Hellman had rented a house on Martha's Vineyard to work on a dramatization of Norman Mailer's *The Naked and the Dead* for Kermit Bloomgarden. While there, she went for a drink one evening at the home of her good friend Leo Huberman, a Marxist editor who was noted for his rare willingness to criticize the Communist party. Staying with Huberman and his wife was a good-looking young longshoreman named Randall Smith, who had served with the Lincoln Brigade in Spain and had worked for the past decade as a union organizer, most recently in the East Coast longshoreman's union. After the recent battles for control of the union, Smith was expelled from the Maritime Union for his communist affiliation. At the same time, he also left the Communist party and broke up with his wife. Totally in flux at the age of thirty, he jumped at an offer from his friend Huberman to come up to Martha's Vineyard and help clear his place of poison ivy.

Over drinks at the Hubermans, Hellman took a liking to Smith and asked him to go fishing with her the next day. They started seeing each other. After a few days, Smith moved into Hellman's rented house at Menemsha. Smith recounts their friendship from its beginning:

"Huberman said to me, change your shirt, Lillian Hellman's coming for drinks. I asked 'Who's that?' 'The famous playwright,' Leo said and went on to tell me all she'd done. I had vaguely heard of *The Children's Hour* but that was about all. When I met her, I didn't find her very attractive, but she won you over by the power of her intellect, her directness, her knowledge of things. She knew more about the longshoreman situation than I did. I don't think she was after me from the start. Unless she was being very subtle. I've been around—I can usually tell. There was no big emotional scene. It was more a matter of, 'We're alone, it's midnight, why don't we fuck?'

"She was working on an adaptation of *The Naked and the*

Dead when I moved in with her. It was giving her a lot of trouble. She'd work all morning and only eke out a few lines. She'd show it to me and I'd say, 'You call that work.' She'd get furious. 'You're goddamn right it's work—the hardest kind!' Around noon she'd quit for the day. We'd fry an egg for lunch, then go out fishing all afternoon.

"I really liked being with her, but I've got to admit I fell into our relationship more because of the glamour and excitement of being with Lillian Hellman. I was broke and she had plenty of money, we could go to restaurants, that sort of thing. And she had this old Cadillac I used to love to drive. It was big and black. . . .

"As for sex, it wasn't as though she was frantic about it, but she liked having it around, if you see what I mean. She had a good chest, but no ass. Her shoulders were broad and her hips very thin. She loved good clothes. I remember a lot of silk.

"The thing that drew me to Lillian was her honesty and integrity. There were no petty lies, no petty bullshit. I'd never met anyone like that before. No, Harry Bridges was like that. You sense integrity in someone, not so much by what they do or say, but the *shadow* of what they do or say. You overhear them on the phone, then you hear them relate the conversation later, that's what I mean by 'the shadow.'

"I only stayed with her a few weeks on the Vineyard, but we saw each other in New York. She'd phone me on a Wednesday or Thursday and invite me up to her farm for the weekend. It was great—good food, plenty to do—she had to keep me from working in the fields, didn't want me to do that. We didn't have an intense affair, she may have been seeing other people.

"Hammett was living down in Greenwich Village at that time and drinking heavily. She wasn't seeing him—I mean, at all—but she was worried about him. She asked me to go see him, pay him visits. He seemed to like me and liked hearing about my longshoreman days. I once used a word that he really liked—'gunsel'— it means a goon. He was fine in the morning, but by the afternoon he was drunk. And he could be mean. When he was drinking, he would get violent with his girlfriends. He was seeing one regularly then, a girl who lived in the neighborhood. We were sitting talking one time and he took his cane and lifted her skirt with it.

I didn't like that. He was always pulling some stunt like that. Still, I saw a lot of Hammett, I was seeing Hellman at that time too. But I never saw them together.

"We didn't talk politics much. We were all sympathetic to communism, but we all deviated from the party line. With both Hellman and Hammett, I have a recollection of them testing me, to see how far I deviated and if I deviated in the same way they deviated. But as a former communist, I used to resent their attitudes—so lofty and intellectual. I doubt if either of them ever went to a meeting or did any work. They were like officers, I had been an enlisted man.

"As for whether Hellman was ever a member of the party— what is a member? It wasn't that organized. I was an active member for over ten years and if they got ten dollars in dues out of me they were lucky. I may have signed a card or something at one time, but it was vague and of no importance. Those things don't say whether or not you were a party member. It's whether or not you were under *discipline*. In that sense, Hellman was completely independent. She didn't hesitate to have an opinion outside the party line.

"Hammett's daughter Mary came to stay with him. She was a little screwed up and started seeing Hellman's analyst, Zilboorg. Mary and I had a romance. (If you see her in California, tell her I'm still alive.) We'd go off together and make love for a few hours. If Hammett knew and he probably did, I doubt he cared. Hellman found out about it and there was hell to pay. 'How could you do that to me?' That sort of thing.

"I went to work out in California, got married again. I hadn't seen Lillian for twenty years when I ran into her on upper Madison Avenue. She was trying to get a cab. I hailed one for her. We exchanged a few words—maybe ten each—and talked about getting together, but we never did."

The arrival of Hammett's older daughter did nothing to pull him from his boozy slough. Instead, she sank into it. They drank together and fought a lot. Although Mary denied it, there was reason to think he beat her up. In her biography Diane Johnson writes: "[People] were afraid he might harm her in his drunken rages, or worse, or perhaps had already. The situation was ugly."

So ugly, in fact, that a visitor to the West Tenth Street apartment, a woman who was also a friend of Hellman's, insisted Mary pack a bag and come with her to Hellman's. Mary agreed, and Hellman, with little enthusiasm, took her in.

Since its publication in 1934, Hammett had made over a million dollars from *The Thin Man* and the various spin-offs; it was his lack of money worries, he claimed to Nunnally Johnson, that undermined his desire to write—one of the several excuses he gave. Now he no longer even tried. Looking old and desiccated, he spent his time in his Greenwich Village apartment in the company of a housekeeper, a secretary and an assortment of saloon pickups and hookers. He kept a case of Johnnie Walker Red Label in a closet—his security, he said—generally consuming over a bottle a night. His drunkenness got to be more than Hellman could endure and she told him she did not want to see him anymore. Hammett shrugged and had another drink.

Hellman got reports on his condition, each more depressing than the last, from his housekeeper, Rose Evans. Eventually, the calls from Evans became frantic: if she didn't come down to Tenth Street and rescue Hammett, he would die. At first Hellman refused—there had been so many of those calls—but finally Evans convinced her how serious it was. Hellman went to the apartment and could see that Rose had not been exaggerating. Hammett had severe DTs—he was convulsing and screaming. They feared the scandal that would result if they took him to a hospital in that condition. With a doctor's help, Hellman got him into sufficient shape at her East Eighty-second Street house to put him in a hospital, where he spent Christmas and New Year's of 1948. When he got out, he was told he could never drink again. Except for a ritualistic martini or two when he was dying, he never did.

Earlier in 1948, before Hammett's collapse, Hellman made another foray into journalism. She accepted an assignment to go to Yugoslavia for the *New York Star* to interview Tito, who had just won the world's attention by being the first communist leader to break with Moscow. At the time, all that was known of the dispute was that Tito had incurred the wrath of the Comintern and had received an ominous letter of censure. The letter was made public, but it was written in such lofty generalities that even the most knowledgeable Soviet observers were unable to understand any more than that the Kremlin was mightily unhappy with Tito. When Tito refused to capitulate—confess his crimes, recant, kiss Stalin's ring or any of the customary preliminaries for returning to favor—the world waited for the inevitable lowering of the iron fist. When that did not happen and it began to appear that Tito was to be permitted his defiance, he became the object of worldwide curiosity.

The implacable polarization of the world between the two great powers, communist Russia and capitalist America, now had taken an unexpected detour. An alternative had appeared that held out hope for avoiding the Russia-America showdown many felt inevitable. Informed observers of the world situation considered Tito's accomplishment to be the most significant historic development since the end of the war; others extended that time measurement back to the Bolshevik revolution.

Once again Hellman found herself at the scene of a pivotal event, but in the six articles she wrote for the *Star*, the interview with Tito took up only part of one of them. She interviewed a few other VIPs—the vice-premier of Czechoslovakia was one—but devoted much of the series to the sort of aimless travel observations permitted big-time writers by editors of small-time publications.

When she was finally alone with Tito, they talked about the danger of war, the Progressive party and the diversity of American opinion about everything. After the interview—to which Hellman devoted nine paragraphs—her escort from the Yugoslav foreign office said it was not necessary for her to have been so "tactful" in her conversation with the premier. She understood from this remark, she wrote, that he meant she could have asked Tito about his fight with Moscow. Hellman laughed and asked the man if he would put his charge of tact in writing to prove to her friends she had not invented it.

Whether or not for reasons of tact, Hellman sidestepped a serious political discussion with Tito. A newspaper had sent her on an expensive journey, and we can assume paid her well for the door-opening prestige of her name (there was a production of *The Little Foxes* in Belgrade while she was there). Yet even her official escort expressed polite amazement that Hellman had not used her journalist's prerogative to ask the questions American readers wanted asked and, it is very possible, Tito wanted to answer, especially in a relaxed conversation with a prominent, sympathetic intellectual.

The strange omission may have resulted from Hellman's inexperience as a world-class journalist. But another possible explanation must not be ruled out. Tito's defection was an enormous setback for the Russians, and Hellman may not have wanted to provide Tito with a forum for ideas that might be hurtful to the Kremlin. Perhaps in her own improvised concept of equal time, she gave Tito, in this dispute, no time at all. She talked politics with him but not about the one thing that made him newsworthy, not to mention history-worthy. If she avoided the subject to spare Moscow, she was more than letting down the *Star* and its readers. She was exercising her own form of journalistic censorship and then laughing it off as "tact."

According to Randall Smith, Hellman was very much on Tito's side in his fight with Moscow; they had had fights about it themselves. In fact, Smith cites this as proof of Hellman's political independence. But while her interview with Tito was friendly and complimentary, it contained not a word to indicate such partisanship on Hellman's part. On the contrary, the subject of "Titoism" only came up in her articles when she interviewed the vice-premier of Czechoslovakia, who stated, and Hellman recorded, the Russian complaint against Tito. Tito's side was not offered in any of Hellman's articles.

There is a strong suggestion of Hellman's political dilemma in her arguing Tito's case in private, yet publicly presenting only Russia's case against him. *Watch on the Rhine* proved she did not fear defying the Party. The pulled punch on Titoism, however, coupled with her sympathetic hearing of the Stalinist complaints against Tito, bespeaks a reluctance to make any public utterance that might damage the Russians. This same inhibition would come up again more markedly during her HUAC ordeal.

While in Europe Hellman met the Spanish playwright Emmanuel Robles and was so impressed by him she decided to get out of her *Naked and the Dead* commitment and instead do an English adaptation of Robles's play *Montserrat*. In this period she also undertook an odd mission: the producer Irene Selznick, who was a friend of Hellman's, asked her to come out to Hollywood to help her persuade Sam Goldwyn to buy *A Streetcar Named Desire* for a film. ("Let's say Lillian was a paid houseguest," Selznick said many years later.) Hellman knew Goldwyn and, from her script for *These Three*, she knew how dodgy material could be made acceptable to the Breen office. But Goldwyn could not be sold.

In the first months of 1949, the Cold War was at its peak. The Russians' blockade of Berlin in June 1948 had brought the two superpowers as close to war as they had been and resulted in the airlift that was still in effect. The North Atlantic Treaty Organization was at the point of ratification and would unite America and the Western European nations in a military alliance against Russia, a response to what was perceived as alarming evidence of Soviet expansionist ambitions, most notably the seizure of Czechoslovakia, the abrogation of the treaties guaranteeing free elections in Eastern Europe, and the attempts to overthrow the democratic governments of Greece and Turkey. On the other side of the globe the communists were winning the civil war in China and the People's Republic would be declared in Peking in October 1949.

Within the country, the American public was still in shock from Whittaker Chambers's accusations the previous August that Alger Hiss, while a high-ranking State Department officer, had been a communist spy. In January 1949, the leaders of the American Communist party were accused under the Smith Act of seeking to overthrow the government by force in a trial that dragged on most of the year and resulted in convictions. Predictably, the FBI was keeping close watch on Hellman at this time, and they noted that she had given a May Day party in both 1947 and 1948. Of particular interest to the agency was her friendship with Kenneth Durant, the secretary of the Russian envoy and the U.S. manager for *Tass*.

At no previous time was the American public more alarmed about the communist threat. Fewer and fewer people regarded communism as just another, if somewhat extreme, political system, and were coming to see it instead as an insidious conspiracy aimed at destroying the American way of life. The spreading alarm gave impetus to the House Committee on Un-American Activities, which had been operating off and on since 1938, and would lead to the Republic-threatening excesses of Senator Joseph McCarthy.

Radicals like Hellman saw this rabid reaction to communism as not just a setback for progressivism, but as the result of trumped-up incitements, fabricated by the country's fascist elements, for the purpose of pushing America into a war with Russia. To those of the far left, the press revelations about the ruthless aggression of international communism were seen as capitalist lies, more trumped-up incitements to war. Instead of shrinking away in the face of spreading Russophobia, they chose to combat it with propaganda assaults of their own.

To communist supporters like Hammett and Hellman, everything the Western nations were doing to obstruct Russia was warlike; so the word chosen by way of contrasting Russia's objectives was "peace." A number of "peace conferences" sprang up that were communist-inspired and feverishly pro-Russian. In 1948 a major conference of this sort had been held in Wroclaw, Poland, which attracted a number of prominent pro-communist intellectuals from around the world. One of the sponsors of the conference had been an American front group called the National Council of the Arts, Sciences and the Professions, in which Hammett and Hellman were active, along with those prominent American liberals who either still believed in Russia's humanitarian intentions or were so frightened by the war rhetoric that they felt appeasement of Russia was the only hope for peace ("Better red than dead"). From the sponsors' point of view the conference had been such a success—that is to say, widely covered in the world press—that they were emboldened to hold another, this time in New York. Thus was born the infamous Waldorf Conference, officially called The Cultural and Scientific Conference for World Peace.

Hellman was one of the chief organizers of the conference, whose political bias was recognized quickly due to the names involved, including many leading pro-communist intellectuals from America, Russia, Europe and Latin America. The biggest name would be the composer Dmitri Shostakovich, who had had his own troubles with the Soviet leadership but had been brought into line and was now a trusted emissary. According to his memoirs, he attended the Waldorf conference at the personal request of Stalin.

Given the anti-Russian temper in America at the time, the furor caused by the conference was understandable. Except for the difference between cold and hot wars—which to many was a tenuous technicality at that point—it was as if Jane Fonda had held a Vietcong rally in Madison Square Garden during the Vietnam war. Lillian Hellman was one of the most prominent names behind the Waldorf Conference and was widely perceived as one of its instigators. In a scathing write-up of the conference, *Life* magazine ran a photo of Hellman with the caption "Mastermind."

The State Department's refusal to grant visas to some of those invited made the conference a newsworthy *cause célèbre* weeks in advance. Thus, by the start of the event itself on March 25, 1949, those most critical of the conference were prepared to demonstrate their opposition. Pickets jammed up against the police barricades that surrounded the Waldorf with signs denouncing "Russian tyranny" or charging more specific crimes such as Stalin's enslavement of Czechoslovakia or the Berlin blockade. Some groups sang "The Star-Spangled Banner," others knelt in prayer.

A group of anticommunist intellectuals led by New York University professor Sidney Hook also rallied in opposition. Suspecting the conference was not open to all viewpoints as claimed, Hook had earlier gotten two members of the program committee to write the director, Harvard Professor Harlow Shapley, recommending that he be invited to speak. Hook received no answer and was unable to reach Shapley. Angered by the brush-off, Hook told the press of his fast shuffle, which he felt proved the conference's determination to include only speakers sympathetic to communism.

When the newspapers carried a denial from Shapley that any of the conference organizers had written him about Hook, Hook was outraged. The opening night of the conference, he forced his way into Shapley's room at the Waldorf, presented copies of the letters and demanded to know why Shapley had denied receiving them. Shapley, who was having cocktails with his wife and another couple, suggested that he and Hook step out in the hall in order to discuss the matter privately. Once outside, Hook heard the door slammed and bolted behind him.

Hook had brought a *Herald Tribune* reporter as witness, and the press account of the incident set the farcical tone of the event—rather like a Marx Brothers' film turned cold-war nasty. Comical as the incident was, it vividly dramatized the conference's role in focusing and solidifying animosities between the communist sympathizers and the anticommunist intellectuals of that time. Hook and his group saw the conference participants as dishonest, disloyal and wrong; Shapley, Hellman, *et al*, saw Hook and his cohorts as enemies of progress and warmongers.

In fact, a number of noncommunist liberals had agreed to take part in the conference, in the conviction that peace was a worthwhile cause, but dropped out as its propaganda aims became more apparent. One of them was Norman Cousins, the editor of *The Saturday Review of Literature*, who had initially accepted an invitation to speak but came to disapprove so strongly of the blatant partisanship that he had canceled. Cousins subsequently changed his mind when he received a telegram from the U.S. State Department expressing the hope that someone in a position to address the group would seize the opportunity for "a vigorous presentation of the democratic and antitotalitarian point of view." Cousins agreed and took up the hint with relish.

Two thousand people attended the opening-night banquet in the Waldorf ballroom. As soon as Cousins took his seat, Harlow Shapley, who was to be master of ceremonies, asked him the nature of his speech. Cousins handed him a copy. An unsigned article in *Newsweek* describes what happened next:

"Shapley looked at the first page, then at the second. His jaw dropped. He rushed over to Lillian Hellman. He and Miss Hellman read the speech together, conversing earnestly. Miss Hellman called over Miss Dorner (Hannah Dorner, director of NCASP), who read it too. Shapley returned to Cousins. 'Norman,' he said, 'it's been an awful lot of work to start this conference . . . but if this is the speech you want to make . . .'"

When his turn came, Cousins first talked about the hostility the conference had aroused; Americans were against it, he said, because of the auspices under which it was being held: "a small political group . . . which owes its allegiance not to America but to an outside government." Boos and hisses broke out in the grand ballroom of the Waldorf-Astoria. Shostakovich, at the speaker's table, looked bewildered and frantically asked his neighbor what was happening. "I ask you to believe," Cousins continued, carefully avoiding mentioning the Communist party by name, "that this group is without standing and without honor in its own country." More boos and hisses. When Cousins said that Americans also wanted peace, but not peace at any price, a woman in the back of the room smashed a dinner plate in fury.

Cousins was permitted to finish his speech, and he even received some polite applause. Most of the audience, however, was angry and felt that the evening had curdled. Hellman took the rostrum. In the clipped tones of a dowager mustering all of her breeding to maintain her composure in the face of unspeakable boorishness, she said into the microphone, "I would recommend, Mr. Cousins, that when you are invited out to dinner, you wait until you get home before you talk about your hosts."

The crowd exploded with laughter and applause. Hellman's wrist-slap made Cousins look churlish and tiresome. Not only had she defused an ugly moment; she had deftly converted Cousins from a harsh accuser to the butt of derision. But, having dealt with Cousins, she was unwilling to let the crowd off completely. Although Cousins's sentiments would have been better aired at one of the seminars, she said, she could not condone his having been booed and hissed.

What Cousins had done could not have been easy. He stood before a large group of people to tell them that he profoundly disapproved of what they were doing. He made charges of the utmost seriousness. Instead of responding to his allegations, Hellman gave back a quip. Cousins had accused these people of betraying their country, of abetting a foreign government that was bent on destroying their own. Hellman accused him of bad manners.

Still, misguided or not, there is something quite impressive about Hellman at this moment in her life. With the winds of McCarthy suppression stirring unmistakably, she had thrown herself behind a major event of the far left, an event that aspired to and achieved high visibility and was anathema to the U.S. Government and to most of the nation's press. She had an important role in deciding who would address the conference and in choosing the agenda for the discussion groups. She sat at the head table—drinking, chain-smoking, conferring with Shostakovich and Shapley—then took the microphone to dismiss contemptuously one of America's most distinguished editors.

It is tempting to view Hellman's bravura performance at the Waldorf Conference as the hubristic political flight that invited her downfall in the McCarthy period. But to give substance to that vision, the gods she displeased would have to be placed on Mount Olympus rather than on Capitol Hill. In her interrogation before the House Un-American Activities Committee, her involvement in the conference was never mentioned.

18

IF NEMESIS was only two years off, Hellman was to have a burst of professional glory in the fall of 1949. Her adaptation of Robles's *Montserrat*, which she directed, opened on Broadway on October 29. *Regina*, Marc Blitzstein's operatic version of *The Little Foxes*, premiered a few days later, while earlier that same month, a production of *Another Part of the Forest* opened in Moscow under the title *Ladies and Gentlemen*.

The Moscow production was well received. *Montserrat* fared less well in New York, opening to mostly negative reviews as a play, with added disapproval for Hellman's direction from the few critics who took notice of it. *Regina* succeeded remarkably, considering Broadway's uneasiness about operas. The score was praised by most critics, although a number of them spoke wistfully of the original play's power, which they felt had been undermined by the music's softening effect. Jane Pickens, a handsome singing actress who had once been part of radio's singing Pickens Sisters, gave a memorable performance as Regina in the critics' view. Tallulah Bankhead, who was ungracious about turning over her role, disagreed. When asked what she thought of

Pickens in the part, she growled, "I didn't even like her when she was one of the Andrews Sisters."

In terms of critical and financial success, Hellman had enjoyed better moments. But in terms of important manifestations of her talents—as a playwright, adapter and director—few theater people could match her display in the fall of 1949. Hellman had had little involvement with the production of *Regina*. Opera and musical theater were not areas in which she claimed any expertise, and she trusted the musical talent of Blitzstein who was a friend as well as a political ally. His 1938 musical, *The Cradle Will Rock*, was a landmark of leftist theater. The director of *Regina*, Robert Lewis, and the producer, Cheryl Crawford, both found Hellman helpful and approving of their exotic transformation of her play. Rather than taking a fiercely protective stance, as was feared, she was apparently flattered that her work was deemed material for opera and decided that the ambitious project was in good hands.

When Blitzstein elicited her opinion about his libretto, Hellman wrote back a detailed critique with many helpful comments. She showed the keen vigilance for false notes that informed her own dialogue, pointing out that certain words Blitzstein had added would not be used by Southerners, that others were "uneuphonious." In the letter, Hellman discussed her characters as though they were real people about whom her opinions were no better than anyone else's. "I don't think Regina is a flirt," she wrote. "She would flirt with Marshall for a reason; she would flirt with anybody for a reason, but I don't for a second believe she would flirt with the men in this town." And then later: "No talk about another woman getting fat. I think [Regina] is long past such small feminine pleasantries." When the opera opened, Hellman complimented the collaborators. *Regina* only ran a few months but has survived among opera enthusiasts in an original-cast recording.

With her mounting of *Montserrat*, Hellman consolidated her reputation as a less than brilliant director and even admits in *Pentimento* that she "directed it in a fumbling, frightened way," intimidated by the star, Emlyn Williams. Perhaps as an apology, she goes on to say that directors have come to their present power mostly through comedies and musicals, but that "few dramas can stand up to another assertive talent even if it is more distinguished than that of the original creator." In this case, however, she was not the original creator, merely the adapter.

During a tryout of the play in Princeton, Hellman despaired of getting the portrayal she wanted from one of the actors and said so to a group over drinks after a performance. Kermit Bloomgarden, who was again acting as producer, defended the man. "He's a method actor, Lillian. You have to give him time to grow into the role."

"What the hell is method acting anyway?" Hellman asked.

"I studied with Lee for a while," Bloomgarden said. "He had us acting an orange."

"An orange, eh?" Hellman replied. The next day the method actor was replaced.

It is doubtful that the most experienced and inspired direction could have saved *Montserrat*, a static and tortuous unraveling of the sort of philosophical conundrum dear to the Spanish. While her adaptation of the play is among Hellman's least successful efforts, her attraction to the work is revealing about the underpinnings of an important and elusive aspect of the Hellman persona—her politics—which at times baffled even close political allies.

Montserrat, a young captain in the Spanish army that occupies Venezuela, has been discovered to be a traitor in that he supports Simon Bolívar's revolt against Spanish rule. When Montserrat's Spanish superiors learn that he knows where Bolívar is hiding, six innocent citizens are rounded up and left alone with Montserrat for an hour (the first act) after which time they will be executed one by one unless he reveals Bolívar's hiding place. Montserrat must decide between betraying Bolívar (and thereby the hopes of millions of oppressed South Americans) or allowing the deaths of six innocent people.

Here Hellman's much vaunted ability to construct—or in this case to recognize—a sturdy plot failed her. Aside from the unrelenting and often extraneous sadism of the action, there is a basic illogicality on which the entire play depends. When Montserrat admits to being a traitor at the play's beginning, he knows his life is finished regardless of whether or not he informs. When the strategy to induce him to talk is made clear, he could kill himself and deprive the Spanish authorities of both the information and any reason to harm the others. Instead he plays along, causes the death of the six and does nothing to avoid his own death at the play's end.

Of all the enigmas and questions raised by the life of Lillian Hellman, perhaps the most puzzling was her dogged conviction that the communists were more on the side of right than her own country through decades of increasingly overwhelming evidence to the contrary. The premises of *Montserrat* closely parallel communist premises: the South American masses are oppressed by cruel and powerful forces; the only remedy is violent overthrow; violent overthrow can only be brought about by one element: Bolívar. The uniqueness of Bolívar as a deliverer that is repeatedly emphasized in the play is perhaps the key. The unsubstantiated but fanatical assertion that he is the one and only chance for social improvement echoes the Communist party's most troublesome idiosyncrasies: its rejection of allies, its obsession with a strict Party line, its rigid discipline and its murderous hostility especially toward other groups and isms, such as the socialists, with similar humanitarian aims.

Once the assumption is granted that the sole hope for the people of South America is Bolívar, then it logically follows that six innocent lives are a modest price to pay for this unique man's protection. Once it is granted that the one and only hope for a better, more just world is communism (with Russia its flagship) then it also logically follows that not just the murder of innocent people, but the purge trials, the pact with Hitler, the suspension of civil freedoms, the takeover of Eastern Europe, or any other exigency are modest prices to pay for furthering the revolution. And once it is assumed that the capitalist body is terminally diseased with fascism, corruption, inhumanity, injustice, exploitation—then even successful efforts toward reform, a half century of progressive legislation and Supreme Court decisions to temper the power of the owners and empower the people, are just window dressing, token palliatives, Band-Aids against cancer.

There is no doubt that Hellman regrets the sad fate of her six civilians in *Montserrat;* she humanizes them, presents them with varying degrees of sympathy and compassion. But she does not shrink from the necessity of their deaths to further the revolution. The implication is strong: she does not like these deaths any more than she liked the purge trials, or other Soviet excesses, but such abominations are excusable when held up against the revolution's potential for improving mankind's lot.

After Hammett's collapse at the end of 1948, he settled down to a more tranquil life, mostly at Hardscrabble Farm, where he gave up drinking and filled the gap with television, which he watched endlessly. Because of a legal battle with Warner Brothers over the ownership of Sam Spade, Hammett had to overcome his hatred of travel and go to Los Angeles, where he visited his daughter Jo, who now had a husband and a baby girl. Hammett was enraptured by his granddaughter and wrangled Jo's permission to bring the baby East for a visit at Hardscrabble Farm. Hellman joined Hammett in falling apart over the child. According to Hammett's biographer, Diane Johnson, anyone who did not agree with Hellman's dictum that the little girl "was the most beautiful child ever, was forthwith on her son-of-a-bitch list."

Nineteen forty-nine and 1950 may have been a high point of contentment at Hardscrabble Farm. Hammett was not drinking at all and Hellman far less than previously. There was plenty of money coming in for both of them and plenty of recently war-scarce items to spend it on. Even sober, however, Hammett was unable to break his writer's block. Hellman did not share that problem; after her adaptation of *Montserrat*, she turned to a new play of her own, *The Autumn Garden*. But even while working, her enthusiasm for her farm did not slacken. She experimented with exotic vegetables, raised chickens and planted a grove of pine trees, perhaps inspired by a pine forest in which Hellman found herself en route to the Russian front and about which she wrote, "I want to be where I am. I want to stay in this forest."

Hammett was not overly troubled by his inability to write, and he relished the farm as much as Hellman. He showed a boyish inventiveness in exploiting its recreational aspects: fishing the lake, shooting squirrels (which Hellman cooked) and setting the turtle traps that prompted a memorable *Pentimento* story. Their relationship, although no longer sexual, settled into what Hellman called "a passionate affection." Each seemed as delighted and fascinated by the other as they had ever been. The war had interrupted their early years together at the farm. This idyll, too, was not destined to last.

The more established Hellman had become as a major playwright, the more the charge of being a melodramatist seemed to rankle. Even before she responded to Brooks Atkinson in *The New York Times*, she had defended her approach to drama in the preface to an edition of her plays brought out by Random House in 1942. Her contention was the same: that great drama abounds in violence and contrived plots. The point is not whether or not violence is used, but whether it is used to dramatize a larger issue or merely to excite unthinking audiences. The blackmail, murder, extortion and such in her plays, she insisted, always furthered some broader statement they sought to make.

Perhaps feeling she had settled the matter, she had then gone on to write her most melodramatic play, *Another Part of the Forest*, and was treated to an even angrier chant of "melodrama." This time she could not point to box-office vigor in rebuttal; the play ran for a lackluster 191 performances. Undaunted, Hellman had again leaned heavily on the blood-and-guts strategy for holding the audience's attention in *Montserrat* and was even more roundly rapped. It appeared that on the issue of melodrama, the critics were not going to give in.

In the spring of 1950, Hellman drastically changed course as a dramatist when she started *The Autumn Garden*, a Chekhovian exercise concerning a group of middle-aged characters ruminating over the mistakes they have made in their lives. The inevitable Hellman device, blackmail, is used only briefly at the play's conclusion, but her other plot preoccupation, money, still does service as a human motivator, although not to the obsessive degree of *The Little Foxes* and *Another Part of the Forest*.

Four years later, Hellman would edit a volume of Chekhov's letters for Farrar, Straus and Giroux, which appears to have been a result of her admiration for the Russian playwright rather than the cause of it. (It was also due to her old friend Louis Kronenberger's giving her a job when she needed it.) She came originally to Chekhov in an exploration of major playwrights who were not accused of being melodramatists, and his influence on *The*

Autumn Garden is unmistakable. Unlike Hellman's other plays, there is no immediate situation to struggle out of, and the aims and desires of the characters, the driving energy of Hellman's and almost every other realistic playwright's plays, is secondary to their evaluations of their lives and their attempts to determine where they lost out on happiness. One aspect of Hellman, her judgmental approach to her characters, is still present and sets her apart from Chekhov—as does the absence of Chekhov's quirky humor and his lyricism. The play is not without humor, but lyricism was something Hellman had never strived for and in some ways was the antithesis of her hard-edged dialogue.

Again Hammett was on hand to help her with the play, and when he read the first draft, he told Hellman that it was worse than bad, it was "half-good." She was so angry and humiliated, she writes, that she took the play and "tore it up"—at least figuratively, since the University of Texas Library has a manuscript of *The Autumn Garden* which is marked in Hellman's hand, "first draft." Torn up or not, she considered abandoning the play but decided to try again, eventually getting it into a form that both she and Hammett liked—except for one speech toward the end when the character Griggs sums up the play's theme of missed opportunities. Hellman said she worked and reworked the speech but could not get it right. Then one morning she came downstairs at the Pleasantville farm to discover that during the night Hammett had written the speech for her and had succeeded in saying what she had wanted to say.

The speech, which examines the notion of everyone's life heading toward "a big moment," is perhaps less Chekhovian than it is a depiction of Hammett's own state of mind in 1950. Griggs says:

> So at any given moment you're only the sum of your life up to then. There are no big moments you can reach unless you have a pile of smaller moments to stand on. That big hour of decision, the turning point in your life, the someday you've counted on when you'd suddenly wipe away your past mistakes, do the work you'd never done, think the way you'd never thought, have what you'd never had—it just doesn't come suddenly. You've trained yourself for it while you've waited—or you've let

it all run past you and frittered yourself away. I've frittered myself away.

The speech is prophetic, for Hammett was shortly to face his own "big moment"—his defiance of the Federal courts, a decision that he came to see as the sum of his life.

The Autumn Garden, with a first-rate cast headed by Fredric March and Florence Eldridge, directed by Harold Clurman and produced by Kermit Bloomgarden, tried out in Philadelphia, then opened in New York at the Coronet Theater on March 7, 1951. The reviews registered a few complaints—unsympathetic characters, unsatisfying conclusion—but for the most part the critics were gracious about Hellman's finally having capitulated and given up writing melodramas. Brooks Atkinson of *The New York Times* had many good things to say about *The Autumn Garden* but complained that it was "boneless and torpid," which sounds suspiciously as if he missed the well-structured plots and melodramatic action of the old Hellman. John Chapman of the *New York Daily News* called it Hellman's best play. Others concurred. A number of critics went on record to call it her most probing and ambitious work, a judgment that spread over the years to a consensus.

The distinguished critic John Gassner said he found the play unsatisfying, elaborating that Hellman had failed "to absorb us completely in the world she had created." Gassner offered a summation of *The Autumn Garden's* point, which, although tongue-in-cheek, was nonetheless apt: ". . . our little weaknesses pile up like calcium in the body and end in a bursitis of character." With all Gassner's reservations, he still preferred *The Autumn Garden* to anything else on Broadway and voted for it to win the Drama Critics Circle Award of 1951 (it placed third). The play closed after 101 performances, just inching over the hundred needed to be dubbed a success.

Most critics noted the influence of Chekhov on the play. But it was Harold Clurman, the play's director, who remarked on an interesting distinction between the Hellman of *The Autumn Garden* and Chekhov. Writing in his *New Republic* column, he said that Chekhov loved his characters whereas Hellman did not.

"She will not embrace her people," he wrote. "She does not believe they deserve her (or our) love. Love is present only through the ache of its absence. Miss Hellman is a fine artist; she will be a finer one when she melts."

Because this stern but fatherly lecture appeared three weeks after the play's opening, it was a tribute to Clurman's greater interest in artistic excellence than promoting his own box office. The play's producer, Kermit Bloomgarden, was naturally appalled.

In 1951 a property came to the attention of Kermit Bloomgarden which he was very anxious to bring to the stage. It was the diary of a teenage Jewish girl written while she and her family were in hiding from the Gestapo in Amsterdam. Bloomgarden wanted Hellman to adapt it for the stage. After reading the moving volume, Hellman agreed it would make a first-rate stage work but did not feel it was her kind of material. She suggested her good friends Frances and Albert Hackett, who had written the screenplay for *The Thin Man*. They took on the project and wrote the theatrical landmark *The Diary of Anne Frank*.

That ended the matter from Hellman's point of view, but it became a major drama in the life of another writer, Meyer Levin, who spent years trying to right the wrongs he felt had been done to him by many people, most of all by Lillian Hellman. Levin had been one of the first to discover the diaries, was avid to dramatize them and had worked out a loose agreement with Otto Frank, Anne Frank's father, that he could have the rights if his adaptation won the approval of "a major Broadway producer."

Levin received an expression of interest from Cheryl Crawford, who had just had a resounding success with the musical *Brigadoon*. Crawford was uncertain about Levin's script, however, and said she wanted to get an opinion from her friend Lillian Hellman. According to Levin, that was when everything started to go wrong. Crawford turned him down and eventually the property fell into the hands of Bloomgarden. Otto Frank was persuaded that Levin's version was hopeless and agreed to let the Hacketts have a shot at it.

Levin spent years trying to get to the bottom of the miscarriage of his plans and wrote a book about his battles in and out of court, aptly titled *Obsession* (not to be confused with his best-seller *Compulsion*), hoping to expose rumors he had heard—confirming his hunches—that the only objection Hellman had to his version was that it was "too Jewish." He said that after many years someone close to the original situation indeed confirmed that was the reason Hellman, Crawford and Bloomgarden had eased him out.

It was a very sad and sorry episode. Hellman, like Crawford and others who read the Levin script, felt that it was "too Jewish" only in the sense that, in prolonged Seder scenes, for example, it dwelled too heavily on aspects of the Franks' family life that would divert audiences from the specific horror they were undergoing. Levin's entire case depended, finally, on a point of artistic judgment: whether or not his version was of Broadway quality. According to Cheryl Crawford, it was not.

For all Hammett's readiness to lend his name or send a check to radical causes and front groups, his active involvement with these groups, which never amounted to much, dropped off to almost nothing in the late 1940s and early 1950s. While his political activities declined, the FBI's interest in them increased. In the spring of 1951 three bureau agents paid a visit to Hardscrabble Farm, and even though they admitted to not having a search warrant, Hammett invited them in to look around. At his request, Hellman drove them over the place and suggested they talk with her tenant farmer, Gus Benson. When Hellman later wrote of their invasion in *Scoundrel Time*, she gave the impression that she was baffled and amused by the FBI's curiosity. The chances are strong that she knew exactly why the agents were there.

One of the organizations to which Hammett had lent his name was the Civil Rights Congress, a group ostensibly dedicated to protecting the voting rights of all threatened with disenfranchisement, but their choice of causes proved the group was interested only in protecting the voting rights of communists. When in 1949, after a nine-month trial in Federal Court in New York City, the eleven top U.S. communists were convicted under the Smith Act, a bail fund for them was set up through the Congress with Hammett as one of the trustees. Their convictions were upheld by the U.S. Supreme Court in June 1951, and four of those convicted jumped bail and fled. When the FBI agents arrived at Hardscrabble Farm, they were in fact looking for the bail-jumping communists.

Four months after actor Colin Keith-Johnson delivered Hammett's "big moment" speech to *The Autumn Garden's* opening-night audience in New York, Hammett's moment arrived. Unable to find the fugitive communists, the Federal Court subpoenaed Hammett as one of the bail-fund trustees and demanded the names of the contributors to the fund. When the four missing men could not be found at the homes of the trustees, the FBI now wanted to track them to the homes of individual contributors. Another trustee, Frederick Vanderbilt Field, had already appeared in court; when he refused to cooperate, he was jailed for contempt, leaving Hammett no doubt about the consequences of silence. Hellman says that Hammett was not in possession of the information the court wanted, having never so much as visited the Congress's offices. She pleaded with him to tell them just that and avoid jail.

Feeling the court had no right to ask him anything, Hammett refused, and at his court appearance on July 9, 1951, he pleaded the Fifth to all the relevant questions. The judge insisted the Fifth did not apply since there was no question of Hammett's incriminating himself, and added that when one stands bail for another, one is pledging not just money, but to do all in one's power to deliver the bailee to court. Hammett was ruled in contempt and from the judge's anger, everyone knew the bail set for him would be high.

Hellman somehow got the idea the figure would be $100,000 and frantically spent the afternoon trying to raise it. She pawned all of her jewelry for $17,000 and got a check from Gerald Murphy for $10,000. Among the friends she approached were fellow playwrights, Ruth and Augustus Goetz, and Ruth Goetz remembers that Hellman said she owed Dash this effort because "He gave me two plays." Ruth Goetz believes that in the passion of the moment, Hellman revealed a far bigger collaborator's role for Hammett than was generally supposed. Yet it would not be beyond hyperbole for her to refer to *The Children's Hour* and *The Little Foxes* as gifts from Hammett. She often acknowledged that he had a large hand in both plays.

After a few hours of telephoning, Hellman was still far from the sum she imagined would be necessary. At the suggestion of Leo Huberman, an old friend and a Marxist, she flew up to his house on Martha's Vineyard, where a plan would be worked out. After hours of deliberations around the Hubermans' dining table—throughout most of which Hellman, by her own account, was in tears—Huberman announced he had obtained a mortgage on his house that would make up the balance. They returned to New York to learn that the judge had denied bail and Hammett would have to serve six months in jail.

Hammett was enjoying it all. He joked about encountering friends as he was being transported and made a show of shaking hands while handcuffed. He approached jail with the same gusto with which he had entered the army—probably for the same reason: it gave drama and purpose to a life that had grown singularly devoid of either.

Perhaps even more significant than his six-months jail sentence were the liens slapped on his income for $100,000 in back taxes. (By the time of his death ten years later, interest had raised the figure to $163,286.) Up to now Hammett, despite his unproductivity, had enjoyed a comfortable income from royalties and the use of his fictional characters. He would never have any money again and would live totally off Hellman.

Before Hammett was sentenced, his lawyer had handed Hellman a note from him telling her not to come to the courtroom, to leave her farm and her town house for a while. "Take one of the trips to Europe that you love so much. You do not have to prove to me that you love me, at this late date." When he left for jail, Hellman did set out for Europe. When she returned, she knew the Hardscrabble idyll had come to an end.

Fundamental to the legend of Hellman's heroism at the time of her HUAC ordeal was that, as a result of her public vilification, she had to sell her much-loved farm. The actual facts are, in a way, even more poignant. She sold the farm in 1951, the year prior to her appearance before the House Committee. She had to do it, among other reasons, because of Hammett's legal expenses. The sale price was $67,000.

Hellman had earned a great deal of money over the past two

decades and had lived well. But the recent years had not been lucrative. Blacklisted in Hollywood, she hadn't written a film script since *The Searching Wind* in 1946. Films, however, had never been an essential source of her income, most of which came from the theater, where there was no effective blacklist. More relevant than the blacklist to her predicament was the poor showing her recent plays had made at the box office. The spurt of Hellman works in the fall of 1949 had generated very little revenue. Her next effort, *The Autumn Garden,* in 1951, had had a short run, and in *Scoundrel Time* she tells of another blow. The IRS had come after her for unpaid taxes.

For one who was earning as little as Hellman in 1951 and who apparently had saved as little as she had, she was living beyond her means. Hammett's legal expenses could have been the clincher to a situation that had been building for some time. But it has become written in stone that, facing an encounter with HUAC the following year, Hellman had to sell her farm. Writers about the McCarthy period can be forgiven for perpetuating the error because of the irresistible symmetry of its chronology. But Hellman also perpetuated the myth in *Scoundrel Time* when she wrote: "I saw what was coming the day the subpoena [to herself] was first served. It was obvious, as I have said, the farm had to be sold. I knew I would now be banned from writing movies."

With her upside-down order of events, Hellman is not trying to make herself look better. What could be more praiseworthy than selling your home to rescue your lover? The IRS was, in fact, coming down on her. She was indeed blacklisted in films, but had known about it for three years (since 1948). The distortion does not inflate the hardship she suffered. But what she does seem to be doing is marshalling all of the bad things that happened to her in those years and depositing them at HUAC's feet—and not just any HUAC, *her* HUAC. It may have been her playwright's instinct to reorder events more logically, to consolidate them and to eliminate untidy details, but the fact is, the farm was sold in 1951, and she appeared before HUAC in 1952.

Yet, for all her rearranging of the facts, the underlying assertion is true: she and Hammett suffered badly from the anticommunist frenzy that gripped the country at the time. And it was this very frenzy that mandated and energized HUAC. But in telling her story, her personal enemy was not a national mood or a string of unsuccessful plays—it was HUAC.

When Hammett was released from jail early in 1952, Hellman met him at the airport with a car and driver and took him home to a dinner of oysters and quail. There were a number of welcome-home parties for him, one at the Jefferson School, which used the occasion for a fund-raiser. Hammett was determined to show he had not been cowed by his punishment, and he pursued his politics as publicly as possible, including teaching at the Marxist school. At the same time, he was aware of the danger in which his bravado placed Hellman.

In her memoirs Hellman says that one time, walking with Hammett down a Manhattan street, she was voicing her fears that his continued association with the Jefferson School would land him back in jail. Without rancor but with a good deal of drama, Hammett expressed gratitude for all she had done for him, but he knew he was now "a trouble and a nuisance" to her; he wouldn't blame her if she wanted to say goodbye. When they reached the next corner, he told her she must decide if she was going to continue on with him, that is, keep him in her life, or not. Stunned at the ultimatum and perhaps mulling over a Hammett-less future, Hellman stopped at the corner and Hammett continued on. Suddenly she sprinted after him, and, to steady them both after the close call, they went off to buy Hellman a drink.

Hammett would have further brushes with the witch-hunters, most notably in 1953 when he was called before the McCarthy Senate subcommittee which was probing communist-tinted literature in U.S. Information Service overseas libraries. During his testimony Hammett enjoyed a small but telling triumph over McCarthy, who asked him whether, if he were spending over a hundred million dollars for libraries with the aim of fighting communism, he would spend some of that money on the books of communist authors. Hammett replied that if he were fighting communism, he wouldn't give people any books at all.

For the time being, however, it was Hellman's turn at the pillory.

19

T HE FUROR that arose over Hellman's slim memoir of her encounter with the House Committee on Un-American Activities, *Scoundrel Time,* written two decades later, centered largely around her charge that her fellow liberals had been silent about McCarthyism and in their cowardly acquiescence had fostered the communism phobia that led directly to the Vietnam war and the "reign" of Richard Nixon. To a lesser degree—perhaps because fewer were in a position to refute her—the circumstances of her own HUAC appearance were also angrily challenged. These areas of dispute, however, make up only a small part of the book, which is mostly an account of Hellman's experiences during an extremely difficult time in her life. As such, it is a gripping and excoriating evocation of the sort of drama that visits few lives.

But as history, or so its critics would set out to prove, it strayed, both in matters of fact and opinion, significantly from the truth. The ordeal began on February 21, 1952, at her house on East Eighty-second Street in Manhattan, when Hellman received a subpoena to appear before the House Committee on Un-American Activities. She had had no doubt the summons was coming. Individuals with less involvement in radical causes than

Hellman had already been called and the pattern had been established that prominence such as hers was an added lure to the publicity-hungry committee. The witch-hunting mood was at its most virulent. The public was still stunned by the 1950 conviction of Alger Hiss, who, in most people's eyes, was in jail not for perjury but for having used his high State Department position to purloin American secrets for the Russians.

Hellman had never been cowardly about her politics, but in the anticommunist frenzy that was sending her political allies to jail, she was now terrified. She consulted several sympathetic lawyers and finally, on the recommendation of Abe Fortas, later a Supreme Court justice, but then in private practice, chose as her counsel Joseph Rauh, a young Washington lawyer who was already making a name for himself as a civil libertarian (he was a founder of Americans for Democratic Action). Although well to the left, Rauh had no use for communism or the Communist party. He agreed to represent Hellman before the committee, and, in working out a strategy for her appearance, Rauh wanted to refute the committee's allegation of Hellman's communism by pointing out the occasions when she had been publicly at odds with the Party—the *New Masses* attack on *Watch on the Rhine* was one, and her sympathetic interview with Tito another. But Hellman had forbidden this tactic, she later wrote, on the grounds that by agreeing to it she would be "attacking them [the Communist party] at a time when they were being persecuted and I would, therefore, be playing the enemy's game."

Hellman was determined not to say anything, however true, that might in the least way be damaging to the communists, even though she was in serious trouble for her politics. Her lawyer, an honorable man, was delighted to find tangible evidence of her independence from the Party. The *New Masses* attack on her play was well known to anyone at all interested in such matters, and indeed had become a *cause célèbre* because of the Albert Maltz flap. The worst it says about the Party was that it occasionally changed its mind on small matters such as a play. Yet trifling as the allegation was, it could have been enormously helpful in Hellman's current predicament. Her forbidding Rauh to use it could not in any way be explained by the matter of principle Hellman evokes.

Hellman presented Rauh with three conditions: She would not name names; she did not want to plead the Fifth Amendment; and she did not want to go to jail. She admitted that jail terrified her, and Hammett, who was dead set against her foolishly playing the martyr, fanned her fear with tales of rats and marauding lesbians.

Rauh wrote a letter for Hellman to send the committee offering a compromise. Hellman didn't like Rauh's wording and rewrote what is now her famous letter in which she respectfully offers to answer any and all questions about herself only if she will not be required to answer questions about others. If the committee would not agree to that, she would have to take the Fifth Amendment against self-incrimination.

May 19, 1952

Honorable John S. Wood
Chairman
House Committee on Un-American Activities
Room 226 Old House Office Building
Washington 25, D.C.

Dear Mr. Wood:

As you know, I am under subpoena to appear before your Committee on May 21, 1952.

I am most willing to answer all questions about myself. I have nothing to hide from your Committee and there is nothing in my life of which I am ashamed. I have been advised by counsel that under the Fifth Amendment I have a constitutional privilege to decline to answer any questions about my political opinions, activities and associations, on the grounds of self-incrimination. I do not wish to claim this privilege. I am ready and willing to testify before the representatives of our Government as to my own opinions and my own actions, regardless of any risks or consequences to myself.

But I am advised by counsel that if I answer the Committee's questions about myself, I must also answer questions about other people and that if I refuse to do so, I can be cited for contempt. My counsel tells me that if I answer questions about myself, I will have waived my rights under the Fifth Amendment and could be forced legally to answer questions about others. This is very difficult for a layman to understand. But there is one principle that I do understand: I am not willing, now or in the future, to bring bad trouble to people who, in my past association with them, were completely innocent of any talk or any action that was disloyal or subversive. I do not like subversion or disloyalty in any form and if I had ever seen any I would have considered it my duty to have reported it to the proper authorities. But to hurt innocent people whom I knew many years ago in order to save myself is, to me, inhuman and indecent and dishonorable. I cannot and will not cut my conscience to fit this year's fashions, even though I long ago came to the conclusion that I was not a political person and could have no comfortable place in any political group.

I was raised in an old-fashioned American tradition and there were certain homely things that were taught to me: to try to tell the truth, not to bear false witness, not to harm my neighbor, to be loyal to my country, and so on. In general, I respected these ideals of Christian honor and did as well with them as I knew how. It is my belief that you will agree with these simple rules of human decency and will not expect me to violate the good American tradition from which they spring. I would, therefore, like to come before you and speak of myself.

I am prepared to waive the privilege against self-incrimination and to tell you anything you wish to know about my views or actions if your Committee will agree to refrain from asking me to name other people. If the Committee is unwilling to give me this assurance, I will be forced to plead the privilege of the Fifth Amendment at the hearing.

A reply to this letter would be appreciated.

Sincerely yours,
LILLIAN HELLMAN

The committee's response was terse. It would not enter into negotiations with witnesses about what they would and would not testify to.

There is a subtlety to the Fifth Amendment that lay behind

this exchange and determined Hellman's eventual course—as it did for many other witnesses. Once you have answered a question that could in any way be considered incriminating, you have waived your right to plead the Fifth Amendment on *lesser* matters relating to this admission. That is, if you admitted to having been a communist, which was a crime at that time, you couldn't then plead the Fifth when asked the names of other communists you might have known. The Fifth Amendment protects against *self*-incrimination, not against incriminating others. The Supreme Court had not yet ruled on the constitutionality of the Smith Act and was vague about what was "incriminating." So witnesses before HUAC had to walk gingerly around any questions that could be so construed, even about actions they didn't mind admitting to, if they wanted to keep the Fifth Amendment in their arsenal.

It was as if the Fifth Amendment had been framed to thwart Hellman's offer. Of course, the opposite was also true: she wrote the letter in the hopes of stretching the Fifth to fit her conscience. When at the hearing she was asked the feared questions, she pleaded the Fifth, as many had done. Her moral victory came through her letter, which one of the committee members inexplicably moved to enter into the record. With a locked door opened by his opponents, Rauh sprang to his feet and handed out copies of the letter to the press, to the fury of the committee chairman. The letter made headlines, and most accounts over the next thirty years would remember little else about Hellman's appearance before the committee except her eloquent and subtly defiant letter.

In describing Joe Rauh, Hellman wrote, "Shrewdness seldom goes with an open nature, but in this case it does and the nice, unbeautiful, rugged crinkly face gives one confidence about the mind above it." Shortly before Hellman's death in 1984, Rauh, then in his seventies, talked about Hellman's *Scoundrel Time* account. An additional thirty years of battling for causes he believed in had left their mark on his face so that the word "unbeautiful" no longer applied.

"I love Lillian," he said, looking pained. "She has the courage of an ox, but her account in *Scoundrel Time* is not the way it happened."

Rauh's main point of contention is that there was never the

slightest danger of her going to jail and that Hellman knew it. He would not allow for the possibility that he, a lawyer, may have had that assurance, but that Hellman—frightened like most people by subpoenas, courtrooms, judges—did not. "I was her lawyer," he said. "I would have known if she had been afraid of going to jail."

Rauh denies a phone conversation Hellman reports in *Scoundrel Time* in which he is warned by another lawyer, Thurman Arnold, that their letter strategy would send Hellman "straight to jail." Rauh insists that any such advice from Arnold, by phone or any other means, never occurred. While allowing that Arnold was a brilliant lawyer, he said, "I wouldn't have solicited his opinion on such a matter and he wouldn't have volunteered it."

Rauh recalls his first meeting with Hellman. "She came into my office and said, 'I will not go to jail. I am not the kind of person who can go to jail. I do not want to plead the Fifth. It would make me look bad in the press. And I will not name names.' So those were the givens I had to work with: no jail, no Fifth and no names. It was like an algebra problem. But then I began to see it as primarily a public-relations problem. I knew that if the headline in *The New York Times* the next day read 'HELLMAN REFUSES TO NAME NAMES,' I had won; if it said 'HELLMAN PLEADS THE FIFTH,' I had lost.

"To me the truly courageous position was the one Arthur Miller took when I represented him in the same situation. He said to me, 'I don't give a shit if they send me to jail, I am not cooperating.' " (Miller was cited for contempt but was later exonerated on appeal.) Rauh thinks that Hellman felt guilty about not having given the committee what he calls, in reference to the film *The Front,* "the Woody Allen speech" telling them "to go fuck themselves." Indeed Hellman herself indicates this same regret in *Scoundrel Time* and indicates as well an uneasiness about the heroism that had been ascribed to her.

According to Rauh the committee was infuriated by the letter and, as a result, was more hostile to Hellman at the hearing than it might otherwise have been. Others feel that the members of the committee were wary of Hellman; they didn't know what she might do, and, given her prominence, they didn't know how the press would respond to what she might do. As for the strategy that she and Rauh devised, Hellman creates the impression in *Scoundrel Time* that her offer—to talk about herself but not about others—had never before been tried with HUAC. In her account, Hellman even gives the credit for this idea to Abe Fortas, who had "a hunch . . . that the time had come, the perfect time, for somebody to take a moral position before those disgraceful congressional committees and not depend on the legalities of the Fifth Amendment."

Of course the Hollywood Ten had already gone off to jail with no recourse to the Fifth but with the moral position that the First Amendment denied the committee the right to inquire into anyone's politics. But even the claim that Hellman was the first to offer partial cooperation—to talk about herself but not about others—is not true. A number of people had done just that, most particularly the prominent Hollywood writer and producer Sidney Buchman, who eight months earlier had offered to speak openly about himself but not about others. Buchman's offer was refused. He was cited for contempt and sentenced to one year in prison, making his case widely known at the time. Only a few days before Hellman's appearance a professor from the University of Buffalo had offered to tell the committee about himself but refused to talk about others. Hellman's attempt at the same thing was rejected and she joined the large group who pleaded the Fifth Amendment.

There is no doubt that, prior to her appearance, Hellman was all but immobilized by nerves. Before heading for Washington, she could not bring herself to tell sympathetic New York friends of the ordeal she faced, even when the subject arose. Waiting in a Washington hotel room, she declined Hammett's offer to come down for support. Certain that her money-making days were over, she took perverse solace in buying an expensive Balmain dress, a hat and white kid gloves—stylish armor in which to stand down the committee. If she was to go down, she would go down, not just as a lady, but as a well-dressed lady.*

---

* Hellman had a belief in the importance of clothes that bordered on the mystical. She once attributed her collapsing in the face of a verbal bullying from Clare Boothe Luce and Dorothy Thompson to having worn the wrong dress.

Hellman was before the committee for one hour and seven minutes. The crucial moments came when Representative Frank Tavenner asked Hellman if she had known Martin Berkeley, a former communist who had testified before the committee that Hellman, among many others he named, was also a communist. She pleaded the Fifth. Later in the hearing, committee member Francis Walter interrupted to argue that because Berkeley had willingly testified to having been a communist, what "bad trouble could Hellman bring on him by saying she had known him?" His logic appeared sound enough, but to admit having known Berkeley might be construed as an admission that she had been a Party member: then she could be compelled to talk about others not already known to the committee.

Another tense moment came when Tavenner read testimony from Berkeley saying that after having seen Hellman at a Party organizational meeting at his house in Hollywood in 1937, he asked his Party superiors what had become of her and the group she came with (Hammett, Dorothy Parker, Alan Campbell and Donald Ogden Stewart) and was told they had been assigned as "members at large." Tavenner asked Hellman if she had ever been a member at large of the Communist party. She declined to answer.

The interrogation proceeded:

TAVENNER: Are you now a member of the Communist party?

HELLMAN: No, sir.

TAVENNER: Were you ever a member of the Communist party?

HELLMAN: I refuse to answer, Mr. Tavenner, on the same grounds.

WOOD (Committee chairman): See if we can be of mutual assistance to each other. You testified that you are not now a member of the Communist party. On the grounds of self-incrimination, you have declined to testify whether you were ever a member.

HELLMAN: Yes, sir.

WOOD: What I would like to know is can you fix a date, a period of time in the immediate past, during which you were willing to testify that you have not been a member of the Communist party?

HELLMAN: I refuse to answer, Mr. Wood, on the same grounds.

WOOD: Were you a member yesterday?

HELLMAN: No, sir.

WOOD: Were you a member last year at this time?

HELLMAN: No, sir.

WOOD: Were you five years ago at this time?

HELLMAN: I must refuse to answer.

WOOD: Were you two years from this time?

HELLMAN: No, sir.

WOOD: Three years from this time?

HELLMAN: I must refuse to answer on the same grounds.

WOOD: You say you *must* refuse. *Do* you refuse to answer whether you were three years ago?

HELLMAN: I am so sorry, I forget. I certainly do not mean to forget. (Wood had already admonished Hellman about adding the notion of compulsion to her refusal with the word "must.")

WALTER: Were you a member of the Communist party in the middle of June 1937.

HELLMAN: I refuse to answer, Mr. Walter, on the same ground.

Hellman's responses to these questions are almost more puzzling than her refusals to respond. By responding to *any* of the questions about Party membership, she was acquiescing to the committee's right to ask them of her (others had heatedly denied that right). All of the arguments about the risk of waiving the Fifth Amendment protection were obviated if she had responded "No" to the questions about her Party membership in the past as she did to those about present membership and the past two years. You are equally protected if you deny the allegation.

A legend has grown up that Hellman hadn't intended to answer any of the questions about Party membership but was confused into doing so, then got kicks under the table from Rauh, which made her switch to the Fifth as planned. The record does not permit this explanation either. After pleading the Fifth to questions about three years ago or longer, she returned to a frank answer, "No, sir," to a question about membership two years ago.

So a kick did not remind her to plead the Fifth—at least not permanently.

Only one thing, it appears, determined the questions she would and would not answer: the years involved. Any question regarding her membership in the Party in the period between 1937 and 1949 brought a prompt invocation of the Fifth. Questions dealing with membership within the two preceding years received a frank denial. It is extremely difficult to avoid the conclusion that Hellman had indeed been a Party member during the years she would not talk about. Joe Rauh said simply, "She told me she had not been and I believed her."

Her reasons for not wanting to admit to Party membership at that time may very well have been precisely what she claimed: an unwillingness to name names and an unwillingness to go to jail. Under the law, admission of Party membership followed by a refusal to name names assured a contempt citation and probably a jail sentence. Yet in her memoirs, written twenty years later in a far different political climate, she also denies ever having been a Party member. She further claims ignorance of whether or not Hammett ever joined the Party, although he made no effort to conceal his Party membership from anyone, and indeed, had no reason to be secretive about it—certainly not with Hellman. Since the Party and its causes were among the few aspects of the real world that interested Hammett in twenty of the thirty years they were together, it raises the question, if this subject was taboo, of what they *did* talk about.

There is also the question of why, if she was not a Party member, Hellman was in such terror of interrogation by the committee. Perhaps she herself recognized the apparent contradiction in her description of her encounter with the committee in *Scoundrel Time*. It is in every way riveting, but in rereading these pages with a more detailed knowledge of her actual testimony, one suspects the hand of a dramatist at work. Just as Hellman reaches the point in her narrative when she is about to explain switching back and forth from the Fifth to straight answers, she interrupts her account to tell of a man yelling from the press gallery, "Thank God somebody finally had the guts to do it!" She never resumes her explanation of her odd responses to the committee; the gallery heckler is such an arresting disruption—in the text, as he would have been in the hearing room—that the dangling clarification goes un-noticed. In her testimony, Hellman had backed herself into a cor-ner, and the shouting man may have been a literary invention to serve not just the narrator's self-view, but to divert readers from an attempt at explanation that had no place to go.

The hearing room was well represented by the press on that day in particular; disruptions and anything else that dramatized the controversial nature of the hearings were duly reported. No mention appeared in any news stories of Hellman's yeller from the gallery. Joe Rauh says loyally, "I don't recall it happening but that doesn't mean it didn't." And the gallery voice raises another problem: With Hellman in the midst of pleading the Fifth Amend-ment, it is hard to figure out what it was someone "finally" had the guts to do.

In her letter, if not in her testimony, Hellman had articulated the moral repugnance of forcing denunciations of friends and col-leagues with greater eloquence and restrained dignity than had been done by anyone previously, and certainly by no one of Hell-man's stature. If the committee was afraid of her, as some claim, it was right to have been. At her hands, it suffered one of its most severe and long-remembered public-relations defeats.

Once again, if one sifts through the fancies and imaginings and wish-had-happens in Hellman's account of things, beneath it all one finds a story that is in essence the one she is telling, only less vivid and gripping. On one hand, she wishes she had gone further, been more defiant, less respectful, less craven. On the other hand, what she did was a lot more than others were doing, and she was doing it with a style and a panache that made it a more telling and remembered artifact of that grim period than the brash combativeness of others whose anger made them lose all caution.

Joe Rauh had his victory too. The next day's headline in *The New York Times* read: LILLIAN HELLMAN BALKS HOUSE UNIT.

Hellman's ordeal with HUAC was not the only drama in her life at that time brought on by the "red scare" mood. Her former lover, John Melby, was under investigation by an internal State Department review board. The initial cause of Melby's trouble was the same as that bringing ruin on a number of distinguished foreign service officers who served in China prior to its takeover by the communists: his belief that Mao's communists would be better for China than Chiang Kai-shek's Kuomintang, a position that was acceptable in 1948 but seen as near treason when viewed from the hysteria of the 1950s.

In Melby's case, his inquisitors focused on his friendship with the notorious fellow traveler Lillian Hellman. Melby was never told the reason for his dismissal from the State Department. From the questions he was asked, however, he feels that his refusal to end his association with Hellman was the cause for his downfall. State Department officials not directly involved, but close to the situation at the time, recall that his trouble arose from denying having seen Hellman at times when it was known that he had; that is to say, his crime, in their eyes, was not cavorting with Hellman, but lying about it. Melby agrees to a conflict between his testimony and what the State Department alleged were the facts. Hellman testified for him, but the questions put to her were aimed at establishing the extent of her friendship with Melby—dates and places of meetings—since, in his words, "they were already convinced she was an out-and-out communist."

Melby's ordeal caused Hellman considerable anguish. What might have been a brilliant foreign service career was destroyed, and a major reason was a liaison with her. Perhaps that was the reason she never wrote about this highly dramatic episode. In *Scoundrel Time*, which she used repeatedly to settle scores and relate her side of disputes, she refers to the shameful persecution of men like Melby, but offers no hint of the special place he held in her life, or the major role she played in his calamity. While the State Department was well aware of her bond with Melby, people close to Hellman at the time knew nothing about her involvement in his hearings. She felt the less people knew about their involvement, the better his chances would be of keeping his job. She did, however, make quiet efforts on his behalf with powerful friends like Averell Harriman, but to no avail. Although Melby left the United States to teach at a Canadian university, he remained devoted to Hellman and kept in touch over the years. When she died, she left him a modest bequest.

It would be several years before civil libertarians and liberals would pronounce Hellman a major heroine in the battle against McCarthyism. At the time she felt that whatever dignity and honor she had managed to preserve were tarnished by the HUAC disloyalty brush. Her belief that she was persona non grata with the public came out in her fear, expressed to Marc Blitzstein, that she would be an embarrassment to a concert version of *Regina* she was scheduled to narrate at the YMHA in Manhattan a few weeks after her appearance before the committee. Blitzstein would not hear of her offer to step aside; he felt it would make them all look cowardly. The night of the concert, a large crowd filled the Kaufman Auditorium at Ninety-second Street and Lexington Avenue. When Hellman walked onto the stage, in the same Balmain dress she had worn before the committee, the audience rose to its feet in a thunderous ovation. Blitzstein said that she looked behind her to see who was causing the commotion.

Hellman tells this appealing story in *Scoundrel Time*. But she also experienced other less agreeable reactions, which she told friends, but left out of her memoirs. One of these suggests that Hellman never understood or believed in the sincerity of those in political opposition to her. In Rome in 1954, she was checking into the Hassler and saw that Gary Cooper was at the desk next to her. Having been friendly with Cooper in Hollywood, she greeted him warmly. Apparently forgetting she had ridiculed him in her "Judas Goats" article, she was flummoxed to see Cooper look at her, then silently turn his back. She repaid him with a stiletto in *Scoundrel Time*, boggling (again) at his HUAC testimony that he had never found communist propaganda in the scripts he'd read because he read them at night.

20

THERE WAS something disturbingly prophetic in Hellman's having written, in 1934, *The Children's Hour*, a play about the destructive power of false accusations. It was a natural idea to revive the play in 1952, when the tally was growing of lives destroyed or badly damaged by allegations that in many cases were false or wildly exaggerated. The parallel was not exact. Mary Tilford knowingly lies out of spite; the Congressional investigators were making their accusations either from a desire for publicity— the only motivation their denigrators allowed them—or from a genuine fear of a massive communist infiltration into American institutions. *The Children's Hour* avoids the question of whether or not lesbian lovers should run girls' schools, and instead rests its outrage on the falsity of the accusation. The victims of the Congressional inquiries were often guilty of the allegations against them; the outrage stemmed from the belief that communist affiliations were either harmless, past history or nobody's business. A strong element, however, was common to both dramas: irresponsible accusations bring calamity to people who don't deserve it.

For the 1952 version of *The Children's Hour*, Kermit Bloomgarden and Hellman cast Kim Hunter as Karen and, for Martha,

Patricia Neal (who, during the run, would meet her husband of thirty years, the writer Roald Dahl, at a party at Hellman's house). Hunter had just completed two years of playing Stella Kowalski in the original production of *A Streetcar Named Desire*. Patricia Neal had gone immediately to Hollywood after her triumph in *Another Part of the Forest* eight years earlier and had made some ten films, among them *The Fountainhead*, in which she gave a memorable performance opposite Gary Cooper.

Undaunted by her earlier difficulties with grumbling actors, Hellman determined to direct the *Children's Hour* revival herself. During the out-of-town tryout of *Another Part of the Forest*, her first directorial stint, she had found herself in a shouting match with one of the company who capped his complaint with "You don't know how to talk to actors!" The line must have rankled. Early in the rehearsals for the revival of *The Children's Hour*, Hellman took each of the principals to lunch with the intention of becoming better acquainted and discussing the play. To each she gave a message: "If I say anything during rehearsals you don't understand, if I am not making myself clear, please come to me and let's talk about it."

Kim Hunter liked working with Hellman and considered her a good director. "You always knew where you stood with her," Hunter said. "She did not mince words." But early in rehearsals they seemed to be heading for trouble. Hunter had a nervous habit of fiddling with her hair. Hellman asked her not to do it. Hunter would forget and do it again.

Hellman finally exploded. "Kim, you've got to stop messing with your hair. It looks nervous. A New England schoolteacher would never do it. Now quit it!"

Hunter, now frightened into rigidity, went to Hellman later. She was still working on delivery of her lines, she said; if Hellman would close her eyes to the gestures, she would polish them once she felt confident about the lines. That sounded reasonable to Hellman. Relieved, Hunter concentrated on her lines at the next run-through.

Hellman was delighted. "That's it exactly, Kim," she said. "The gestures and movement are now perfect."

One of the reasons Hellman wanted to direct the revival herself was her longtime belief that Herman Shumlin had missed the point of the play by putting the emphasis on Mary and the evil she embodied. Hellman apparently came to this conclusion after a hard study of the text with an eye to reworking the last act that had bothered so many of the earlier critics. After much thought she concluded the fault was not in her writing, but in Shumlin's direction. She decided not to change the text at all.

At a party Hellman gave at her East Eighty-second Street home for the *Children's Hour* cast, she told the group of her belief during an informal discussion of her directorial aims. She read them a number of reviews of the original production which said, in effect, that Act One was terrific, Act Two all right, but that in Act Three the play fell apart. (Hellman's theory could have been reinforced by other 1934 reviewers who cited the absence of Mary from Act Three as a serious flaw.) She was seeking to reverse this critical opinion, Hellman told her company. "I want the critics to say Act One is OK, Act Two is better and Act Three is the whole play." The way to achieve that, Hellman was convinced, was to shift the focus from Mary to the plight of the two teachers. She wanted people to see it as a play "not about lesbianism, but about a lie."

Hellman's thesis was vindicated by the reviews, which were highly favorable, many voicing more unrestrained enthusiasm than the earlier reviews. Several critics cited recent history as the explanation for the play's greater power, but no one, this time, mentioned the third act as being weak or anticlimactic.

The play, which opened in December of 1952, had a good run and provided a substantial income for Hellman as author and director at a time when she needed it—within a few months after her HUAC appearance. While it was fortunate at the time, it does violence to Hellman's later tales of the financial ruin HUAC had visited upon her.

There is no doubt that Hellman had lost, for the time being, her Hollywood source of income, and when she did get screen work—from Alexander Korda in 1953—she was offered about a fifth of what she had previously earned. The legal expenses, both for herself and for Hammett, were large. But it would appear that the Internal Revenue Service had an even greater hand than HUAC in her financial plight. According to her memoirs, the IRS reappraised the taxes due from a movie sale and determined that she owed another $175,000. At a dinner party at the time, she said the total amount she owed the IRS was $190,000. Either was an enormous amount in 1952.

The IRS will neither confirm nor deny any statements concerning an individual's tax situation, even if made by the individual himself. Ruth Goetz recalls Hellman's having been advised by a tax accountant that an earlier movie sale had been exempt from taxes, in the same way that selling a house can be exempt under certain circumstances. If the amount owed was accurate, Hellman was probably not exaggerating when she said she had been wiped out by the tax people—even with the sale of the farm.

An improbable claim made by Hellman was that she was so impoverished after returning from her film-writing stint in Europe (for which Korda never paid her in full), she had to go to work as a saleslady at Macy's. In her *Scoundrel Time* version of her desperate action, she says only that she worked half-days in a large department store. (To several interviewers, however, the last to Marilyn Berger on PBS, Hellman specifically mentioned Macy's.) She also says that she went to work there under an assumed name and, unable to endure it for more than a few days, she quit.

While Hellman was not as recognizable as a film star, by the mid-1950s she had still been seen many times in newspaper and magazine photographs over the twenty years since her first play. In all likelihood she would have been recognized by one of her co-workers, a number of whom surely followed the Broadway theater. That such a prestigious figure was working behind a sales counter was a bit of in-house gossip that would have spread quickly throughout the store. Employees who were at Macy's in that year have no recollection of Hellman's presence. Casting even more doubt on Hellman's hard-times vignette is that two people close to her at the time, John Melby and Albert Hackett, said they had no knowledge of her working in a department store.

Although there is no hint that Hellman ever considered selling her town house, the fact is that she did face financial hardships all through the 1950s, at least compared to her former style and standard of living: movie blacklisting, Hammett to support, IRS problems. But even to a sympathetic listener, especially in later years when she was again wealthy, describing her predicament might require wordy and tiresome explanations—whereas to state simply that you, one of America's foremost playwrights, had to work as a Macy's saleslady is a pithy, wrenching image that succinctly conveys the same message of hardship.

If some lies are told because of a fear that the unadorned truth is boring, others may be told because the truth is long-winded. It appears Hellman was once again using the shorthand, and perhaps the license, of the dramatist.

Shortly after getting out of jail, Hammett decided he disliked New York intensely. He and Hellman found a suburban home for him, the guest cottage at the Katonah home of some friends, which they turned over to Hammett for a nominal rent. Although the hope was that he would finish work on his novel, *Tulip*, he did nothing more than quickly convert the place into an impenetrable litter of piled magazines, books and newspapers and settle into a recluse's life. By Hellman's account, she would visit him once a week, but others close to them said that she hardly ever went to see him. In this, she might be burying a painful recollection: Hammett's hosts said that he didn't want her to come and would make excuses to put her off.

Hellman claims in her memoirs that, as some sort of sacrifice to the god of dissidents, she had sworn off sex until Hammett was out of trouble. For a woman who usually had at least one affair in progress, the sacrifice was no small one, and she appears to have made it—and to have stuck to it for a period in the early fifties.

Her sexual drive wasn't altogether dormant. She told the director Joseph Anthony, with whom she would shortly be working on *The Lark*, a story about herself that is revealing as much for its candor as its content. Hellman had been having her hair done at the beauty parlor by a young man new to her. She found herself attracted to him, and after some time, overwhelmingly so. She got out of the shop without making a fool of herself, but once at home, she could not get him out of her mind. Beside herself, she telephoned the shop and asked for him. Her hair was not right, she said, and she had to go out shortly. Would he come over to her apartment and fix it? Anthony remembers that the man agreed to the house call, but insists he is not drawing a curtain across the conclusion—only that he cannot remember what Hellman said the outcome was.

For all of Hellman's financial problems, a simple HUAC-proof remedy was always at hand: to write another hit play. At various times she had made remarks to the effect that she didn't go out looking for play ideas; they came to her. That is, she would suddenly, without a conscious effort, be staring at a good idea. In 1953 and 1954, when she badly needed such an encounter, it did not occur. It was then that she made her first tentative step toward the publishing industry and signed a contract with Farrar, Straus and Giroux to edit and write an introduction to a volume of Chekhov's letters as part of a series her old friend Louis Kronenberger was overseeing.

Her excellent essay on Chekhov is a preview of the tough-minded yet gracefully written memoirs to come. Already attracted to and influenced by Chekhov as a dramatist, she also seems to have found in him justification for her own political state of mind. She quotes the famous Chekhov line she had alluded to elsewhere: "A reasoned life without a definite outlook is not a life, but a burden and a horror." Chekhov is not differentiating between the reasoned life and the unreasoned one. He is limiting his observation to those who lead reasoned lives, that is to say intellectuals, and divides them into those who have *a definite outlook* and those who don't. In other words, for Chekhov, it is not sufficient to be intellectual—you must consign your intellect to a definite outlook. And for Hellman, such a framework could be seen as allegiance to a system of thought, possibly a political ideology.

Later she addresses the seeming lack of political content in Chekhov's plays, seeking, perhaps, justification for political beliefs as a "definite outlook," including her own. "There can be no doubt, on the evidence, that Chekhov was a man of deep social ideals and an uncommon sense of social responsibility. This has been true of almost every good writer who ever lived and it does not matter that the ideal sometimes seems to be a denial of an ideal, or that it springs from hate, or has roots in snobbishness, or insanity, or alcohol, or just plain meanness." The essay is one of the few times Hellman discussed ideals and social responsibility—which she considers essentials for good writers—and it is intriguing that she goes on to list evils from which these virtues might spring, including hate, alcohol and meanness, which she saw as failings of her own.

Ideals were much on Hellman's mind in the first years of the fifties. In the spring of 1955 she flew to London to see Christopher Fry's adaptation of Jean Anouilh's play about Joan of Arc, *L'Alouette*, with the idea of doing her own adaptation. The theme of a woman being coerced by the state to testify to things she was unwilling to say had a rather direct connection with Hellman's own experience at that time. Oddly, that parallel was mentioned by none of the reviewers when the play opened, perhaps sparing Hellman, who was no saint, from charges of grandiosity, whereas almost all of them had remarked on the McCarthyism parallels in *The Children's Hour*.

Hellman had reservations about the play, as did its author and his agent about her as an adapter, but she needed the money, and, as she later wrote, she was determined to prove her dramatic prowess. She set to the task with enthusiasm, but as usual ran into trouble. At one point she wrote Anouilh and asked if he would like to collaborate with her. He wrote back that he felt unqualified, not knowing the tastes of the Broadway audiences, and he was confident to leave the matter in Hellman's "capable hands." It was a strange, perhaps tactful, reply from an eminent playwright; Hellman might have pointed out that Shakespeare, Ibsen and Shaw had not known the taste of the Broadway audiences either, but had done well with them.

Hellman's French was not good enough to write her own translation, so she got help from graduate students at Columbia, but then contacted her friend Harry Levin, a professor of comparative literature at the Harvard Graduate School, to find some students who could do a colloquial translation of enough of the speeches to give her a feel for each character. Two students were found and the deal was made: fifty pages for $100. But when the work was presented to Hellman, she refused to pay on the grounds that the students had double-spaced their translations, and "if they knew anything about the theater," they would have known that dialogue is single-spaced. Both sides stood firm, ugly words were exchanged and the possibility of legal action was raised. Unfortunately for Hellman, one of the students was John Simon, later to become a powerful theater critic in New York.

During one of the angry phone conversations between them, Simon said, "Miss Hellman, you're talking like a Calvinist."

"I'm Jewish," she snapped, and stuck to her refusal to pay the full amount.

Not long after, according to Professor Levin, Hellman was further affronted when speaking at Harvard. During a question-and-answer period, a student rose from the audience and asked Hellman if a possible reason for her plays' loss of their earlier quality was that she was undergoing menopause. A gasp went up from the audience and a whoop of delight from Hellman.

As her work progressed, Hellman's enthusiasm for the play, now called *The Lark*, began to fade. One of the men Hellman greatly admired and who was for her a political mentor was the eminent psychiatrist Henry Sigerist. Hellman had known Sigerist when he taught at Johns Hopkins. Feeling threatened by the McCarthy purges, he had moved to Switzerland in the early fifties. In the summer of 1955 Hellman wrote in a letter to him, "In October we'll go into rehearsal with an adaptation I've done of Anouilh's *L'Alouette.* I haven't too much hope for it, but I thought I needed the money—which is a good way not to make any."

She did make money, part of which went to the IRS and part for the purchase of a new property on Martha's Vineyard, where she had rented houses the summers of 1954 and 1955, and bought one in 1956 after *The Lark* opened on Broadway. The main house, dating back to the mid-eighteenth century, sat on a bluff overlooking the water. The property was three acres and had a private beach ("if you can discount the army of young who fornicate, I guess, during the nice summer evenings," Hellman wrote in a letter to Irene Worth). She went on to tell Worth that she "loved this island and this house the way you sometimes love when you get something you want that you never thought you'd have again." There was also an octagonal three-story guesthouse that had once been a small mill. Hammett claimed it for his quarters. If Hellman had guests he didn't care for—which was most of the time—he would hide out there for days.

The summer of 1955 was a difficult one for both Hammett and Hellman. In August Hammett suffered a heart attack, and although he returned to New York and would regain a certain degree of activity—teaching at the Jefferson School, for example—his health deteriorated rapidly. His hair was white and his face gaunt. Hellman told friends that she would like to live on the Vineyard year round but couldn't because of Hammett's weakened condition. The last four years of his life he was practically bedridden and dependent on Hellman for everything.

Dividing her time between the Vineyard and New York, Hellman finished her adaptation of *The Lark*. Kermit Bloomgarden, who had induced Hellman to undertake the project in the first place, was again her producer. He signed Julie Harris to play Joan and the young director Joseph Anthony to stage it. If Hellman had finally admitted her own failings as a director, she was not ready to relinquish her latest play into the hands of another combative ego with a looming reputation. Anthony had no Broadway credits and could not be considered a match for a formidable woman who was also one of America's top playwrights. He suspects that the wide disparity in their rank was a great part of his appeal to Hellman.

Anthony remembers being summoned by her to the Vineyard house to discuss his thoughts about directing *The Lark*. Shortly after he arrived, she took a phone call, and while he sat in the room with her, she got into an involved conversation with a woman friend, or possibly an employee, that grew more and more heated. "She was soon yelling into the phone," Anthony said. "Something about the woman letting her down when she needed her—and then there were tears. She was totally oblivious to my being there. It became so embarrassing that I got up and walked outside. But even from far down on her lawn, I could still hear Lillian yelling into the phone. It went on for an hour. I was getting so mad at being kept waiting that way, I almost left. When it finally ended we resumed our conversation about *The Lark* and she never mentioned the call. Not a word of apology."

Anthony had other complaints: "During rehearsals, Lillian was outrageous in the way she would overrule me in front of the actors. I finally went to her and said, 'Look, I want to direct this play in a way that will satisfy you, but if you feel I am doing something wrong, please tell me in private. You're undermining me completely with the actors.'"

Hellman was not pleased with his stand, but agreed. Anthony thought the matter was settled; Hellman was not so easily disciplined. For a serious discussion about a bit of interpretation, Anthony would often call the actor or actress to the footlights and, from the first row, quietly say what he wanted. After several such discussions, an actor took pity on him. "Don't you know what she's doing?" he said. "She's sitting right behind you as you talk to us. If she agrees with what you're saying, she nods her head; if she doesn't, she shakes it from side to side."

This time Anthony's complaint to Hellman was more forceful: if she didn't stop, he would quit. Hellman tried to get him fired. But Bloomgarden refused, and relations between playwright and director remained icy until the show was about to open out of town. At a last-minute rehearsal, an actor who had been a running nuisance stopped the action to say that he felt awkward just standing motionless at that moment and needed a bit of business. Could Anthony suggest something?

In total exasperation, Anthony snarled, "Jerk off!"

Hellman, who had been sitting next to Anthony, erupted with her now famous rusty-ratchet laugh. According to Anthony: "Lillian was roaring, totally out of control. The rehearsal stopped dead. She couldn't stop laughing. She choked out, 'Get me to the ladies' room. I've wet myself.' We got her up the aisle and to the john. Finally she'd pulled herself together and returned to her seat. The rehearsal began again. The minute the nuisance actor said his line, Lillian exploded *again!* She had to leave. After that little episode Lillian and I got along fine."

Whatever deprivations Hellman felt she was suffering in her private life, she was not disposed toward self-denial when she was working. During out-of-town tryouts of *The Lark*, she insisted that Bloomgarden provide her with a limousine and driver and always have fresh flowers in her hotel room. Some of her demands were not so trivial. On a late-night train ride after the play had opened to good reviews in New Haven, Bloomgarden told his director a frightening tale that suggested saying no to Hellman was not easy. She had insisted on the addition of an expensive curtain that was not provided for in the show's budget. To get the money, Bloomgarden borrowed from the proceeds of his hit *The Diary of Anne Frank*. "That was strictly illegal," he said. "If *The Lark* had folded, I could have gone to jail. And we ended up scrapping Lillian's damn curtain—never used it!"

The Lark did not fold. It opened at the Longacre Theater on November 17, 1955, and was praised by almost all the critics. Even the few grumblers admitted the play was good theater, and Julie Harris's portrayal of Joan was applauded by everyone. Its run of 229 performances put it comfortably in the hit category, and Hellman's finances once again comfortably in the black.

The Lark had called for incidental music, and Hellman prevailed on her good friend Leonard Bernstein to write it. For some time Hellman and Bernstein had been discussing another "French" idea of hers: a theatrical adaptation of Voltaire's satiric novel *Candide*. Hellman wanted Bernstein to write incidental music for that as well; but when he reread the book, he became wildly enthusiastic and talked Hellman into expanding it from a play into a musical. Full of misgivings, she went along with the idea.

James Agee was selected as lyricist, then replaced by Dorothy Parker, who was so unnerved by Bernstein's officious energy she bowed out. For a time, Hellman and Bernstein decided to write the lyrics themselves. With the help of his wife, Felicia, Bernstein wrote one song, "I'm So Easily Assimilated," and Hellman wrote the words to "Eldorado." (Although both songs remained in the show throughout its revivals, at one of the frequent desperation meetings prior to the premiere there was talk of eliminating "Eldorado." Hellman, clearly crushed, told the others, "I don't claim to be a poet or a lyricist. Do what you want.")

John La Touche was taken on as lyricist but was dropped due to, among other reasons, friction with Hellman. Finally, the team accepted Hellman's choice: the talented young poet Richard Wilbur. Since Wilbur was tall, handsome and intellectual—a type of man to whom Hellman had little resistance—he may have caused additional romantic softening of her customary obstinacy. (She dedicated her next play, *Toys in the Attic*, to him.) When Hellman approached Wilbur about writing the lyrics, he played down his qualifications. "But Lillian, I've scarcely even seen a musical."

"Neither have I," she said. "At least not all the way through." She was being congenial. She once told another friend she had seen the 1940 Rodgers and Hart musical *Pal Joey* seven times.

Among the many disagreements that sprang up among the collaborators was how free-form the songs should be. A drop-in visitor to Hellman's house on Martha's Vineyard in the summer of 1956 found the three collaborators at work: Bernstein was at the piano, Wilbur was poring over a notebook, and Hellman was stretched out on a sofa. While Wilbur wrote, Bernstein fell into a full vocal rendition of Gershwin's "Someone to Watch Over Me." When he finished, he turned on the bench and addressed the others. "Now *that's* what a popular song should be."

Without moving, Hellman snarled at the ceiling, "Out-of-date!"

The score for *Candide*, in affecting an operetta style, would be far more "out-of-date" than Gershwin, but it would also brim over with brilliant Bernstein music. Whatever else its problems as musical theater, *Candide* had one of the most melody-rich and inventive scores ever written for Broadway.

Except for the two songs with words by Hellman and Bernstein, the lyrics of the final score were mostly Wilbur with a slight La Touche residue* and a few phrases of Dorothy Parker. While the collaborators rejoiced in the brilliance of Wilbur's lyrics, he came to exasperate Bernstein with the meticulous care he would give to each word at times when speed was needed. "He shuts himself off in a phone booth and talks to God!" Bernstein exclaimed. For his part, Wilbur found it exasperating to be asked for additional verses one evening and discover the next morning that Bernstein had dashed off his own before Wilbur had written his. While amenable to incorporating the lyrics of others, Wilbur fought against anyone's tampering with his. Away from the company for a time, he wrote Hellman, "If you catch [Lennie] rewriting my lyrics, clip his piano wires."

Hellman is on record as calling *Candide* her most unpleasant experience in the theater. Never an enthusiastic collaborator, she found herself working with a clutch of creative talents, three of them major, in a form she had never tried—musical theater. The project was plagued with problems from the outset and required

---

* La Touche's words remain primarily in two songs: "You Were Dead, You Know" and "My Love," the latter, according to Wilbur, was half his and half La Touche's.

craftsmen who could make sudden turns, something at which Hellman admitted she had never been any good. At one point while the show was being put together, she remarked to a friend, "It's like working in the Five and Ten. They say 'Do this' and you do it. Then 'Do that' and you do it." Under the pressure of the out-of-town tryout, she docilely acquiesced to line cuts and changes she previously would never have accepted without a fight. Looking back on this period later, she found an explanation: "I think," she told a friend, "I gave in so easily because I was a little bit in love with Guthrie" (Tyrone Guthrie, the show's director).

In interviews at the time, and later in her memoirs, Hellman repeats her belief that she yielded too readily to requested changes. The implication is that had she not been such a cooperative team player and stuck to her artistic guns, *Candide* might have been a success. Thomas Hammond, who was the show's company manager and who had been with it from the beginning, contradicts that view, while maintaining his fondness for Hellman: "From the day Lillian completed the script until two years later when we opened in Boston, she did not make *one* change of any substance." Still, Hellman's papers at the University of Texas have twelve complete drafts of *Candide* by Hellman and others who worked on the production firmly deny this.

The producer of the show was a rich woman named Ethel Linder Reiner, who had had little Broadway experience. She invited a young man named Lester Osterman to join her as associate producer. Osterman had done well on Wall Street and in real estate but had even less theatrical experience than Reiner—in fact, none at all. Osterman recalls that his first meeting with Hellman, at a party at her house, was not pleasant.

"I told her how much I liked *The Children's Hour* when I was a kid. I liked it so well when I saw it at a matinee, I told her, I went back to see it a second time that night. She just looked at me skeptically and said 'Oh, did you? What was it about?' I said 'Miss Hellman, you don't know me and I think you are being rude, but if you really want to know . . .' I went on and gave her the plot right down to the final scene. She was silent a moment, then said in the same unfriendly voice, 'I suppose I should say I'm sorry.'" (Osterman overlooks the possibility that Hellman, who was then fifty-one, may have been irked by his having seen her first play as a "kid.")

Osterman was active in assembling *Candide,* but when the show went off to New Haven for its tryout, he remained behind on the assumption that Ethel Reiner could handle whatever problems arose. After a few days Osterman received a frantic call from Thomas Hammond. "You've got to get up here right away, Lester. The show's going down the drain."

Osterman protested that he wasn't the producer.

"Ethel won't leave her hotel room," Hammond wailed. "They won't listen to her anymore. None of them are speaking. It's you or nobody."

Osterman drove to New Haven and arrived toward the end of that evening's performance. Immediately after the curtain, he called an emergency meeting of the collaborators and principals in his hotel suite. When everyone was assembled, Hellman strolled in and said in her most surly I'm-a-pro-and-you're-not voice, "Now what the hell is this meeting all about?"

Osterman said, "I'll be glad to tell you what it's about, Miss Hellman. I arrived tonight in time to see the last fifteen minutes and I was almost knocked down by people trying to get out of the theater."

Hellman glowered at him for a moment and the group braced for trouble. Then she said, "I guess that's a pretty good reason for a meeting."

When *Candide* finally arrived in New York on December 1, 1956, audiences and critics were both perplexed and disappointed. It closed after seventy-two performances. Brooks Atkinson felt the original book did not lend itself to stage adaptation. Indeed, there is a repetitiveness to many of the scenes, in which only the location changes; philosophical and satiric points are advanced but the action repeats earlier patterns and ends up where it began.

Lester Osterman's wife, Marjorie, herself a writer, and eventually a good friend of Hellman's, had a more esoteric theory about the failure. She felt any creative coherence was shattered by irreconcilably different approaches to the world's ills. Voltaire's Gallic approach of satire and bitter derision, shared to a degree by Bernstein and Wilbur, was at complete odds with Hellman's "Teutonic" approach of "Something's wrong here and something must be done!" Probing as this analysis is, it is belied by the many later attempts to repair Hellman's book, none of which have been totally satisfactory.* Most people agree on the brilliance of Bernstein's music and Wilbur's lyrics. The finger therefore points to Hellman's script—since, unlike Brooks Atkinson, most people feel the fault can't possibly be Voltaire's. It is this last assumption that may have caused so many talented people so much trouble for so long—or rather the assumption that *somewhere* in a great prose work must lie a great stage piece.

The day of the closing performance of *Candide*, a mysterious phone call raised hopes of a reprieve for the show and involved Hellman and her colleagues in a brief drama of the sort that sets the playwright's life apart from those of other writers. A man with the voice of an underworld thug phoned Osterman to say that his boss "a Joisey businessman with a lotta dough" wanted to use some of it to keep *Candide* running. The caller would not give his boss's name, but said that the man would be at the theater that night with a good-looking blonde and he would make himself known to Osterman.

Throughout the first half of the evening, Hellman and the Ostermans tried to catch the eye of every man with a blonde. Finally, during the second act, Osterman whispered to Hellman that he had indeed been contacted and was off to Ethel Reiner's apartment to negotiate with the mysterious angel. The man wanted Hellman to come because of his admiration for her, but Reiner, still feuding, vetoed the suggestion. "Take the others to the Famous Kitchen," Osterman told Hellman, referring to a favorite company hangout, "and wait word from me there."

Hellman, Tyrone Guthrie and Marjorie Osterman went to the restaurant, set themselves up at a table with a bottle of scotch and started their vigil. Every half hour Marjorie would go to the pay phone and call her husband, who would report that the meet-

---

* Playwright Hugh Wheeler, who would completely rewrite Hellman's book for a revival, received a phone call late one night from a not altogether sober Hellman saying that although she was entitled to a percentage of the royalties from the current run, she would give her share to charity because she was unwilling to "keep a penny earned from that piece of trash you wrote."

ing was going well and that they should continue to sit tight. Eventually the owner had to close for the night but said they could remain if they didn't mind candlelight—he had to turn off the power. Before leaving, he contributed another bottle of scotch to the cause of keeping *Candide* open. More phone calls, more encouraging reports and more hits of scotch. At one point Hellman began growling about the goddamn theater, where you have to sit in a closed bar by candlelight waiting for a New Jersey hood to tell you if your play is going to run or not.

By the time word came from Osterman that the benefactor's requests were reasonable, that the deal was set and *Candide* would remain open, Hellman and her group were too drunk to care. The next day, the man put in one additional condition: that he be repaid before the other investors. Hellman and her collaborators felt that was entirely reasonable, since without the newcomer the other investors would lose everything. Ethel Reiner, however, refused, and *Candide* closed.

21

OF HELLMAN's various ploys to make money through means other than writing original plays, perhaps the least known was a serious effort during the late 1950s at producing. Her forays into stage directing had had different motivations: to protect her own work and to eliminate the bickering. But as she moved into other areas—the Chekhov book was a start—she would increasingly blame her digressions on her playwright's exasperation with the terrible power of critics she did not respect.

Another rationale suggests itself. *The Autumn Garden,* her next-to-last original play, had clearly taken a toll on Hellman. Although the critics had generally hailed her new dramaturgical style and the box office was respectable for such a glum play, she never again wrote in the Chekhovian vein. Abandoning that direction despite its fair success would seem to indicate that it was a dramatic mode in which she did not feel comfortable—or that she had exhausted the *Weltschmerz* vision that inspired the genre. Her next three plays were adaptations of others' work: *Montserrat, The Lark* and *Candide*—four, if the aborted *Naked and the Dead* project is included. This was a great deal of theater activity for one who claimed disenchantment with Broadway.

The adaptations and her move into theatrical producing, still leaving her at the mercy of critics, point to a different motive for not writing plays: fear that she had dried up as a playwright.

During the run of *Candide*, Hellman asked Lester Osterman if he intended to remain in the theater after the show closed. He said he hadn't much thought about it, but probably would. Hellman then asked if he would be interested in forming a producing operation she had in mind, a playwrights' cooperative in which the profits of any play produced would be distributed to each playwright in the group. A similar operation had been tried earlier with the Playwrights' Company but had been abandoned for a variety of reasons, none of which was the unsoundness of the idea.

Osterman said he would indeed be interested. When *Candide* closed, he and Hellman rented a two-room apartment in the Hotel Devon on West Fifty-sixth Street, hired a secretary and began contacting the country's leading playwrights. The suite had a small kitchen in which Hellman cooked elaborate lunches— bratwurst, gumbo, shrimp dishes. Aside from her original antagonism toward Osterman, he was an unlikely partner for Hellman. The son of the president of Bond Stores, he came from a privileged background and leaned toward political conservatism. After one of a number of heated arguments, Hellman declared politics off-limits for them. On the positive side, she was impressed with Osterman's business prowess, and impressed as well with his authoritative takeover of *Candide* in New Haven.

At first they had success recruiting playwrights. Arthur Miller thought he would go in. William Inge said yes. Tennessee Williams was leaning toward the notion until his agent, Audrey Wood, forbade it. But eventually the playwrights' cooperative scheme bogged down, so they broadened their concept. They would, Hellman announced, persuade top novelists to write plays and produce the results. A number of letters went out, but little came of that notion either. One of the writers Hellman solicited was Albert Camus, who almost immediately sent them a play. Osterman recalls with a shudder the letter Hellman wrote Camus telling him he would never write for the theater. "You wouldn't write your office boy a letter like that," he said.

One night, after a disagreement about a particular play, Osterman received a phone call from Hellman with a firm announcement. "I am the one who is experienced in the theater, Lester. From now on, I will decide what plays we do."

After acknowledging that he had far less theater experience, Osterman said, "But I can't let myself be reduced to an apprentice. I can't buy that. Let's call the whole deal off, Lillian. No one gets hurt. Let's make a clean break."

Hellman got angry, heated words were exchanged; then she hung up. An hour later she called back. "I've changed my mind. We'll keep things as they are."

"You can't change your mind," Osterman said. "You've shown that's the way you feel, Lillian. No matter what you say, I'll know you have those feelings underneath."

"You're just saying that to break it off."

"I am not! You brought up the whole subject!"

Osterman admits the partnership was like a crazy love affair and agrees that, with Hellman, more may have been involved than a pure business deal. "Lillian had so many facets. She could be one thing socially, one thing politically, one thing in business. She was a mosaic of a person."

Another time they were interested in producing a French play called *The Egg*, and Hellman was keen to cast Mort Sahl in the lead. When they went to see Sahl's act, Osterman thought he was completely wrong for the part. Hellman insisted they go backstage and talk with him. Osterman refused; he said it would be embarrassing. "Lillian got furious," he recalled. "She accused me of vetoing Sahl because of his politics. I said that was absurd. I could care less about his politics. Lillian and I were always getting into things like that. She would find motives and make a drama out of every disagreement."

Osterman had other recollections: "I think Lillian may have had an affair with Jed Harris." (She had, according to Ruth Goetz.) "When I made some reference to him once, she got very tense and told me never to mention his name to her. Another odd thing that came up: Lillian could not get insurance—life insurance, personal property, anything. It had something to do with her troubles with the Government. She was considered a bad risk. She was a great worrier, too. Especially about her work. Later, when she was up on the Vineyard writing *Toys in the Attic*, she would call me all the time. If she had a problem with the writing, everything was wrong with the world; when her writing was going well, she was sweetness and light. . . .

"Our breakup came during *Toys in the Attic*. Lillian asked me to produce it. After a time, she decided I was too inexperienced and she wanted to bring in Kermit Bloomgarden to co-produce. I said O.K. Meanwhile I found another property I was eager to produce. It was a black play called *The Cool World*. I knew I couldn't make a dime on it, but I thought it was important. I got Robert Rossen to direct. He's a terrific director [the film *All the King's Men*] and he was perfect for this play.

"When Lillian found out about it, she was beside herself. She screamed that I had signed Rossen only to get at her. How did I know that she considered him an archenemy because he was a friendly witness to HUAC? I knew nothing about it. What did that have to do with his directing the play? It was nuts to think I had hired him to direct a play I was producing only to get at her.

"Somehow we got through that, but things were never the same between us. One day we got into a shouting match over some little thing in front of the *Toys* company. I had had it. I told Kermit he could have the play, I'd keep ten percent. That was it for me."

Although her temper was quick to flare, Hellman always regretted her fights with Osterman and would consult her psychiatrist immediately after they had one. When the break finally came, she began having lunches on the sly with Marjorie Osterman, whom she would ask where the friendship had gone off, and whether there was a chance for reconciliation. In her later writings about herself, Hellman would express something approaching pride in her anger, acknowledging that it had been a lifelong problem for her, but at the same time implying that it was usually justified by some manifestation of the world's imperfections. These tantrum postmortems during the Osterman partnership indicate that, in some instances at least, she saw her temper as a liability.

Marjorie Osterman became good friends with Hellman and has more pleasant recollections than her husband:

"Lillian was a wonderful hostess. Her concern for her guests went beyond the food, which was always marvelous. She paid a lot of attention to the mix of people, who sat next to whom, and if an arrangement didn't seem to be taking off, she would change it right in the middle of the party. One thing I had some trouble with. She felt our job as women was to please the men. She once told me that. When we were going to her house for dinner, she would ask what Lester liked to eat, never what I liked.

"She was also very formal and would introduce people as 'Mister' or 'Miss' So and So. She made me think about social class for the first time in my life. She told me that she and I were both from the upper middle class.

"She had terrific energy. She'd get up early and write all morning, then spend the afternoon doing housework alongside her housekeeper, Helen. She always had to be doing something. If you were just sitting having a conversation, she'd take a handkerchief and start dusting the table next to her chair. She read constantly. When she visited us in Connecticut, she would take long walks in the woods, then come back with unrecognizable things she'd picked and which she insisted were vegetables. She would cook them and make us eat them.

"Lillian helped me a lot with my writing and she was very kind in her criticisms. I remember once she told me that I had to master the use of the word 'like.' Then she said Dorothy Parker used to tell her that if she was reading a book with the idea of reviewing it, and she came across a misuse of 'like,' she tossed the book in the wastebasket. 'I know it's silly and old-fashioned,' Lillian said, 'but why run the risk of antagonizing anyone with something like that?' "

Marjorie Osterman emphasized Hellman's truthfulness and her insistence on it from her friends. One year the Ostermans received a large package from Hellman with strict instructions not to open it until Christmas. Some later remark led Hellman to believe they had seen the gift (a small Oriental rug). She extracted a confession of peeking, then had trouble shaking off her dismay that Marjorie would go back on her promise.

Hellman loved to argue, Marjorie Osterman recalls; the issue could be profound, or the best way to marinate fish. She often gave the impression the arguing was merely for sport. Playwright Howard Teichmann has a similar recollection. He was at a dinner party with Hellman when an aspect of the Arab-Israeli conflict arose. Although most of those present were Jewish, Hellman took the Arab side on the issue and single-handedly held at bay an increasingly irate table. Teichmann is sure she was amusing herself.

In the late 1950s Hellman made several trips to Europe, mostly for pleasure, but once to see the opening of *Candide* in London, where it fared better than it had in New York. With Hammett in deteriorating health and in her new role as a businesswoman, Hellman's political activities were diminished, if not dormant. It may have been the period during which she was re-evaluating her rigid Stalinism, although she never mentions in her writings when—or why—that change occurred.

Hellman's FBI file has a curious report of a visit paid to her Manhattan town house by two agents on April 8, 1957. The report does not make clear what they were interrogating Hellman about, but stated that she "appeared to be quite friendly to the interrogating agents and was very courteous." It then says that Hellman proceeded "to give the following information:" The next two paragraphs are blacked out.

As intriguing as the question of what she might have told them is the tableau of Lillian Hellman genially passing along even innocuous information to the FBI. The explanation may be nothing more than that she found one of the agents physically attractive, or that with the McCarthy fires out she no longer automatically regarded her government as a treacherous enemy. Any hint of middle-aged mellowing would be false, however. A few years later, Hellman would be as combative with Washington as she had ever been. The interview remains a mystery, and, whether or not it was of any significance, it must be lumped with the many contradictions and anomalies that made good sense to Hellman (to her the highest goal), but still baffle attempts at a full understanding.

In *Pentimento* Hellman says that her experience with *Candide* had nearly brought on what she feared was a terminal writer's block, but that she had been jarred from it by Tyrone Guthrie and the distinguished critic Edmund Wilson, former husband of Mary McCarthy, and now, along with his present wife, Elena, a close friend of Hellman's. Both men told her to stop the foolishness and get back to work. Hammett, not to be outdone in making Hellman productive, gave her the idea that became *Toys in the Attic*.

Hammett envisioned a play about a man whose loved ones want him to become rich and successful. He does it to please them, only to find they don't like him that way; so he bungles his success and ends up a worse failure than before. Whether or not Hammett had in mind Hellman's father, whom he knew well, is not mentioned, but Hellman took Hammett's theme and wove it into a story that follows in a number of particulars the histories of her father, her mother and her maiden aunts.

The setting is the New Orleans boardinghouse of two maiden ladies who dote on their only brother, Julian, help him out of scrapes and root for the success they feel is his due. Julian has married a misty young woman whose rich mother set him up in a shoe business that went bust. Up to this point, the facts are consistent with the lives of Hellman's parents. In the play, however, Hellman has Julian return home inexplicably rich. His dream-come-true arrival back at his sisters' boardinghouse launches a complicated plot that develops a number of themes: people don't want to get what they hope for; the people who love you can cause more trouble than enemies; people grow dependent on others' dependence on them. There are also enough subplots for a massive novel of Southern decadence.

While Hellman was enthusiastic about Hammett's hapless hero, she saw his story in terms of the women around him and turned her attention to the effect their motivations had on his fate. She began work on the play in February 1957, just as *Candide* was closing, and completed the first draft in June 1958. It was not until the following December that Hellman decided it was ready for production.

The play was entrusted to Kermit Bloomgarden, who assembled as good a cast as the American stage could produce. Maureen Stapleton played one sister, the other was Anne Revere (who had been in the original *The Children's Hour*, thus putting her in Hellman's first and last original plays); Jason Robards was Julian, and Irene Worth his mother-in-law. Howard Bay designed the set and Arthur Penn directed. It was a congenial company. Hellman rarely liked actresses, but had two good friends in this cast, Worth and Stapleton, in addition to Anne Revere, a longtime colleague and political ally. Jason Robards would later remark that he thought Hellman "one of the sexiest dames" he'd ever met—an opinion not likely to cause friction between him and Hellman. Robards was drinking heavily in those days but could be counted on to pull himself together when necessary and give a brilliant performance.

With all the good feeling prior to the Broadway opening, Howard Bay recalls a minor disturbance that came from outside. When the play was trying out in Boston, Hellman, Penn and Bay were having lunch at the Ritz. Both Hellman and Bay thought one of the actors was getting out of hand and that Penn should come down harder on her. In defending his forbearance, Penn grew lyrical about the sensitivity of actors. "Actors are like delicate vessels," he said. "You must handle them ever so gently or you will smash the vessel."

Just as Hellman was about to make a rude noise, Laurence Olivier, also in Boston with a play, came up to their table. Without saying hello, Olivier growled at Penn, "Would you mind telling your leading lady not to call me up drunk at four o'clock in the morning!" As Olivier huffed off, Hellman and Bay almost fell out of their chairs at this report on one of Penn's delicate vessels.

Once after a rehearsal, when the company was still assembled onstage, Hellman took the floor and started a discourse on what she was trying to achieve with the play. She got tangled in her thoughts, stumbled and lost volume to the point of inaudibility. Hellman had never had any taste for discussing her work or been particularly adept at analyzing it—weaknesses that may have gone far toward her failure as a director. On this occasion, the cast was made uneasy and exchanged glances in puzzlement. Afterward, Hellman and Bay went for a drink at a bar next to the theater. A while later, Maureen Stapleton's voice boomed out of the darkness at the back of the bar: "Hey, Lillian. You should never address the troops!"

The tone of the New York critics when the play opened on February 25, 1960, was generally approving, but some critics showed their dissatisfaction in offhand concluding remarks such as "not one of Hellman's best plays"—which, of course, begged the question of whether the play was good or bad. When *Toys in the Attic* opened in London late the same year, the English critics showed no such reticence and thoroughly trounced it. The success of the play in New York owed a great deal to the powerhouse cast and the dearth of dramas in which such virtuosity might be displayed. Hellman was also held in respect by New York critics, who offered such kudos as "brilliant" and "hellishly hypnotic" while couching their dissent in polite cavils and never cutting loose with such angry London howls as "an anthology of bathos" and "no more dramatic push than a tea trolley."

In writing *Toys in the Attic*, Hellman had taken yet another dramatic tack, abandoning the loose, reflective style of *The Autumn Garden* and moving into the murky areas of Southern gothicism; this gave her former melodramatic devices a more than passing resemblance to the plays of Tennessee Williams, which for the past ten years had enthralled Broadway. The public had developed an appetite for his lyrical probings into Southern depravity, repressed sexuality and the terrible vulnerability of the sensitive. Other important playwrights such as William Inge and Jane Bowles had also delved into these themes so that the Williams vernacular dominated serious American drama. Hellman, a Southerner with as good a claim to familiarity with decadence as anyone, may well have felt Williams had invaded a turf as much hers as his.

Coming along at that late date with a play that on the surface seemed to treat similar matters, it appeared that Hellman had rummaged through her own personal "attic" to find material for a Tennessee Williams play. Indeed, a climactic moment in *Toys in the Attic*, when one spinster sister accuses the other of having always wanted to go to bed with their brother, is the kind of revelation of sexual dishonesty that Williams employed so effectively. But while the exchange provides a dramatic climax to the play, it is not central to any of its major points; it is little more than a Williamsish flourish. Other similarities are equally superficial. Hellman was not cutting her play to fit this year's fashion, she was merely ornamenting it for that purpose.

The basic drama owes more to Eugene O'Neill than to Williams, but more still to the Lillian Hellman of *The Little Foxes* and *Another Part of the Forest*. It is full of the dark and heavy plot devices—shady deals, betrayal, violence—that Hellman juggled so deftly. The main difference is that, in the new play, money is the bartering medium for the love that all the characters want; in the earlier plays, money is an end in itself.

Hellman and Williams were as different as two playwrights could be, and to the small extent that Hellman did emulate him, she faltered. Williams would plumb the depths of his quirky characters and find truths that applied to everyone; Hellman plumbed the depths of her quirky characters and found quirks. Her great strength as a playwright was in her slamming encounters with surface reality—greed, blackmail, slander, power plays. If there were secrets to be unearthed, as in *Another Part of the Forest*, they were secrets because a character chose to keep silent, not because they were psychologically blocked from admitting them.

Her two attempts to go beneath the surface and excavate repressed truths—*The Autumn Garden* and *Toys in the Attic*—were not failures, but they were not Hellman. She was dressing up in other people's clothes. The clothes didn't look ridiculous on her— she was too intelligent and self-critical to allow that to happen— but neither did they fit well enough for her to look her best.

There was some evidence that this was Hellman's conclusion as well. *Toys in the Attic* was highly successful. The reviews were, for the most part, strongly approving; it ran for 556 performances, the second-longest run of any Hellman play, and it won the 1960 Drama Critics Circle Award. Yet Hellman, who still had twenty years of productive life, never wrote another original play—or another serious play. She had nothing to do with the film version of *Toys in the Attic*, which suffered from a poor transcription by James Poe and probably would have failed even if a more appropriate actor than Dean Martin had been cast as Julian. Hellman's only remaining work for the theater was a farce adapted from a novel and so far removed from anything else she had written—and so clumsy—that it appeared an act of desperation. She seemed to be a woman trying to get out of the theater but unable to find the exit.

One of the aspects of Hellman's life that most annoys her enemies is her representation of her thirty-one-year relationship with Dashiell Hammett. They imply it was greatly exaggerated or greatly prettified. In her memoirs she talks openly about other lovers, about living apart from Hammett and complete breaks with him. But if these deviations from the ideal raise questions about the definition of a "relationship"—what are the rules, the boundaries, the permitted absences, the obligations—such questions would seem to be put to rest in Hellman's case by her loving treatment of him in his difficult last years.

Hammett had lived in the Katonah cottage for five years, visiting back and forth with Hellman and spending the summers with her on Martha's Vineyard. But when it became apparent even to Hammett that he could no longer live alone ("I've been falling"), he announced that he was going to put himself into a Veterans Hospital. Appalled at that prospect, Hellman consulted Gregory Zilboorg on the best strategy for getting him to move in with her. Zilboorg's advice was to convince him she needed him.

Hellman's half of her Eighty-second Street house had two large, sunny front rooms—one was the living room, the one above it was her library-workroom, which she prized. She converted the latter into quarters for Hammett and moved her typewriter into a small bedroom at the rear of the house. He came to live with Hellman in the spring of 1958, and would remain in her care, financial and every other sort, for the final three years of his life. If Hellman would later be accused of doctoring the truth for her own enhancement, she was often silent on highly commendable acts of generosity. It was *her* idea to give up her workroom to Hammett, but she never spoke of it. In fact, she once grumbled to Ruth Goetz, "Hammett's taken over the whole goddamn house!"

For a while Hammett would still go out—he attended the rehearsals for *Toys in the Attic*—but eventually he stayed in bed most of the time. Hellman continued her normal life, which was energetically social. Simone Signoret recalled a dinner at the Eighty-second Street house when Hellman quieted her guests by saying, "Please keep it down. There's a dying man upstairs."

Hammett's final year was agonizing. He couldn't get out of

bed and knew he didn't have long. He refused to see old friends and wanted Hellman with him all the time. In 1957 an interviewer had asked him how he spent his time and he replied, "I am learning to be a hypochondriac." Now there was no question of hypochondria; his emphysema grew so bad that breathing became an exhausting effort and he could sit up in bed for only short periods of time.

He was finally taken to Lenox Hill Hospital, where he died on January 10, 1961, thirty years after Nunnally Johnson had observed that Hammett was a man who "had no expectation of being alive much beyond Thursday." It had taken a lot to kill him: he had a cancerous tumor of the lung (which the doctors had not told him about), as well as pneumonia and a diseased heart, liver, kidneys, pancreas and prostate gland.

When Hellman phoned John Melby to tell him of Hammett's death, she expressed relief, which Melby took as further evidence of the exaggeration of Hammett's importance in her life. But perhaps Melby was unaware of Hammett's horrendous condition in the final months and the agony it caused both him and Hellman, both of whom knew his death was imminent and unavoidable. With so many months to rehearse the loss, relief would seem the only reaction possible.

There was a funeral service at Frank Campbell's on Madison Avenue, attended by old friends among whom were Dorothy Parker, Quentin Reynolds, Leonard Bernstein, Arthur Kober, Patricia Neal, Bennett Cerf and Kermit Bloomgarden. Hellman spoke, calling Hammett "a man of simple honor and great bravery."

On January 13, 1961, Hellman, Kermit Bloomgarden and Howard Bay took Hammett's body by train to Washington, where he was buried in Arlington National Cemetery. Hammett's sister was present and a few cousins. An ex-soldier who had been stationed with Hammett in the Aleutians arrived, and no one could figure out how he heard about the burial. In the months to come, efforts were made by some angry veterans to evict Hammett from Arlington on the grounds that anyone who had advocated the overthrow of the U.S. Government should not rest beside soldiers who had lost their lives preserving it. But by now the energy for harassing Hammett had dissipated, and nothing came of those efforts.

Since Hammett died owing $220,000 ($180,000 of that to the Government), making a will would seem to have been an empty gesture. Yet he was quite specific in his bequests. He divided his estate into four parts and left two parts to his daughter Jo, one part to his daughter Mary and one part to Hellman. Eventually Hammett's estate would be worth a great deal of money and Hellman got it all.

22

HAMMETT WOULDN'T let Lillian be a celebrity," said Howard Bay, who had known them both well for over twenty years. "When he died, she bought herself a new mink coat and really did it."

The image of Hellman, heavy with mink, on the way to lunch dates with Claudette Colbert, Warren Beatty and Mike Nichols is tempting, but probably as far from the truth as a picture of Hellman, covered in black, observing a prolonged period of mourning. Her life did change quite a bit, however, after Hammett's death. By her own admission he had always served as a brake on what he saw as her shoddier impulses, shaming or kidding her out of them—but now that he was gone, she could indulge those forbidden weaknesses. In some ways, socially for instance, she was like a junk-food addict who has the bad luck to fall in love with a nutritionist. But in time there would be other, more significant changes that marked the post-Hammett period in Hellman's life.

His death also revived the question about the degree of his influence on her plays. She had certainly written bad plays with his help, but she never wrote a good one without it. Not only was

286

her next and final play a failure, it was a form—absurdist farce—
that Hammett, who had an enormous range of literary interests,
had shown no interest in whatsoever. Nor had Hellman.

A dynamic and enigmatic man had swept into Hellman's life
before Hammett's death, a rich Philadelphia businessman named
Arthur Cowan, who would now become even more a fixture in
it. During the relatively short time they were close (he died
in 1964) Cowan's impact was sufficient to earn him a portrait in
Pentimento, a preserve occupied by only four of the innumerable
individuals important to Hellman. (She wrote such word pictures
of seven people altogether: Bethe, Willy, Julia and Cowan in
Pentimento, Helen, her housekeeper, Hammett and Dorothy
Parker in *An Unfinished Woman*.)

Cowan was erratic, funny and winningly given to expensive
presents and surprise treats. He was also brash, unpredictable
and prone to public scenes. He could be brutally rude. In London, meeting an elderly American woman who had lived there
most of her adult life, he asked her why she had such a phony
English accent. Cowan would launch similarly gratuitous attacks
on Hellman's friends with such frequency it raises the suspicion
that, for her, he may have been a surrogate assassin. He could
also turn his hostile outbursts on Hellman herself, which caused
numerous breaks in their friendship but never ended it. In his
mysterious business dealings and contradictions about his background, Cowan also represented for Hellman the sort of truth-
eluding figures that are the preoccupation of her last book, the
novel *Maybe*.

Like other people who have made a great deal of money,
Cowan was surprised that a woman of Hellman's fame and talent
should not be rich, and, because he liked her, it annoyed him. He
took charge of her investments and spent lavishly on her—costly
gifts, dinners, trips—and she relished it all. Cowan was not all
money and brass. He could, according to Hellman, make extraor-
dinarily generous gestures to comparative strangers in difficulty.
He sought out intellectual companions and was a large contributor to *Poetry* magazine.

Even though Hellman was in her early fifties when she met
Cowan and he was about five years younger, they had a sporadic

affair during which he made little effort to conceal his involvements with other, younger women. He convinced Hellman of the special place she held in his life, insisting that of all his women she was the only one he respected. For her part, Hellman was amused by Cowan and loved the attentions heaped on her by the zany millionaire. In front of him, Hellman would say to friends, "Arthur wants me to marry him. Do you think I should? You know he has this scar down his stomach. . . ."

From the fond *Pentimento* portrait, there is no doubt that much about Cowan amused and fascinated Hellman. It is also clear from future friendships that Hellman was entering a period in her life when she was intrigued by the idea of being squired by men who carried fat portfolios around in chauffeur-driven limousines. She had, from time to time, been drawn to men with money, and that leaning may have been stimulated by her deliverance from the burden of Hammett's legal and medical expenses.

Cowan's arrival on the scene occurred at a time when Hammett had become a near recluse and had lost interest in whom Hellman was seeing—although he was aware enough of Cowan to consider him dangerously crazy. Hellman had always liked many people; Hammett had not. Some she liked well enough to see on her own, Dorothy Parker, for instance. But while Hammett was still active (and while his more rigid Marxist sensibilities were intact), there were no businessmen with limousines, no self-made tycoons, in Hellman's life. With Hammett out of the picture, there were a number of them.

Another change effected by Hellman as a result of Hammett's death was selling her Martha's Vineyard house, which was now too large. She did retain a portion of the beach front and on it built a smaller house, into which she moved in the summer of 1962 and in which she would eventually die. She asked Howard Bay to design it, and he turned out a flat-roofed, two-level house with much glass, opening onto house-long decks over the beach, the upper one with a view of the Vineyard Haven harbor. The house with its toned-down modernity smacked more of Malibu than Martha's Vineyard, where deviations from the weathered-shingled New England style were rare. She had changed houses, but not neighbors: the Herseys, the Styrons, the Brusteins were still close by.

Before Hammett's death, Hellman had accepted an invitation to deliver a series of lectures on writing at Harvard. Her plan had been to take him with her and put him in a nearby nursing home. When Hammett died before the scheduled lectures, Hellman went ahead with the commitment, moved into a Cambridge apartment with her housekeeper, Helen Jackson, and took an active part in the intellectual social life that abounded there. In that heady atmosphere, she happened to read a novel by Burt Blechman called *How Much?*, a satire on Jewish American life that triggered recognition in Hellman of her own family. She decided the book was a comic landmark and she would adapt it for the stage.

One of the pitfalls of becoming a theater legend who has written a number of hits and who is venerated in many places, including Harvard University, is that you are very hard to stop. Hellman had never been easy to dissuade from a course she had chosen, but there were usually one or two people in her life to whom she would listen. Many of them had been phased out— Shumlin, Sam Goldwyn—and the principal one had just died. If someone did caution her against such a radical divergence from her customary dramatic vernacular, he or she was ignored. Hellman would write *My Mother, My Father and Me*.

It is also ironic that while writing her last and perhaps her poorest play, she began receiving the deluge of honors that would festoon her final decades. Brandeis awarded her its Theater Arts Medal for outstanding lifetime achievement, Yeshiva University gave her an Achievement Award and Wheaton College named her to receive an honorary doctorate. In December 1962 she was elected to the American Academy of Arts and Letters to replace poet Robinson Jeffers. While she was still busy at the craft on which her fame was based, her greatest admirers appear to have been hustling her off into the over-the-hill emeritus limbo generally reserved for those whose creative contributions are well in the past. In fact, Hellman's career as a dramatist was all but over, but it perhaps says more about the accumulated impact of her overall accomplishment than any public perception that she was finished that, in the leanest years of her productive life, from *Toys in the Attic* in 1960 to *An Unfinished Woman* in 1969, she was awarded more honors and attention than she had received when she was writing major Broadway plays. Now approaching sixty, she was starting to take on the raspy-voiced, no-nonsense demeanor that would intensify with increasing age, and which would become the Hellman persona made widely known by the memoirs and recreated by Zoë Caldwell in *Lillian*.

Simone Signoret, who had met and liked Hellman on a trip to New York, decided to translate *The Little Foxes* into French and put it on in Paris, playing Regina herself. Hellman was pleased with the idea, but when she and Cowan arrived in Paris in December 1962 "for the last two weeks of rehearsals," she was aghast at what Signoret had done with her play. Hellman disliked everything—the casting, the set, the costumes, the theater, the translation—and said so at length a decade later in *Pentimento*, chiding Signoret, whom she admired as a film actress, for her serious-theater pretensions.

In her own memoirs, *Nostalgia Isn't What It Used to Be*, Signoret takes strong exception to Hellman's account of the episode and previews the battles others would fight over Hellman's versions of events. Admitting that Hellman had at the time openly criticized many aspects of the production, Signoret bitterly protests Hellman's assertion that she arrived two weeks before the opening. Despite constant pleas for Hellman to come to Paris, which met with regrets from Hellman and assurances of her confidence in Signoret, Hellman arrived *the day before* the opening, according to Signoret, when it was too late to make any changes.

Her dismay at this alteration of facts moves Signoret to a plaintive rumination: "Does one really forget? Or does one rearrange? Or does one contrive? It is a question I will soon be asking myself. It's a question I am asking Lillian Hellman today." Then dropping the "Miss Hellman" and other strains for civility that have marked her account up until then, Signoret blurts: "Lillian, you know perfectly well you only arrived the day before the opening."

As Signoret admits, it is Hellman's memory against hers, but

Signoret had a company of actors to back up her recollection—a fact she does not mention. She also cries foul at Hellman's disparagement of her translation, pointing out that Hellman spoke "no French at all" and had selected three experts to appraise and approve Signoret's translation.

Clearly, Hellman's strongest recollection of the production was a feeling of unstoppable disaster, and Signoret's artistic wrongheadedness becomes much more obstinate, and the outrage to Hellman much worse, if she really had been on the scene for two weeks rather than one day. Assuming Hellman was wrong on the dates and Signoret right, the question then becomes: Did Hellman deliberately falsify the record to vent her anger with Signoret, or did her anger cause her unintentionally to jumble the record?

When the script for *My Mother, My Father and Me* was complete, Kermit Bloomgarden assembled a powerful cast headed by Walter Matthau, Ruth Gordon and Lili Darvas. Arthur Penn was signed to direct but, after quarreling with Hellman, was replaced by Gower Champion, who had recently had an enormous success with his staging of *Bye Bye Birdie*. There was little liking between Champion and Hellman either. She once told Howard Bay she suspected Champion had never read her script.

When the play was about to try out in Boston, a reporter for one of the local newspapers wrote in a news-of-the-theater column that *My Mother, My Father and Me* was having directing problems, that the director had been fired and that Hellman was directing the play herself. Hellman phoned the paper in a rage. Without denying the story, she demanded a retraction. The writer said that if the story was true, he would not retract it. Hellman said she would see that he did. Over the following weekend the newspaperman went to New York and visited a number of gay bars. On Monday Hellman phoned and said if he didn't print the retraction she would tell his boss where he had been the past weekend. Because the writer was open about his homosexuality, Hellman's blackmail attempt fell flat.

So did the play, and Hellman often blamed its failure on a newspaper strike that was in progress when the play was scheduled to come to New York from Boston. But enough reviews did get into print from *The New Yorker* and the news magazines to suggest that she should have been grateful for the strike; she certainly should have been after the play closed, when the newspaper reviews were finally printed. Except for a few admirers, the critics were appalled by the play and saw in it evidence of many fundamental flaws in Hellman ranging from humorlessness to anti-Semitism for her derisive depiction of the family.

Hellman would not admit to error on this one (as she more or less had with her other disaster, *Days to Come*). When the show was closing, she said to Howard Bay, who had designed the sets, "Someday we'll do this right." Later she circulated a petition among her more influential friends in theater and literary circles, asserting that the play was good but had been done in by a bad production. Edmund Wilson signed it, but Robert Brustein refused, and his friendship with Hellman went into a period of deep chill. Her remarks about the play in *Pentimento* are equally unrepentant.

The fault, however, may not have been entirely her own. While much emphasis has been placed on Hellman's lack of qualifications to write this sort of comedy, little notice has been given to deficiencies in the original material. Whatever merits Blechman's book may have had when it was written, by 1961 the subject was familiar ground that had been better worked by such deft satirists of Jewish family life as Philip Roth. It was as if Hellman had been so immersed in Chekhov, Dostoyevski and Engels that she was only now discovering such shopworn targets for fun as the American mom, teenage *angst* and consumerism, as well as adopting the absurdist dramatic style that was well established in New York theater by Edward Albee's *American Dream,* among other successes.

With the failure of *My Mother, My Father and Me,* Hellman announced she was finished with the theater, saying she could no longer tolerate its cavalier treatment of serious work. A look back over the shifts in her playwriting career suggests another reason for such a major decision. While most of her early plays written in the "Hellman" style had been successes, she had been hounded by the critics into other styles: the Chekhovian *The Autumn Garden,* then the Williamsish *Toys in the Attic* and finally the

Albeeish *My Mother, My Father and Me.* That the second of these was a solid success would seem to indicate that Hellman's disillusionment went beyond the rejection of her last play. More than the critics or public, she felt she had lost her theatrical voice and was unable to find another that suited her.

Throughout her playwriting career, Hellman had always maintained relatively cordial relations with her fellow dramatists. Unless she had a specific reason for animosity like Clifford Odets's cooperation with HUAC, she was either silent about her colleagues or vocally admiring—as she was about Tennessee Williams. With several prominent playwrights she had regular social relations, particularly George S. Kaufman, Ruth Goetz and Paul Osborn.

She could be actively helpful to rival playwrights: she had turned *The Diary of Anne Frank* over to the Hacketts; she encouraged Jay Presson Allen to write *The Prime of Miss Jean Brodie.* At one of Hellman's dinner parties in 1963, Robert Lewis recalls, her maid broke a rule and interrupted her at the table to say that a very upset man was on the phone and insisted on speaking to her right away. Hellman took the call to find William Inge, whom she knew only slightly, on the line. Inge was going into rehearsal with his new play, *Natural Affection,* he told Hellman, and could not decide between two third acts he had written. Would Hellman, who was "such a great constructionist," read the two versions and resolve the impasse? Stunned, she said she would have to think it over and call him back.

After her guests had gone, Hellman began mulling over the request. If she did as Inge asked, she would have to give him her reasons for the decision, which would require hard thought and pull her away from her own work. On the other hand, a colleague was in serious trouble, probably desperate, or he wouldn't have sought the help of someone he hardly knew. But what if the play was a flop? Inge could blame her. Hellman lost sleep going back and forth on the problem.

By morning she had decided to help Inge. She dialed his number and found a groggy Inge trying to figure out why Lillian Hellman was waking him. When she reminded him of his SOS the night before, he told her she was nice to call but it was no longer necessary. After they had talked the previous night, a friend had dropped by and told him which act to use. *Natural Affection* was not a success.

To Arthur Miller, however, perhaps her closest competition as a realistic dramatist, Hellman was far from sympathetic. For the May 1964 issue of the short-lived *Show* Magazine, which was then widely read by theater professionals and enthusiasts, Hellman wrote a devastating parody of Miller's recent play *After the Fall*. The play had been something of a scandal in show-business circles because of the cruel portrait of Miller's ex-wife, Marilyn Monroe, and for the lengthy parade of excoriating self-revelations. It had not been well received by the critics but was enjoying an extended run thanks to a blue-chip production and the gossip value of the script. Hellman's article was entitled "Lillian Hellman Wants a Little Respect for Her Agony" and was subtitled: "A famous playwright hallucinates after a fall brought on by a current hit." In the third-person lead (written by Hellman) it is explained that because of the strongly autobiographical nature of Miss Hellman's play *Buy My Guilt*, which is currently being performed in converted tiger cages at the Bronx Zoo, she has received a number of letters from friends who are incensed at seeing themselves portrayed. The rest of the piece is made up of her responses to these friends.

To one who complains of her revealing their illicit affair and his drug addiction, she writes: "It was agony to put all this down, but that's what a great writer is here on earth to do. Truth, and only truth, and more truth." Another attempts suicide after being portrayed in her play as a communist. He writes that it was not true. Hellman replies: "I know that full well, but how was I going to disguise you in the play except by making you a party member?"

The piece, despite its unmistakable inspiration, is a deft and funny stab at all writers with grandiose pretensions, but particularly at those who feel their noble mission justifies sacrificing family, friends and ex-spouses in the pursuit of their "truth." In an interview sometime later, Hellman admitted to having been disgusted by what she saw as Miller's heartless exploitation of his troubled ex-wife. Whatever Hellman's reasons, it was an unprecedented attack by one playwright on the work of another. Miller could not have been other than outraged.

Twenty years later, declining to discuss Hellman at any length, Miller said, "Lillian always resented my emergence on the playwriting scene and she resented even more my not making a quick exit from it." Then, without any reference to her parody, his rancor heated up: "Lillian came on with every man she met. I wasn't interested and she never forgave me for it."

Hellman was apparently fascinated by Miller's marriage to Marilyn Monroe. Once in the fifties when she and Miller were still friendly and both under siege from HUAC, Hellman came away from a phone conversation with him convulsed with laughter. A friend who happened to be present asked what was so funny. "I was talking with Arthur Miller," Hellman said, "and he said to me, 'I've got to get off the phone now. Marilyn just put breakfast on the table.' The picture tickles the hell out of me!"

The reason for her attack on Miller may have been simple jealousy. If Hellman had felt threatened by any of the playwrights to emerge after the war, it would have been Miller. While Tennessee Williams was exploring a very different terrain of human emotions and doing it in a very different style, Miller, like Hellman, was an Ibsenite realist with a radical vision, and was exploring the causes of social ills in the family nexus. When critical enthusiasm for Hellman was at one of its two lowest points, with *Montserrat*, Miller burst onto Broadway with *Death of a Salesman*, a play many knowledgeable people did not hesitate to rank ahead of any of Hellman's. Hellman may also have envied Miller's more courageous stand before the House Un-American Affairs Committee.

Appalled by the way Hellman had mishandled her money, Arthur Cowan gave her financial advice and encouraged her into another business speculation that would prove to be both very profitable and very controversial. Since the U.S. Government had no hope of collecting the $163,286 still owed by Hammett's estate, Hellman and Cowan felt a deal could be made and they moved to buy the rights to his work from the estate, which was held by the IRS. They offered the Government $2,000 and were turned down. But the IRS agreed with them that the rights should be sold; it was decided to put them up for auction, with Hellman, as literary executor, officiating and with a minimum bid set at $5,000.

In order to buy the rights, Hellman still had to obtain written consent from Hammett's daughters. She wrote them several letters, persuading them of the wisdom of her offer. Her main argument was that if they were to retain the rights, they would be liable for their father's considerable debts. This was not true, as the Government had acquiesced to the sale of the rights in order to *close* the Hammett account. The only other lien against the estate of any size was Hellman's claim for $40,000 for "advances to decedent in his lifetime."

Hammett's daughters finally agreed and the auction took place in the offices of Hellman's lawyers. Cowan and Hellman bought the rights for the minimum bid, each putting up $2,500. When Cowan died a few years later, Hellman said that he left her his half, although in *Pentimento* she would write that no will was ever found. In her deposition to the probate court, Hellman said that she was considering writing a biography of "the deceased" and thought it would be better if the rights to his work were in her possession and free of liens. Privately she told John Hersey and other friends that her real reason for acquiring the rights was to protect them for the Hammett girls, who were hard up and might be tempted to sell them for nothing.

Whatever the case, Hammett's work almost immediately began making money—all of which Hellman kept. Paperbacks of his novels had just been rereleased at the time of his death. A year after Hellman obtained the rights, she edited a hardcover edition of Hammett's short stories under the title *The Big Knockover*. There were other paperback editions of the novels, all of which had steady sales. *Publisher's Weekly* later reported that *The Dain Curse*, Hammett's least popular novel, had sold an average of 12,000 copies a year for a six-year period during the 1970s. In 1978, Don Congdon, then Hellman's agent, sold the rights to *The Dain Curse* to CBS for a mini-series for a quarter of a million dollars.

At no time did Hellman ever turn over any of those considerable earnings to Hammett's daughters. When she died, she did leave them generous amounts, but nowhere near the percentages their father had wanted them to have. But for the twenty years she possessed the rights until her death in 1984, Hellman kept the proceeds for herself, years during which she was very comfortable and Hammett's daughters were not.

Curiously enough, the one daughter who would talk about it, Jo Marshall, feels no animosity toward Hellman and was delighted to be remembered in her will at all. "I figured that Lillian was my father's wife for all practical purposes," she said, "and that she was entitled to a widow's rights." When asked if Hellman had ever given her money over the years, Mrs. Marshall replied, "Maybe a fifty-dollar check at Christmas."

Hammett's biographer, Diane Johnson, was convinced that Hellman's actions were motivated by nothing more than greed. Others would argue, as Jo Hammett Marshall did, that Hellman was owed the money. Hellman herself put the cash outlay to Hammett at $40,000. And it is possible that once she had recovered that amount, she intended to make other arrangements, then neglected to do so. It is also possible that since her income from royalties came from a wide variety of sources, she was unaware of just how valuable the Hammett rights had become. But Hellman was far from naive about money, and she could hardly have failed to notice the $250,000 from the sale of *The Dain Curse*. Everything about her acquisition of the Hammett rights smacks of a shrewd, deliberate and not very principled business maneuver.

When the subject was discussed in a 1973 interview with Nora Ephron, Hellman simply said that buying the rights had been Cowan's idea. Later in the interview, however, she interjected the notion of protecting the work from misuse when she confessed she had gone against Hammett's expressed wishes when she republished his short stories. Others were not permitted such a liberty. When a black theater group put together a musical version of *The Maltese Falcon*, Hellman had it closed down without seeing it (she wouldn't come to New York and the troupe wouldn't come to Martha's Vineyard), even though her agent, Don Congdon, said it was good. Hellman was undoubtedly sincere in seeking to protect Hammett's work. The ethical difficulty is that the money it earned was, in the deepest sense, Hammett's, and he had made his wishes explicit in his will: one-quarter to

Hellman, three-quarters to his daughters. Had he wished, he might have set it up so that Hellman would get the money during her lifetime, and that at her death it would pass to his daughters. But he did not. In addition, his wishes were written at a time when no one, least of all Hammett, thought the amounts would be large.

Given the portraits of both of them Hellman paints in her memoirs, it is difficult to imagine that they discussed the matter at all, let alone argued about it. Hammett had made what he considered to be a simple and equitable distribution of his estate. From her later actions regarding the rights, however, Hellman clearly did not agree with him. In this, as in so many other matters, she had the last word.

23

I N 1967, HELLMAN, whose reputation as a serious playwright was at a low ebb, had a solid New York success that, oddly, brought her work as much negative reappraisal as it had yet received. Mike Nichols, at the time probably the most successful and highly regarded director in America, mounted a major revival of *The Little Foxes* at Lincoln Center with a star-heavy cast that included Anne Bancroft, George C. Scott and Margaret Leighton. To her admirers, the blue-chip mounting of an early play represented an important step in Hellman's climb to cultural permanence; to the denigrators who saw her as a middlebrow remnant of a defunct theatrical epoch, it was a call to arms.

Of Hellman's five most recent plays, only one had been a solid success. Three of them, including her latest, were failures. In 1965 she had returned to screenwriting and had written a film for producer Sam Spiegel called *The Chase*, an adaptation of a Horton Foote novel set in a small town that aspired to be a metaphor for the Kennedy assassination. It was the worst kind of failure with both reviewers and the public, despite a cast that included Marlon Brando, Robert Redford, Robert Duvall and Jane

Fonda. Many things contributed to the debacle, but the consensus seems to have been that the various creative forces were overruled by Spiegel, who had rigid ideas about what he wanted the film to be. As the screenwriter, Hellman, who had been absent from films for twenty years, was finally subjected to the kind of strong-arm bullying that from the beginning had marked the screen careers of such writers as F. Scott Fitzgerald and William Faulkner. Now, after an almost unequaled record of screenwriting successes, Hellman joined the army of prominent writers who had given their names and their talents to a costly bomb.

As a writer for both the theater and films, Hellman appeared to have reached a point in her life when she was expected to pack up her rave reviews and her typewriter and, if not die, as had a good number of her colleagues (Clifford Odets, Maxwell Anderson, Robert Sherwood), at least fade discreetly from sight along with Elmer Rice and Thornton Wilder and accept a status as an out-of-the running relic of another era.

Even the major dramatists who came along after Hellman like Tennessee Williams and Arthur Miller were beginning to stumble. Such burned-out achievers are permitted an occasional off-Broadway revival, a score-settling memoir and as many honorary degrees as they want. To honor them with full-scale Broadway revivals was something else. That smacked of pretensions to permanence, intimations of immortality. When Hellman was so honored, a sharp reaction was inevitable.

Throughout her playwriting career, Hellman, even when one of her plays was being panned, had been treated respectfully by the critics. They may not have liked the play at hand, but her preeminence as an American dramatist was rarely questioned. The backlash from the intelligentsia began with the film version of *Toys in the Attic* when Stanley Kauffmann wrote that occasionally a film adaptation comes along that is so bad it calls into question not only the original work but the reputation of the playwright who wrote it. With the revival of *The Little Foxes*, the newspaper reviewers who decide a play's fate at the box office were enthusiastic. But among the intellectual community, the lynch mob was growing, led by two formidable hit men: Elizabeth Hardwick, a respected writer who reviewed the play for the influential *New York Review of Books* (when married to Robert Lowell, Hardwick had been a casual friend of Hellman's) and Hellman's former translator, John Simon, who was now reviewing for *Commonweal*.

Hardwick came down hardest on the production, but had nothing good to say about the play itself, nor about Hellman's plays in general. She first told Hellman what her play was *really* about—"a besieged agrarianism, a lost Southern agricultural life, in which virtue and sweetness had a place, and, more strikingly, where social responsibility and justice could, on a personal level at least, be practiced." Hardwick then deplored the clichéd, mythical Old South that Hellman evokes through the character of Birdie. (Those who admire Tennessee Williams's plays should be glad that Hardwick didn't spot Birdie's falsity until after he created a good number of highly prized "Birdies," most particularly Blanche and Amanda.) Hardwick also deplored the missed dramatic possibilities of Regina's husband, Horace, in that Hellman does not allow him to feel the slightest temptation for the easy money that motivated the others.

Of the many grounds on which *The Little Foxes* can be faulted, however, its historical accuracy is not one of them. If there is a single aspect of her story Hellman knew practically firsthand, it was affluent, middle-class, antebellum Southerners. The Hubbards are the Marx family down to the last antimacassar. Hellman was born five years after the time of the play—which is to say that when Hellman was twenty, Regina would have been fifty-five. Hellman knew her characters.

As for Horace, to ask for more vacillation on the part of a supporting character indicates why Hellman was a dramatist and Hardwick was not. Horace's instant rejection of the Hubbards' money-making scheme is totally believable as a dying man's long overdue stand against values and ambitions he has silently deplored for years. In addition, Hellman makes it clear he thwarts his wife to repay her for monstrous wrongs done to him; hesitation about a possible profit would undermine his psychologically sound motivation. To criticize Hellman for not realizing the dramatic possibilities of a secondary character is like criticizing Shakespeare for not seeing the dramatic possibilities that Tom

Stoppard later saw in Rosenkrantz and Guildenstern. The two men were writing different plays, as, apparently, Hellman and Hardwick were.

John Simon swung the old cudgel of "melodramatist," but with greater force than any of Hellman's earlier critics, and with a Harvard-graduate-school certitude about his categories. Simon saw the distinction between a melodrama and a drama as clearcut and obvious as that between an opera and a variety show. (And even that analogy suggests the precariousness of such rigid labels.) That Hellman should be considered one of America's foremost playwrights, Simon believed, spoke only of the dearth of American playwrights.

The Lincoln Center production of *The Little Foxes* enjoyed such success that it was moved to a Broadway theater early in 1968 for a good run. But Hellman blood was in the water, and a critical feeding frenzy was in the making. Its culmination came in 1972 when Little Brown brought out an edition of her complete plays at roughly the same time that a professor at Indiana University, Richard Moody, published a book on Hellman, including some biographical information but far more lengthy and laudatory discussion of her plays. Neither publishing event would ordinarily have caused much of a stir, but both got big critical play by those committed to stopping the bandwagon that seemed to be hauling Hellman toward immortality.

The major broadside came from *The New York Times Book Review*, which gave lead space to Charles Thomas Samuels to write a combined appraisal of the Moody book and *The Collected Plays*. Samuels quickly dispatched the book about Hellman as "deplorable and inept," with its skimpy biographical information all lifted unquestioningly from Hellman's memoirs. He then got down to the grim business of destroying Hellman's reputation as a serious playwright. Among his main points were that Hellman did not get revived, that she was not discussed in the right journals and that she did not have a subject. He also felt that she pandered to her audiences, defanging her villains so the audience returned home feeling comforted and safe. He mentioned a number of theatrical devices Hellman employed—overheard conversations, "retrospective confessions," clandestine contracts—and dismissed them as cumbersome stage machinery that disqualified her as a serious playwright. But more significant than any of Sam-uels's points was the positioning of the attack so prominently in *The Times Book Review.*

Three weeks later the *Times* turned over its book review's essay space, "The Guest Word," to critic Renata Adler for a re-buttal to Samuels's attack. Adler escalated the debate into a fierce *ad hominem* blast that, among other things, pointed out writing errors on Samuels's part that "should not be characteristic of a published prose style." She then speeded up her attack with an examination of the theatrical devices Samuels objected to and, with more wit than precise analogy, showed how his prohibitions, if broadly applied, would lose for us most of the world's great plays. There was, however, nothing humorous in Adler's dismissal of Samuels's review as "a pure instance" of critical ineptitude.

Another two weeks went by and "The Guest Word" was given to Samuels to respond to Adler. He chided her on the un-gentlemanly personal nature of her remarks, then defended a number of his positions with a reasonableness that had the effect of softening his original accusations against Hellman. Oddly, Ad-ler had made no mention of his two most patently untrue charges: that Hellman's plays were not revived and were not discussed in serious journals. This last was particularly ludicrous in light of the five-week battle over Hellman's plays Samuels and Adler them-selves had been waging in *The New York Times.*

The debate about Hellman's place as a playwright would go on for the rest of her life and well after it. Any attempt at evalua-tion, however, must start with an acknowledgment of how few prominent playwrights outlive their own period. Of the hundreds of authors of successful plays in the 350 years since Shakespeare, only a relatively small number are recognizable to us today and even fewer of their plays are ever performed. From the last one hundred years alone, there are scores of poets and novelists who are known and read today, but only a few playwrights who are regularly revived—Ibsen, Chekhov, Strindberg, Wilde, Shaw—and even those turn up only sporadically. Of all the literary forms, playwriting seems to be the most rooted in its own period, the most transitory.

During Hellman's years of greatest strength, the 1930s, she

was highly regarded but by no means preeminent. She was certainly outranked by Eugene O'Neill, as well as Maxwell Anderson, Robert Sherwood, Clifford Odets, Elmer Rice, William Saroyan and Thornton Wilder. Except for O'Neill, these playwrights have all but disappeared from American stages, and Hellman, while never considered in O'Neill's class as an artist, can approach his record for revivals.

It is perhaps Hellman's refusal to go the way of a good second-rate playwright that irks her critics more than anything else. A partial explanation of her staying power may be found in the formidable personality of the woman herself, a possibility that became stronger after the publication of her highly successful memoirs with their resounding evocations of her battles, adventures and brushes with history. But the advent of the television talk show obviated interesting personality as a motive for exploring an author's work when, by switching the dial, you could have the personality itself. The reason for the modest endurance of Hellman's plays must lie in the work.

When he was drama critic for *The New York Times*, Clive Barnes had an interesting theory about why Hellman incites a number of critics to mayhem. He felt that the well-madeness of her plays was its own worst enemy in that it tempted the audience of a Hellman play to "accept and analyze it on the highest level." But the plays do not reward such an effort, which, Barnes inferred, left playgoers feeling duped and therefore hostile. His subtle analysis seems off in one respect: it can't be the well-madeness of Hellman's plays that invites criticism at the highest level—*Blithe Spirit* and *Angel Street* are well made—it is more likely her unrelenting seriousness. What Hellman stumbled on— as Edward Albee did in *Who's Afraid of Virginia Woolf?*—was that the dark side of the human condition, if presented with energy, intelligence and brio, can be entertainment of a high order.

We are excruciated by such plays, and we are exhilarated as on a drive in a fast car. To a large degree we are made to reflect, in part to satisfy ourselves that some lofty and recondite message is *not* at hand, and in part on the nature and origins of the human foibles that are being so vividly portrayed. But once aroused to reflection, we are reluctant to settle for pat conclusions like "the world has villains," so we burrow on to find more specific meanings, such as "the Hubbards are an indictment of the capitalist system." After being so brilliantly stimulated, we refuse to accept the absence of a brilliant message.

In a 1960 interview with *The New York Times*'s Seymour Peck, Hellman said, "I don't know that I was ever very much concerned, in a literary sense, with the world. I don't think playwrights should write about society . . . I've always written about people." Assuming that Hellman was honest in disclaiming polemical motives in writing *The Little Foxes*, or any of her plays except *Watch on the Rhine* (and even that play, she says, did not start out as an antifascist tract), it is still no coincidence that those who imposed a message on her came up with a political conclusion—the rottenness of the capitalist system—that was indeed a belief of Hellman's.

If the immediate drama that has captured the author is presented honestly and unequivocally, it is not surprising that the author's larger vision will emerge, whether or not it is reduced to a motto and pinned over his or her typewriter. (Once asked if a certain play was political, critic Kenneth Tynan replied, "When one character asks another for a cigarette, there are political implications.") A case could be made for Hellman's approach: Let the big themes shift for themselves, and concentrate instead on the theatricality, the logic and the sense of pacing of the story in order to grasp the audience's attention and emotions, and hold those emotions until the final curtain. If it turns out that the larger themes generated by a play are indeed unconscious on the author's part, how many demerits should he or she be docked as a creative artist? And will such docking make any difference to the people who decide what plays are revived? Probably not. It is an unfair game, since we do not always have a Seymour Peck around to extract confessions on the absence of creative premeditation from our most eminent writers.

With or without the big themes and elusive messages, Hellman's "fast drives" through human greed, ruthlessness and self-delusion prove that seriousness and unpleasantness don't have to be profound to justify themselves. The people who like her plays can always find in them the deeper themes, and those who dislike them will continue to insist they are about nothing.

The knack of commanding involvement was, perhaps more

than anything else, Hellman's strength as a playwright. There is clearly a mystery to that talent because such giants as Thomas Wolfe, Henry James, Ernest Hemingway and T. S. Eliot tried for it and failed. It surely is connected with the ability to create clear-cut characters who engage our emotions—positive or negative— economy of dialogue and a relatively quick (by the end of the first act) establishment of the plot: who wants what and what the obstacles are.

Elizabeth Hardwick's complaint that Hellman in *The Little Foxes* missed the opportunities for nuance and intellectual delving that are offered by the character of Horace is perhaps a serviceable paradigm for a major difference between a play and a novel. (Hardwick admits her interest in the theater is primarily literary.) Unlike a play, a novel is not working against the clock; it can be read for a while, then considered for a while, perhaps with passages reread. The playwright must deal with audiences squirming in uncomfortable seats who can only be asked to take in so much in one evening, identify with only so many characters, follow only so many plot twists, weigh only so many moral dilemmas. If all of a play's characters are given dimension, hard choices, vacillating personalities, the result would be the intellectual equivalent of a Busby Berkeley finale—too much happening onstage for the eye to take in.

Hardwick's complaint may also provide a valuable clue to what makes a dramatist. By passing up whatever literary temptations Horace presents, Hellman may have been exercising her talent for writing plays that work. Once again it is difficult to know whether she did this consciously or instinctively, and on that point she offers no help. From her manuscripts at the University of Texas it is clear that she had a compelling urge, no doubt abetted by Hammett, to get on with the business at hand cleanly and quickly. Every revision cuts out "fat"—excess dialogue, excess background, excess characters, excess plot complications.

There is no reason why the ability of a playwright to recognize enervating superfluities must be intellectualized. In Hellman's case, clearly it was not. In a 1942 interview she said that she came to feel that she had one character too many in *Watch on the Rhine*—just as she had in *Days to Come*—but she was unable to figure out which character was unnecessary. Such a notional approach to creation raises (or lowers) the fashioning of a play to the mystical; it certainly takes it out of the realm of hard analysis.

Hellman is proof that playwrights must possess, in addition to whatever other talents they may have, a certain noncerebral instinct that tells them when an element is "wrong," "doesn't work," "slows down the action"—or any of the many clichés that conceal a bafflement about why something hurts rather than helps a creative work. The important thing is that this ruthless editorial sense be there. Whatever it is, Hellman had that sense to a degree shared by few others.

The business of economy and pacing that are so essential in the theater points to another Hellman strength, rarely cited: her dialogue. Few dramatists have shown her ability to move the action ahead with such speed and logical thrust without seeming forced and unnatural. Repeatedly in Hellman plays there are scenes in which the lines do not move the action ahead in steps but in leaps, yet never do the characters seem to be leaping—they are merely talking.

One of the techniques Hellman uses to achieve such a rapid pace is the elimination of the niceties and obfuscations that clutter most conversations. It is not so much the economical use of language, although that too is symptomatic, it is the speed of candor. Her characters say precisely what they feel, and it is often the sort of assertion for which an ordinary talker would require five buildup lines. Hellman skips the buildup lines, leaving only the hard sinew of the most direct sort of communication. The effect is exhilarating when it is achieved to the degree that Hellman regularly achieved it, and it is an aspect of her better plays, as much as their deft construction, that has earned them respect and that keeps an audience, as more than one critic has observed, holding its breath.

In reply to the most frequently made charge against Hellman's plays, other than their being melodramas—that they were "well-made," with the pejorative implication of contrivance—the critic Allan Lewis in a discussion of *The Little Foxes* came to her defense by picking up on Hellman's own defense that fictional writing by its very nature is contrived. "All writers rearrange life and impose their own will on the chaos of reality," Lewis wrote.

"The test in the realistic theater is whether the characters seem to be self-propelled as they do in *The Little Foxes.*" In defending Hellman against this familiar charge, Lewis also called attention to another of her strengths: her characters are not just Hellman in different disguises, but believable individuals with a life and motivational system of their own.

In her introduction to the Chekhov letters, Hellman writes that it still seems to surprise some people that authors inevitably come to like all of their characters. Whether or not that is the commonplace Hellman suggests, it loses its commonness when coming from the mouth of the creator of such nasty pieces of work as Regina Giddens, Ben Hubbard and Mary Tilford, among others. But it certainly is a strong clue as to why Hellman's villains are so arresting: she betrays an underlying sympathy for them, an ability to see things through their eyes.

As for the accusation that her plays are not about anything, one is tempted to have recourse to the many favorable Hellman critics who say that her plays are about "the problem of good and evil"—but that empty analysis is tantamount to saying her plays are about "the problem of human beings" and would tend rather to substantiate the charge of their being devoid of subject.

There is no doubt, however, that a strong moral current runs through all Hellman's work, as it did through so much of the serious American drama of the thirties, forties and fifties. It is the making of charges—something is wrong here—and then spending two or three acts finding out who or what is to blame. Talking about the playwrights of the thirties, Malcolm Goldstein in *The Political Stage* wrote: "They wished to analyze the social forces that created killers, perjurers, slanderers and other antisocial beings." In the following decades, the playwrights' list of culprits would be broadened to include the family nexus and American values. But the ever-present assumption was the basic assumption of liberalism: whatever the particular horror, a cause could be rooted out, condemned, then changed or eliminated.

The notion that the seeking out of guilt is the dominant theme of so much contemporary theater was developed by Robert Brustein in his brilliant essay "The Crack in the Chimney." Brustein expanded the judgmental nature of mainstream American theater to include the forties, fifties and sixties, citing in particular such playwrights as Arthur Miller and David Rabe. Brustein wrote about their dramas: "The event to be excavated is still the guilt of the (generally older generation) protagonists; and the drama retains the air of the courtroom, complete with arraignments, investigations, condemnations, indictments, and punishments."

Brustein then relegated such fault-finding plays to a secondary rank in the artistic hierarchy. His essay convincingly argued that Ibsen, who is thought to be the prototype of the social-realist dramatists like Hellman and Arthur Miller whom Brustein finds so accusatory, had made quite the opposite point: that the sources of guilt are not readily accessible to the inquiring mind. Brustein said, "Great artists have traditionally understood that the true explanations are beyond concepts of blame."

(When he wrote this essay, Brustein had already become friends with Hellman on Martha's Vineyard, saying with pride that he was one of few theater people admitted to her circle. His disdain for the judgmental drama that she epitomizes may explain why she never, according to Brustein, solicited discussions with him about her plays, while frequently asking his opinions and advice about her prose.)

When looking over the critical evaluation of Hellman's theater work as a whole, the tendency for even the most kindly tabulator is to pass over the admirers, whose existence can be assumed, and get to the denigrators who are chipping away at the edifice. If her rank as an artist is arguable, her prestige and eminence are facts. Even before the memoirs, she was honored by as many leading universities as any American playwright; her plays are performed regularly and around the world, and her position as a dramatist is debated periodically in intellectual journals, which is remarkable. Who in recent decades has argued about the work of Sherwood or Odets?

What is often forgotten, particularly by those who want to relegate Hellman to an inferior niche or to the dustbin, are the many serious critics who have been unstinting in their admiration of her work. Among those who over the years have praised Hellman as a playwright are Walter Kerr, Wolcott Gibbs, John Gassner,

Louis Kronenberger, Jacob Adler, Allan Lewis and Edmund Wilson. Such literate enthusiasts should be mentioned if only to avoid the impression that the debunkers are in the majority.

No tallying of yeas and nays, however, has any bearing on changing tastes in drama or Hellman's chances for longevity. The didactic playwrights of the thirties have been shelved. Except for Tennessee Williams, the major playwrights of the postwar years are meeting the same fate. Perhaps the only reason to think that Hellman's plays might possibly last is that a few of them *have* lasted a short time beyond the period of their original success. That puts them in a very small and exclusive minority.

Hellman herself would also last, if not as a continuing theatrical voice (her playwriting days were over), certainly as a very theatrical presence on the American scene. With a persistence that bordered on the awesome, she threw herself into carving out a new literary niche for herself even as critics argued her claim to the old. She seemed to stand apart from, or above, the argument. Even in the comparatively few pages in her memoirs that she would devote to her career in the theater, she attempted no self-elevating analysis of her plays or of herself as a playwright. She was not so passive when attacked, but even then she assigned the task of reprisal to her friends in the literary establishment. Before countering the Samuels attack on Hellman in *The New York Times*, Renata Adler recalls receiving incessant phone calls from Hellman stalwarts Richard Poirier and a more recent friend, writer Peter Feibleman, urging her to argue Hellman's case because she was old and frail and couldn't fight back herself. The picture of a defenseless Hellman, whatever her age, was somewhat fanciful—as is the notion that writers of youth and vigor invariably battle their critics themselves.

The controversy over whether or not Hellman's dramas were worth reviving would continue for years, as would the revivals. But the running argument was mild and restrained compared to the controversies to come over Hellman herself.

24

THE PLAYWRIGHT Howard Teichmann was teaching at Barnard in the late 1960s when his old friend Lillian Hellman was asked to deliver a commencement address. He telephoned and offered her a lift up to the Columbia campus for the ceremony. When she got into the car and greeted him with a kiss, Teichmann could tell she had had a drink or two.

"That goddamn bitch Dorothy Parker," Hellman raged as if continuing an interrupted conversation. "You won't believe what she's done. I paid her hotel bill at the Volney for years, kept her in booze, paid for her suicide attempts—all on the promise that when she died, she would leave me the rights to her writing. At my death, they would pass to the NAACP. But what did she do? She left them *directly* to the NAACP. Damn her!"

Throughout Parker's last years, Hellman had felt guilty about neglecting her, admitting she found her life "too messy." Parker drank heavily, had frequent accidents and was in other ways a troublemaker. (Running into Parker after one of her well-publicized suicide attempts, George S. Kaufman looked at her bandaged wrists and said, "You'd better be careful, Dottie. Next time you might hurt yourself.") Perhaps Hellman had had her fill of such chaos with Hammett. Still, she maintained a strong affection for Parker and indeed helped her out financially. According to her biographer, Marion Meade, Parker had other benefactors, some of them a lot wealthier than Hellman.

Assuming the bequest to Hellman of her rights was in fact promised, seriously and soberly, Parker might still have felt that Hellman's financial difficulties were behind her, that she was affluent once again and would no longer be interested in what might be an insignificant amount of money. Or Parker, in her fervent enthusiasm for Martin Luther King, may have changed her will without feeling she was betraying Hellman. It is equally possible she simply forgot about the promise. Whatever the reason, Hellman did indeed feel betrayed and was angered even further that the NAACP would benefit from Parker's will, since she considered the group far too conservative.

Hellman had always been quick to anger and always difficult in her business dealings. Considering her disdain for capitalism, it probably followed that she had an instinctive distrust for businessmen and that, where money was concerned, that distrust reached to friends as well (the break with Shumlin was over money). Suspicious of financial chicanery, she had no trouble finding other forms of perfidy in business associates to justify her mistrust. Lester Osterman discovered that when Hellman viewed as a deliberate affront his hiring Robert Rossen for a play in which Hellman was not involved. At the time of the Mike Nichols revival of *The Little Foxes*, Hellman broke with her agent of many years, Robert Lantz, because she felt his representing both her and Nichols constituted a conflict of interest. The agent who succeeded Lantz, Don Congdon, commented, "Lillian was always taking umbrage at something to which the rest of us normal folk would say 'So what?' "

For an agent to represent two or more people who happen to be collaborating on a production is common in show business; indeed, many productions are assembled on that basis. That the conflicting client in this instance, Mike Nichols, was a good friend of Hellman's points up the degree of her mistrust. The agents who represented her throughout her career all found her difficult. Kay Brown, who represented Hellman for many years prior to Lantz, was said to have been relieved when Hellman left her.

The Samuel French Company, Hellman's longtime agents for amateur and secondary productions of her plays, finally had had enough harassment from her and resigned as her representatives. Abbott Van Norstrand, the company's president, would not discuss Hellman's grievances that prompted her badgering, but he gave a good indication when he sputtered heatedly, "We haven't stayed in business for a hundred and sixty years by being crooks!"

Even before she became a best-selling author herself, Hellman was, like most authors, vociferous in her complaints about her publisher's marketing efforts. In an angry letter to Random House editor Joe Fox, she said that not one of Martha's Vineyard's three bookstores had a copy of *The Big Knockover,* the book of Hammett's stories she had edited. Still, she ended the carping letter on a conciliatory note, a tidbit of glamorous self-deprecation: "You can see that frugging with Sarge Shriver didn't put me in a fine humor."

Several years later, when Hellman read that the 1941 film version of *The Little Foxes* was to be shown on television, she made one of her famous irate calls to her agent to learn if her contract for the film rights also allowed for showing it on television. When it turned out that no such permission was specifically granted, Hellman sued CBS for a half-million dollars. That her grievance also applied to every movie aired on television didn't deter her in the slightest.

The assumption at that time in the film business was that, having paid the author for the film rights, the filmmaker was then entitled to sell the film to television or anyplace else. Hellman argued that a television showing should be a separate deal. The suit was finally decided against her in 1970, but while it was in progress it was watched with more than casual interest by every film producer and television station in the country.

Taking major corporations to court over established business practices when she felt gypped was Hellman at her feisty best. All too often, however, wrangles and dealings over money brought out her worst. The fascination with money that began with childhood dinners at the homes of her mother's rich relatives and provided the dominant motive in her strongest play had hardened into a virulent acquisitiveness in Hellman's own life that seemed to overrule her more generous impulses. She had been poor as a child, then had earned a great deal of money, spent profligately and endured a period of financial hardship. Perhaps because she saw money as protection, and those without it as victims, she was willing to go to such lengths to insure against ever being poor again.

Alternative sources of revenue were increasingly on Hellman's mind with the failure of *My Mother, My Father and Me*. She continued to refer to that fiasco as her reason for giving up the theater, elaborating on the horror of delivering a year's hard work to the mercies of not just philistine critics but to bad direction, bad casting and newspaper strikes. For Hellman such vicissitudes were nothing new, but writing absurdist comedy was, and it is doubtful that she would abandon a highly successful career as a *serious* playwright because of the failure of a farce. A stronger clue to her ultimate decision to write books was in a remark Hellman made to an interviewer in the mid-sixties. She told of having recently read an article about the theater which mentioned the six or seven major American playwrights of the twentieth century. Her name was not on the list. That upset her so much, she said, she decided to switch to prose and settled on the notion of writing her memoirs. (After such a slight, Hellman would have been gratified by the first sentence of her front-page obituary in *The New York Times*, which began: "Lillian Hellman, one of the most important playwrights of the American theater . . ." No qualifications as to decade or gender—just "important.")

Still, it would have been highly uncharacteristic of Hellman to react to an affront by slinking off in another direction. In 1936, when the critics harshly rejected her second play, *Days to Come,* she responded by writing *The Little Foxes.* Toughened by thirty years of critical buffetings, she probably would not have been driven from the theatrical field by a journalistic snub. Why, then, did she decide to write about herself?

There is no doubt that Hellman had always been drawn to prose; nor is there doubt she was indeed disheartened by the uncontrollable variables of theatrical production and what she saw as the sinking taste level of Broadway audiences. She needed to earn, and even more, she needed to work. But what pushed her into not just prose, but a memoir, was probably her belief that she had already tallied up an impressive accomplishment in the theater; attempting to sustain her reputation with a new play every two years was a losing game, and an unnecessary one. She could remind the public of her record (which she perceived as starting to fade from public memory) with a review of her life. That this life could make other claims to interest was strong reinforcement to her strategy.

Gore Vidal once remarked that television had changed everything for authors. Traditionally, he said, writers went on television to sell their books. Now, because of the opportunity television afforded writers to communicate with far vaster numbers of people than their books would ever reach, they wrote books in order to appear on television. In one appearance on *The Tonight Show*, Vidal said, he reached more people than Hemingway had with all his writing.

While Vidal's analysis deals only with communication in the most literal sense and begs the question of creating art, there may have been something similar in Hellman's thinking: deciding what your ultimate goal is—that is, *why* you write your books, plays, films or whatever—and seeing if there aren't other routes to that goal. At this point in her life, Hellman's "goal" was not so much "reaching" large numbers of people—she had too little respect for most people for that. She was more concerned with her stature, her place among writers, her niche in posterity. A solid, widely read autobiography would consolidate her known victories, bring to light some unknown ones, and, if the writing was found to have merit, expand the range of her literary prowess.

Hellman was sixty-two when she began *An Unfinished Woman*. As a writer of prose, she turned out to be just as fretful as she had been as a playwright. But she now had no Hammett to pester for advice. William Abrahams, her editor at Little Brown, who would become a good friend, received phone calls from Hellman at any hour for help in resolving writing problems, an echo of her noisy agonies with Hammett while at work on a play. Abrahams, invariably accommodating, was understandably irked that Hellman gave him no acknowledgment in the book.

If Hellman was worrying about her place among twentieth-century American authors, she didn't have to worry about her place among the New York literary elite. She was close friends with many of the day's most important writers—Edmund Wilson, Theodore Roethke, William Styron, John Hersey, Norman Mailer. She was a prized guest at the most prestigious social events and she gave many parties of her own. Norman Podhoretz in his memoir *Making It* tells of meeting Hellman at a party given by the Lionel Trillings and being invited in turn to one of Hellman's. For him, the casual invitation marked an important passage from the purely intellectual circles he already frequented to the intellectual *cum* success and money that Hellman epitomized.

Hellman's world was broad. She didn't merely limit herself to stroking sessions with the old money of the New York literary and theater elite, but was receptive to new blood. Admiration for a recent book or film could send her out on a quest, invariably successful, for a new friend. For a Jules Feiffer or a Mary Tyler Moore, a phone invitation from a gravelly voice claiming to be the legendary Lillian Hellman was all but unrefusable. The few people who have such flat-out social power use it sparingly; Hellman used it with relish. It was not just her legendary status among the stars of upper Bohemia that drew to Hellman whomever she wanted; she was a serious hostess who worked assiduously to see that her guests enjoyed memorable food and company. Hellman had always thrived on social activity, but in the post-Hammett period she indulged the impulse fully.

Her social alliances could even, in some instances, take precedence over her political ones although many of the people she had known socially in earlier years, having behaved dishonorably in Hellman's eyes during the McCarthy period, were still bitterly ostracized. (Encountering Abe Burrows as she was leaving a Philadelphia restaurant, Hellman spat in his face.) Others, whose behavior she publicly condemned, she privately courted, most prominent among them the intellectual superstars Diana and Lionel Trilling, whom Hellman would write of as bitter adversaries during the McCarthy years. Norman Podhoretz recalls that the Trillings received a conciliatory note from Hellman saying that they shouldn't allow their political differences to destroy an old friendship. Diana Trilling remembers that, during the early fifties, her husband ran into Hellman, who expressed regret at not seeing him and asked if they couldn't resume their friendship. Trilling had told Hellman that because of their disparate politics, relations now would not work. But Hellman dismissed that as a reason for estrangement. Warily, Trilling agreed to a dinner, which went well enough and the friendship was resumed.

Hellman would show a willingness to effect a similar drawing-room truce with a bitter Vietnam war adversary, McGeorge Bundy, whom she had known at Harvard, had seen again in Washington when he was with the Kennedy Administration, and who became a regular guest of Hellman's in New York and on Martha's Vineyard. Some of her friends were not so forgiving. Arriving at a Hellman cocktail party on the Vineyard, Robert Lowell spotted Bundy and turned to leave. "I haven't done all I've done to oppose the war just to turn around and have drinks with one of them." Bundy insists, however, that no such thing could have happened, on the shaky grounds that Lowell was a cousin of his.

Hellman had a leaning toward poets and took considerable pride in her friendships with Theodore Roethke, Robert Lowell, Richard Wilbur and others, which reveals a modest side to her nature and perhaps reflects her youthful guru-seeking side. Among such artistic heavyweights, Hellman's commercial theater output was a small, if not a negative, credential. She could have limited herself to the scintillating theater and film world in which she was a queen. That she aspired to a milieu in which her admittance was provisional—somewhat like that of a colorful and well-connected groupie—shows that Hellman's ego was not the kind that prevented her from seeking the company of talents most people, and probably she herself, considered superior to her own.

The end result was that Hellman had as impressive a "circle" as any in America. Podhoretz tells of being at a cocktail party Hellman gave in 1966 for Senator George McGovern. According to Podhoretz, McGovern was so impressed at being fussed over by what he saw as the cream of the nation's artists and intellectuals, he may have conceived the idea of running for President that evening. (The possibility was reinforced by a later conversation between McGovern and Podhoretz.)

For a place of honor in New York's success aristocracy, Hellman had more credentials than most. She had a solid block of creative achievement; she was intelligent, concerned and involved in events; she lived well and entertained well. She was gregarious and fun to be around. She loved playing the social game, and few played it as well. The weighty names among whom she drank and supped elevated her partying safely above the level of frivolous diversion. Hellman came late to this high-powered playground, but it remained a dominant part of her life until her death.

In 1966 Hellman made an emotional trip to Russia, her first visit in twenty-two years; she returned again the following year. Because her relentless political activities on behalf of her pro-Russianism appeared rooted in ideology, it is often overlooked how sentimental it was. Hellman had many good friends in the Soviet Union, particularly her translator, Raya, with whom she had corresponded over the years. (The letters were monitored by the CIA.) She had at least one major love affair there—Melby—and her plays were admired by the Russians.

On her 1967 visit, however, she found that most of her Russian friends had become dissidents, and she herself was critical, for the first time to any degree, of official Soviet positions. (The previous year she had joined a group of some 150 American writers to sign an open letter to Premier Kosygin asking clemency for two Soviet authors on trial for having published abroad.) While in Moscow, she was invited to address the Writers' Congress being held there at the time. She accepted on the uncharacteristically mistrustful condition that she could say whatever she wanted.

By her account of this episode in *An Unfinished Woman,* she waited, speech in hand, in the great hall where the delegates were meeting, refusing to let anyone see it. When it became obvious she would not be permitted to speak until someone read her speech, she yielded it, then found her turn was passed over. The next day she left Moscow in a huff. In her words: "I left the hall, went back to the hotel, telephoned *The New York Times,* gave them the speech, packed my bags and took a morning plane to Paris. My speech was published here and in Europe."

Hellman is mistaken. The speech, if it existed at all, was not published in New York. She may have been thinking of a *New York Times* interview with her about her trip in which she made no mention of being barred from addressing the Congress; instead she spoke of the ferment among Soviet writers, who are "determined to make the fight for their own freedom to write as they wish to write." It was an optimistic prediction from one who later claimed to have just been roundly censored by Soviet authority. Its naive hopefulness notwithstanding, the observation implied more criticism of conditions in Russia than was customary from Hellman. And the later account of being barred from speaking may have been her dramatist's way of telling the world that she now understood about free speech in Russia.

The numbers of pro-Russian Americans had been dwindling ever since the purge trials of 1937 and Stalin's pact with the Nazis in 1939. The *coup de grâce* for most of those who still clung to a belief that the Soviets were more righteous and humanitarian than their own government was Khrushchev's 1956 speech in which he confirmed the brutal repressions and genocide of the Stalin regime. According to John Melby, who was seeing Hellman at the time, she grudgingly acceded to the probable truth of Khrushchev's allegations, but came down hard on the Soviet Premier for stabbing in the back the man he, Khrushchev, had to thank for his present eminence.

With remarkable agility, Hellman passed quickly and without comment over Khrushchev's thick catalogue of monstrous crimes that she, perhaps unwittingly, had endorsed, and alighted on a hint of bad character on Khrushchev's part: disloyalty to a former superior. In her pro-Russian bias, her morality had always been selective. But perhaps she could not abruptly change a thirty-year habit of seeking out mitigation for Stalin's brutal acts, or seeking out bad behavior on the part of his adversaries to distract from them.

During her 1966 Moscow trip, even Russians were surprised by Hellman's pro-Russian bias. She was dining with a group of Russian friends, one of whom had spent several years in Siberia for having spoken out against the brutal and uncivilized behavior of Russian soldiers in Germany at the end of the war. Hellman told the group a story she had heard from Ambassador Averell Harriman. As the war was drawing to a close, Roosevelt had asked Harriman to convey to Stalin his wish that the Allied Armies be ordered to behave properly when they entered Germany. When Harriman delivered his message, Stalin had laughed and said he would pass along the order but "he did not believe men who had been fighting for years could be kept from rape and loot."

Aside from this picture of Joseph Stalin as a man who chuckled at the impossibility of controlling those under him, the anecdote suggests the contortions Hellman's sense of right and wrong could take when the powerful magnet of Russia disrupted her ethical field. There is a disturbing sense that she agrees rape is unavoidable, even excusable, for men who have been fighting for years. Although she makes no mention of the Americans and other nationalities who had also been fighting for years, would she have felt rape was all right for them as well? It is not surprising that, according to Hellman, the Russians at her table reacted to her story with silence.

It is almost impossible to know if Hellman's political views were really changing at this time, just as it is unclear what they had been. There is no doubt her public posture of unreconcilable radicalism was softening slightly, but the defend-Russia reflexes never died altogether. Budd Schulberg can remember getting into a heated discussion with Hellman at a party in the late sixties about whether or not the Russians were confining or otherwise silencing writers who were too outspoken against the Kremlin. Hellman said that was all anti-Russian propaganda. Schulberg pointed to the number of writers, such as Isaac Babel, who were listed in the Soviet writers' directory one year, then dropped the next year without a word, and sometimes without a trace. "Lillian grew furious," Schulberg said, "and started yelling 'Prove it! Prove it!' "

There were signs, however, that Hellman was moving into a less partisan stance on East-West relations and was turning her energy from defending or promoting *their* system to improving her own. Early in December 1968 she attended a series of seminars at Princeton with a hundred intellectuals to exchange views on "The United States, Its Problems, Impact and Image in the World." The meeting was sponsored by the Institute for Advanced Study and the Paris-based International Association for Cultural Freedom. Among those attending were Henry Kissinger, Jean-Jacques Servan-Schreiber, Andreas Papandreou, John Kenneth Galbraith, George Kennan, Norman Podhoretz and Roy Innis.

Looking around the room during the first meeting, Hellman

said to the person next to her, "This conference should be called 'Making It,'" a cynical reference to the title of Norman Podhoretz's memoirs published the year before about his emergence as a prominent voice in American intellectual circles. Hellman was showing her disdain for the presence in the august group of such newcomers as student activist Sam Brown, *Harper's* editor Willie Morris and Harvard instructor Martin Peretz, who would soon become the publisher of *New Republic*. When Servan-Schreiber got up to speak, Hellman asked her seatmate, "What are Servan-Schreiber's credentials?"

She was told that he had written a best-seller.

"Who hasn't?" Hellman snorted.

Aside from the fact that at that point *she* hadn't, her questioning of others' eligibility for inclusion revealed that she hadn't the least misgivings about her own congruity with these statesmen, historians, economists and political leaders, although she was the only one of the major names present whose "credentials" were exclusively from the arts. Belief in the logic of Hellman's presence was shared by the press, which, in its extensive coverage of the meetings, always placed her name prominently among those attending.

It was the first time Hellman had taken part in a highly conspicuous gathering that was not primarily pro-Russian. While still safely on the what's-wrong-with-America ground, she was among people most of whom were well known for their belief in the existing system. In her snideness about the conference she may have been suffering the unease of the turncoat, and was not really questioning the credentials of the others, but rather their politics. Hellman was not going to go gently into the mainstream.

One of the major speeches was delivered by George Kennan, now a highly distinguished writer and professor and a former U.S. Ambassador to Moscow who, twenty-four years earlier as an Embassy under secretary, had rescued a very sick Hellman from Moscow's National Hotel. Kennan gave a despairing picture of what was happening to America. After hammering away at the usual ills—poverty, pollution, race relations—he then focused on youth, which he saw as "floundering around in its own terrifying wilderness of drugs, pornography and political hysteria."

At the conclusion of his speech, Hellman rose to rebut him,

primarily on his views about young people. She started off wondering how two people like Kennan and herself, of the same generation, could have such opposing views of American society. (In *Scoundrel Time* she would wonder the same thing about Lionel and Diana Trilling, a form of contradiction she apparently reserved for respected friends.) First criticizing her own generation as being mere dabblers at social change, she then extolled the present-day students. "God knows many of them are fools, and most of them will be sellouts, but they're a better generation than we were . . . since when is youth not allowed to be asses? Many of us spoke today as if Freud never lived." Winding up her rambling remarks, she said, "There's nothing to be despairing about except the American liberal."

It was not one of Hellman's clearer pronouncements; her somewhat gratuitous condemnation of liberals could be taken as another symptom of her discomfort in this company. Her admiration for those who sought radical change, however, was real. And when Hellman accepted her applause and sat down, student leader Sam Brown got up to say that he now knew what it was like to fall in love with an older woman.

25

DURING THE SUMMER of 1968 on Martha's Vineyard, Hellman completed the final draft of *An Unfinished Woman*. When it was published the following June, Little Brown gave her a large dinner party at New York's Four Seasons restaurant. There was much to celebrate. The advance reviews had been enthusiastic, the word of mouth even better, and bookstores were ordering heavily. The only critical complaints about the book, for the most part, concerned the things Hellman left out. Several cited the theater as the basis of interest in Hellman and felt she should have concentrated on her professional life instead of making only fleeting references to it. Others applauded Hellman's refusal to write the expected clichés and found much virtue in her sketch of a life rather than a career.

A number of critics praised Hellman's modesty, even more her honesty, which many felt was one of the book's standout features—among them V. S. Pritchett, Joseph Epstein, Doris Grumbach, W. G. Rogers and Caskie Stinnett. Since few, if any, of these writers were in a position to know whether or not Hellman's account of herself was unfailingly truthful, it was clearly something in her style that so frequently brought forth this judgment.

For one thing, Hellman repeatedly raises the subject of truth, although not to the degree she would in *Pentimento* or with the force of a preface to a later edition of her three memoirs in which she says, "What a word is truth. Slippery, tricky, unreliable. I tried in these books to tell the truth, I did not fool with facts." *Pentimento* would be peppered with such reflections, and in her last book, *Maybe,* the elusiveness of truth is the primary theme. *An Unfinished Woman,* however, has fewer such direct references to truth, but many examples of Hellman's struggle to get things right. She is quick to say if she is unsure of something, and often says she has totally forgotten something else. Her gentle and winning self-deprecations go far toward building an atmosphere of candor. Given the clumsily self-serving, unabashed posturing of most autobiographies, it is not surprising that Hellman's book was taken by many to be a model of honesty and humility.

The writing was also widely admired for its on-target succinctness. While Hellman had a knack for expressing large thoughts in a few small words—"Mailer wasted time being famous"; and, referring to her love for Hammett, "the short cord that the years make into rope"—at times the monosyllabic brevity bordered on self-parody, particularly in exchanges with Hammett, when both sometimes sound like Indian chiefs grunting simple truths by a bonfire. There is also a self-indulgent tendency to digression, often in the midst of gripping events. The many asides that interrupt her account of Spain during the civil war are usually rewarding, but sometimes it is hard to figure out why. And when held up against the things she might have reported from Spain, they fail miserably.

In the thirty-four pages she devotes to her 1937 visit to the Spanish war, five of them are taken up with a crazy old man and his woman keeper whom Hellman meets in a public park. While her three encounters with the couple are intriguing, they strain hard for significance, symbolic or merely evocative, but never achieve more than a color that can't even be called local: the pair could have been encountered on a park bench in London or New York. Hellman's powerful narrative skill makes us overlook the pointless distraction from a subject of far greater interest.

Details of her theater work were not the only sizable omission from *An Unfinished Woman.* Hellman does not give a name or a face to any lover but Hammett, although she had many of prominence—Shumlin, Ingersoll, Kronenberger, the financier George Backer. One of them, John Melby, actually questioned Hellman on this omission after reading *An Unfinished Woman*. Why had she not mentioned their affair with its added HUAC drama? Hellman's response to him was that she never wrote about the living. She would later say the same thing, in fact, in the final chapter of *Pentimento*. While her self-imposed prohibition is not strictly true, it might have been true about her love affairs. But adding to the suspicion that something inhibited her other than respect for the living was the anonymity she also imposes on lovers then no longer alive, like David Cort and Jed Harris.

Simple, old-fashioned discretion should not be discounted, even in one so nonchalant about sex as Hellman. But it is hard to reconcile with her sexual forthrightness in discussing others, including her family (her father's infidelities) and her friends (Louis Aragon's late swing to homosexuality). And she talks openly about her sexual relationship with Hammett, which began when she was married to someone else and to whom she was never married. If her reticence about her love affairs was discretion, it was a highly selective and complex one.

For some of Hellman's lovers, their affair with her was a high point of their lives, and they were not grateful to have been written out of her life. Hellman, like most celebrities, was keenly aware of the potency of her fame to the unfamous, that people connived to be in her circle, to be seen in public with her, were delighted to receive a note from her. That her lovers might have no objection to appearing in her book increases the suspicion that Hellman was not exorcising these major involvements out of consideration for them, but rather from a fear of diminishing the Hammett-Hellman legend. After his death, that legend became increasingly important to Hellman—and perhaps the outside involvements less so. If that was the case, she might have indulged herself in the distortion to avoid the *public's* distorting the other affairs; that is to say, giving them an importance close to Hammett's. And that Hellman *knew* was untrue. Still, it amounts to a significant revision of the biographical truth.

Another noteworthy omission from a memoir written in the late sixties was any discussion of herself as a woman operating in a man's world. Even if Hellman encountered no professional disadvantage because of her sex, as she would say elsewhere, it is inconceivable that she never experienced sexism, toward herself or toward a friend, noteworthy enough to mention. And while she makes many references to her Jewishness, she never offers one anecdote in which that is central. Surely, as she was growing up in New Orleans at the beginning of the century, or in New York prior to World War I, something might have occurred that distinguished the Hellman family from their neighbors or Lillian from her schoolmates. When one considers the scores of memoirs in which a central theme is maintaining a Jewish identity in a gentile America, it is strange that the subject never arose for Hellman.

Hellman also never mentions her looks, which, for one so amorously inclined, must surely have been a cause for some reflection. It is, of course, an understandable omission, but in her casual references to a number of lovers, the impression is created that she is a woman who could get any man she desired. Perhaps she could, but the reasons for her amatory success would have to come from the recollections of others. "It was simple," a close friend said. "She was sexually aggressive at a time when no women were. Others were promiscuous, God knows, but they wouldn't make the first move. Lillian never hesitated, and she cleaned up!" The remark would give some credence to Arthur Miller's wild assertion that Hellman came on with every man she met, or to a tale Martha Gellhorn told of waiting for Hemingway in the lobby of a Paris hotel in 1937 while he paid a courtesy visit to Dorothy Parker's suite. He returned looking disheveled, and explained the lipstick on his collar with "Lillian Hellman was up there and she's the most extraordinary female I ever met!"

Although a thorough knowledge of Hellman's life makes *An Unfinished Woman* notable for the important matters Hellman omits, that the critics bemoaned relatively minor omissions was a tribute to the strengths of what she includes. Hellman's New Orleans childhood is wonderfully evoked, the portraits of Hammett, Dorothy Parker and her housekeeper, Helen Jackson (who died the year following publication), are loving but never mawkish. She impressionistically sketches other fascinating friendships—Sergei Eisenstein, her Russian translator, Raya—and throughout she gives the impression of a woman who has avoided the allurements of glamour and false prestige in a search for more meaningful elements in her life: work, true friends, worthwhile causes.

More than any other of this memoir's assets—and it would be just as true of the ones to follow—the greatest pleasure comes from the feeling that you are spending time with a truly splendid individual. Not only does Hellman present a woman with the highest standards of honor, decency and a no-nonsense sensitivity, she shows a playwright's instinct in her portrayal of herself: when to be self-effacing, when to be funny, when to be generous, when to be unabashedly mean. The person she creates in these books, whether or not an accurate likeness of Hellman, is a superb example of humanity. That alone makes them an exhilarating pleasure to read.

No one doubted the honesty of Hellman's self-portrait in *An Unfinished Woman*. It does, however, contain a number of anecdotes that, when read with the skepticism many would later feel, cause a degree of wonder at the credulity originally awarded her recollections. In the chapter on her housekeeper, Helen, Hellman writes that when she was about eleven or twelve, she got on a streetcar with her black nurse, Sophronia. They started toward the rear Negro section of the car when Hellman, on an impulse, sat behind the driver and pulled Sophronia down with her. A fracas followed. The driver ordered them to the rear, Hellman refused, screaming that Sophronia was better than he was, a white woman slapped her and the driver evicted them both.

If those who thought that Rosa Parks, in a similar act of defiance, had launched the Civil Rights movement in 1955 were surprised to learn that Hellman and Sophronia had indeed launched it four decades earlier, none of them said so out loud. After Hellman's death and countless attacks on her veracity, William Luce trustingly included this history-jarring episode in his one-woman play, *Lillian*. Even then, only one critic, Howard Kissel, noted the enormity of Hellman's claim.

In another assertion that went unchallenged, Hellman reports that while in Moscow, word comes to her that Marshal Stalin, whom she had not asked to see, has granted her an interview. Hellman respectfully declines, pleading that she has nothing to say to him and to take up his time would be an imposition. When twenty years earlier Hellman returned to New York from Russia, she held a press conference in her Manhattan town house to talk about her trip. *The New York Times* reported her as saying she had tried to see Stalin, but got back the message from his secretary "Very sorry . . . but too busy with the Poles." Her *Collier's* article about the same trip makes no mention of Stalin either way—his refusing to see her or her refusing to see him.

Hellman's belated claim in her memoir is hard to believe on other grounds. If, as she says, her invitation to the front lines caused a sensation among the diplomats and press of Moscow's foreign community, it would have been nothing to the sensation that an invitation to meet Joseph Stalin would have caused, particularly among the ambassadors, most of whom had never so much as been in the same room with Stalin after years of representing their countries to the Soviet government. Melby recalls that Hellman told him of the invitation, but Kathleen Harriman Mortimer definitely does not. She says it is unlikely that anyone around Spasso House could have been invited to meet Stalin and "the rest of us not known about it, particularly the Ambassador." In Hellman's account, the invitation arrived by phone through the Spasso House phone operator, who listened in on all conversations. After the call from Stalin's appointments secretary, Hellman went outside her room at the embassy to decide what to do and spotted the phone operator "already half up the stairs to report my call to Mr. Harriman."

It would appear the phone operator never got there, since no one but the loyal Melby knew anything about the invitation. To be sure, Hellman would have been capable of keeping such matters to herself, but she undermines that possibility by her claim that there were no secrets at Spasso House. When her story of the invitation is read with the knowledge that there is no mention of it in her previous accounts and that others on the scene deny it, one wonders how it could have been believed in the first place. Anyone with even the slightest feeling for history (Hellman had a great deal) or the slightest journalistic impulses (Hellman wrote three journalistic books and numerous articles) would consider an opportunity to meet one of the most famous and reclusive men of history to be the climax of an eventful life.

As for her fear that accepting the invitation would be an imposition, whatever nicety of feeling that attitude suggests is overruled by the condescension of Hellman, in effect, telling Stalin that although he wishes to meet her, he is wrong to have that wish. And what is the result of the story? We are left giddy with the spectacle of a life so full and a nature so cool as to turn down, for reasons of *politesse,* a historic invitation.

While a case accumulates that Hellman enlivened her memoirs with flattering recollections of dubious veracity, she also omits a number of comparably flattering happenings—aspects of her Russian trip, for example, that are established by the testimony of others. She had a serious love affair with an outstanding young man in wartime Moscow, a setting of novelistic romance. She was treated like royalty by both the Russian and American governments, the only American to be so honored. She skips over all that. Perhaps by modestly omitting such ego-boosting facts, Hellman felt she bought for herself the right to cheat on others—a bargain with the truth to mitigate the sin of falsifying. Whatever the explanation, the conclusion seems to be that Lillian Hellman, having been "found out," remains as complex and as elusive as ever.

A curious story in the section on her visit to the Spanish civil war suggests possible origins for her fictionalizations. Shortly after arriving, Hellman twisted her ankle and was taken back to her room by a young American acquaintance, a soldier on recuperative leave from the International Brigade. When Hellman inquired about his wound, he told her it was in the penis. In her memoirs, she ruminates on this: "I never thought of anybody being wounded in the penis. How little I know about any of this."

It is an odd observation to come from so literary a woman as Hellman. A wounded penis is the arresting central image in Hemingway's *The Sun Also Rises,* a novel whose publication eleven years earlier had caused a sensation in American literary circles. Hellman was now in the country of the book's setting and was about to have dinner with its author. She may well have been employing literary license and relating an encounter with one wounded soldier in order to evoke all the war's wounded, but the juxtaposition of unmeshed facts suggests the subconscious inspiration of the literary devices of the memoirs.

There is also an episode in *An Unfinished Woman* that, when checked out against another on-the-record version of the same story, also written by Hellman, perhaps shows even more about the mechanisms behind Hellman's juggling of the truth. After returning from Russia in 1945, Hellman accepted a commission to write about her trip to the Russian front for *Collier's*, then a rival of *The Saturday Evening Post* as a large-circulation national magazine. The article differs from her version of that same trip in *An Unfinished Woman* in significant and revealing ways.

In both instances she was writing for a similar audience—the general American reader—that is to say, the ordinary American reader with no particular political leanings or special interest in Russia. The propaganda motive for promoting a wartime ally would have been absent by the time of *An Unfinished Woman*, except that Hellman's impulse to extol Russia, or more specifically the Russians, never left her. In any case, the variations in the two stories are not in the way Russia is depicted, but in the way Hellman depicts herself.

Many elements are present in both versions: the rigors of the trip, the cordial reception by Russian military leaders at the front, the high spirits of the Russians as they move toward victory. There are also details of a more literary cast that survived in the telling after twenty-five years: the beauty of a snow-heavy pine forest, the luxury of a steam bath at the front, high-spirited dinners with the Russian generals, and a farewell gift from the Russians of an inscribed cigarette case.

In the *Collier's* version Hellman includes a marvelously endearing description of her costume at one moment on the Vistula front: "Ski pants, two sweaters and a blouse, long woolen underwear which bulged in strange places, woolen stockings, socks, shoes, boots, an American Army sheeplined coat with hood, and a large shawl to keep the hood in place." She assured the Russian officers that all American women did not dress that way. There are also self-deprecations in the later account, but they are of a more ponderous, less jocular kind.

The major differences concern what happened during the trip: some of the most dramatic episodes in the 1969 account are absent in the 1945 version. In both versions Hellman tells of spending the first night in Lublin at a nice hotel that was warm, well guarded by soldiers, but curiously empty. She later learns that it was the headquarters of the legendary Marshal Zhukov. In 1945 she had a wonderful night's sleep, but in 1969 the sleep was disturbed by the sound of "many men in heavy boots running by the hotel." A parenthesis explains: "There were still pockets of trapped Germans in the city and the suburbs." Perhaps Hellman did not feel it would interest *Collier's* readers in those last months of the war that her sleep had been disturbed by the sound of fleeing Germans.

More significantly, she leaves out of her *Collier's* piece a visit to the recently captured concentration camp at Maidanek, an omission hard to explain, since in 1969 the horror of what she saw moved her to some of the most florid writing Hellman ever produced: "I was down in the blackness of deep water, pushed up to consciousness by monsters I could smell but not see, into a wildness of lions waiting to scrape my skin with their tongues, shoved down again, and up again, covered with slime, pieces of me floating near my hands."

It is not a dream; it is Hellman's attempt to verbalize her emotions on seeing the ghastliness of the death camp. She goes on to describe the bins of shoes arranged by size and color, how she idly touches a pair of red shoes. She points out that the large ovens were for the adults, the small ones for children. In the 1945 article, there was no mention whatever of visiting the camp. Given Hellman's capacity for principled obstinacy even when big money was involved (buying her freedom from Goldwyn for $30,000 rather than make changes to *North Star*, for instance), the possibility can be ruled out that she had censored her piece to accommodate *Collier's* editors—who certainly had no reason to spare the Nazis at the end of a long war with them, just as the full horror of the concentration camps was becoming widely known in America.

Perhaps the most dramatic moment in the account in *An Unfinished Woman* was the only occurrence in either version that places Hellman on the front lines or within shooting distance of the Germans. She visits a General Chernov in his "two-room dugout." They have tea and talk about his days in the czarist army and about his surrender and recapture of Kovel in the present war. As conversation flags, he asks her if she would like to see the

German soldiers, who at the time were of considerable interest to the rest of the world.

He takes her to a small "glass opening" in the dugout wall, adjusts his binoculars, then moves her into position. As he gives her the binoculars, he places her hand over the top as a shield and she is so surprised to see the Germans "five hundred feet from us" that she drops her hand. That produces an immediate barrage of "grenades and heavy guns." The general pushes Hellman to the floor, explaining that moving her hand had caused a reflection, which, in turn, told the Germans of their whereabouts. Hellman berates herself for her foolishness.

It would seem that if a major American magazine had asked Hellman to tell of her visit to the Russian front lines and if during the visit she not only stood face-to-face with the enemy, but elicited their gunfire as well, it would be germane to the article. In the *Collier's* piece, however, Hellman says only that when taken by the general to watch some maneuvers, he gives her binoculars, then tells her to lower them as there are snipers in the vicinity. She refers to the sounds of German gunfire from "across the river" but does not claim to have actually seen any Germans or been fired on by them.

In *An Unfinished Woman* Hellman also tells of having been in the headquarters of a Russian general when some captured Polish soldiers who had been fighting with the Nazis are brought in for questioning. Their obsequious replies are immediately shown up as lies by such incongruities as soft hands on a professed coal miner and Russian boots on a man who claimed to be a reluctant fighter against Russians. It is not a scene from real life—it is a scene from a play, a Hellman play. Whatever it was in 1969, Hellman did not feel it would interest *Collier's* readers in 1945.

There are a number of other additions to the later account, but one more variation in particular hints at Hellman's own alarm at the liberties she was taking with the record. According to her *Collier's* version, when she decides to return to Moscow from the front, the general she is then with, General Kusmean, bids her goodbye the night before her departure. He will not see her again as they are moving out early in the morning. They are going into Warsaw. Hellman asks if she can come along. The General laughs and says that if she will wait right here for a week, he will capture Warsaw and come back to get her for the victorious entrance into the city. Hellman declines, jokingly saying he might take more than a week. She then concludes the article by saying it was surely a coincidence, but precisely one week later the Red Army entered Warsaw.

In the account written in 1969, the bantering tone is dropped from this exchange. On the eve of her return to Moscow, the general sends Hellman a firm invitation to accompany him into Warsaw and *on to Berlin*. She awoke at six the next morning and wrote the general a note declining his offer, which, she said, she would remember all her life. She explained that she "hadn't the courage for such a journey, not in fear for my life, but in fear of my nature, and hoped that we would both live long enough for me to understand myself and be allowed, if that should happen, to explain it to him."

"Fear of my nature" is a jarring phrase for any reader who might already suspect he is knee-deep in one of the most troubling aspects of Hellman's nature—the Walter Mitty fantasies woven into an already interesting reality. What in her nature could have frightened her more than the risk of death at the hands of the Germans? Was it what she herself might do to the Germans if given a machine gun? Unlikely as that possibility may have been, it is even more unlikely that Hellman would have "feared" it.

Or perhaps her fear was more realistic: that if she permitted herself *in the memoir* to indulge the fantasy of marching with the Russians to Berlin, it would incite her into more grandiose fantasies, lacking even the slightest footing in reality and raising the specter of psychosis. It may be that Hellman is not writing her note of refusal to a Russian general, but to herself—saying, in effect, stop, leave it alone, you've gone far enough.

An Unfinished Woman was a best-seller and won the National Book Award for Arts and Letters. Hellman's accomplishment was remarkable. The memoirs of a playwright whose period of greatest success was thirty years earlier would not be a likely candidate for a best-seller. Such books emerge regularly, enjoy modest sales with libraries and theater buffs and then quietly disappear. While Hellman had not exactly created a new literary form, *An Unfinished Woman* bore more resemblance to a series of literary sketches than to an autobiography. Whatever the form, it suited her well, and it suited the public even better. Kermit Bloomgarden ran into Howard Bay about this time. "You've got to hand it to Lillian," Bloomgarden said. "Of all the big playwrights—Tennessee, Inge, Arthur Miller—none of them are going anywhere. She's the only one still doing something."

If Hammett's death had given Hellman the permission to be a celebrity, *An Unfinished Woman* made it official. Up to now Hellman was basically a theater name, little known to the nation at large. Now readers in Ohio and Texas were learning of the boardinghouse on Prytania Street, Sophronia, Hardscrabble Farm, her visit to the Russian front lines, her romantic liaison with Hammett. However begrudgingly, people had had to acknowledge her accomplishments as a playwright. Now they had to reckon as well with a personality who had led a life of rare glamour and excitement.

Hellman relished her broadened image. In April 1970 she attended a conference on the Far East in San Francisco sponsored by the Association for Asian Studies, sharing the dais with John Fairbank, then of Harvard, and her former lover, John Melby, whom she had arranged to meet for a sentimental reunion. In the next few years she regularly accepted lecture and teaching engagements; she chaired writing seminars at the University of California in Berkeley in 1970 and again in 1971. In the spring of 1971, she conducted similar month-long seminars at M.I.T., and at New York's Hunter College in 1972.

Since Hammett's death, Hellman had wrestled with the idea of writing a book about him, but could not arrive at an approach that made sense to her. At a party on Martha's Vineyard, she fell into a discussion about the dilemma with Thornton Wilder, who later wrote Hellman suggesting that she do a fictional portrait. She wrote back thanking him for the good idea and went on to ruminate about mixing fact with fiction: "I have been hampered, of course, by the truth, or what I thought was the need for it. (Maybe I only mean I can't imagine things that didn't happen with things that did.)" In a touching footnote to her letter, Hellman tells Wilder how pleased she was at their encounter, admitting to an uneasiness she has always felt regarding him. "I think I have always been shy with you," she wrote, "because I was so long ago impressed. Maybe hamburgers for just the two of us would cure that one day." She eventually abandoned the idea of writing further about Hammett.

During this period, she made a major change in her living arrangements. She sold the house on Eighty-second Street and, in the spring of 1970, moved into a tenth-floor co-op apartment at 630 Park Avenue at Sixty-fifth Street, which would remain her principal residence until she died. It had a large living room, a full dining room and two bedrooms, one of which Hellman turned into a workroom. She decorated the rooms with the same highly personal meld of period furniture, family items, relics from her plays and her travels, books everywhere, and many photographs—most conspicuously in the living room, one of herself as a child, one of Sophronia, and a large framed one of Hammett at his most dashing.

Even though Hellman was far less a Russia enthusiast than she had been, traces of her hostility to anti-Russianism remained. Shortly after the publication of *An Unfinished Woman*—and one year after the Russian invasion of Czechoslovakia—she wrote a scathing piece for *The New York Times* denouncing Russian political exile Anatoly V. Kuznetsov. While others in the West were applauding those Russians who found it insupportable to live under the oppressive Soviet system and had managed to get out, Hellman voiced her contempt for one who, according to her, was only interested in saving his own neck. He should have remained in Russia, she said, where his protests might have done some good.

It was yet another manifestation of her inconsistency where Russia was involved. Hellman herself, in her brush with the U.S. Government, had pleaded the Fifth Amendment and treated the House Committee with respect rather than denouncing it as other HUAC witnesses had done—and as she later said she wished she had done. Except for the implied protest in her famous letter to the House Committee, she had not "spoken out," her reason being fear of a brief jail sentence. When Kuznetsov had shown similar caution in Russia, where the danger and the punishment, as Hellman well knew, were far greater, she denounced him as a coward and a traitor. Brushing quickly past the terror and repressions that are the overriding message of Kuznetsov's story, she focused on what she saw as an ignoble response on his part. That she denounced this man, not at a Party meeting, but in the pages of *The New York Times,* shows she felt totally confident of the righteousness of her position. Again, it seems that when criticism of Russia or communism was involved, Hellman lost all ability to see parallels or maintain evenhandedness in making her moral judgments.

Over the years, Hellman, perhaps more than most celebrities, had built up a devoted network of powerful friends; one longtime Hellman associate, while acknowledging that collecting celebrities had always been an enthusiasm of Hellman's, believes it became a conscious campaign on her part as she grew increasingly concerned about the Vietnam war.

In the late 1960s she had little trouble enlisting those she wanted into her social stable, which became a holding tank for later service in her causes. For the political activists and pundits, such as those at the Princeton conference, her theater fame made her a welcome addition to their circles, or even better, their organizations' letterheads. Show-business celebrities venerated her, many for her feisty political stands, even more for her old-money status as a solid achiever in a profession increasingly populated by talk-show ephemerals. Underlying such opportunistic considerations was Hellman's powerful personal appeal, which she knew how to wield to win the affection of those she wanted to influence. With a dramatist's sense of the moment's requirements, she could be outspoken for an effect of shocking humor or winning candor, she could be harshly self-deprecating while bluntly flattering to others, and, with men, she could flirt shamelessly. Adding strength to those familiar wiles was her no-frills, dead-serious demeanor, which removed any suspicion that wiles were being used.

When under attack, Hellman was quick to rally the aid of her friends for a counterattack, to marshal her troops as she did when *The New York Times's* reviewer trashed her collected plays. When she found herself increasingly embattled in her final years, the need for such calls to arms grew, and the power and prestige of her troops grew as well. By her nature and by her friendships, she became no lady to trifle with. The use of the Hellman support network was by no means limited to personal disputes. She would take to the telephone over anything in the newspapers she found sufficiently upsetting. In 1970, she found herself increasingly alarmed at the abuses and excess of aggression of the FBI and the Justice Department in harassing dissenters from the Vietnam war.

Hellman took action. She set out to establish a committee of prominent figures who would serve as watchdogs to keep an eye on a government she felt was careening arrogantly out of control. In a short time she had over a hundred names for her committee, which was named the Committee for Public Justice. Making up the committee were such members of the Hellman inner circle as John Hersey, William Styron, Mike Nichols, Jerome Wiesner (president of M.I.T.) and Hannah Weinstein (a film producer who had become one of Hellman's closest friends). Also involved were a good number of lawyers, some of national prominence, and such concerned figures from the arts as Warren Beatty, Shirley MacLaine, Leonard Bernstein, Paul Newman, Robert Silvers (editor of *The New York Review of Books*) and Neil Simon.

The cartoonist Jules Feiffer was another Hellman friend enlisted into the organization. Later commenting on Hellman's feat, he said, "She got on the phone and brought together a group of lawyers and professors and writers and statesmen and a millionaire or two and formed the Committee for Public Justice. She chaired the meetings, helped raise the funds, got others to raise more funds, thrashed out agendas, and set up across the country a series of well-covered public meetings which described in detail the calculated erosion by the FBI, the CIA and the Justice Department on the First Amendment and other constitutional rights. No other writer I know would know how to do this. . . ."

At first Hellman took a rather inconspicuous role on the committee, and Roger Wilkins, then of the Ford Foundation, was named chairman. At a press conference held January 1, 1970, to announce the launching of the committee, former Attorney General Ramsey Clark told reporters the committee grew out of a shared belief that the United States was entering "a period of political repression." He named the FBI as its main target. When Wilkins resigned, Hellman shared the chairmanship with Orville Schell, but it was understood by everyone that the organization was her fiefdom. Hellman toured the country holding meetings and drumming up membership. To serve as bait for these events, she often enlisted one of the film stars, but in many cities Hellman and her cause were bait enough.

The committee had an early success with a conference on the FBI that was held at Princeton in 1971. With a Hellman flourish, an invitation was sent to J. Edgar Hoover, who huffily declined on the grounds that the questions the conference was raising were in themselves unpatriotic. But many prominent people attended, and the meetings got front-page treatment in American newspapers and were covered as well by the international press. With such victories, the committee attracted many bright and knowledgeable young people, a good number with legal and governmental experience. A newsletter was started called *Justice Department Watch* in which "invisible" actions were reported that could affect civil freedoms. When the Watergate scandal broke out in the summer of 1972, the Committee for Public Justice could point to precisely the kinds of power abuse it had been fighting for two years.

When Nixon resigned, Hellman's committee threw cold water on the self-congratulatory mood then prevalent among liberals by pointing out that Watergate should not have occurred in the first place and might have been prevented if the committee had started its work earlier and with more resources. Hellman hired as executive director of the committee a twenty-seven-year-old lawyer named Dorothy Samuels, who later brought interesting light on a second motive Hellman had for forming the committee. She was still obsessed, Samuels said, by what she considered the betrayal of other liberals during the McCarthy purges. Indeed, she would shortly start writing *Scoundrel Time* in which this was a major theme. "Lillian felt that similar repressions were at hand," Samuels said. "If the liberals had their names linked to a committee dedicated to fighting such governmental excesses, it would make it hard for them, when things got bad, to turn tail and run as she felt they had before."

Clever and well reasoned as that strategy may have been, it

conjures up an interesting picture of Hellman soliciting her friends over the phone to join her organization, explaining its high purpose, at the same time knowing that she was slyly blocking them from their more cowardly natures. It is tempting to speculate whether or not the distinguished names on the list, most of them friends of Hellman's, had any inkling that they were being outmaneuvered, checkmated in a sense, cajoled into Hellman's group so she could lock the door on them when the persecutions started up again.

Hellman was very much in favor of the committee's holding large, highly publicized functions, and in later years (the committee dissolved in 1982), when money was tight, that would become a running argument with other board members who felt the money was better spent on more substantive things like the Justice Department newsletter. "Lillian and Hannah (Weinstein) were all for renting Madison Square Garden and holding a monster rally," Samuels said. "We felt that was a waste of funds—as well as being from another era." Since most of the active members were lawyers, they were less for the showy, town-meeting approach to problems than for projects like the highly successful Justice Department newsletter and other projects with legal ramifications. Often Hellman and Hannah would try to dismiss such undertakings as "lawyers' issues."

Dorothy Samuels, while admiring Hellman, found her an extremely difficult boss. "She was always making dramas out of nothing. She would take things people had said and twist them around until they became dramas of some sort. Orville Schell finally resigned as her co-chairman. He couldn't take the bickering that Lillian thrived on. She got very down on Ray Calamaro, an executive director who preceded me. She was so nasty to him, we all thought he must have turned her down. Whatever it was that set her against him, he finally quit and went to work at the Justice Department.

"One day I got a frantic call from Lillian. I was to come to her place immediately. She had to talk with me. I was busy and asked if we couldn't talk over the phone. 'No,' she said tensely. 'This is too big for the phone.'

"I went over to her apartment. She had been in Washington, she told me, at a dinner party where she had been seated next to an official at Justice. She had asked him if a young lawyer who had worked for her committee could use that credit to land an important post with the Justice Department. Her dinner partner had said, No way. 'Don't you see?' Lillian told me. 'Ray was an FBI plant.'

"It was absurd. Among other reasons, Ray had many credits to qualify him for his new job, but because she didn't like him, Lillian didn't hesitate to jump to a wild conclusion and libel him in that way. It was incredible to see Lillian in action at the board meetings. She flirted and flattered the men, most of whom were important in their own right. When she was out to win someone over, first her body would change. She would take a position on the sofa, curl up her legs, a smile would come over her face and she'd purr, 'Well, Bob, you make such a good point, but . . .'

"At the same time she was horrible to me. She seemed to take a delight in beating up on me in front of the men. She'd go on and on about some little thing. She watched literally every penny that we spent and demanded accountings before the bills were in. She would be brutally rude and accusatory to me at these meetings. One day it got so bad that one of the men, Bob Silvers, came up to me afterwards and apologized. I told him that if it upset him, why didn't he speak up at the meetings? He said I was right. At the next meeting, Hellman started in again on me. Bob interrupted. 'Lillian,' he said, 'stop it.' She did." Silvers himself recalls his intercession as a milder one in which he defended Samuels by praising her work, but otherwise he affirms the story.

Subsequent administrators of the committee had similar tales of brutalization by Hellman, particularly Nancy Kramer and Betsy Seidman. Kramer recalls a fund-raiser at Leonard Bernstein's apartment at which Hellman asked her if she had performed a certain task. Kramer said she had. In front of about fifteen early arrivals Hellman screamed, "You're a liar!" Kramer, who was the organization's executive director and a lawyer, ran from the room too stunned and humiliated to reply. When Hellman learned that the task had indeed been carried out, she apologized, but, Kramer recalls, "gruffly and in front of no one."

Stephen Gillers, who served for a time in the same job, never had anything but the most civil relations with Hellman. When he resigned the job, he became a board member as well as a personal friend of Hellman's. Any suggestion of a sexist bias in her choice of victims is negated by Hellman's scathing treatment of the first director, Ray Calamaro. The development of Gillers's personal relationship with Hellman was typical of the kind of friendships she fostered more and more in her later years. Gillers would call and ask if he might come by to see her. An appointment would be made sometime in the next few days for a drink at her apartment and he would arrive, often with flowers, for a private conversation. Gillers recalls talking about a wide range of subjects—often political matters that touched on the committee's work, but just as often anything that happened to interest Hellman in the day's events or from what either of them was reading at the moment.

"I was very interested in Shakespeare at that time," Gillers later said. "Lillian and I would discuss his plays for hours. Her favorite, she told me, was *Coriolanus*; next was *King Lear*. She seemed to have an affinity for bereft or forsaken kings. Lillian was not an intellectual about politics, but she had an uncanny ability to define relationships between people and to put emotional issues into clear language.

"An extraordinary thing about Lillian," Gillers went on. "She never showed the slightest interest in my private life, never acknowledged that I might have one, in fact. For instance, during the period we were friendly, I divorced one wife and married another. Even though Lillian was with both on a number of social occasions, I don't think she noticed the change.

"I would sometimes cringe at the way she behaved to underlings. But everyone's a mixture. I loved her. She had a verve and a drive rarely seen even in young people."

For all of the committee's success and its support by people of considerable eminence, there was never a moment when it was anything but Hellman's show. Not only had it been her idea, it was she who attracted the names and raised the money. As a result, the others constantly had to contend with Hellman's whims and sudden concerns. One board member can remember Hellman's calling her in a frenzy to say the Committee for Public Justice should drop everything it was doing and devote itself to the problem of inflation, a subject that in no way related to the committee's announced agenda. It presents the humorous picture of Hellman, outraged at the new price of a can of coffee, whistling for her posse of corporate lawyers, college presidents and film stars to take immediate action.

While such impulses necessitated a good deal of talking Hellman out of a passing tempest, the committee kowtowed to her in other ways. Milton Gordon, a television tycoon and sometime Hellman escort, flew the committee's directors to Martha's Vineyard on a private plane for a meeting because that's where Hellman was at the time. Majestic in a large-brimmed hat and white linen dress, she greeted her board at the airport and took them to lunch at her house. Hellman had not only brought the underground into the sunlight, she had done it at a stylish resort.

The Committee for Public Justice initiated legislation and had many successes. But the most telling testimonial to the group's effectiveness came several years later from no less a source than a prime adversary, Richard Nixon. After he was forced from office, Nixon was called to testify in a suit brought by National Security aide Morton Halperin (also a member of Hellman's committee) against Henry Kissinger and others for tapping his phone. Nixon testified that wiretaps were used only when absolutely necessary because of J. Edgar Hoover's fear of public exposure; when they had discussed that fear, Nixon said, Hoover had mentioned the Committee for Public Justice conference on the FBI and the press coverage it had received. Few citizens' watchdog groups have ever received such an endorsement from such high quarters. If Nixon is to be believed, it seems that when Hellman and Hoover had stood eyeball to eyeball on Constitutional rectitude, Hoover blinked.

In a chain of causality even more bizarre, John Ehrlichman claimed that the Nixon White House had been "forced" to assemble the notorious "plumbers," because the wary Hoover refused to do the dirty work Nixon and his men deemed necessary. If the Committee for Public Justice was the cause of Hoover's newly found probity, a case could be made that Hellman and her group set into motion the events that culminated in Watergate.

26

THE MAJOR SWINGS in Lillian Hellman's life suggest a neat decade-frame outline: early success in the 1930s, consolidation of that success in the 1940s, the 1950s a low point, the fighting back to prominence during the 1960s and a triumphant 1970s with the final years of glory only partly marred by a crescendoing rumble of denigrators until her death in 1984. Hellman's reputation as a playwright was solid. Her reputation as a political heroine grew as the McCarthy-period dust settled and many looked back in dismay at the sorry record of official trampling on rights on one side and cowardice and villainy on the other. With the success of her first memoir, she also emerged as a woman of fascination and stature.

All these auspicious trends were ratified with the publication in 1973 of her second book of memoirs, *Pentimento,* a collection of portraits of people who had been important in Hellman's life. The book's reception was even stronger than that of *An Unfinished Woman* and it remained on the best-seller list for over four months. *Pentimento* based its claim for attention on the writing itself. With her first book, as with most memoirs, the public was attracted by a curiosity about the life story of a prominent figure. With her second, readers came to it because she was a writer people wanted to read. *Pentimento* moved Hellman solidly into a new area of prestige—that of literary figure. The early plays, rather than being the memoirs' *raison d'être* and wistful reminders of a talent she had lost, became a hard rock of achievement on which to build her new eminence as an author. She was now a successful writer of books, which, with her plays, gave a spread to her accomplishment that few writers achieve.

The most important reviewers were the most laudatory about *Pentimento*. Eliot Fremont-Smith cited the book's "extraordinary richness and candor and self-perception." John Leonard in *The New York Times Book Review* said "the whole shines with a moral intelligence, a toughness of character, that inspires even as it entertains, and the prose is as tough as an electron microscope." Christopher Lehmann-Haupt in the daily *Times* said the portraits of others "add up to nothing less than a portrait of Miss Hellman, an autobiography of her soul." Richard Poirier in the *Washington Post* wrote that *Pentimento* marked one of the rare occasions "when the moral value of a book is wholly inextricable from its immense literary worth."

While the acclaim of such critics all but assured a best-seller, they were, with their praise for *Pentimento* on literary grounds, tacit sponsors for Hellman's provisional acceptance in the highbrow world she had never been able to achieve with her plays. Although her entrance into intellectual Valhalla was marred by the sound of gnashing of teeth from those who in some way found her talent or her image lacking, many of the anointed welcomed her as one of their own, henceforth to be praised and attacked as an equal.

Hellman constructs *Pentimento* around portraits of four people who were important in her life; her cousin Bethe, her Uncle Willy, her friend Julia, and her lover Arthur Cowan. There is a long section called "Theatre" which briefly sketches elements of her life connected with each of her plays (and seems to have been written in response to the many critics of the first book who complained of the lack of such information). The book concludes with a story called "Turtle" about a snapping turtle trapped by her and Hammett whose refusal to die causes Hellman to think about the nature of life.

There has been much comment about the ingenuity (and modesty) of Hellman's writing about others as a way of portraying herself. But with the exception of Arthur Cowan, there is little reason to believe her characters are the "subjects" of their sections even though Hellman entitles them with their names: "Bethe," "Willy" and "Julia." These stories are about Hellman first and foremost, and an aspect of her development centers around her relationship with each. "Bethe" is the story of Hellman's awakening sexuality; "Willy" is Hellman's first love; "Julia" is a story of Hellman's being inspired to a heroic action by her heroic friend, Julia. In none of these tales do the other characters emerge with any sharpness, except for Arthur Cowan, who appears to be the only one Hellman set out to portray. Whatever vividness the others have—and this is particularly true of Julia—comes more from the exotic bare facts of their resumés rather than any precision of observation on Hellman's part.

Instead of trying to create deft portraits of memorable individuals, Hellman's purpose seems to have been to show the influence three people had on her life and development. In the chapter many regard as the book's finest and most gripping, the Julia story, Julia's splendid qualities—courage, altruism, awareness—are givens. The pivotal character is Hellman, who is faced with the dilemma of disrupting a comfortable high-life existence to run a dangerous mission as an act of loyalty to an old friend. The camera is at all times on Hellman, with Julia hovering in the background never quite in focus. It is a fine, even brilliant, way to write a memoir. What is odd is the number of people who were misled by the chapter headings into thinking Hellman was avoiding herself as a subject and concentrating on others.

"Turtle" is a perplexing story that suggests heavy-duty symbolism and major themes. Hellman is delightfully self-mocking in her attempts to broach these larger themes to Hammett, but finally the reader tends to side with Hammett in his suggestion that Hellman leave the subject alone. Still, the story is a charming and amiable portrayal of an intellectually curious person grappling with serious questions and being frustrated in her failure to get anywhere with them.

At the book's start, there is a twelve-line explanation of the title. "Pentimento" is the image that shows through on an oil painting when the surface paint becomes transparent with age; it is an earlier painting that the artist "repented" and painted over. It is a lovely image for a memoirist's attempt to get at the past, both as it originally happened and as it had been painted over at a later time. That Hellman herself would raise the concept of two truths, "what was there for me once, what is there for me now"—indeed, imbed it in her one-word title—is highly ironic in light of the later charge that her books were distortions of the truth, not because of the many obfuscations of time, but because, like a painter, Hellman repented "the old conception," that is to say, reality.

The honors and awards increased as Hellman approached and entered her seventies. She received Ph.D.s from Yale, Smith and Columbia. Her Alma Mater, New York University, honored her with a Woman of the Year award. She was appointed to the editorial board of *American Scholar*. A half-million-dollar offer was made for the film rights for her two memoirs, which Mike Nichols wanted to compress into one film. Hellman at first accepted the offer, but then canceled when she learned she would not be given final editing rights. Nichols had become a close friend and she had no difficulty in trusting him to translate her life faithfully to the screen; the problem arose when she learned that Nichols could be replaced on the project. She said she could not run the risk of abandoning her characters—Julia, Bethe, Willy, her parents, Hammett—to an unknown quantity. She also voiced concern that her personal story might be distorted. "My own life," she said, "is more important to me than money. It is a question of moral responsibility." Her refusal of a half million 1976 dollars would seem to substantiate that boast.

A high point of the pro-Hellman ground swell was a gala evening in her honor to benefit the Committee for Public Justice. The event, which was held at the Circle-in-the-Square Theater in Greenwich Village, would center around a dinner, speeches and scenes from Hellman's plays. From a fund-raising point of view, the idea was excellent, since Hellman was now strong "box office" and the organization would have no trouble lacing the room not just with celebrities, but the caliber of celebrities that Hellman endorsed.

As was her custom, Hellman went over the guest list—some 5,000 names—with a political Geiger counter and eliminated several people for low marks during the McCarthy period. She also wanted to eliminate Jacqueline Onassis on the grounds that she didn't want the evening to be *"that* kind of event." (The invitation had already gone out.) Hellman vetoed the selection of a major film star—a friend of hers—as a performer in a dramatic scene from one of her plays because he "wasn't a good enough actor." Even when being canonized, Hellman's theatrical professionalism took precedence.

The event was helpful to the Committee for Public Justice, but it was a triumph for Hellman. The press started talking about the evening days in advance, columnists fought for interviews with Hellman, and the following day the celebrity-heavy gathering was given broad newspaper and television coverage. The evening itself went smoothly until the speeches began and the self-stimulated crowd lost interest in the remarks of M.I.T. President Jerome Wiesner and resumed their chattering. Hellman, outraged that one of her most distinguished friends should be affronted by film stars, directors and other such riffraff, grabbed the microphone, stood on a table, and sharply told everyone to shut up. Then as she was climbing down, she said in a voice everyone could hear, "Drunken bastards."

Leonard Bernstein turned to the person sitting next to him and said, "Now *that* was vintage Hellman."

After the scenes from Hellman plays were performed, there was a picture-taking session. While photographers were arranging their subjects, Warren Beatty happened to arrive. The photographers seized him and pushed him before the cameras. Seeing him appear at her side, Hellman rasped, "Warren! You didn't do a goddamn thing for any of this, yet you show up in time to have your picture taken. Typical!"

Without saying a word, Beatty grabbed the five-foot-three Hellman in a bear hug, lifted her into the air and held her aloft, her feet dangling. She looked down at him—frail, wrinkled, seventy—and said, "If you only knew how wonderful it was to be held in your arms."

As a gesture of appreciation for allowing the free use of their theater for the fund-raiser, Hellman sent the theater's two owners a case of wine, then almost immediately asked Dorothy Samuels to reimburse her for the cost—$160. In the aftermath confusion, Samuels forgot. Hellman did not. She reminded her several times, raising the possibility that Samuels, perhaps subconsciously, wanted to see how far she would go to collect or if she would drop the matter. For Hellman, all other work of the Committee for Public Justice ceased—FBI abuses, CIA invasions of privacy, wiretapping atrocities—until she got a check for $160.

Few writers ever live to receive an outpouring of love and respect such as Lillian Hellman received that night. While such testimonials, along with the other honors and attention she was receiving, might have mollified some writers and helped them to forgive earlier grievances, Hellman saw her new affluence and prestige as a strong base from which to settle old scores. She would shortly publish *Scoundrel Time,* an account of her persecution twenty years earlier by the House Committee on Un-American Activities and her abandonment by those she thought were her allies. Bygones were not to be bygones.

The writer Peter Feibleman had become increasingly important to Hellman in the post-Hammett years. Thirty years her junior, as a child he had known Hellman in New Orleans, and he resolved to become her friend when he returned from having lived in Europe a number of years with several novels under his belt. In the book about food he and Hellman wrote together shortly before she died, *Eating Together,* which is really a memoir of their friendship, he talks frankly of pursuing a gruffly disinterested Hellman, softening her toward him with expensive dinners, and finally getting her to accept him in her life.

Feibleman became the closest companion of Hellman's last years. They visited back and forth between his Los Angeles home and her East Coast ones, they assisted one another in their work, traveled together, spoke outrageously to one another and fought like longshoremen. But overriding the welter of improbabilities in the friendship was a binding element: they were enormously amused by each other. Another man with whom Hellman became close in those years was Blair Clark, a television news executive who was active in a number of liberal organizations.

In a 1973 interview with Gloria Emerson in *The New York Times,* Hellman turned pensive about growing old. She had lost her capacity for anger, she said. Then, on reflection, she realized she hadn't lost it altogether. "Last week I hit a boy with an umbrella." Hellman was being coy. Her capacity for tantrums and raging battles was still very much alive. She had terminal blowups with many who had been close to her, and more often than not the fights were about money. Such a fight ended her relations with Arthur Kober's daughter, Catherine, to whom Hellman had always been "Aunt Lillian." At one time during her difficult childhood, there was talk of Cathy's going to live with Hellman.

Many years later Catherine Kober inherited, through a legal fluke, $10,000 from Max Hellman's will. The sum had been left to Arthur Kober, from whom Max had borrowed money from time to time; with Kober dead, the money went to his daughter. Catherine, who had recently married, discussed with Hellman what she should do with the money and got Hellman's approval to put it toward a new house she and her husband were about to buy. That plan fell through when her marriage ended. Some time passed and Catherine then told Hellman she was going to give the $10,000 to charity and decided on the American Foundling Hospital. Hellman was not against the money's going to a good cause, but was firm that the good cause could only be her Committee for Public Justice. Catherine balked. Hellman yelled. When Kober went ahead with her intentions, she received a vitriolic letter from Hellman with lines like "You have no moral right to that money" and "You are a terrible person." It was clear that Hellman wanted to terminate their relationship over the matter, which hurt Catherine deeply. She later sought ways of patching things up with her "aunt" but could arrive at nothing she thought workable.

Another of those flash rages Hellman could sail into without a thought to consequences involved Arthur Kober, who, for many summers before his death, visited his old friend Nan Werner on Martha's Vineyard. As his birthday often fell during the visit, Mrs. Werner began the tradition of giving Kober a large party, at which Hellman would always be present. At one particularly festive birthday party, author Richard Crighton read a poem he had written for the occasion, a doggerel summary of Kober's life.

The verses were funny and the group was enjoying them heartily. Touching on the Hollywood years when Kober was married to Hellman, the poem referred to her wearing the pants in the family. Hellman went into a rage. The line was totally untrue. It was malicious. It was contemptible. Despite many attempts from Crighton and others to mollify her, to assure her no harm was meant, Hellman said she could not stay at a party with a person who could make such a vulgar, dishonest slur. Her storming out not only ruined the party, it forced the two guests who had brought her, John and Barbara Hersey, to leave as well.

On the surface at least, the other guests, the cream of Martha's Vineyard's affluent brains, were aghast at Hellman's behavior. But behind the tongue-clucking at such unseemly deportment may have been a secret admiration for one who was able to vent fury, however unreasonably, when every social convention forbade it. Chimpanzees come to be leaders of their colony by noisy, angry and unprovoked "displays." The power Hellman had over her circle was surely based on the respect given her talent, her intelligence and her pluck, but an element of her sovereignty must also be found in her almost unique ability to make scenes, her fearful "displays." In her public dealings, her litigious bent commanded the awe and fear of those she encountered; on a private level, her propensity for furious explosions had a similar effect.

As Arthur Kober grew older, he had the strong impression that Hellman's warmth toward him had cooled, that she was less available to him. He would write her when he was going to be on the Vineyard and get no reply. When Nan Werner urged him to phone her, he would say, "No, I'll wait till she calls." Some of Kober's friends suspected Hellman's unfriendliness resulted from his drop in status. His one Broadway success was forgotten and his stories no longer appeared in *The New Yorker*. But outsiders were too quick to write off the friendship. When he was in Lenox Hill Hospital dying of cancer, Werner came into his room for a visit to find Hellman sitting by the bed holding Kober's hand. "Arthur had the most beatific smile on his face," Werner said. "It was a beautiful picture, very touching. I mumbled something about coming back later, but Lillian said she was just leaving."

Cathy Kober points out how loyal Hellman had been to her

mother, Kober's second wife, when she was dying of a lingering illness. Maggie Kober had been a particular favorite of Hammett's and the two households had been close during the Hardscrabble Farm period, but later were seeing far less of each other. But when Maggie Kober's illness became grave, "Lillian was right there and stuck by my mother," Cathy said, and then, thinking it over, added, "In some ways Lillian was a foul-weather friend."

Hellman's fury could be roused by a slight at a checkout counter, a child stepping on her foot or an adult brushing against her in a crowd. Sometimes it escalated from a verbal disagreement. Hellman's friends knew that when, in a dinner-table discussion, she said, "Excuse me, but . . ." in a particular icily controlled tone, it signaled major trouble. Hellman was well aware that her anger was a problem. She told interviewer Marilyn Berger that she had invented an imaginary character, Nursie, whose function it was to keep her calm. When she got upset, teetering on a tantrum, Nursie would tell her to play a set of tennis or take a hot bath. That helped for a time until Hellman began turning her rage on Nursie.

Hellman reported that one night at her house on Martha's Vineyard, her close friend Peter Feibleman was awakened by shouts coming from her room. Convinced she was fighting off an intruder, he rushed to her room to find Hellman alone. "Don't mind me," she said brightly. "I'm just having a fight with Nursie."

Relations apparently grew so strained between Nursie and Hellman that she had to invent a third character, Madam, who would mediate between them.

Although some of Hellman's outbursts at people around her could be excruciating, others could be quite endearing. She was on her way to a Hollywood party with Peter Feibleman, who told her that, if she didn't mind, they would stop and give a lift to superagent Sue Mengers. Hellman said fine. When Mengers got into the car, she gushed over Hellman: she told her how much she had always wanted to meet her, how she admired her. So great was her admiration, in fact, she had just quoted Hellman to Newsweek.

"Oh, really," said Hellman. "How?"

Mengers explained that the magazine was asking her about her friend David Begelman, the head of Columbia Pictures, then in disgrace for having embezzled studio funds. *Newsweek* wanted to know if their friendship would survive the scandal. "I told them of course it would, that I do not cut my friends to fit this year's fashion."

Hellman erupted. "You did what? How dare you use my line for that third-rate crook? I said that about fine people who were in serious trouble, who were persecuted. You would put that slob in their category? . . ." And much more in the same vein. Hellman got so worked up she began hitting Mengers with her handbag.

If her capacity for rage was still in working order, so was her appetite for fun. In the words of one friend, Hellman was "festive oriented." Her approach to fun was not spontaneous, but usually carefully planned. In fact, she seemed to relish making plans as much as carrying them out. If it wasn't a lunch or a dinner party, it was a weekend in Cambridge, a Martha's Vineyard house party, a Lucullan beach picnic or a trip to California.

Hellman loathed the cold weather and spent the last ten winters of her life in Los Angeles. Since she had never much liked Southern California, she kept trying to find a warm alternative. In the winter of 1974, Hellman, together with her old friends Albert and Frances Hackett, rented a house in Sarasota, Florida, for a good part of the winter. S. J. Perelman was to spend the winter with them, but left after a few weeks, describing the stay to Ruth Goetz as a "nightmare." He couldn't take Hellman's bossiness, it seems, and said that her spicy New Orleans cooking made him sick. The Hellman-Perelman friendship was, in fact, complicated by some forty-year-old scars: Hammett had once had a brief affair with Perelman's wife, Laura.

Albert Hackett remembers the sojourn with amusement, but it apparently was not enough of a success for Hellman to repeat it. She made an exploratory trip to Key West where the Wilburs, the Herseys, the Lashes and a number of her other Martha's Vineyard friends had winter homes. She liked it enough to give local hotel owner David Wolkowsky a $500 down payment on an apartment for the following winter, but when the time approached she decided her eyesight, which had been deteriorating, was too bad to undertake unfamiliar terrain.

In New York Hellman was seen more and more in the company of young single men with a leaning toward the sort of outrageousness that produced the hearty Hellman belly laugh. Rumors circulated that she pressed some of the closer of these good-times companions into amatory service. Robert Brustein speculates that they, in turn, saw in her the stern yet nurturing-with-home-cooking mother. But with or without such Freudian allurements, they also saw in her a woman of monumental fame who was funny, unpredictable, exhilarating company. At a small dinner with some of these cronies, one of the company persuaded Hellman to smoke marijuana. The evening was a raucous success, and when Hellman was dropped off at her Park Avenue building at about 2 A.M., her companions were astounded to look back from the car to see her emerge from the apartment building and start walking down Park Avenue. Before they could decide how to stop the elderly Hellman from heading off into the night, the building's doorman chased after her and brought her back.

27

WITH THE DEATH of Arthur Cowan in 1964, Hell-
man would not again involve herself in romantic affairs. Her es-
corts—Blair Clark, Peter Feibleman, Milton Gordon—were now
close friends, the friendships uncomplicated by erotic compo-
nents despite the inevitable rumors to the contrary. She would
often be conspicuously present at a Broadway opening or lunch at
Le Cirque or the Four Seasons with her good friend Hannah
Weinstein, where the two diminutive women, enveloped in mink,
hair freshly coiffed, would appear to be the pampered wives of
successful businessmen idly filling their days, rather than an important film producer and a famous author about to rock the nation's intellectual establishment with her new book.

Scoundrel Time is a slim volume, 121 pages by Hellman and
a thirty-four-page introduction by Garry Wills. Early in the text,
Hellman makes clear that the book does not claim to be a history
of the McCarthy period or even a polemic on the issues; she will
instead limit herself to an account of her experiences as an unwilling witness. Even that account takes up only a portion of the
book and is fleshed out with flashbacks about her political history
and flash-forwards about the aftereffects of her HUAC encounter.

Its modest scope is punctuated by two or three judgmental statements, terse and angry, about the behavior of others during the crisis. The invective is never aimed at those on the opposite side of the hearing table, who are dismissed with contemptuous asides, but rather at fellow liberals who, in Hellman's eyes, betrayed the most minimal standards of liberal honor by not coming to the defense of the harassed.

If Hellman's book is limited in its ambitions, Garry Wills redresses the balance in his grandiose introduction, which surveys and adjudicates the world situation since the conclusion of World War II. Wills's view of Russia as the innocent victim of Washington's—and particularly Harry Truman's—malevolent designs produces a picture of befuddled passivity on the part of the Russians that even the Kremlin would have trouble accepting. The result is so far from prevailing views of reality and so condescending to those who don't view it as he does (including, on certain matters, Hellman) that it approaches the messianic. After Wills's thirty-four pages of breathtaking revisionism, Hellman's narrowed focus and reserved tone is as welcome as the calm that follows an epileptic fit—and indeed that may have been her motive in enlisting Wills. She vividly evokes the fear she understandably felt at facing the committee, her determination not to let her fear induce her to take a course that would later cause her shame, and her relief at getting through the ordeal with body and honor intact.

In her general political observations, Hellman claims not to have been a political person. She also claims to have been wrong about Stalin and for too long to have mistakenly denied his "many sins." (Her use of that word, "sins," is in itself interesting, since, to a free spirit like Hellman, a sin is something forbidden by wrongheaded authority, something harmless and pleasurable like overeating or sleeping with your neighbor; to have it also encompass the murder of several million Russians would seem to be overtaxing three letters.) The offhand nonchalance with which she dismisses forty years of rigorous Stalinism is so stunning, it obscures the guarded partiality of her disavowal. The deceased and discredited Stalin is all she renounces—not Russia, and not communism. Neither does she offer any information about when she changed her mind or what caused the change. Both are subjects of more than passing interest about a woman whose unshakable devotion to the Stalinist cause made up a good portion of her identity in the eyes of the public.

In other actions during the late 1960s and 1970s Hellman took a stand against Russia's treatment of writers, but nowhere in *Scoundrel Time*, her political testament—or anywhere else for that matter—does she find fault with other aspects of the Kremlin's policies, policies that posed considerable problems for most liberals. The harassment of Jews would be one example, the crushing of the Hungarian revolution another. Even her offhand admission that perhaps Stalin was not an admirable leader came twenty years after a Soviet premier had denounced him to the world as a murderous criminal. If the book raises more questions about Hellman's politics than it answers, and if many of her facts are debatable, few could argue with its dominant thrust: the McCarthy period was a shameful one for the United States, and Hellman faced with courage and dignity an ordeal that she should not have been forced to face.

Scoundrel Time was published in March 1976, and the reviews were almost without exception highly laudatory, both for the book and for the Hellman portrayed in its pages. It shot immediately onto the best-seller list, where it remained for twenty-three weeks. During this same period, the honors and awards for Hellman and interest in her work increased markedly. *The Autumn Garden* enjoyed a much praised revival at the Long Wharf Theater in New Haven. In May Hellman received an honorary Ph.D. from Columbia University (despite her *Scoundrel Time* slam at a Columbia icon, the late Lionel Trilling) and delivered the commencement address at Mount Holyoke College. In August she was awarded the prestigious MacDowell Medal for her contribution to literature.

The denunciations of *Scoundrel Time* were slow in arriving. Except for a few bilious reviews in the small periodicals, those who would later become so hostile to the book—the liberal intellectuals Hellman attacks—did not at first pay much attention to it. What caused alarm was its remarkable success and the growing possibility that it would become the accepted version of the McCarthy period. Everybody is entitled to his opinion, the thinking seems to have been, until that opinion threatens to harden into orthodoxy.

The opening shot came from Murray Kempton in *The New York Review of Books*. He generally liked the book and admired Hellman but considered her "inclined to be a hanging judge of the motives of persons whose opinions differed from her own." In a footnote Kempton showed his only anger at Hellman: for characterizing his friend James Wechsler as a friendly witness. But eventually a barrage of refutation—almost an anti-Hellman cottage industry—surged forth from several quarters. It was an all but unprecedented outpouring of political argument and analysis of a book which, except for Wills's preface, contained none of its own.

The irony is larger than just the absence of political discourse in *Scoundrel Time*. Nowhere in Hellman's prodigious output was there ever polemical writing as such. The characters in her plays who make ethical or political pronouncements are never countered, as they would be in the plays of Shaw or Ibsen, by articulate spokesmen for opposing views. In *The Children's Hour* Karen lectures an abject and shattered Mrs. Tilford; Kurt Muller lectures his worshipful children, and so on. On the relatively rare occasions when Hellman offers her views, dialogue ceases and the soapbox appears.

Her memoirs tend to avoid even such one-sided arguments, but in the few snappish sentences that precede her harsh judgments she rarely alludes to the existence of opposing positions, although she is, like any author, ideally situated to rebut them or denounce them as false. Instead, Hellman doesn't acknowledge the existence of possible rationales for opposing positions, but sees only self-interest or perfidy. On one of the few occasions in *Scoundrel Time* when she does explain the thinking behind her position, she stumbles quite badly. Illustrating the kind of injustices anticommunist hysteria can lead to, she cites the Pumpkin Papers of the Alger Hiss trial.

"Facts are facts," writes Hellman, "and one of them is that a pumpkin, in which Chambers claims to have hidden the damaging evidence against Hiss, deteriorates. . . ."

Hellman uses this homey observation to wrap up a case that

kept many lawyers busy for over a year and, thirty-five years and two trials later, is still not solved to everyone's satisfaction. The most elementary knowledge of the case would have told her that Chambers claimed only to have placed the microfilms in the pumpkins *the night before* he handed them over to the prosecutors. The error is uncharacteristically careless of Hellman in her writing, but it suggests how casually she examined the charges of communist misconduct before deciding, as she invariably did, that they were false.

Most of the outrage against *Scoundrel Time* centered around two brief sections. In the first, Hellman accuses the liberals of "joining" McCarthy, and it also contains as an aside one of her few denunciations of Stalin: "Many of them [the American intellectuals] found in the sins of Stalin Communism—and there were plenty of sins and plenty that for a long time I mistakenly denied—the excuse to join those who should have been their hereditary enemies. Perhaps that, in part, was the penalty of nineteenth-century immigration. The children of timid immigrants are often remarkable people: energetic, intelligent, hardworking; and often they make it so good they are determined to keep it at any cost." And later, after accusing the intellectuals of failing to speak out against McCarthy, she wrote: "None of them, as far as I know, has yet found it a part of conscience to admit their Cold War anti-Communism was perverted, possibly against their wishes, into the Vietnam War and then into the reign of Nixon, their unwanted but inevitable leader."

It indicates much about Hellman's stature, even with her enemies, that her few quick judo chops in *Scoundrel Time* eventually provoked such an avalanche of well-researched indignation from such formidable intellects. The first all-out attack came from Harvard historian Nathan Glazer, who wrote an essay on *Scoundrel Time* for *Commentary*. At the outset he denied strenuously that the anticommunist left had been silent about McCarthyism. Glazer cited numerous examples of writing against McCarthy, including some of his own, adding that "to be forced to defend oneself in this way is no less demeaning than being forced to sign a loyalty oath."

Glazer was particularly angered that Hellman should attack liberals or anyone else for failing to come to the defense of basic liberties. Having denied her charge on the basis of fact, he questioned Hellman's credentials for even raising the issue, pointing to her participation in the 1949 Waldorf Conference. He wrote: "I thought then—and I think now—that the defense of freedom required one to expose the Communist organizers of this meeting, required one to demonstrate the obscenity of speaking of world peace under the auspices of a movement whose leaders ran a huge system of slave camps for dissenters, who extirpated even the most modest efforts at independence of mind, who just about then were executing the leading Jewish poets and writers of Russia (even though those poets and writers had served them well). What was Lillian Hellman doing in that company?"

Glazer pointed to the alarming spread of communism internationally at the time of McCarthy, then moved to the more complex problem of communist incursions in American institutions—not the colleges and film studios which the headline-hunting Congressmen thrived on—but organizations like the NAACP and the CIO, which quietly battled to prevent communist takeovers. These issues, said Glazer, "disappear" in Hellman's account. "She can find no justification for a public concern about communism." As for the people who testified before the committee, Glazer said that, for all but the Party members, who were told what to do, there was an array of reasons, often complex, for testifying or not testifying. "Even this minimal degree of complexity disappears in Lillian Hellman's account," he wrote. All who testified were simply villains only interested in saving their careers.

Irving Howe then joined the fray, writing for *Dissent*. He made many of the same points Glazer made, but focused on different aspects for his greatest outrage. Referring to Hellman's sentence claiming Nixon and the Vietnam war were the unavoidable results of anticommunism, he said, "It is an astonishing sentence with gaps in the argument through which battalions of historical complications could march." Howe joined Glazer in scoring Hellman (and Wills) for denying there was any communist threat in the 1950s, stressing particularly their failure to mention the Russian invasion of Czechoslovakia in 1948. "It would be like writing a study of the upheavals of the late 1960s without mentioning the Vietnam war!"

Howe also pointed out that the man who saved Hellman at

the time of her HUAC ordeal was Joe Rauh, a pillar of the anti-communist left, of which she and Garry Wills are so scornful. (Rauh himself says, "Not just me, everybody who helped her, Abe Fortas, Stanley Isaacs—we were all of the anticommunist left.") Howe had numerous other complaints, and he ended his piece with an answer to one of Hellman's main *Scoundrel Time* themes: while having been mistaken in "taking too long to see what was going on in the Soviet Union, I do not believe we did our country any harm" (and the McCarthyites did). Howe wrote:

DEAR LILLIAN HELLMAN,

You could not be more mistaken. Those who supported Stalinism and its political enterprises, either here or abroad, helped befoul the cultural atmosphere, helped bring totalitarian methods into trade unions, helped perpetrate one of the great lies of the century, helped destroy whatever possibilities there might have been for a resurgence of serious radicalism in America. Isn't that harm enough?

The most full-blown counterattack against Hellman came from Sidney Hook, the New York University philosophy professor and a pioneer among the anticommunist intellectuals who had stormed the Waldorf Conference when denied the opportunity to speak. A high point of his twelve-page fusillade was a catalogue of Stalin's "sins" that he said Hellman either defended or condoned with silence. They provide a handy directory to the historic events that kept the pro- and anti-Stalinists so bitterly opposed for so many years:

> Moscow purge trials
> Deportations and resulting famine in the Ukraine
> The Nazi-Soviet Pact
> The invasion of Poland and the destruction of the
>   Baltic States
> The invasion of Finland
> The 1940 surrender to Hitler of German Jewish communists who had fled Germany in 1933
> The execution of two Jewish antifascist leaders as
>   "spies for Hitler"

The Katyn massacre of Polish officers
The mass execution of returning Russian prisoners
  of war
The overthrow of the Czech democratic government
The Zhdanov purges
The Berlin blockade
The crushing of the Hungarian revolution
The Berlin Wall
The incarceration of dissenters in insane asylums

Hook capped his catalogue of Soviet atrocities with the lament that Hellman failed to speak out against Soviet anti-Semitism when "even the American Communist party, the most supine of the Kremlin's pensioners, had shown enough independence to make a feeble protest. . . ." Hook charged that Hellman's account of her HUAC appearance was "a compound of falsity and deliberate obfuscation." Many others, he wrote, had made the same offer to the committee: to reveal all about themselves provided they did not have to speak about anyone else. There was no justification for Hellman's taking the Fifth, he said, if she had not been a communist.

Hook reached a climax of indignation when he addressed Hellman's charge that liberals had joined forces with McCarthy from fear or opportunism. While other liberals could deny ever having "joined" McCarthy, Hook didn't deny an affinity of purpose, mainly to expose the communist danger, but resented the implication of jumping onto a hysterical bandwagon. His reason: he and others had been fighting communism for many years before McCarthy came on the scene.

Hook would make somewhat of a hobby of Hellman-baiting. He gleefully pounced on an exchange between Dan Rather and Hellman on a *60 Minutes* interview a short time later. Rather asked why she was so quick to criticize her own country, yet had never criticized Russia. Hellman replied that Russia's leaders had never done anything to her; she lived here and not there. "She didn't live in Spain," Hook observed, "yet she criticized Franco; she didn't live in Germany yet she criticized Hitler . . ." Hook went on to string out his rebuttal as if to savor to the fullest his crystalline logic, which he felt fully exposed Hellman's lack of it.

While no one did such a detailed job of rebutting *Scoundrel Time* as Hook, his essay did not approach the effect of an article that ran in *The New York Times*—surely the reason for its greater impact—by Hilton Kramer in October 1976. Kramer commented on the number of recent resurrections of the McCarthy period: two films (Woody Allen's *The Front* and a documentary, *Hollywood on Trial*), an off-Broadway play based on HUAC transcripts, *Are You Now or Have You Ever Been,* by Eric Bentley, and several books, including *Scoundrel Time.* Kramer accused almost all these works of revisionism and of bending history to accommodate the current liberal prejudices of the post-Watergate, post-Vietnam years. It was for Hellman, however, that he reserved the most scorn: "Who could guess reading the soigné prose of *Scoundrel Time* that Miss Hellman was once one of the most vigorous public defenders of those [Stalin] 'sins' which even Khrushchev did not hesitate to call crimes. . . ." Kramer then spoke about "the other blacklist . . . the one that Woody Allen will certainly never make a movie about" through which anticommunist liberals were barred by communist pressure from editing and teaching jobs. As to why many liberals did not come to the defense of Hellman and others, Kramer quoted *Partisan Review* editor William Phillips: "Some *were* communists and what one was being asked to do was to defend their right to lie about it. . . ."

Finally, one of the angriest responses to *Scoundrel Time* came from the eminent critic Alfred Kazin, who groaned in *Esquire* that "fact and reason won't prevail against the public that ignorantly swallowed *Scoundrel Time* as the last word on McCarthyism." Kazin later said the book was "historically a fraud, artistically a put-up job and emotionally packed with meanness."

The whole conundrum of Lillian Hellman's politics is rather like the ambiguity-induced dilemma in *The Children's Hour.* What is under discussion: two heterosexual women wrongly accused of lesbianism, or two lesbians wrongly persecuted for their condition? While many aspects of a life are nobody's business, life held out for judgment, as Karen's and Martha's lives were in *The Children's Hour,* and as Hellman's was in her memoirs, has a better chance at a fair verdict if the jurors know what's what. Was Hellman a communist, or wasn't she? If she was not a communist, an examination of her record reveals a strongly unbalanced ethical sense, an extremely faulty memory and a remarkable capacity to ignore facts. She also emerges as irresponsibly determined to remain uninformed, and brutally unfair in her judgments. And worst of all, underneath the stern, judgmental nature, one begins to perceive the outlines of an erratic emotionalism that is sharply at variance with the cool, muscular intelligence Hellman projects.

Her political postures—and that would include her silences almost more than her stated positions—take on a much needed logic if it is assumed that Hellman was a Party member. They are also far easier to reconcile with an image of Hellman as a person of integrity. Other obvious problems with that assumption—her occasional deviations from Party line—disappear if it is further assumed she enjoyed a customized membership that loosened the discipline.

As just one example of how Hellman's actions take on a more logical complexion: if she decries unconstitutional legal actions against communists but cheers the same actions against Trotskyites or even KKK members, she emerges as either unintelligent or unprincipled. If, however, she was a communist engaged in a struggle for an order beyond the Constitution and democratic processes, then such a stand has a logic and an ethic that transcend what is being admitted openly. For her to decry violations of a Constitution she would like to discard may be viewed as cynical, but not stupid, or, in the Communist party context, not unprincipled.

Making sense of so many of Hellman's attitudes and actions is perhaps the strongest evidence of her longtime Party allegiance. Of course there is much additional evidence. Her FBI file runs to nearly a thousand pages; much of it is repetitious, much of it innocuous—the kind of communist-front participation in which many noncommunists became involved. But there is also a substantial amount that, if believed, places Hellman squarely in the Party.

In addition to the well-known testimony of Martin Berkeley, three other informants claimed knowledge of Hellman's Party membership, among them the former managing editor of the *Daily Worker*, Louis Budenz, who said that since he joined the Party in 1937, he had been told of Hellman's membership and her availability to him, as an editor, to support Party causes. A man who worked with Hellman on her Committee for Public Justice told others that his father remembers Hellman at Party meetings, "not as a silent tag-along with Hammett as she writes in her memoirs, but taking charge as she does with the meetings of our committee."

While assignment of Hellman to Communist party membership clears up many questions and anomalies about her positions over the years, it also raises other questions. Why would she have lied about it? Many distinguished people admitted to former Party membership and retained places of honor and respect in America. Hammett made no secret of it. As for danger, no rank and file Party member, however illustrious, was ever prosecuted under the Smith Act and no ordinary American communist ever felt threatened by specific governmental punishment such as dissenters receive regularly in other countries. As for blacklisting and other forms of harassment, in that area Hellman, with her book and theater revenues, had far less to fear than most people. But even allowing for fear, how would that justify maintaining the falsehood thirty years after blacklisting ceased to be a threat?

One reason for deception could have been a concern on Hellman's part about her image. Many Americans, particularly the affluent audiences to whom her plays were directed, considered Party membership unthinkable, even in the 1930s. But it is more likely that if Hellman was a member, Party leaders decided to keep her membership secret in order to exploit to the fullest her prominence. Open knowledge of Hellman's Party allegiance would have greatly reduced her effectiveness as a public spokesman on issues. As an unaligned and independent figure of national stature, her statements and stances on world affairs carried far more weight than if she were known to be under Party discipline. She would appear to be speaking from conscience rather than from the Party line. And while many people accused her of doing the latter, the accusation was hurled with such frequency and at so many people (with, in many cases, so little basis) in the 1930s and 40s that it lost most of its credibility.

Hellman's maneuverability would also have been diminished in other ways if she were known to be a Party member. It would have been impossible, for example, for her to mediate between

Henry Wallace and the communists in his campaign, had Wallace thought of her as, or if she had been known to be, a communist along with the others. Diana Trilling and others have cited her effort at mediation as evidence of Hellman's official status in the Party; otherwise, how would she even have known who the Party leaders were, let alone have been able to assemble them for a meeting? So great were the advantages of secrecy to both Hellman and the Party, she may well have been encouraged in her few well-aired deviations from Party policy—primarily her writing *Watch on the Rhine* when she did. Her other deviations were stated only in private—far from rare among Party members. And if the Party decreed secrecy about her membership, that secrecy would have extended to everyone she knew, including other Party members (although probably not to Hammett). That Hellman had solid career reasons for subterfuge merely strengthens its likelihood, but it is inconsistent with her character that she would have taken so deceptive a course for career reasons alone.

Her writing *Watch on the Rhine* at a time when the Russians and Nazis were allies is often pointed to as proof of Hellman's freedom from communist affiliation. But before that is accepted as proof, an important distinction must be made between Party discipline in America and in Russia. As far as is known, the American Communist party did not use strong-arm tactics—no roughing-ups, no prisons, no executions. The worst a wayward member could suffer—Albert Maltz would be an example—was excoriation in the Party press. For Hellman that would present no great threat. For the Party, losing Hellman would.

In his fascinating memoir of his Party involvement, *From Left to Right*, Frederick Vanderbilt Field discussed the vagueness of his transformation from fellow traveler to full member:

> Little by little I became aware that I was becoming a full-fledged member and was being treated as such. There was no decision "Today I will become a Communist," but after a couple of years I could look back and say, "Lo and behold, I have become a Communist."

While Field presented a believable picture of the informality of Party membership, his account served only to show the variations possible—particularly for potential supporters as valuable as

Field and Hellman. If it can be assumed that Hellman was some sort of member, a large difference remains between her status and Field's. He did nothing to conceal his connection and was considered a communist by other communists. Hellman, on the other hand, was not.

That leaves only the possibility that she was a secret member, and it seems highly likely that she was, at least for a few years. Her responses to HUAC probably give an accurate picture, that she, like Hammett, joined in the late thirties, and dropped out in the late 1940s. The possibility must be considered, however, that she never dropped out, or dropped out and rejoined, and that when she denied having ever joined the Party in *Scoundrel Time*, she was indeed a Party member. This last alternative presents the further possibility that she lied to the House Committee when she told them she was not currently a member. While that would have seemed to put her in severe legal jeopardy (and would explain why she and Rauh disagreed on the extent of her jeopardy), Hellman may have known of reasons why her membership would have been impossible to prove in those years, as opposed to earlier ones, or indeed, as in Field's case, how impossible it would have been to prove at all. If her intention was to deceive on that point, it may explain why she chose Joe Rauh to represent her. Rauh was an anticommunist liberal, the political breed Hellman makes clear in *Scoundrel Time* she despises above all others. She might have been willing to overlook her enmity for a tactical advantage: Rauh was widely known for refusing to represent Party members; merely having him as counsel was in itself a partial exoneration.

Among the reasons for suspecting not just a one-time but a lifelong membership would be Hellman's continued reticence to criticize Russia even when many Russians and the American Communist party showed a willingness to do so. Another would be her setting up in her will a fund for the promulgation of Marxism. It was done in Hammett's name, to be sure, but it was *her* will; he had made no such bequest. Another minor action on Hellman's part that indicates a continuing loyalty to Russia and communism occurred the year following the publication of *Scoundrel Time*. Hellman's old and dear Russian friend, Raya, had married a man named Lev Kopelev who was a minor official in the

Russian government. For mild dissidence, Kopelev had been imprisoned in a gulag for a number of years, but managed to get out of both prison and Russia. He wrote a book about his experience which was to be published in English under the title *To Be Preserved Forever*. Hellman was asked to write an introduction.

For most writers that would have presented no problem. The husband of a valued friend of long standing had written a book, not journalism or abstract opinion, but an account of his own experience. Kopelev was a Russian and himself a friend; there could be no question of capitalist lies or reactionary distortions. But Hellman's introduction makes the extraordinary statement that she has not actually read the book yet, but, because Kopelev and his wife are such old and valued friends, she is sure it is fine. It is not possible that the translated manuscript was unavailable to Hellman, nor is it possible that such a voracious reader, and one who had time to write a preface, could not also find time to read her friend's book. In addition to being unbelievable to casual readers, not reading the book would cause severe social problems between Hellman and the Kopelevs: unfamous writers are touchy about their famous friends not reading their work.

Hellman's strange introduction smacks strongly of a compromise resolution to a knotty problem: how to accommodate old friends without in any way giving the slightest appearance of endorsing testimony of Soviet repressions. Such equivocating, had it been done in 1937, would have been easier to explain; that Hellman would find it necessary to go through such contortions in 1977 suggest strongly that she was still "somebody's girl."

There are large ramifications to the supposition that Hellman was a lifelong communist. One is the number of years when deception and lies would have been the foundation of her existence, and the possibilities her success along these lines later opened up for her in management of the truth. Another is the ethics of enlisting the support of friends in various political projects when that support might have been withheld had Hellman's Party connection been known. Then too, the friendship itself might have been withheld.

When Hellman made pronouncements and judgments on matters of great public controversy like the Alger Hiss case, the assumptions about her attitude or that of any other American would be that spying for the Russians was a bad thing for a U.S. citizen to do. Since all are agreed to that, the discussion could then move rapidly to whether or not the accused was guilty, whether he was fairly prosecuted, what the damage was for the nation. But if, in fact, Hellman considered spying for the Russians a commendable act, her remarks on the case—and she made many condemning the government's case—become hypocritical and cynical. In fighting "unannounced" battles, Hellman was creating a warring and divisive atmosphere between people of conscience that distracted from the large problems that both she and her adversaries were concerned with: poverty, racial injustice, the arms race. It is also extremely difficult to argue with someone when you don't know the real reason for his or her positions.

The moral dilemmas are endless. The strong opposition to such duplicity is best summed up by Sidney Hook when he articulated the underlying principle of the anticommunist left: "They insist on the central distinction between 'heresy' whose defense is integral to a free society and 'conspiracy' whose secrecy is inimical to it."

The attacks on *Scoundrel Time* continued. William F. Buckley joined the posse with two diatribes, making up in bruising wit what he lacked in liberal sympathy. He compared Hellman to Albert Speer, saying they differed only in that "Speer repented his professional service in behalf of totalitarianism in two considerable books, while Hellman's apology for her generation-long unpaid defense is discharged in a formalistic sentence in her book, otherwise devoted to vilifying every American, liberal or conservative, who attempted to tell the truth about the hideousness of the Soviet regime."

Shortly after her death, Hellman's good friend Robert Brustein wrote: "I never took her politics very seriously, and was always amazed when people, particularly American intellectuals, still waging fifty-year-old wars, treated her as a dangerous political thinker." If Brustein was referring to *Scoundrel Time*—and the old-wars reference indicates he was—he misunderstood the furor it caused. Hellman's observations were not *dangerous,* they were damaging, lethally damaging to the reputations of the writers who struck back. It cannot be pleasant to read in a best-seller that looms as the definitive history of a period that you had behaved with cowardice and dishonor during that period, especially when you are convinced you had not. Certainly, protests should come as no surprise, no matter how old the war. Hellman, after all, was the one who had resurrected the subject. By charging with dishonor men and women who took their honor seriously, she gave them no choice but to fight back or slink off in shame. That they fought back mightily was noticed by few. Hellman, with her best-seller and her access to national media, attacked with a missile launcher; her adversaries, with the exception of Hilton Kramer, retaliated with peashooters.

There is something almost comic about the wrinkled, seventy-one-year-old Hellman, with her passion for fine clothes and Creole cooking, driving the finest intellects in the country to their typewriters and their reference books to write lengthy and scholarly obloquies against her brief remarks in *Scoundrel Time*. And they were writing them with a heat that suggested not only truth and honor were at stake but some lofty reputations as well.

Comic or not, it is the picture of Hellman that most people had—feisty, government-baiting, fearless, go-get-em, pissed-off old crone—that may have rendered her invulnerable to the onslaughts, regardless of the seriousness, documentation and authorship of the charges brought against her. Hellman's public was not about to have their heroine taken from them by a lot of boring historians and jealous intellectuals who never wrote a film script, never stood up to Congress and never lifted a finger for Julia.

That Hellman felt unscathed by the attacks was implicit in the imperious silence with which she greeted them. She had a fine summer accepting honors and degrees, entertaining friends at her house on Martha's Vineyard, bottom-fishing for scup and flounder, infuriating her fancy neighbors by forbidding them to cross her property to get to the beach, and counting the royalties of the book.

Her next appearance before the public at large, a few months after the release of *Scoundrel Time*, seemed a mocking finger held aloft at the writers who had vilified her: national magazines ran full-page advertisements showing Hellman wrapped in a Blackglama mink coat with no identifying caption—only the familiar line "What becomes a legend most?" Hellman herself misunderstood the slogan, giving it the subjective reading of "What human raw material is most likely to develop into a legend?" rather than "What garment looks best on a legend?" Either way, her legendary status had been validated in mink, infuriating her enemies and perplexing her admirers.

28

I F HELLMAN had deftly sidestepped the furor *Scoundrel Time* caused, she finally got pulled into it in a highly personal way: a public fight with an old friend. In the book's attacks on liberals it generally speaks of them as a group, without being specific. Two mentioned by name are the late Lionel Trilling and his wife, Diana, whom Hellman refers to as "old and respected friends." She leaves no doubt, however, that her respect tumbled when the Trillings failed to speak out on her behalf in 1952. Her estimation fell even lower when she read that Lionel Trilling had referred to Whittaker Chambers as "an honorable man." Hellman had great difficulty understanding how two people who came "out of the same age and time" could have such different political and social views from her own. The sentences, little more than a polite boggle at her friends' opinions, launched the season's juiciest literary scandal.

Hellman had known Lionel Trilling casually for many years, but did not become friendly with both Trillings until the early 1950s; relations were at their warmest *after* Hellman's HUAC appearance. Since it was understood they disagreed politically, topical issues were never discussed, specifically no references to the

Trillings' "silence" about HUAC during their meetings or in their correspondence (which Diana Trilling plans to publish). During the 1960s, the friendship waned, but when Diana Trilling rented a house on Martha's Vineyard the summer following both Lionel Trilling's death and the publication of *Scoundrel Time*, Hellman was, to quote Diana Trilling, "unexpectedly cordial." One day, while having breakfast together, Trilling told Hellman she was soon coming out with a book that would respond to Hellman's charges in *Scoundrel Time*. Hellman told her friend she should print whatever she wanted as long as it was the truth.

In September 1976, with many on Martha's Vineyard closing up their houses for the winter, an item in *The New York Times* announced that the Trilling book was being canceled by the publishers, Little Brown, who were also Hellman's publishers. In interviews, Trilling said that Little Brown had first asked her to remove sentences critical of Hellman; when she refused, they canceled the book. An immediate outcry went up in the press based on the strong suspicion that Hellman had wielded her clout with Little Brown to prevent the publication of negative remarks about her. Accusations of censorship flew, particularly from other writers. Hellman immediately denied any involvement with the book's cancellation and professed ignorance of its contents. She was backed up by Little Brown's editors, who admitted that Hellman was indeed the reason for their decision, but only because she was a lucrative author they did not wish to offend, not because of any pressure from her. They added that Trilling's remarks about Hellman were of a personal nature rather than ideological. Censorship was not at issue, Little Brown claimed, since they knew Mrs. Trilling could get her book published elsewhere—as indeed she did. When a reporter read the most offensive passage to Hellman—that many books had emerged about the McCarthy period but with "always-diminishing intellectual force"—she laughed and said, "I don't give a damn."

When the Trilling book, *We Must March, My Darlings*, finally appeared, it proved a considerable anticlimax, especially to those hoping to see Hellman get a black eye. Trilling made the usual rebuttals to Hellman's *Scoundrel Time* allegations, with the additional points that Senator McCarthy's obvious opportunism did not disprove a communist threat, that the McCarthyite purges played into the Kremlin's hand ("McCarthy was the greatest gift Russia ever had from this country") and that he couldn't have flourished as he had if leftists like Hellman had acknowledged earlier the grim truth about the Soviet dictatorship.

Although Trilling's points were hard-hitting, they were couched in more civil terms than the earlier attacks on *Scoundrel Time* and were all but concealed beneath thick layers of mandarin prose. Sometimes the hostility emerged, as when she referred to Hellman's HUAC letter as "a masterpiece of moral showmanship." But rather than stirring up the controversy, the publication of Trilling's book had the effect of quieting the scandal. While the controversy was raging, however, it had given the press and public a trial run for bigger feuds with Hellman to come.

Almost a decade after the cancellation of her book by Little Brown, Trilling claims no evidence that Hellman engineered it, but feels her failure to protest it publicly is almost as reprehensible. She also remains in awe of what she sees as Hellman's remarkable ability to get others to do her bidding. "When I went to Martha's Vineyard that first summer, I am sure Lillian put out the word for everyone to be nice to me. I can't think when I've been entertained so often and by so many distinguished people who were not really friends of mine. The William Styrons not only had me to dinner a number of times, they had the young college couple who worked for me. The following summer, after my fight with Lillian, none of them had anything to do with me. It is incredible to think of people of such prominence jumping to her bidding that way. Lillian was the most powerful woman I've ever known, maybe the most powerful *person* I've ever known."

Trilling says that several people told her Hellman put out the word: Anyone entertaining Diana Trilling would no longer be welcome at Hellman's house. The implication is that Hellman got on the phone the second summer, as Trilling suspects she did the first, and instructed William Styron, John Hersey, Jules Feiffer, Jerome Wiesner and the rest to drop Trilling. None of Hellman's friends on the Vineyard admit to getting such instructions. It is more likely that they simply knew how strongly Hellman now felt about Trilling and decided the most prudent course with their volcanic friend was to sidestep the controversy and cancel the new Trilling friendship as Little Brown had canceled the Trilling book. Any friend of Hellman's knew that "bad trouble" could erupt unexpectedly with her; why run the risk of courting it by socializing with someone on Hellman's hit list? Trilling stuck it out a few more summers on Martha's Vineyard, then went off to Cape Cod saying, "Lillian defeated me socially."

In assessing the undeniable power Hellman had over her friends, her temper and her fearlessness about venting it clearly played a part, particularly among the refined and dignified sensibilities that made up Hellman's circle. When Richard Wilbur and his wife declined an invitation to Hellman's because they felt they were going out too much, Hellman assumed enough about their reasons to denounce Charlee Wilbur noisily when she encountered her in the Vineyard Haven grocery store. Most people subjected to such an ordeal would consider carefully before declining any future Hellman invitations.

Norman Mailer also felt the force of Hellman's wrath. Mailer had responded to Diana Trilling's request for comments about *We Must March, My Darlings* that could be used in promoting the book, and at a lunch party at Hellman's Park Avenue apartment he mentioned that he had done so. In front of the guests, Hellman exploded, saying she was aghast. Then, perhaps from fear of ruining her own party, she said she wanted to talk with Mailer alone after lunch. When the other guests took their coffee into the living room, Hellman took Mailer into her bedroom and closed the door. He emerged fifteen minutes later glum and flushed. That afternoon, Mailer phoned Trilling's publishers and said he wanted to alter his comments. The effect of his changes was to neutralize them so they were of no use.

While a good deal of Hellman's social life had an empire-building character, much of it was for fun and a hedge against the restlessness that plagued her all her life and was a prelude to flat-out boredom. For Hellman, however, the line was blurred between fun and expanding her influence. Her frequent dinner parties were meticulously cast, then recast, with an eye to the expansion and strengthening of her power network as well as providing a stimulating mix of amusing and accomplished people. As many hostesses know, but Hellman more than most, the two motives can be inseparable.

Once a guest list was established, Hellman would attack the composition of her menu with the same fury she had applied to troublesome third acts. Leek soup and Stroganoff? No, two courses with cream. How about her old reliable baked ham? No, she had served that the last time she had had the Steegmullers. Would Hannah Weinstein's chocolate cake be too heavy after shrimp gumbo? She would call Hannah and ask her opinion. Hannah was in London? Didn't matter. This was important. If Weinstein's verdict was not the one Hellman had already arrived at, the two friends would argue angrily on the transatlantic cable for twenty minutes.

No Hellman dinner party came about without incessant long-distance calls, juggled guests, returned meat and produce, at least two tantrums at whoever was helping her, whether a third world domestic or a visiting brain surgeon, and, in the last hour, three changes of dress. Often, in the minutes before the first guests arrived, there was also an outburst of hostility toward the people who were about to expect food and drink from her. ("What do I want to entertain them for?") The fidgeting and adjusting did not end with the guests' arrival. If she thought conversation was flagging at one end of the table, she would rearrange people mid-meal. Once the curtain was up, however, she implemented her anxieties as a hostess with an Old South graciousness that caused no ripples.

In earlier years, most of Hellman's leisure activity had been tied up with the lover of the moment. But as she grew older she relied more and more on friends for her diversions. When an associate from her Harvard days, McGeorge Bundy (the friendship had survived McBundy's role in the Vietnam war), mentioned to Hellman that he was taking his family to Montreal for Expo, Hellman indicated she would like to join them. Bundy remembers that Hellman was a delightful traveling companion and was particularly kind and patient with his children. In the summer of 1973, she toured Europe with her Little Brown editor, William Abrahams, and a friend of his. She had earlier attended a theater festival in Berlin with Mike Nichols, and she took frequent jaunts with Peter Feibleman, whom she now referred to as her "adopted son."

Sometimes Hellman showed a confusion about her platonic friendships and would relate to them with her old romantic psychic apparatus. Her feelings for Richard de Combray, a handsome bachelor four decades her junior, seemed to exceed the bounds of simple friendship. She offered expensive gifts and bestowed unexpected favors; one year she announced that his birthday present was to be a trip to Greece, she to come along. Even when she later grew decrepit, she would, according to her nurse, change her dress three or four times before de Combray was to arrive for dinner. She once stared at him in silence, then said, "I wish I looked like you."

Hellman had always enjoyed the personal appearances that went along with accepting honors, but more and more she would turn these occasions into pleasure outings for herself and her friends. She accepted an invitation to speak at a series of lectures sponsored by the New Orleans Public Library. On a number of occasions Hellman had grumbled about how little attention her native city paid her, and so made a party of her homecoming. She got the library to invite Peter Feibleman to speak at the same time and persuaded two other friends into joining them for the fun and Cajun food: her chum Claudette Colbert (who apparently tired of her tag-along status and left early) and a more recent friend, Max Pavlesky, a supporter of liberal causes who had quickly made a fortune in a computer-related business. In her serious writing days, that sort of speaking obligation, if accepted at all, would have been carried out as expeditiously as possible. Now Hellman not only enjoyed such public attentions; she seized upon them as excuses for prolonged parties.

A high point of her stepped-up recreational agenda came in October 1976 when she was one of a group Max Pavlesky took up the Nile on a chartered yacht. Among the high-powered guests, the seventy-two-year-old Hellman was the reigning power. Dressed in sunsuits and picture hats, she delighted in keeping her fellow yachtsmen off balance, but graciously allowed Pavlesky, who affected Bedouin dress much of the time, the fiction of being in charge. Among the passengers was *New Yorker* writer George

Trow, who offered some sharp-edged recollections of Hellman on the Nile:

"Once on board the steamer, Lillian and I became friends quickly. We were alike in some ways. We both liked to be included in everything; but once included we liked to be critical of our companions; and finally, we referred our experience to social conventions. We didn't expect (or want) many social conventions to be in force, but we wanted an echo or a memory.

"All the 'big' issues of Lillian's life—the controversial ones— were outside our relationship. I knew a woman of the old upper bourgeoisie who valued playfulness and a certain arrogant spirit. . . . She was fun, real fun, serious fun. You were here; she was there and this was fun. Things *took place* around her."

In discussing the blindness that was starting to dominate Hellman's existence, Trow referred to it as the biggest of her "big" issues. "She railed against it," he said. "She tried every gadget—and hated them all. . . . She could not find the books she wanted on the *Talking Books* list. She *was* brave, and she did use her anger as a way of keeping things in order by getting angry at what seemed to make no sense. I think the big issues for Lillian were generosity versus greed; sense versus craziness. 'Crazy' was the worst thing something could be—and sometimes what most things were for Lillian."

Hellman's trips, like the one to Egypt, would usually be punctuated by a stopover in London to see her many friends there. Foremost among them were Lord (V.S.) and Lady Pritchett, with whom she would relish a roast-beef dinner at Wheeler's or some other favorite restaurant and make unsatisfactory trips to the theater. Beckett was one of the few playwrights to win Hellman's highest accolade: "He's good."

On March 30, 1977, Hellman was a presenter at the Academy Awards ceremonies. The Hellman bandwagon which had gained speed with the brisk sales of *Scoundrel Time* now arrived in Hollywood and was joined by the drumbeats for the Jane Fonda-Vanessa Redgrave film, *Julia*, that Fred Zinnemann was then shooting. During the Awards ceremony, Fonda's impassioned introduction of Hellman cited many of her great achievements but stressed her bravery in the face of political oppression. The signal was clear to the crowd; they were not merely honoring a fine playwright; they were dissociating themselves from, perhaps asking forgiveness for, their industry's cravenness during the 1950s purges.

Onto the huge stage stepped a tiny old lady wearing a nononsense dark evening dress, bookish reading glasses covering a corrugated face that carried the scars of Siberian flights, HUAC terrors and Hammett's binges, whose name meant for these people a number of plays they had grown up with, a number of films they had studied and a number of books they were embarrassed not to have read. Hollywood rose to its feet and gave Hellman a prolonged standing ovation, the only standing ovation of the evening. Hellman took the occasion to chastise Hollywood for its superficiality and its materialism. Accolades and a nationwide audience notwithstanding, she was not to be silenced or bought off so cheaply by that tainted crowd.

Not everyone in America was so ready to honor Hellman. On the CBS Evening News the next night, Eric Sevareid devoted part of his commentary to denouncing Hellman. He was talking about a phrase coined by German terrorists, the "shame barrier," which they had to pass through before they could blow up schools, bomb airplanes and the like. There had been an example of that same psychology, Sevareid said, at the recent Academy Awards ceremony when "playwright Lillian Hellman passed through the shame barrier by accepting applause, not for her art, but for her political activities in the McCarthy era. And Miss Fonda, who introduced her, was stopped by the memory barrier. She did not know, apparently, that Miss Hellman was a systematic supporter of Stalinism, in spite of its mass horrors, for many, many years, and a savage critic of American liberals who opposed both McCarthy and American communists. These liberals earned not applause, but the satisfaction of being historically right." Speaking about his commentary many years later, Sevareid said that in all his years of journalism, it was the only time he had used his position to go after a private individual.

Perhaps of all the honors Hellman had enjoyed over the years—and few Americans ever enjoyed as many—her apogee as a popular public figure came with the release of the film *Julia* in

October 1977, which followed faithfully the forty-seven-page chapter of that title in *Pentimento*. Because of the success of the film, a far broader audience than the relatively small numbers of book readers now knew of the adventurous and romantic private life of the celebrated playwright. The beautifully made motion picture starts out with Hellman living with Hammett (played by Jane Fonda and Jason Robards) on Tavern Island in Long Island Sound at work on her first play; the guru-disciple relationship is presented so appealingly and is so well played, it will probably serve for most of the people who saw it as the definitive depiction of the Hellman-Hammett liaison. Even with a beautiful Hellman and a sober Hammett, it came closer to the mark than Nick and Nora Charles.

The film then traces Hellman's friendship with Julia (played by Vanessa Redgrave) through childhood visits, the mutual discovery of literature and the adult separations that began with college and became permanent when Julia settled in Vienna to study psychiatry and joined the antifascist underground. The script included the casual reference that Hellman had made in the story to an erotic component in their love for each other. It was, she said, "too strong and too complicated to be defined as only the sexual yearnings of one girl for another. And yet, certainly that was there."

Escaping a Hammett drinking binge in 1934, Hellman then goes to Europe to work on *The Children's Hour* and tries to visit Julia in Vienna. Word has arrived from Vienna that Julia is in the hospital, a casualty of the socialist riots in which hundreds of workers were killed. Hellman goes to her but sees her only briefly; Julia is too bandaged to speak.

The climax of the film begins three years later, in 1937, with Hellman, now a famous playwright, en route to Moscow for a theater festival. While diverting herself in Paris with Ernest Hemingway and Dorothy Parker and her husband, Hellman receives an emissary from Julia, asking her to run a dangerous errand for the underground: to smuggle $50,000 in cash into Berlin on her way to Moscow. The money will be sewn into a Persian lamb hat she is to wear. With much trepidation, Hellman agrees.

On the train, two other people in Hellman's compartment turn out to be members of the conspiracy. Arriving in Berlin, she is met by others in the station and is steered to Julia, who is waiting in a nearby restaurant. Julia, who has lost a leg, is on crutches. She tells Hellman to place the hat on the seat between them, orders caviar and explains that the money, which is hers, will be used to buy back lives from the Nazis. Hellman learns that Julia has a baby daughter whom she has named Lilly.

With other chaperones from the resistance, Hellman continues on to Russia. The following year she learns that Julia had been badly wounded by the Nazis in Frankfurt and was transported to London, where she died. Hellman goes to London, is unable to learn anything about the fate of Julia's daughter, and brings Julia's body back to America to find her family has rejected any involvement. Hellman has Julia's body cremated.

The film opened with a splashy New York premiere to benefit the Committee for Public Justice. The first wave of reviews was highly enthusiastic; a second wave contained various complaints—old-fashioned direction, too little of Julia, evasiveness in the script—but no one questioned the truth of the story itself; it was assumed that the real-life Lillian Hellman had, in fact, made such a trip. A number of essays appeared extolling the long-overdue presentation of female friendship, which indeed was the heart of the movie. A few complained that the film glorified Hellman too much. In interviews Hellman claimed to have been surprised that she was referred to by name, assuming, she said, that for a "story" picture, she would be assigned a fictional name. That assertion, however, requires, among other difficult things, belief that Hellman never saw a script of *Julia*. That was denied by both Jane Fonda and the scriptwriter, Alvin Sargent, who said that Hellman had read the shooting script. Fonda went on to say she met with Hellman only once, stopping on Martha's Vineyard en route to Europe to discuss the script. Hellman at that time had only minor complaints: she was portrayed as swearing and smoking too much, two things she said she did not do, Fonda laughingly recalled. Hellman made no objection to her name being used.

One of Hellman's attributes that made her a more brilliant self-promoter than other writers was her craftsman's precise sense of when she risked going too far in building her image. When the claim is a highly flattering one, excess is particularly dangerous because rather than positing with your audience generosity, courage, nobility or whatever, the overload capsizes the entire portrait into brazen egomania. Few people have ever told the world so much of their best qualities with so few accusations of conceit. In the story "Julia," Hellman shades her bravery in the fear and uncertainty about her mission to Berlin. In the film, however, her heroism on the trip and her nobility in reclaiming Julia's body and searching for her child may have seemed a little heavy-handed to Hellman. A remedy would be to deny any intention of using her real name in the film. But she did not deny, nor did anyone yet suspect, that the story itself was not real.

In the aftermath of *Scoundrel Time,* with so many thoughtful people trying to decide if Lillian Hellman was an Aaron Burr or a Joan of Arc, she became involved in another controversy, far less conspicuous, that suggested she was neither, or rather that she had personality traits that transcended such abstract considerations as political convictions. An off-Broadway play that dealt with the McCarthy period, Eric Bentley's *Are You Now or Have You Ever Been,* made a riveting theater evening by weaving excerpts from the Congressional Committee's transcripts into a tableau of the personal and national drama caused by the hearings. The high point of the play came with the reading of Hellman's letter to the House Committee.

Such a tour de force did that turn out to be for Rosemary Murphy, the lucky actress given the task, that someone connected with the successful production got the ingenious notion of inviting other actresses to take turns reading *the letter.* Many of New York's most renowned actresses lined up eagerly for the opportunity. Murphy was followed by Colleen Dewhurst, Tammy Grimes, Barbara Baxley, Peggy Cass—and not only actresses residing in New York—also some, like Liza Minnelli, who were merely passing through. Each had a turn in refusing to cut her conscience, generally one week per actress.

The play was a serious New York effort, with a topflight cast, and was totally consonant with Hellman's view of the McCarthy period. The full houses of sympathetic theatergoers went wild with admiration when Hellman's stirring words were read. There were no pesky questions about others who did the same thing, about Hellman's political history, about the letter's failure to absolve her from taking the Fifth. Night after night, the stage was cleared of everyone but the actress playing Hellman and the audience responded by awarding Hellman the heroism for which she had applied with her memoirs. Moreover, the job was now being done for her by respected professionals who simply read a letter that was in the public record and had been handed out as a press release at the time she wrote it. One would imagine Hellman to be delighted. Instead she phoned her agent, Don Congdon, in a fury. "Do they have the right to read the letter without paying me?" she asked.

Congdon agreed she should be recompensed and said he would pursue the claim—as a matter of principle, since both he and Hellman knew that only a few dollars a week were involved. The producer refused to pay any royalties. Both he and Hellman dug in their heels, causing a ruckus that reached the newspapers. The play's author, the distinguished critic Eric Bentley, was quoted as saying, "I think Lillian has a chip on her shoulder." A deal was finally arrived at, but Hellman had stood ready to close down a play that anyone else with the slightest interest in self-glorification would have paid to have produced. It was a little as if Abraham Lincoln had asked the U.S. Treasury to pay him for using his likeness on the penny.

Although Hellman generally put business ahead of other considerations, sometimes her rigid stands cost her money. When she saw in the paper that *Toys in the Attic* was being revived off-Broadway without her permission, she went after the production with a killer determination. That it was a bona fide serious effort that might earn her a nice royalty was of no relevance to her. Her play agents had violated their agreement with her (she had approval of any New York area productions) and they had to be punished. She closed the production.

She was also regally indifferent to the fate of other theater people where her work was concerned. A Chinese director who had been working in Colorado had a dream to mount a production of *The Little Foxes* in Peking. He approached Don Congdon and said the best he could get together as a royalty would be $1,000. Hellman told Congdon the offer was ridiculous and to forget it. "I felt sorry for the guy," Congdon said. "He had already translated half the play and made progress with the bureaucracy in Peking. But things like that never moved Lillian in the slightest. I reminded her that Arthur Miller had recently gone to China with *Salesman* and had had a good experience. Lillian said she didn't care for Arthur Miller any more and didn't much care what kind of experience he'd had."

Congdon told Hellman he thought it would be prestigious for her to have a play running in Peking and it would probably get her a free trip to China. She still wasn't interested. Congdon then delivered the bad news to the Chinese director. But a few weeks later Hellman phoned to tell Congdon she had changed her mind. She would agree to the Peking production if the director would guarantee two first-class tickets from New York to Peking via Hong Kong, two first-class hotel rooms in both cities and a royalty of $8,000.

"I knew the guy couldn't do all that," Congdon said, "but I passed the word along to him. He was delighted and said he would try. He phoned to say yes to the plane tickets and the hotels—and that he was halfway to getting the royalty Lillian wanted. Some time went by and she called to announce that she had changed her mind again, she wasn't going to China. I should call off the whole thing, including the play. Where her work was concerned, she didn't give a shit about anyone else."

Congdon was also involved in the Zev Bufman revival of *The Little Foxes* that eventually came to New York in May 1981 with Elizabeth Taylor playing Regina. Many people, including some old friends of Hellman's, saw in her agreeing to Taylor in the part proof of her willingness to betray her artistic principles where big money was concerned. That suspicion was reinforced when it became known that Hellman had vetoed some outstanding stage actresses before agreeing to Taylor. But according to Howard Bay, Hellman, in her theater dealings, always appointed someone her official counselor and leaned heavily on his advice. For many years it was Hammett and, to a degree, Shumlin. When those mentors were no longer around, Hellman became friends with Mike Nichols and, in Bay's words, "decided he knew everything." It was Nichols who had suggested Elizabeth Taylor for the part.

The revival did end up making Hellman a great deal of money, but in an unexpected way. At a point when the production looked as if it might do well at the box office (it didn't), Hellman had a terminal falling out with the producer, who bought her out for a rumored one million dollars. That was a far greater amount, it developed, than she would have made from the show through normal royalties.

Whatever the money involved, Hellman had some misgivings about Taylor. Both women liked each other. Plus, Hellman was as respectful of superstardom as most people are, and Taylor was outspoken about her admiration for Hellman. One night, after arriving in town from the Washington tryout prior to the New York opening, the principals had dinner with Hellman at Jim McMullen's restaurant on Manhattan's Upper East Side. The actors were discussing the few run-throughs they had scheduled before opening, and Hellman remarked that she would come to see one of them. Taylor, nervous about Hellman's reaction, seemed to have been thinking of their production as a surprise gift they were laying at Hellman's feet. It never occurred to her that Hellman, then in her mid-seventies and losing her eyesight, thought of herself as a fellow collaborator with certain authority over the proceedings. Taylor groaned and asked that she please not come until opening night, meaning only that she wanted Hellman to see the production at its best.

Hellman took it differently. She thought she was being pushed aside in classic bar-the-playwright style. She grew livid and screamed at Taylor with all the pent-up hostility of an old and ugly great lady of the theater for a young and beautiful film star who might be contaminating her work. It was a horrendous moment for all present, and Hellman, who by then had to be helped in and out of restaurants, left in a clumsy huff. Since there was no doubt which of the two was more important to the production, Taylor was assured that an apology would be elicited from Hellman. Seeing the misunderstanding, and perhaps more, Taylor insisted the whole thing be forgotten.

Hellman's financial victory over Bufman was not enough to assuage whatever she considered his transgressions. One day, while reading the paper, she saw an announcement from Bufman that he was taking his production to London. Hellman had her agent on the phone in an instant. "Can he do that without my permission?" she asked. She was told that he couldn't. There was a silence on the phone as Hellman contemplated the barrel over which she had Bufman; then from the receiver came a long, maniacal laugh.

29

HELLMAN WAS ALONE in her apartment watching "The Dick Cavett Show" in January 1980 when she heard Mary McCarthy proclaim her a liar to the American public. When the show was over, she telephoned John Hersey whom Hellman felt McCarthy had also slandered ("He trivialized Hiroshima"). "Well, John," Hellman said, "are we going to sue?" The idea had not occurred to Hersey and he urged Hellman to forget about it. She refused.

Of all the writers who accused Hellman of dishonesty, curiously the only such attacker she chose to battle with legal action was Mary McCarthy. McCarthy was important enough, but she had delivered so many such roundhouse slams throughout her career, particularly as the theater critic for *Partisan Review*, that her invective was often taken as hyperbole. A typical example, which happened to contain a left-handed compliment to Hellman, was in a 1946 review of Eugene O'Neill's *The Iceman Cometh*. McCarthy wrote: "After the oily virtuosity of George S. Kaufman, Lillian Hellman, Odets, Saroyan, the return of a playwright who—to be frank—cannot write is a solemn and sentimental occasion." Oily or not, by opposing her to the disabled O'Neill, McCarthy implied that Hellman *could* write.

Dick Cavett was undoubtedly aware of McCarthy's history as a giant-killer, and was surely prodding her to do her stuff when he asked her if there were American writers who she felt were overrated. It was akin to asking J. Edgar Hoover if he felt America had any subversives. Cavett was ensuring that the next quarter hour of air time would be filled, and in all likelihood with the sort of literary gore that was McCarthy's specialty. She snapped at the bait and started her catalogue of the undeserving. When she came to Hellman's name, Cavett expressed surprise. And here again he may have been exercising his interviewer's right to incite a guest to mayhem, although he later said he had questioned the Hellman inclusion only because of his admiration for her.

McCarthy was ready with amplification. Hellman, she said, was "a bad writer, overrated, a dishonest writer."

Cavett asked what was dishonest about her. "Everything," McCarthy replied. "I once said in an interview that every word she writes is a lie, including 'and' and 'the.'"

When Cavett, who knew Hellman and had had her on his show in the past, got wind of her rage and her plans to sue, he phoned and invited her to come on his show to answer McCarthy's charges. Hellman angrily declined; she would look foolish, she said, going on national television to claim she was not a liar. Instead she proceeded with a defamation suit against Mary McCarthy for $2,225,000, naming Cavett and Channel Thirteen, the PBS affiliate, as co-defendants. McCarthy's statement, according to the complaint, was "false, made with ill-will, with malice, with knowledge of its falsity, with careless disregard of its truth, and with the intent to injure the plaintiff personally and professionally." McCarthy was staying in a London hotel when she received a phone call from Herbert Mitgang in New York informing her that Hellman was suing her. McCarthy started laughing. When Mitgang told her the amount, McCarthy, who was not rich, laughed even harder.

The lawsuit was widely covered in the press and immediately became a *cause célèbre* in the literary world. Many of the reports cited animosity between the two women that stemmed from political differences during the Spanish civil war. Hellman expressed surprise that McCarthy would attack her so vehemently since she "hadn't seen her in ten years and . . . never wrote anything about her." McCarthy concurred that they hardly knew each other; her judgment, she said, was based primarily on reading Miss Hellman's memoirs.

The careers of the two writers, which paralleled each other chronologically, illustrated the different levels of literary success in America. McCarthy, while six years younger than Hellman, emerged in the late thirties as a bright ornament of the *Partisan Review* crowd, the most formidable of New York's intellectual street gangs. She was brilliant, good-looking and the lover of the magazine's co-editor, the legendary Philip Rahv. Like all in those circles, McCarthy was fiercely political and militantly radical, but was one of the first wave of that group to lose faith in communism.

In a short story of McCarthy's called *The Perfect Host*, published in a book of her short stories called *The Company She Keeps*, she described a run-in with a group of Stalinists at a New York dinner party. The woman at her semifictional table, McCarthy dimly recalls, was based on Hellman. The party was destroyed when McCarthy denounced "Hellman" and the others for being unpaid agents of the Soviet spy network. The impression was created that this was just another 1930s New York brainy set dinner party, but forty-five years later the denunciations still flew—including the suggestion, made by McCarthy in 1985, that Hellman had been an operative for the KGB.

While McCarthy came to have misgivings about the Loyalist leadership during the Spanish civil war, as did George Orwell and a number of other liberals, that position was neither far enough from Hellman's, nor indeed so unusual, as to launch a lifelong blood feud. Their political enmity became more pronounced at the time of the 1949 Waldorf Conference, which Hellman so prominently supported and which Mary McCarthy so vigorously denounced as a communist propaganda extravaganza.

McCarthy, however, had many such political enemies for whom she did not bear the special loathing she had for Hellman. There was undoubtedly some jealousy. Despite a number of highly praised novels, McCarthy had never enjoyed Hellman's broad commercial success, nor had she received so many honors and awards or received a standing ovation in Hollywood. Her one best-selling novel, *The Group*, was thought by many (including

McCarthy) to represent a lapse of standards. Although she was in many people's eyes a better writer than Hellman—and certainly prettier—she had not approached Hellman's level of fame or popularity. The basic difference seemed to be that McCarthy was a highbrow who had unsuccessfully flirted with middlebrow culture, while Hellman was a middlebrow who had made inroads into the highbrow world.

McCarthy, naturally, denied any personal animus toward Hellman and claimed she simply disapproved strongly of her writing and her character as viewed from an impersonal distance. But she admitted to some disagreeable encounters. In 1948, when Stephen Spender was conducting a seminar at Sarah Lawrence, he asked his students to name two female writers they would like to meet. They named Hellman and McCarthy. McCarthy arrived while Hellman was addressing the class and stood in the rear; she thinks Hellman mistook her for a student. When she heard Hellman tell the young women that John Dos Passos had abandoned the Spanish Loyalists because he didn't like the food in Spain, she became incensed. Dos Passos, by most accounts, had complex reasons for losing faith in the Loyalists and had struggled with his decision. "She was just brainwashing those girls," McCarthy said. "It was really vicious. So finally I spoke up and said, 'I'll tell you why he broke with the Loyalists, you'll find it in his novel, *The Adventures of a Young Man,* and it wasn't such a clean break.' [Hellman] started to tremble . . . it was a very dramatic moment of somebody being caught red-handed."

Stephen Spender also recalled the encounter but added an interesting footnote on Hellman: "Of course, being Lillian, she imagined we had invited her worst enemy, Mary McCarthy, as her fellow guest, out of malice." If Spender's recollection was correct, it would appear that Hellman was on record as detesting McCarthy thirty years before hostilities erupted on national television. And McCarthy had more than impersonal reasons for her dislike for Hellman.

McCarthy's plan for her defense against Hellman's suit was to take the position that any statements she had made on the television show were presented as opinions, not facts. She was asked by Hellman's lawyers to list every example of Hellman's dishonesty. McCarthy declined on the grounds that such a search would be too difficult and her files were at her house in Paris. Instead she offered some examples of what she called Hellman's "intellectual dishonesty."

1. Her representation of herself as the first to refuse to name names before HUAC.
2. Presenting James Wechsler as a friendly HUAC witness when, in McCarthy's view, he had been hostile.
3. Hellman's claim to have been unaware of the purge trials during her visit to Russia in 1937, when the trials had been going on for two years.
4. The impression she creates in *Scoundrel Time* that the only fault in her Stalinism was a passive failure of understanding of the Soviet regime, never giving readers a hint of how actively she supported it.
5. The unbelievability of "Julia."

McCarthy also presented a list of people to whom she felt Hellman had been deliberately unfair and who were no longer alive to answer her "intemperate charges": Henry Wallace, Ernest Hemingway, Errol Flynn, Clifford Odets, Morris Ernst, Lucile Watson, Tallulah Bankhead and Alan Campbell. Whatever the merit of McCarthy's sampler, both in terms of the suit and in terms of Hellman's overall honesty, Hellman seemed to think she was on firm ground in denying she was a liar. About this time she telephoned Joe Rauh on another matter, and in the course of the conversation she brought up her libel action.

"Did you hear about my suit?"

Rauh said that he had.

"What do you think?"

"Lillian, I think it's a big mistake."

A pause—then, in a deeper tone, "Why?"

Rauh recognized the fighting mode, but took a deep breath and forged ahead. "Lillian, every one of us has told a fib now and then. If this ever got to court, they could bring up every word you ever wrote or said and examine it for its truthfulness. Do you really want that?"

Hellman became furious; after a number of heated words, she ended the conversation in anger. Perhaps in Hellman's mind she *was* a totally truthful person who had nothing to fear by pursuing the suit. That does not rule out the possibility that she lied as a matter of course; such self-deception has occurred in others as intelligent as she, and who placed as much importance on personal probity. But she may also have had another motive in pursuing the litigations. McCarthy's lawyer, Ben O'Sullivan, heard that Hellman intended to push the case to trial—it would possibly take a matter of years because of numerous complexities—then drop it. Hellman was now rich, McCarthy was not. Defending a legal action is expensive. Others began to suspect that Hellman was extracting her revenge by the mere act of draining McCarthy's assets with prolonged lawyers' costs.

The literary world at first welcomed the dispute between the two women as a refreshing change from the outworn political and artistic arguments that no one much cared about anymore. And while the putative origin of the scrap was a most worked over and venerable issue—pro- and anti-Stalinism—the public slugfest of two such distinguished ladies had an exhilaratingly rowdy air about it. In their world, the traditional method of settling old scores—the one Hellman had adopted—was to sprinkle cutting asides throughout a memoir. McCarthy had done what she censured Hellman for not doing: making her accusation while the accused, Hellman, was still around to refute it.

Bystanders watching the battle soon began to speak up. Many people saw serious questions of free speech in the lawsuit and felt Hellman had sacrificed any claim to being a civil libertarian. Robert Kraus, writing on the subject for *Harper's,* subtitled his article: "If you can't call Lillian Hellman a liar on TV, what's the First Amendment all about?" A number of articles appeared on the controversy, and papers like the *Washington Post* and the *Boston Globe* wrote editorials about it. Some were angry, others compassionate, but almost without exception the commentators felt Hellman was wrong to have initiated legal action. Some suggested that she was trying to use her money and the law to clobber a critic into silence, others felt that McCarthy's statement was a literary judgment which the courts were not competent to adjudicate, and still others saw the whole thing as a no-win situation for Hellman and an undeserved hardship for McCarthy.

The New York Times ran an article that presented a collection of brief opinions of the litigation from a number of writers.

It mentioned that Norman Mailer had declined comment. A month later, he leaped in with an open appeal in *The Sunday Times Magazine* addressed to both women, for whom he claimed admiration and affection. Heroically, Mailer tried to haul the argument to the mountaintop with the grandiose claim that "no writer worthy of serious consideration is ever honest except for those rare moments—for which we keep writing—when we become, bless us, not dishonest for an instant."

While many writers rubbed their eyes, others saw it as a gallant effort to declare both women right. But even if one could accept Mailer's shift of the issue from truth as opposed to falsehood to the loftier matter of artistic truth, he was still missing, perhaps choosing to miss, a glaring difference between not writing the truth, which suggests a failed effort at the truth, and writing lies, which means a deliberate effort to deceive. McCarthy's response to the lawyers' interrogatory had made it clear she was not talking about shooting for the truth and missing—she was talking about a conscious attempt to deceive.

For his pains, Mailer suffered the fate of many peacemakers. Hellman's literary hit man, Richard Poirier, wrote a letter to the *Times* editors denouncing Mailer's stand. Mailer wrote a letter denouncing Poirier that went to Hellman and a few other people. In return he received a letter from Hellman calling off their friendship.

Little noticed in the furor surrounding first the Diana Trilling fracas, then the Mary McCarthy suit, was the publication of a small book by Hellman, her last solo piece of professional writing. It was called *Maybe* and was billed as "a tale." The story centers around a beautiful friend of Hellman's named Sarah, and Hellman writes it in the first person, talking freely about her own life with Arthur Kober and Hammett, and bringing in such other nonfictional people as her father, her aunts and various friends. The many biographical references all jibe with the known facts— to a degree causing some Hellman commentators to number her memoirs as *four* rather than three. Still, the book's style is that of fiction. Hellman, in her last piece of serious writing, does not differentiate.

Sarah herself seems more a creation of the imagination than

a real person. Throughout the many years that Hellman has known her, she has proved to be elusive, mysterious and deceptive. Hellman admits to not trusting Sarah and to generally disliking her, but is more than a little obsessed by her. It is very much like the Julia story—flashbacks, quick glimpses, long gaps—but with Julia now a villainess rather than a saint. Sarah shifts in and out of focus, telling lies, denying truths and generally making herself very hard to record with any accuracy. Hellman not only tries for the truth, she struggles valiantly with the task. But the main theme of the story is how difficult it is to know the truth about anything.

There is a fascinating subplot, if the book is indeed autobiographical. Hellman admits to having been worried all her life that she had a particularly strong odor "down there." The fear took hold of her when her first lover, a casual sexual partner, mentioned it while breaking off his short affair with Hellman. Stung, she takes to bathing three and four times a day, and over the years asks innumerable people, even her tenant farmer at Hardscrabble Farm, if she smells funny.*

It develops that Sarah also had an affair with the same nasty young man. Hearing that Hellman is destroyed by his allegation, perhaps incapacitated from further sexual activity, Sarah says blithely, "Oh, he said the same thing about me." For Hellman, Sarah's offhand remark is deliverance from a crippling torture. That is, it is deliverance until she reflects that the obviously sweet-smelling Sarah might be lying out of kindness. Thus, wondering whether Sarah is being truthful or whether her nature

---

* Ordinarily, the body odor of a subject is outside the legitimate or relevant areas of biographical investigation. Hellman not only raised the issue, but in a sense wrote a book about it—and indeed introduced the subject in a funny *Pentimento* account of a fight between her parents over whether Max Hellman or his daughter had been called "the sweetest smelling baby in New Orleans." So the matter was researched with the following results: Two stage directors who had worked with Hellman, Joseph Anthony and Gower Champion, complained of her having a pungent odor; two of her lovers were asked about the matter. One said he was aware of no such thing, but that Hellman had an uncanny *sense* of smell and could tell who had been sitting in a chair before she did; the other also denied Hellman had any unusual odor, but added that it would have been easy for her to conceal it from him. In spite of these puzzling responses, the investigation was dropped right there.

would allow compassionate gestures, becomes for Hellman a lifelong curiosity.

There would be enough self-revelation in the ninety-one pages of *Maybe* to keep a psychiatrist busy for months if its truth were established. The story is told with Hellman's usual tight, engaging style, but with more than the usual number of asides in which she agonizes over the difficulty of getting at the truth about anything. Finally all other reactions in reading the story give way to an awareness that Hellman is striving for profundity, that the book is a rumination on the nature of reality. When that awareness takes hold, the fun stops. Unfortunately, the metaphysical insights don't begin, and we are left with a small book posturing for magnitude like an incomplete existential novel. Still, the Hellman persona of the memoirs comes across as vividly as in the best moments of those books and does so through an engaging mystery. Few of its critics noted that Hellman, under siege for her distortions of truth, might have been offering an explanation, perhaps even an apology. Or that an ambiguous "maybe" was her last word on the truthfulness of all her memoirs.

The first accusation in print that Hellman had *deliberately* lied was in Tallulah Bankhead's 1952 autobiography, in which she emphatically denied Hellman's interview assertion that Bankhead had refused to do a benefit of *The Little Foxes* for Spanish civil war refugees. Bankhead's charge, while widely circulated, was never seen as more than the vitriol of a public dispute. For the next three decades, Hellman's writings and public statements were given the same tacit credence as those of other prominent figures.

A few of Hellman's friends quietly raised eyebrows at certain claims in the memoirs, like Herman Shumlin, who had not believed "Julia" because he knew Hellman could not have been in Europe in 1934, since she was working with him. The only reviewer to question the honesty of anything in Hellman's memoirs at the time of publication was John Simon, who wondered why Hellman claimed to have changed names in "Julia" when only first names were used. He also found suspect Hellman's reasons for changing them: that the Germans might still harbor resentment against their "premature anti-Nazis." Simon found that an odd explanation to put forward at a time when Germans were clearly honoring them. His mild skepticism, however, would become the first shot in a barrage of later attacks on the truthfulness of Hellman's memoirs. Perhaps the discrediting would have come in any case, but except for Simon's relatively mild demurs, no one else raised any suggestion that Hellman so much as exaggerated, let alone indulged in wholesale fabrication in her first two memoirs. And that remained true throughout the seven years following *Pentimento*'s publication—until the Mary McCarthy remarks.

While the attacks on *Scoundrel Time* were loaded with allegations of dishonesty, the charge is common in political argument and tends to take on a special meaning: biased reconstructions, convenient memory and the like. That these attacks also accused Hellman of lying, not just on behalf of her convictions, but on behalf of her role in events (to be the first to offer HUAC only partial cooperation, for example) was generally overlooked in the ideological fray. By suing McCarthy, Hellman forced one of the country's sharpest and most energetic minds to pore through the entire Hellman *oeuvre* in search of lies.

McCarthy received significant assistance from sympathetic friends. She learned that Martha Gellhorn, an established journalist and Ernest Hemingway's third wife, had taken strenuous exception to Hellman's account in *An Unfinished Woman* of her visit to Spain in 1937. (Gellhorn had not yet written her article for *Paris Review* attacking Hellman.) Another friend, the poet Stephen Spender, told her of a woman in Vienna in the 1930s who very much fit the description of Hellman's Julia, but who, unlike Julia, was still alive. Spender had had an affair with the woman, the Muriel Gardiner Buttinger who had returned to America from Europe in 1939 with her resistance-leader husband. She had become a prominent psychiatrist whose honesty and credibility Spender, who had remained close to her over the years, vouched for without hesitation.

At Spender's instigation, Muriel Gardiner phoned Mary McCarthy. It did not require much conversation for McCarthy to be certain that Gardiner was indeed Hellman's Julia, but she chose not to get into the overall dishonesty of the story—that Hellman had never met Gardiner and that the entire friendship was a fantasy. McCarthy instead limited herself to specifics of Hellman's story that Gardiner, as an experienced underground operative, convinced her could not have happened. As a result, McCarthy was able to add to her interrogatory response to Hellman's suit a number of improbabilities in "Julia":

1. That eight underground agents would have been employed to shepherd a neophyte through a dangerous mission (that any one of them could have done better than the neophyte).
2. The high visibility of the operation: fur hat, a woman on crutches, exchanging the money in a public restaurant, ordering caviar.
3. That Berlin, the Nazi capital, would have been chosen for the exchange site.
4. That the individual chosen for the mission would be a celebrated Jewish antifascist.
5. The reasons Hellman gives for changing characters' names (unconvincing because anti-Nazis are now heroes; Julia has been dead for twenty-five years; her family, detested by Hellman, is mostly gone; and she never gives last names).
6. That no one ever came forward in the years following *Pentimento*'s publication to say that they also knew Hellman's remarkable and heroic Julia.

While never published, McCarthy's interrogatory was filed with the court records of the libel suit and was available to anyone who cared to read it; it may well have been the basis of subsequent published attacks on Hellman's honesty. Whatever the reason, the sport of searching for Hellman lies caught on. The first to publish an all-out attack was Martha Gellhorn, who lived in London and, at the time of the McCarthy interview, was planning to write an article for *Paris Review* that would refute statements in an earlier article published there on the Spanish civil war. That article had been written by McCarthy's friend and Muriel Gardiner's former lover, Stephen Spender, a coincidence that evokes a picture of the members of the literary *haut monde* as not just incestuous but as passing their time challenging one another's honesty.

Gellhorn's article was expanded to encompass distortions of the Spanish war by numerous writers, including her ex-husband

Hemingway, but would focus on the Spender piece. Perhaps because of her conversations with McCarthy, or perhaps simply as a result of her research, Gellhorn's article—a masterpiece of vitriol entitled "Guerre de Plume"—was given over in largest measure to assaults on Hellman's version of reality. She took only six pages to finish off Spender's "apocryphisms," a word Gellhorn altered and gleefully wielded as any part of speech she wished. They were a mere warm-up for the sixteen pages she devoted to Hellman, introducing the main event with the sentence: "In my specialized study of apocryphism, Miss Hellman ranks as sublime."

Gellhorn made her points with authority, since she herself had been present at a number of the episodes in *An Unfinished Woman* that she challenged; plus, she bolstered her firsthand knowledge with painstaking research. There were many things about Hellman's account that Gellhorn pointed to as highly improbable, but it was the alleged impossibilities that gave strength to her assault: encounters and events that she said could *not* have happened.

> 1. Hellman's attending a party with Hemingway in Hollywood when he went there to show his film *The Spanish Earth*. According to Gellhorn, Hemingway took the film to Hollywood only once: in July 1937. And Hellman writes that she *first* met Hemingway in Paris in late August or early September 1937, which is consistent with Gellhorn's recollection.
>
> 2. Hellman's description of a fracas between Hemingway and Hammett at the Stork Club in Manhattan at a time when Hemingway was in Cuba writing *For Whom the Bell Tolls*. He didn't visit New York for another year.
>
> 3. Hellman's *Pentimento* account of Arthur Cowan, in the 1950s, giving her $1,000 for her to pass along to her friend, the communist writer Gustav Regler, who was "ill in Paris without any money." Hellman mentions sending Regler money of her own as well and receiving a thank-you note from Regler's wife. Gellhorn said that Regler was then living in Mexico City and had been since 1940.
>
> 4. Hellman's giving the impression she spent several weeks in Hemingway's company in Paris in 1937. Gell-

horn was then living illicitly in Paris with Hemingway and they were not seeing anyone. He went off one evening to have drinks with Dorothy Parker and Alan Campbell as an "anti-gossip ploy," Gellhorn said, and Hellman may have been present. Gellhorn also said she was away from Paris for three days, during which time Hemingway may have seen Hellman, but he did not mention having done so.

5. Hellman's story of Hemingway's coming to her room the night before she left for Berlin with his manuscript of *To Have and Have Not*. According to Gellhorn, Hemingway was already in Spain by that date. She also pointed to Hellman's *Pentimento* account of the same night, in which she reports having slept soundly with no mention of famous visitors and all-night reads.

6. With the story "Julia," Gellhorn made an elaborate reconstruction of the time frame, using Hellman's own statements about when she did this or that, how long she was in a certain place, etc., to prove she could not have done half of what she claimed.

7. Hellman's harrowing account, from a diary entry dated October 15, 1937, of being caught in the streets of Valencia during a bombing raid. Gellhorn looked up the news reports in *The London Times* and *The New York Times* and established that Valencia had been badly bombed on October 3 and not again until December 11, over two months later. (Hellman was in Spain from ten days to two weeks.) Gellhorn then attempted to head off any claim of a mix-up of dates: in the October 3 raid some sixty civilians were killed in the port area, where the worst bombing occurred. Hellman refers to sixty people being killed in the port area in her October 15 raid. Gellhorn found it inconceivable that a foreigner who was in Spain to see the war, particularly Franco's atrocities against innocent civilians—an aspect of war then new to the world—would not tour the bombed area and see the damage for herself. She concluded that Hellman could not have experienced a Valencia bombing.

8. The dinner party Hellman attended in Madrid with Hemingway and Gellhorn, in which Hellman is disgusted at the others for going out on the balcony to

watch "the beauty" of a bombing raid. Gellhorn again established from news accounts that there could not have been a bombing raid that night; even if there had been, the bombs used by Franco's planes caused no light and were therefore invisible at night. But Gellhorn's real complaint about that part of the memoirs was the way in which Hellman portrays herself "at her noble best. Everyone else, not to mince words, is a shit." The picture certainly lingers of Hellman, with a bravery bordering on madness, going out into the raids to do a radio broadcast—word has arrived from the station for her not to come as they have received more than one direct hit—while Ernest Hemingway takes time off from enjoying the bombing display to plead with an unhearing Hellman not to risk certain death. There is no record of any broadcast by Hellman.

Gellhorn made a number of other points, picking up on a few details that showed "Hellman's incomprehension of that war was near idiocy" (beef from "bullfight people" for the Hemingway dinner, impossible-to-get lettuce found in a bombed-out house, and so on). Her accusations escalated to Hellman's not only filling her tales with inventions out of whole cloth, but doing so in a woefully ignorant fashion. Hemingway was also taken to task by Gellhorn for becoming in his later years "a shamefully embarrassing apocryphiar." But that doesn't lessen her anger at Hellman for relentlessly portraying Hemingway—and everyone but Hellman—as a posturing fool.

Gellhorn's diatribe attracted attention beyond the narrow audience of *Paris Review. The New York Times* ran an article under a large-type headline: "Hellman Word Assailed Again." George Plimpton, editor of *Paris Review*, heard through mutual friends that Hellman was in a rage about the article. He wrote her an apologetic letter calling Gellhorn's attack "gratuitous," and offered Hellman as many pages of the following issue as she wished to refute the charges. He added that he should have sent Hellman the article "the minute it came in."

Only under unusual circumstances are subjects of articles allowed to read what has been written about them before publication. One of the circumstances might be if the subject was a friend of the editor, which was the case here. Others assumed Plimpton feared Hellman's litigious nature, although he denied that to be so. But even if Plimpton was not motivated by fears of legal action, the subliminal message of the suit against McCarthy was that Hellman was a dangerous person to offend publicly. Lawsuits were just one of the more extreme forms of retribution available to her. For Plimpton, the vision of the beloved old playwright on a national talk show making a scathing remark about him or his magazine might well have been enough to inspire a nervously conciliatory letter to her. When asked about Plimpton's letter, Hellman struck a posture of amused indifference. "People get funnier and funnier," she told a reporter. As for Plimpton, he assumed Hellman was mollified, but he was not of a mind to take unnecessary chances. At a large party in Manhattan a few years later, he found himself alone in a town-house elevator with Hellman, who was now almost blind. He stayed at one side of the car and tried not to make any noise.

Everyone in publishing and the other media knew there was considerable peril in scrapping with Lillian Hellman. The McCarthy lawsuit (which was headed for trial when Hellman died but was then dropped) merely added financial disaster to possible retaliations. McCarthy's pretrial legal costs quickly mounted to over $25,000. A defense fund for her was established by Robert Silvers of the *New York Review of Books*. As the fund-raising was getting underway, an angel appeared, a young heiress of literary bent, who underwrote McCarthy's entire legal debt. Had some sort of help not arrived, McCarthy freely acknowledged, she would have had to sell her home in Maine. Financial backers in the case may not, however, have been limited to the defense. According to McCarthy, Hellman was offered an "offense fund" of up to $500,000 by one of her tycoon friends who had said to her, "Let's have some fun with this thing."

30

HELLMAN'S PHYSICAL CONDITION was deteriorating rapidly. Despite many operations, her eyesight was almost gone. She suffered a heart attack in 1982 that was so mild she didn't realize it had occurred until informed of it by her doctors, but it was still serious enough to result in the installation of a pacemaker (which Robert Brustein said once "popped out of her papier-mâché chest"). She also had emphysema and painful arthritis that made unassisted walking impossible. She was not particularly stoical about her ailments; she complained constantly to those around her, her physical condition dominating her thoughts. For much of her life her moods had depended on the progress of her work; now they depended on how she felt on a given day. Still, she refused to allow her ailments to ground her, and she continued making arduous and ever more complicated forays to restaurants and friends' houses until the day before she died.

Most evenings during the final years, she would eat dinner at home, prepared by her housekeeper, Therese, often with a friend or two, then go to bed early. Richard de Combray was a frequent dinner guest and sometimes stayed with her after the other guests had gone.

I would sit with her on the side of her bed or on a chair just next to it. Her bedside table kept getting larger to accommodate the accumulation of medicines she was taking—for her eyes, her digestion, her heart, ointments for the bruises she would suffer from having fallen yet again, usually on the street, for there never was a woman who fell down as frequently as Lillian did: fall down, lie there for a moment, and get helped back up to her feet. She never did any real damage to herself with these falls, probably because she usually wore a coat of some fine fur. Also on the night table were sleeping pills, lotions, piles of books, tape recorders, and a special radio sent to her by an organization called In Touch, geared to a mysterious frequency and meant to entertain the blind, a kind of audial magazine.

After we'd exhausted the conversation begun at dinner (during which her health and doctor problems had been relentlessly examined—for as with most ill people, she never tired of discussing her ailments) it came time to leave. This was frequently difficult because it meant leaving her alone in a darkened room with her troubles and it was clear to me that she was in a constant yet unexpressed panic about her deteriorating condition. Anyway, on certain evenings I would try to calm her by offering to sing a lullaby. This invariably brought such a wonderful and childlike response that she would slip into the charming baby talk most of her friends had come to know and delight in. When she seemed to be asleep, I'd get up and begin to steal out of the room, longing, I must say, to hit the streets and get some air— her room was always stifling—and I'd *feel* one of her eyes snap open.

"Going?" she'd ask, not in a sleepy voice.

"Yes. I thought you were asleep."

Then followed the long moment which so characterized Lillian. She lay there like a ship's figurehead, and I could feel the struggle going on between the two essential ways she had of expressing herself: the deeply generous and affectionate elements in her nature battling with those manipulative and self-centered characteristics for which she is generally known and remembered. One response would have gone like this: "I'm not surprised. I'm sure you have better things to do. You promised earlier that you'd read to me, but never mind, never mind. You don't read well anyway, if you don't mind my saying so. You read too fast and I can't follow half of what you're saying, probably because you're in such a hurry to get out of here. You're the most social man in America. You're never home. Never for one evening. I doubt you even keep a carton of orange juice in your ice box. No, don't anger me by denying it. . . ."

Or she would say, turning that great profile in my direction, "Yes, darling, it's late. And I loved your singing to me. You're a cute kid. Which reminds me. I have a T.L.* for you but I can't think of it now. I'm too tired. But I'll remember when we talk on the phone in the morning. Now get home safely. You really ought to wear a longer coat in this weather. My God, that one isn't even a coat, it doesn't cover your rear end! You'll get a chill! It's winter, darling, winter! You never dress properly. And you forgot to kiss me goodbye. Be careful of my pacemaker, and on your way out, turn out the lights in the hall. . . ."

In May 1983, with her health growing worse, and with the McCarthy lawsuit still pending, Hellman received what would become the severest blow to her beleaguered reputation. Muriel Gardiner Buttinger's memoirs were published by the Yale University Press under the title *Code Name Mary*. It brought into the open the accusation that there was a real Julia who had *not* been a friend of Hellman's. For her part, Gardiner tried to minimize such an acute embarrassment. In her preface she wrote that when *Pentimento* came out ten years earlier, many of her friends had told her that, because of the parallels, she must have been the model for Julia. She had replied to them what she repeated now: although she agreed that the similarities were remarkable, she could not have been the model because she had never met Lillian Hellman.

* A "trade last," a compliment which will be traded for one the recipient has heard about the speaker. De Combray recalls once challenging Hellman about making deals over compliments; she got angry at first, then admitted that Hammett had once offered to pay her to "keep her damn T.L.'s to herself."

Gardiner did not mention in her book that when she had read "Julia," she wrote Hellman a polite letter in which she apologized for what might be taken as "an intrusion" and told Hellman not to respond if she preferred. Gardiner pointed out the similarities between Julia's life and her own: wealthy American family, studies at Oxford in the early thirties, a move to Vienna to be psychoanalyzed by Freud (Freud's daughter, Anna, was a good friend of Gardiner's and wrote the introduction to her memoirs), psychiatric studies at the University of Vienna, and dedicated involvement in the city's antifascist underground.

In the letter Gardiner also mentioned their mutual friend, Wolf Schwabacher, with whom she and her family shared a house after returning to the United States in 1939. Gardiner asked Hellman if Julia might be a composite of several of her friends in addition to people she had merely heard about. The closest the letter came to challenging Hellman was Gardiner's expression of surprise at never having met Julia, since their lives paralleled each other's so remarkably. There was no reply. When the matter became public, Hellman said she had no recollection of receiving such a letter.

From an advance copy of Gardiner's book, Jane O'Reilly of *Time* magazine was among the first to notice the amazing similarity between Gardiner and Julia. She decided to investigate and found that Gardiner was still living in the Pennington, New Jersey, house that she had shared with Schwabacher and also had an apartment on Manhattan's West Side. After interviewing Gardiner, O'Reilly was convinced she was Julia. Before *Time* ran her piece, however, *The New York Times* went into print with an article that, if not outright accusatory of Hellman, was highly skeptical of her denials. The reporter phoned Hellman on Martha's Vineyard and asked how she could explain the similarities between Gardiner and Julia. The coincidences gave Hellman no trouble.

"She [Gardiner] may have been the model for somebody else's Julia," she snapped, "but she was certainly not the model for mine."

With Hellman taking such a rigid stance, Gardiner began to think she perhaps had been too polite in her letter. The same *Times* article quoted her as saying, "I don't make any claims of being Julia, because I couldn't possibly prove it." But when the director of the Austrian Archives of the Resistance, Dr. Herbert Steiner, was in New York, Gardiner asked him if there had been any other American women working with the resistance. He said that he knew of none. To make certain, he phoned a number of former members of the resistance when he returned to Austria and asked them if they had ever encountered another American woman in their work during the prewar years. The answer was always the same: "No, only 'Mary.'"

Gardiner volunteered that there were two other American women at the University of Vienna's medical school, but that she was the only one studying psychiatry. According to Viennese-born writer Frederic Morton, the antifascist resistance in Vienna was not a widespread operation, but was limited to a relatively small number of people. Thus, it would be not one, but two confined Viennese worlds that both Muriel Gardiner and Hellman's Julia were part of—the University psychiatric department and the anti-Nazi underground.

When Hellman was challenged about Julia, she could have said that she changed not only Julia's name but the dates, the country or anything else that put distance between her and Dr. Gardiner, but she did not. She maintained only that she had changed names; everything else was true. To many people, including Gardiner, it was inconceivable that two such women—with identical backgrounds and engaged in the same highly specialized activities—could have been in Vienna at the time and not met, or at least have been aware of each other.

Many of the improbabilities in the Julia story were first pointed out by Mary McCarthy, but there seemed to be an unlimited supply. One not mentioned in McCarthy's affidavit was perhaps the most telling: it was no problem for an American to get money into either Austria or Germany in 1937; Gardiner had been doing it for years and continued to do it for another year through the Chase Bank. That alone would have obviated any need for the dangerous mission Hellman claims to have run for Julia.

As an experienced underground operative (she preferred the word "conspirator"), Gardiner insisted on the absurdity of the Berlin mission as depicted in "Julia." She pointed to minor contradictions in the story that others had also noted. One was Hellman's statement that she changed Julia's name, then in the middle of the story having the young Julia fancifully claim that John Donne wrote his poem about Julia for her. (It was Herrick, not Donne, in any case.) Another was Hellman's phoning Julia at medical school in Vienna, then phoning her again ten years later to find Julia is still in medical school. Gardiner stated that it took five years, at most six, to get a medical degree there. Gardiner further pointed out an inconsistency that others had overlooked. On the last page of the *Pentimento* story about her Aunt Bethe, Hellman, writing in 1968 about 1931, said, "I never went back to Germany. . . ." Forty-nine pages later in the same book, she starts the Julia story about a memorable trip to Germany in 1937.

The link between Gardiner and Hellman, the lawyer to both women, Wolf Schwabacher, died in 1951. His son, New York attorney Christopher Schwabacher, was interviewed by the *Washington Post* when Gardiner's book came out, and he verified that his father had indeed been close to both women, that he had represented Hellman in her efforts to lift the Boston ban of *The Children's Hour* in 1935, and was at the time a gregarious bachelor who socialized with his clients. The son also confirmed that Schwabacher shared a house with Gardiner and, as her lawyer, had worked assiduously in 1938 and 1939 to arrange her Paris marriage to Joe Buttinger to expedite his coming to America. The son also affirmed that his father talked often about his heroic client and made her inspiring drama known to a wide circle of people. That Kurt and Sara Muller, the couple in *Watch on the Rhine*—which was written the year after the Buttingers' return to the United States—so closely resembled the American heiress and her resistance-fighter husband should remove any doubt that Hellman, like many people, had heard of Muriel and Joe Buttinger.

Throughout the debate that then erupted about the Julia story, Hellman's position could have been greatly reinforced if one of her friends had come forward and said that Hellman had mentioned Julia on at least one occasion during the past thirty years, but none did. Hellman herself could have silenced the furor abruptly by the simple act of telling Julia's real name. The name could then have been checked against the archives of the Austrian resistance, the University of Vienna enrollment (or whatever city and university Hellman chose to put her in) and hospital and cemetery records. Hellman refused to do that on the grounds that Germans were still persecuting their "premature anti-Nazis" (they were, in fact, honoring them) and that Julia's mother might still be alive. That was perhaps the oddest reason of all, since Julia's mother had gone to live in South America, she had disowned Julia and the child, Hellman hated her and the woman would have to be, if alive, over a hundred. But most people, encountering her rationale when reading "Julia," or hearing it again on an interview on PBS, thought how splendid of Hellman to "protect" her dead friend, not stopping to consider that she was protecting her only from the honor that should have been hers and that every reader awarded the Julia of *Pentimento*.*

The conclusion is inescapable that Muriel Gardiner not only lodged in Hellman's consciousness in 1939, but that she remained there for thirty-four years, next appearing in 1969 in *An Unfinished Woman* as her friend and co-worker at Liveright, Alice, who, Hellman wrote, was killed in the Vienna riots of 1934 (detailed American newspaper accounts of those riots make no mention of any Americans being killed), and finally coming to full flower as Hellman's dearest friend in "Julia."

One of the many questions that arise from an acceptance of Hellman's guilt in commandeering Gardiner's life to enhance her own would be the recklessness of making such wanton use of so prominent a person. Although by no means famous in the way that Hellman was, Gardiner was far from a nonentity. Since becoming something of a legend as a beautiful young heiress engaged in highly dangerous anti-Nazi activities, Gardiner returned to the United States to build a distinguished career in psychiatry. Immediately at the end of World War II, she again went to Europe and was one of the original organizers of what would become the International Rescue Committee. She edited a book about Sigmund Freud's famous patient, the Wolf Man, that would be a landmark in psychiatric literature. She was on the board of direc-

---

* When asked if any of those who worked on the film *Julia* ever doubted aspects of the story, Jane Fonda replied, "No, we didn't, but we were all very curious about who Julia was."

tors and was a principal backer of the Freud Archives and Museum in London. She also wrote a highly regarded book on murderous children called *The Deadly Innocents*. In 1980 she was decorated with the Austrian Government's Cross of Honor for her work with the underground. Her husband, Joe Buttinger, received the only higher Austrian decoration, the Golden Cross of Honor.

If Hellman had consciously set out to requisition the life of someone she knew had existed, the most minimal caution would have compelled her to learn what had become of the remarkable woman she had heard about in 1939. That she did not would indicate that Hellman either thought she was a creation of her imagination and therefore safe to use as she wished, or, the more dire possibility, that she actually believed Muriel Gardiner had been her friend.

In May 1983, the month that *Code Name Mary* was published, Dr. George Gero phoned Muriel Gardiner in New Jersey. The housekeeper said that Dr. Gardiner was not at home. The caller said he wanted to speak with Dr. Gardiner on behalf of Lillian Hellman to ask her for a statement denying she was Julia. The housekeeper said that Dr. Gardiner was away for a few days, but that she would relay the message. After Gardiner returned, she received a call from Dr. Gero, who reminded her of their having met through the Freud Archives (Gardiner vaguely remembered). He repeated Hellman's request for a denial, but he did not mention that since the death of Gregory Zilboorg he had been Hellman's analyst. Gardiner responded that she would have to "disappoint" Miss Hellman; she had never claimed to be Julia and she never claimed not to be.

A short time later, by Gardiner's account, she was not feeling well, so she remained in bed. The phone rang. A voice that Gardiner took to be a man's said, "This is Lillian Hellman."

"Is this Miss Hellman herself?" Gardiner asked, now accustomed to intermediaries.

"Yes."

In a pleasant tone of voice, Hellman said that she would like very much to meet Dr. Gardiner. Did she come to town? Could they have lunch? Gardiner explained that she was ill, her doctor was away for a few days and she wanted to wait for his return before deciding to leave her bed. Hellman was understanding, but asked if in that case she might come out to Pennington to see Dr. Gardiner. When Gardiner said that would be all right, Hellman added, "I would like to bring with me a very charming young man I am sure you would enjoy meeting."

Gardiner, who was now highly mistrustful of Hellman, immediately took her to mean that she was bringing a lawyer. Gardiner replied that it would be all right if Hellman brought a friend, but in that case she too would have a "friend" present.

A young cousin of Gardiner's who worked for her as a secretary, David Lowe, was present when another phone call came from Hellman. This time Gardiner explained that her doctor had diagnosed her condition as pneumonia; she would have to put off their meeting. Hellman, according to Gardiner, said she understood and then added, "Mrs. Buttinger, I wanted to explain to you why I never answered your letter."

The connection was not good, and Hellman, who was seventy-eight, complained of not being able to hear Gardiner's response. Did Gardiner mind if Hellman put her secretary on the line? Gardiner said that she understood, she too had hearing problems. (Gardiner was eighty-one.) Gardiner made a suggestion. Why didn't Hellman ask her secretary to explain about the letter? Hellman thought about that and decided it was a good idea, then added in a tone Gardiner did not feel was meant to be menacing that an even better idea might be to have her lawyer explain to Gardiner about why she hadn't answered it. Hellman then added that she would think over her new idea and call back. Gardiner, who remained in her bed with a telephone at her side for six days, never heard from her again. Hellman lived for another year.

Gardiner, who died in February 1985, may well have misread Hellman's request to bring "a young friend." At that point Hellman was blind and unable to go anywhere without someone at her side. Still, she could have indicated a willingness to talk alone with Gardiner once her companion got her to the meeting. The young friend Gardiner planned to have present was her cousin, David Lowe, who is not a lawyer. What was actually said in these phone conversations comes only from the account of Muriel Gardiner, a woman with a reputation for truthfulness. And that Hellman on two occasions contacted Gardiner was witnessed by several other people, particularly David Lowe and Gardiner's housekeeper. Hellman was famous for responding to those who threatened her either by ignoring them or by an onslaught of verbal menace. She telephoned Gardiner, however, in a conciliatory frame of mind. Her uncharacteristic cordiality to a woman who was, by her very existence, a challenge to her truthfulness, strongly suggests that Hellman perceived the trouble she was in: Gardiner was in a position to establish the dishonesty of Hellman's most famous memoir chapter and, because of the film, the best-known episode in her life. That Hellman's honesty was now a subject for litigation gave a certain urgency to Gardiner's unspoken threat.

A number of Gardiner's friends, among them Robert Silvers, were aware of Hellman's efforts for a meeting and urged Gardiner not to accede to one. Their fear was that Hellman would seek to elicit some sort of statement from Gardiner that could be used, primarily in the McCarthy suit, as a denial that she was Julia. Gardiner was leaning against a meeting but, as Hellman did not call again, never had to decide.

Hellman's psychiatrist, Dr. Gero, in a conversation after Hellman's death, said flatly, "Muriel Gardiner was not Julia. That is a fact." But when apprised of some of the contrary evidence, he shifted significantly. "Well, I know Muriel Gardiner was not Julia because Lillian assured me she wasn't." If Hellman was conscious of the fantasy basis to her friendship with Julia, she was sharing her embarrassment with no one, not even her psychiatrist.

The exchange between Hellman and Gardiner, which was never known except to a few people, does not prove that Hellman knew she was lying when she wrote the story. There may have been a part of her mind that would have allowed her to continue comfortably and indefinitely with the memory of her noble friend Julia; but the harsh reality of her lawsuit against Mary McCarthy, and Gardiner's potential effect on it, may have forced Hellman to acknowledge the story's imagined origins and to take steps to control the damage. There does not seem to be any other motive for her wanting to meet Gardiner, even to be civil to her. But their meeting never took place, and with both women dead, all that remains are the intriguing possibilities of the dialogue that would have occurred had Lillian Hellman ever had her first meeting with "Julia."

The emergence of Muriel Gardiner and the piece by Martha Gellhorn, who concluded her attack on *An Unfinished Woman* with a glancing reference to questions still teeming in her head concerning "Julia," opened the gates for further assaults against Hellman's veracity. In June 1984, Samuel McCracken, assistant to the president of Boston University, published an article in *Commentary* titled "Julia and Other Fictions by Lillian Hellman." With the aid of two researchers, a somewhat eyebrow-raising effort for a magazine article, McCracken demonstrated how numerous stories in Hellman's memoirs could not be true. He admitted drawing heavily on the Gellhorn article, particularly for the sizable problems concerning Hellman's dates in 1937, but came up with a number of anomalies and impossibilities on his own.

McCracken warmed to his task by first attacking minor specifics of Hellman's "Julia" account: seeing *Hamlet* in Moscow (no *Hamlet* that year), the name of Julia's funeral parlor (no such establishment), and so forth. He did perhaps more damage by poring over old train and boat schedules. Hellman says she left Berlin for Moscow at the Zoo Station, but McCracken pronounced that impossible because Moscow trains did not stop there. Hellman also asserts that she left Berlin the same day she arrived because her passport did not permit an overnight stay. McCracken found that the earliest she could have gotten to Berlin if she left Paris in the morning was 11:44 P.M.; the last train for Moscow left at 6:13 P.M. There are many such problems with Hellman's travel schedule.

Why, when Julia was wounded in Frankfurt, McCracken asked, was a dying woman taken to London—which would have involved an arduous Channel crossing by boat or, even less likely in 1937, an airplane trip—instead of obtaining assistance for her in France, Belgium or Holland? Hellman claims to have brought Julia's body back to America on "the old *de Grasse*" which McCracken called "an odd choice for a lady traveling with a corpse," since the *de Grasse* sailed from Le Havre, did not stop in England, and would have involved a second unnecessary Channel crossing for the dead Julia. Mary McCarthy, however, contradicted McCracken here; *her* research indicated that the *de Grasse* stopped at Plymouth, which would still have necessitated extra travel for Hellman and the coffin.

The time of Hellman's rush to England to retrieve Julia, May 1938, was the precise time when Hammett had collapsed in Hollywood and had been flown East to be in Hellman's care. Hammett remained in serious condition in Lenox Hill Hospital until June. If she was forced to leave his bedside to go to the dead Julia, said McCracken, she might have at least mentioned the dilemma in her account. Instead she states that a presumably healthy Hammett encouraged her to make the trip.

There was much more of a similar nature in McCracken's inquisition. Why is there no record of Julia's arrival and departure from England? Sick women cannot be brought into England without inquiries; corpses cannot be taken out. Hellman does address herself to one of these technicalities, the faked death certificate, but in a way that raises even more questions. After pointing out a number of additional inconsistencies, McCracken paused to exclaim: "Almost every detail is improbable to a degree that would disgrace a third-rate thriller, or plainly contradicted by the historical record."

McCracken saw material for a psychiatrist in the brutal fate of Julia and her equally violent end in her earlier incarnation in Hellman's memoirs as Alice, the fellow worker at Horace Liveright. Alice was killed in the Vienna riots of 1934, Julia lost a leg, but survived only to be mortally wounded in Frankfurt. But if McCracken was trying to build a case for Hellman's suppressed hostility toward her most noble character, he had to reconcile his theory with the numerous sudden deaths and maimings that make Hellman's memoirs hazardous for even its walk-ons. Chapter endings are the most dangerous.

A number of pages in McCracken's essay were devoted to the alleged misrepresentations and false claims in *Scoundrel Time*, particularly regarding Hellman's political beliefs. Much of that ground, however, had been well worked over by the book's earlier critics. But in his examination of Hellman's statements about Arthur Cowan's will, McCracken came upon a new area of Hellman revisionism, one that, while small, suggests an explanation for her inventions totally different from the usual assumption of self-aggrandizement.

In her *Pentimento* portrait of Cowan, Hellman says somewhat derisively that Cowan frequently dangled before her his will and the money he would be leaving her. According to Hellman, when Cowan died, no will was ever found. Thus the Cowan portrait concludes with the enticing picture of important money destined for Hellman—if only the will could be found. With some investigation, McCracken discovered that Cowan had indeed left a will, which was duly registered in his city of residence, Philadelphia. He bequeathed money to various women friends, but none to Hellman.

McCracken stumbled on another contradiction. The will made no mention of Cowan's 50 percent interest in the Hammett rights, which he bought when Hellman bought the other half, and which Hellman, on another occasion, said he "willed" to her. There was, however, a letter from Cowan's sister, an executor, relinquishing all claim to the Hammett rights in favor of Hellman. McCracken felt that probably came as a result of Hellman's convincing the sister that such was Cowan's intention. With or without that explanatory detail, McCracken's research into Cowan's will turned up the possibility that Hellman had been treated carelessly, if not shabbily, by Cowan. But with a few deft sentences she converts that hurtful reality into the far more intriguing and more palatable missing will.

Although McCracken did not say so, there is an aspect to that particular alteration of fact that sets it apart. In other instances Hellman altered facts in matters that bore directly on her public persona—her historic friendships, her involvement in great events, her courageous exploits. Because of the many testimonials from friends who insisted that Hellman never lied to them even over small matters, it might then appear that she lied only to the public, never to those close to her. But whether or not Lillian Hellman was remembered in the will of Arthur W. Cowan, a man of no particular renown, was a matter that could be of interest only to Hellman. By totally revising the truth of that personal matter in her memoirs, Hellman was lying not to the public, but to herself.

Thus, at least some of Hellman's fabrications may have

stemmed from a murkier area beyond the all-but-routine myth-making of celebrated figures. Perhaps she altered the truth not only to enhance her public image—to leave with posterity a portrait of the woman she would have liked to have been, a life she would have liked to have led—but to meet a psychological demand for a less painful reality. There is a significant difference between a person engaged in dishonest public relations and one who is fundamentally delusional. In Hellman's case, she may have worked out a compromise with her psyche: to realize wish-fulfillment fantasies and salve painful truths by revising her history in her memoirs and perhaps thereby forestalling a collapse into psychosis.

Such a dire analysis would depend on the degree to which Hellman knew she was lying. Diana Trilling, driving to the beach at Martha's Vineyard one time with Hellman, was stunned to hear her say, "But then, Diana, you're two years older than I am." Trilling looked at Hellman in the hope that she was joking and was amazed to see she wasn't. For many years it was well established between them that they were the same age. In talking about a bad experience Hellman had in the intensive-care unit of a Boston hospital, Richard de Combray said, "Maybe she dreamed it, for in those last months she'd frequently mix up dreams and fantasies and realities, although she certainly had those tendencies all along." Hellman's anger at Joe Rauh for advising her to drop the libel suit against Mary McCarthy indicated she did not know she was vulnerable on the matter of honesty, that she thought of herself as a totally truthful person whose every utterance could withstand the harshest scrutiny.

Perhaps the most revealing story of Hellman's certainty about at least some of her alterations of reality concerned her great friend William Wyler. When Wyler died a few years before Hellman's own death in 1984, she told his New York Times obituary writer an anecdote to illustrate not only Wyler's generosity but his forgetfulness about it. In the early fifties, when she and Hammett were in financial trouble, Wyler had called her and said, "Lillian, I hear you and Hammett are broke. I like Dash and I love you. I am opening a bank account in your name and depositing thirty-five thousand dollars. Every six months I will check the balance and make sure it is brought back up to thirty-five thousand."

Years later, at a dinner party for the Wylers, when Hellman told the group of his generosity, Wyler had said, "Lillian, I don't know what the hell you are talking about. I never opened any account for you."

Hellman concluded that Wyler's kindness was of so little importance to him, it slipped his mind. But it would appear that Hellman, with her gift for developing plot, had imagined the attractive story, had come to believe it, and in later years was so convinced of its truth that she was willing to hold it up against a denial from the central figure. Her overtures to Muriel Gardiner, on the other hand, indicate strongly that, when forced by such an implacable reality as a lawsuit or the prospect of public ridicule, Hellman had no trouble differentiating between fact and fantasy.

With the strong possibility that Hellman manipulated the truth, the question arises of whether Hammett was aware of her failing. (Hellman quotes him as saying "Liars are bores.") There do not seem to be any instances of her bending the truth while he was alive, which suggests he may have been a brake on that impulse. Indeed, his fierce attitudes toward honesty may have had a primary appeal for Hellman, who knew she had problems along these lines and may have realized her need for a strong disciplinarian along with a "cool teacher."

A literary preoccupation of Hammett's raises a strange possibility. In discussing Hammett's having used her as the model for the delightful Nora Charles in *The Thin Man*, Hellman admits sardonically that he had told her she was also the model for the other two female characters. These women are liars, but particularly the more important of the two, Mimi Wynant, who lies constantly. In fact, in *The Maltese Falcon* and *The Thin Man*, the most memorable characters, after the Charleses and Sam Spade, are two sexy women, Brigid O'Shaughnessy and Mimi Wynant, both with indefatigable lying as their strongest characteristic. It is tempting to speculate that Hammett had a fascination with women who lie; he certainly did in his writing. While one would hardly expect villains in crime stories to be models of honesty, Brigid O'Shaughnessy and Mimi Wynant seem to go beyond normal criminal deceptiveness and stand out in the memory as inexhaustible fonts of imaginative lies. Many types of villains are available to the mystery writer. Indeed Hammett created some memorable ones—Gutman, the Sydney Greenstreet character in *The Maltese Falcon*, for instance—but none of the other possibilities for villainy captured with equal persistence the creative fancy of Dashiell Hammett. In his own life, he seems to have had quite the opposite predilection; he was fiercely honest himself and required equal honesty from others. But while the judgmental Hammett might require honesty in those he dealt with, the bored, amusement-hunting Hammett might have found titillation in a chronic transgressor.

At one point in *The Thin Man* Nick Charles is moved to a lyrical outburst about Mimi's lying: "The chief thing . . . is not to let her tire you out. When you catch her in a lie, she admits it and gives you another lie to take its place and, when you catch her in that one, admits it and gives you still another, and so on. Most people—even women—get discouraged after you've caught them in the third or fourth straight lie and fall back on either the truth or silence, but not Mimi. She keeps trying, and you've got to be careful or you'll find yourself believing her, not because she seems to be telling the truth, but simply because you're tired of disbelieving her."

Although Hammett claimed to have had Hellman in mind when he wrote the character of Mimi, whether or not Mimi's lying was one of her borrowed characteristics must remain a speculation. Still, it is irresistible to consider together the two phenomena: an author who repeatedly revealed a fascination with lying ladies involved in a lifelong love affair with a woman who would be repeatedly accused of being one herself.

31

WHEN HELLMAN had the *Commentary* article by McCracken read to her, she picked up the phone, now her principal weapon, to reach Richard Poirier. With some difficulty she located him and asked if he had read the piece. He said that he had. "Well," she snapped, "what are we going to do about it?"

Poirier, whose mind at the moment was far from feelings of shared beleaguerment, made sympathetic murmurs while he thought how to respond. He came up with an idea. "It seems to me, Lillian," he said, "that is a job for your official biographer." Poirier was referring to William Abrahams, Hellman's editor at Little Brown on all of her memoirs, and the trusted friend she had recently named her official authorized biographer.

Hellman thought for a minute, then said, "You're right," and hung up. About an hour later, Poirier's phone rang again. This time it was Abrahams calling from San Francisco.

"Thanks a lot," he said.

Even though McCracken's attack on Hellman ran in the small-circulation *Commentary*, it caused a fair amount of talk and provided several weeks of ammunition for the "get Lillian" gossip platoons. Her physical condition would have seemed sufficient punishment for whatever crimes her enemies attributed to her. Her retaliatory instincts, however, remained keen. With Mary McCarthy she had counterattacked mightily (the litigation had passed an important judicial review, to the surprise of many, and was headed for trial); with Gellhorn she had raged loud enough to alarm George Plimpton; and with Muriel Gardiner, a far trickier matter, she had groped for an accommodation. She still had plenty of fight, but loyal lieutenants like Poirier and Abrahams were growing weary.

Her determination to fight back was not the only one of Hellman's forceful character traits to survive her physical decay. On Martha's Vineyard, the summer before her death, she made a triumphant personal appearance. A young film enthusiast, Roger McNiven, ran a series of classic films in West Tisbury that were followed by a talk from someone either connected with the making of the film being shown or knowledgeable about it. A friend of McNiven's who knew Hellman, seeing he had scheduled *The Little Foxes,* asked why he didn't invite her to speak at the screening. McNiven said he couldn't pay, and he had heard she was too feeble. The friend said she would ask Hellman, and returned with an acceptance. The night of the film, Hellman arrived with four young women and a masseuse in attendance. She sent McNiven off for some pillows. When he returned to his office, he found Hellman stark naked face down on a table, about to be massaged. The women indicated for him not to make a sound so that the nearly blind Hellman would not know he was there. (According to other friends, Hellman had exhibitionistic tendencies, and would not have cared.)

Drinks had been brought in thermoses, and Hellman repeatedly called for a fresh drink or a cigarette. When she was dressed again, she asked for McNiven. "You know, Roger," she said, "I don't do this kind of thing for nothing. . . ."

He was ready for anything.

"My fee is twenty-five dollars."

McNiven said that would be no problem. Hellman made many more demands, the last of which was that she be carried to the front of the auditorium so she could see the picture better, adding that every fifteen minutes or so she would have to be carried to the back for a fresh drink and a cigarette. Hellman's eyesight may have left her unaware of the stir she caused, but she went up the aisle as unobtrusively as the Pope at a group audience. McNiven thought that if during the discussion period she treated the audience as imperiously as she had been treating those in attendance on her, the talk would be a disaster. Midway during the screening, one of Hellman's companions said she didn't think Hellman could stick it out much longer. McNiven asked Hellman if he might stop the film so that she could speak right away. Hellman agreed.

"She was incredible. On stage she changed completely. She gave thoughtful, lengthy answers to all the questions, was generous in her praise for Bette Davis and Wyler, discussed Gregg Toland's deep-focus technique and how it had been used to heighten the drama. Everyone was fascinated. After she finished, she told me that she would like me to show *The Thin Man* sometime so she could speak about that. At the end of the evening, the audience went wild. They stood and cheered as she was carried up the aisle. I made my way to her to thank her. She looked down from her chair and said, 'Roger, you don't have to worry about the twenty-five dollars.'"

On September 2 of that summer, 1983, residents of Martha's Vineyard were astonished to pick up their copy of *The Vineyard Gazette* and read the following advertisement:

MY NAME IS
LILLIAN HELLMAN.

I would like to ask you to join me in signing this letter to the Telephone Company.

"We wish to protest the equipment that the Massachusetts Telephone Company owns on this Island. We pay high rates, but we get bad equipment and bad service. In this summer 1983 I, Lillian Hellman, have proof that out of 67 long-distance calls, more than 39 were interrupted, either because I could not hear or a disconnection happened. There is great difficulty in local calls as well."

Please send me your name and I will add it to the letter to be forwarded to the Telephone Company.

This is no demand, but I would be grateful if you

would contribute a small amount to this advertisement which cost $183.60. A check should be sent to P.O. Box 138, Vineyard Haven. If the amount runs over, your check will be returned to you.

The ad was reminiscent of Hellman's Committee for Public Justice days in the way she almost lost her thread of outrage as she bogged down in the matter of her cash outlay. And there was a slight suspicion, sad and poignant, among those who saw the ad that Hellman's real grievance against the Massachusetts Telephone Company was that she was deaf and old.

Hellman spent the last winter of her life with Mrs. William Wyler, whose large house on Summit Drive in Beverly Hills had a guest wing in which Hellman set up an independent household. She brought along a nurse and her cook, Theresa, the Jamaican who had kept house for her for several years.

"Lillian and I led separate lives," Mrs. Wyler recalls. "It was not a houseguest situation at all. We each had our own activities and would meet for dinner perhaps twice a week. Sometimes I would invite her to have dinner in my dining room that my cook prepared and sometimes we would eat in her part of the house, something her cook prepared. Lillian installed her own phone. Sometimes if I wanted to speak with her, I would knock on her door, but more often I would telephone her and she would telephone me.

"What most impressed me was the way Lillian responded to her ailments. She had the pacemaker and emphysema. Although she was nearly blind, she could see things at different ranges. For instance, at dinner she could not see what was on her plate, but she could make out something across the room. I'm not sure why, but she could barely walk and always had to have someone at her elbow. When we discussed her coming to stay with me, I mentioned the flight of stairs that led to her part of the house; she thought that would be no problem, that she had managed the stairs at Martha's Vineyard. But when she arrived, my stairs proved too difficult. Instead of just keeping to her room, she hired a student from UCLA to drive for her and to carry her up and down the stairs.

"If I had the health problems she had, I would just curl up my toes and close my eyes, but Lillian got herself dressed, made up and went out *every day*. Frequently she would go to a restaurant with a friend, or she would have her hair done, or she would go shopping, often to one of the beautiful produce markets we have out here. She especially loved the Irvine Ranch Market in the Beverly Center where she was pushed around in a wheelchair and she would examine all the produce and make a few purchases. She did something like that every day. I felt that this was her decision, her fight to stay alive, not to let go."

On a bright spring day in May 1984, Hellman, who was then seventy-eight, was pushed down Madison Avenue in a wheelchair. Her head thrown back, her mouth open wide, her eyes closed, she looked dead, or in the process of dying. The following night she attended a party given by Patricia Neal for her daughter at Visages, a very loud, very trendy, very crowded discotheque. A reporter, perhaps surprised at seeing an elderly blind woman in that setting, asked Hellman if she was enjoying the party. "I don't generally go to nightclubs," Hellman replied. "But I'd go anywhere for Pat Neal."

A Martha's Vineyard charter fishing-boat captain, Jack Koontz, had for several years shared a boat with Hellman and had taken her fishing every Saturday during the summers. In her last year, when she was blind and extremely frail, Koontz had to secure her in a chair when a speedboat approached to keep her from being knocked down by the wake. If the boat came close, Hellman would struggle to her feet, give the speedboat the finger and scream four-letter words. The week before she died Koontz received a phone call from her to arrange their next fishing date.

Peter Feibleman, who was working on a recipe-and-reminiscence book with Hellman almost until her death, tells an even stronger story of Hellman's indomitability. Alerted that the end might be near, Feibleman flew from his home in Los Angeles and arrived at her house on Martha's Vineyard. Before going in to greet her, he was briefed on her condition by the most recent nurse. (Hellman had a bad habit of biting her nurses' fingers.) Miss Hellman, he was told, was in great pain. She was blind, half paralyzed, had suffered strokes, had rage attacks, crying fits, couldn't walk, couldn't eat, couldn't sleep or even find a sitting position that wasn't agony. The nurse was convinced she was dying.

When the briefing was over, Feibleman entered Hellman's room and greeted her as nonchalantly as possible with, "How are you doing, Lillian?"

"Not good, Peter," she replied, "not good."

"So what's the matter?" he asked, granting her the sick person's right to catalogue ailments.

"This is the worst writer's block I've ever had."

The night before she died, Hellman was carried the short distance from her house to the Herseys for dinner. At one point she turned to Robert Brustein and said, "You know, Bob, you and I should spend a little time alone together." Brustein recalls the line, but discounts any romantic hint. Others present at the time think otherwise.

When John Hersey telephoned Milton Gordon on June 30, 1984, to say that Hellman had died, Gordon replied, "She didn't die, someone reached down from up there and grabbed her by the throat."

Despite the official loyalty of her close friends, there were many such private denigrations, impromptu asides, from others in Hellman's circle. A year after her death, friends of long standing would preface their discussion of Hellman with a disclaimer such as that of V. S. Pritchett's wife: "We were all rather *chopped* about Lillian." (Even without knowing that relic of British slang, it was clear Lady Pritchett meant "of two minds.") Or the more sweeping negation of another friend: "She was not a nice person, you know." Such remarks generally would be followed by an illustrative horror story.

One friend, also a well-known writer, was so bothered by this conflict in herself about Hellman that she compiled a list of pluses and minuses, and then decided the minuses won by far. "I judge people by the number of corpses they leave behind," she said, "and Lillian left a lot of corpses." The friend was not speaking of the damage done by Hellman to avowed enemies—peers like Mary McCarthy and Diana Trilling—but to the many less powerful people on whom she inflicted lasting wounds. Twenty years after Hellman screamed that she was a liar in front of a roomful of dignitaries, Nancy Kramer was still troubled by the scene, wondering how she could have deserved it, how she should have reacted. Cathy Kober still ached at the dressing-down letter she received from Hellman. The numbers of such Hellman casualties, the walking wounded, were large.

Hellman's prominence, as well as her fire-spewing eloquence, may have made her attacks more devastating than she realized. But from their nature, the diatribes seem to have been calculated to do maximum harm, which is, of course, the nature of rage. In Hellman's case, however, she may have felt that as her fury subsided, so would the damage. Or she may not have cared; contrition was not part of her makeup. There was a pain that had to be redressed. Still, large as was her list of victims, it was small compared to the hundreds of people who felt their lives enriched by knowing Lillian Hellman and impoverished by her death.

Hellman was buried under a large pine tree on a gentle rise at one end of the Abel's Hill Cemetery in Chilmark. The outpouring of love and respect at her funeral both at the graveside and in the press across the country—*The New York Times* placed the obituary on the front page—was remarkable even for a public figure, but particularly for a writer, ordinarily less visible than other celebrities. Since Martha's Vineyard was a difficult place for distant friends to get to quickly, the plan was to have a small funeral right away, on July 3, followed by a large memorial service in New York in the fall (the memorial service did not take place).

The funeral's arrangers, primarily Peter Feibleman and John and Barbara Hersey, had not reckoned on the devotion of Hellman's many friends. People arrived from around the country, turning the event into the sort of famous-name congeries Hellman would have relished. Warren Beatty flew from Los Angeles to pay his respects alongside Carly Simon, Norman Mailer, Mike Wallace, Ruth Gordon, Katharine Graham, James Reston, Mike Nichols (who chartered a plane to fly up from New York), Carl Bernstein, Patricia Neal, Jules Feiffer, William Styron and many others of similar prominence. The numbers were swelled by large groups of tourists who had come to photograph and gawk at the famous.

Eulogies were delivered by Feibleman, William Styron, Pat Neal, Annabel Nichols, Jerome Wiesner, Robert Brustein and

John Hersey. Styron said, "I think we had more fights per man and woman contact than probably anyone alive. We were fighting all the time, and we loved each other a great deal for sure, because the vibrations were there. But our fights were never really, oddly enough, over abstract things like politics or philosophy or social dilemmas; they were always over such things as whether a Smithfield ham should be served hot or cold, or whether I had put too much salt in the black-eyed peas."

Of all the eulogies, perhaps the most moving was that of John Hersey:

"I'd like to say a few words about Lillian's anger. Most of us were startled by it from time to time. Anger was her essence. It was at the center of that passionate temperament. It informed her art. The little foxes snapped at each other, we could see their back hairs bristle, we could smell their foxiness—they were real and alive because of the current of anger that ran through them, as it did through so many of Lillian's characters. What I want to say is that this voltage of Lillian's was immensely important and valuable to our time. It electrified a mood of protest. The protest was that of every great writer. 'Life ought to be better than this.' . . .

"Dear Lillian, you are a finished woman now. I mean 'finished' in its better sense. You shone with a high finish of integrity, decency, uprightness. You have given us this anger to remember and use in a bad world. We thank you, we honor you, and we all say goodbye to you now with a love that should calm that anger of yours forever."

After the ceremony, there was a reception for about seventy people at Hellman's house. The Herseys and Feibleman selected the guests, a task that strained memories as to who had just arrived on Hellman's hate list and who had just been reprieved. An effort was made to serve the kind of food Hellman would have served: a baked Virginia ham, spaghetti al pesto from homegrown basil, thinly sliced cold roast beef, deviled eggs, assorted cheeses, French bread, salad and vegetables from her garden.

Hellman's will, which had been updated two months before she died, contained some surprises in the division of an estate of close to four million dollars. Her principal beneficiary was Peter Feibleman, to whom she left $100,000 in cash, 50 percent of all royalties from literary works and her Martha's Vineyard house (minus $100,000 of the proceeds if he chose to sell it). She also left cash bequests of from $1,000 to $40,000 to eighteen friends and employees, among them John Melby and Raya Kopelev. The bulk of her money went into two trust funds. One was the Lillian Hellman Fund to encourage the arts and sciences with grants and gifts for deserving applicants, the other was the Dashiell Hammett Fund, which also gave grants and gifts but stipulated that, in making awards, the trustees should "be guided by the political, social and economic beliefs which, of course, were radical, of the late Dashiell Hammett who was a believer in the doctrines of Karl Marx."

Most of the newspapers picked up on this curious proviso, perhaps because few prominent Americans had, in recent years, remembered Karl Marx in their wills, and because Dashiell Hammett, who was being commemorated in this unusual way, had made no such request in his own will. Hellman left each of Hammett's daughters $35,000 in cash and the rights to their father's works, dividing those rights into three shares, with two shares going to Jo and one share to Mary. In that way, the wishes expressed twenty-three years earlier in Hammett's will were finally being carried out—to a degree. The rights had been well picked over and would be worth substantially less now than they had been in the two decades since Hammett's death when Hellman had enjoyed all the proceeds from his writings. Except for the $70,000 Hellman left the daughters, the money she got from Hammett—the quarter of a million for *The Dain Curse* movie sale, the proceeds from his book of short stories and so on—was now going into trusts and bequests of Hellman's choosing, not Hammett's.

Despite the outpouring of love and respect at Hellman's funeral and in the newspaper testimonials, the attacks against her veracity continued, although perhaps somewhat muted, and a growing body of people in writing and publishing, as well as the readers of the more serious publications, were coming to the conclusion that she was indeed an "apocryphiar" of no small dimension. Up until now most of those convinced of her dishonesty were people with other inducements to thinking the worst of her—professional rivals, political adversaries and those for whom broad success was in itself suspect. As for her many distinguished friends, even after her death they were fiercely loyal, generally dismissing the attacks as the envy of the less talented and the less celebrated.

Among Hellman enthusiasts in the public at large, the documented demonstrations of her dishonesty seemed to have no effect whatsoever. To some who valued Hellman as a writer, whether or not she told the documentary truth was unimportant when held against the overall strength of her works. That was especially true of those readers who had not gone to her books for factual reporting, but rather for a deft and engaging evocation of a career, a character, a time and place. How serious would it be if some of it were untrue?

The necessity to argue in defense of writers of nonfiction sticking to the truth is, for many, unthinkable. Yet justifications for falsification are put forward and should be answered. Some of the justifiers—Norman Mailer was one—invoke the goddess of art to claim that a degree of falsity may be necessary in the higher quest of literature. That argument is, however, undermined by the existence of a literary category—fiction—that permits every manner of creative freedom, from complete invention to minor alterations in otherwise true events. Fiction writers are free to mix any proportions of reality and invention they choose. Other justifiers take a more modest stand and plead that, as long as the overall picture is valid, what difference does it make if some of the details are false? That is a harder question to answer, but in Hellman's case far more than details are at stake.

To call a piece of writing nonfiction does not by any means guarantee its accuracy, but it does call into play an immediate obligation on the part of the writer to make the writing as accurate as possible. That obligation binds most journalists and other writers of nonfiction, not just because they have scruples, but from fear of professional, and even legal, consequences. In the long run, reputations in this field rest, as much as anything, on the writer's record of accuracy. In the short run, one discredited fact, even a minor one, can cause a reader to put aside a book or, even worse, bring down a dismissive review upon an otherwise worthy book. Such an obsession with accuracy, drilled into young journalists by battle-scarred editors, is based on the argument used by defense attorneys, probably with equal injustice, to discredit damaging witnesses who have been caught in an inconsequential lie: "If you find a piece of rotten meat in a stew, you don't fish it out and continue eating; you reject the whole dish." With Hellman's memoirs, the discovery of a few fabrications raises the unpleasant prospect of how many undiscovered ones may remain. (Mary McCarthy has evidence that the "Willy" chapter of *Pentimento* is just as untrue as "Julia.") Should her books, proven to contain some untruths, be rejected like contaminated stews?

There are things to be said in favor of Hellman's memoir inventions. The stories of derring-do naturally are more exciting when they are presented as real events that happened to the very real Lillian Hellman. Even Muriel Gardiner admitted that Hellman brought her story to a broad public it would otherwise not have found. Her own account of her life was turned down by two American publishers for not being sufficiently dramatic. When it was finally published by Yale, it had modest sales. But while that would tend to confirm that storytelling relies on artistry as much as on gripping material, it doesn't prove the artistic necessity for Hellman to present Gardiner's tale as events that actually happened to Hellman herself. She could have written about the real Gardiner or she could have fictionalized her story, as indeed she did in *Watch on the Rhine*. Whatever documentary excitement is added by having those adventures occur to the celebrated Lillian Hellman would seem to be outweighed by the vainglory of making false boasts.

Perhaps the primary reason untruth is a serious matter in Hellman's case is that she was a respected public figure writing about matters of more than passing importance, particularly in *Scoundrel Time*. In that book she was offering her version of one of the nation's major traumas—the McCarthy period—and she was casting hard judgments on both governmental authority and the conduct of other prominent figures. That takes her writing out of the realm of diversion and into the area of history, where the truth is elusive enough without deliberate alterations in the record.

With the writings of a well-known and respected public figure like Hellman there is also an acute danger that the inventions—on any subject—may become part of the permanent record.

As an example, Hellman's vivid but discredited story about the party given for Ernest Hemingway in Hollywood by the Fredric Marches is repeated (and credited to Hellman) in the Hemingway biography by Carlos Baker, a book Martha Gellhorn refers to sarcastically as "the King James version." The anecdote, now validated by two such authorities as Hellman (firsthand) and Baker (scholarly), becomes an indelible part of the Hemingway lore. The same story in *An Unfinished Woman* has a haunting sketch of Scott Fitzgerald and provides a penetrating revelation of Fitzgerald's feelings of intimidation by Hemingway. That anecdote will undoubtedly be picked up by future writers on Fitzgerald to help gauge the dynamic between the day's two major literary figures. Whether or not Hellman's anecdote is true becomes a matter of more importance than whether or not it is diverting.

Hellman herself falls victim of the distorting fallout from invented happenings. While writing *The Children's Hour,* she relates, she became so upset by Hammett's drinking that she went to Paris for two and a half months to work in peace. It was during that stay that she made a sudden trip to Vienna to visit her friend Julia, who had been wounded in antifascist riots and was in a hospital in serious condition. The entire two-and-a-half-month European sojourn does not, however, fit into Hellman's 1934, a year in which she wrote her first play while also working as a reader for Herman Shumlin. She claims to have left their summer-rental beach house for Europe, which means she went abroad sometime during the summer. Hellman placed the completed manuscript of *The Children's Hour* on Shumlin's desk in September and it went into rehearsal in October. Other facts render the 1934 hospital visit to Julia impossible. The street fighting to which Hellman refers is clearly the famous attack on the Dollfuss government on the socialist workers' apartment blocks, which was the only violence in Vienna that year. It took place on February 12. Hellman had left the *summer*-rental beach house she shared with Hammett to go to Paris. Once in Paris that summer, she had spoken several times by phone to a healthy Julia before learning that she was wounded.

Of course Hellman's geographic location when she wrote *The Children's Hour* makes little difference. What does make a difference is if she wrote it with Hammett at her side or on a different continent. The European trip, whether confused with another trip or invented outright, thus muddles the circumstances of her first solo dramatic writing, a matter of interest to future drama historians. It even raises a darker suspicion: that Hellman, rankled by all the talk of Hammett's help, deliberately sought in her memoirs to "remove" herself from him during the creative period.

Dishonesty in recounting one's personal history can confound efforts at understanding. Hellman once told Yolande Fox, a former Miss America, that she had experienced the most brutal anti-Semitism growing up in New Orleans. The subject arose when Fox told Hellman about the prejudice she had felt in Alabama as a child with a French Catholic background. Hellman went on to say that it was the scars from this mindless cruelty that made her, as an adult, so mean and combative. Thus she contradicted directly her account of the same subject in her memoirs, where she says she was all but unaware of her Jewishness until she was an adult, and that she has nothing but the warmest recollections of her New Orleans youth. Either story can be true; both cannot. Perhaps Hellman, on a comradely impulse of shared pain, gave herself childhood persecutions that were worse than those Fox had undergone. Or perhaps she gave Fox a unique glimpse of the truth about her childhood, and the idealized picture of the memoirs and countless interviews was the reconstruction. Fox is convinced it was the latter. "Lillian and I were both in analysis and she admitted that the anti-Semitism she experienced was an area she was unable to resolve."

Another telling argument against fabrications in allegedly true accounts emerges when Hellman's memoirs are reread with a degree of skepticism. Odd happenings and coincidences that seemed delightfully serendipitous on first reading now become jejune plotting and clumsy manipulation. One of the most memorable moments in the three memoirs occurs in *Scoundrel Time* when Hellman and Hammett are preparing to leave the farm they have been forced to give up. They look up from their work inside the house to see forty or fifty deer emerge from the woods to nibble, idly and without fear, leaves and buds around the house. The deer remain in plain view near the house for over two hours while Hellman and Hammett sit silently watching the animals' moving farewell. The story, which is told with considerable artistry, is beautiful and mystical. So much of its beauty, however, depends on the unearthliness of an actual happening. If it was a product of imagination, any six-year-old child could have done as well.

A problem with making up stories like "Julia" is that the discovery of their falsity discredits stories that are perhaps true, like the deers' farewell. True or false, "Julia" is a good story. But the memoirs have many other stories that are good only if true; they are not creditable enough to hold up under the burden of skepticism and not interesting enough to survive disbelief. Once distrust takes hold of a reader, he finds himself in an unmarked wonderland.

Nora Ephron, who knew Hellman, writes in her book *Heartburn* of the unbelievability of the Hellman-Hammett relationship as presented in the memoirs. Ephron bases her disbelief on the violation done her own view of the man-woman possibilities by the hard-drinking, tough-talking, until-death bond that Hellman describes. It would seem unfair of Ephron to rely on such subjective disproof, but surely reinforcing her rejection of the affair's characterization was an awareness of Hellman's burgeoning reputation for doctoring the truth. There is a bitter irony in others disbelieving what is important to you because you fabricated on matters of far less importance. It is a dilemma, however, that every fibbing child has had to face.

During the television interviews for PBS, Hellman casually told interviewer Marilyn Berger that she had become pregnant by Hammett, that he had wanted her to have the child but she would not. She adds that the same occurred during her marriage to Arthur Kober. Since both men were dead, and good friends of both Hammett's and Hellman's do not recall any mention of this, the question is left hanging of whether Hellman, who professed to love children, had really refused to have children despite the protests of the men involved or if her childlessness became easier to accept if she made it her own choice. (Berger appeared so startled by the strange announcement, she neglected to ask Hellman why she had ruled out motherhood.)

Another reaction comes with a skeptical rereading of the memoirs. So many improbabilities and contradictions emerge that the second-time reader can't help marveling that it was all believed on first reading. There is a natural disposition to believe representations in a book published by a reputable publisher, and by an established writer, even more by a writer as likable, admirable and self-deprecating as the Hellman that emerges from the text. Another prop to credulity is the ever-present fact of Hellman's prominence and achievement. Lies are told by criminals, politicians and naughty children, not famous playwrights. Once the possibility of falsehood is introduced, the entire edifice crumbles.

The small effect the revelations about Hellman's honesty had on her popularity is a phenomenon and says something about the creation and maintenance of mythical figures. There seems to be a trial period during which the public is watching and exercising a certain amount of judgment, a weighing of appearances. But when those appearances add up to a character the public likes— in Hellman's case the tough, ugly little woman, the steel-trap mind, concerned, courageous, loyal, feisty, riddled with principles, swimming against the stream—the public rivets the character over the actual person like a suit of permanent armor against which a hundred articles of debunking exposé will seem the merest scratching against steel.

The impregnability of the fantasy character is not unlike our resistance to believing damaging accusations against close friends, but with an important difference. It is normal to marshal all possible rationalizations to shunt aside accusations directed at people we like. But with actual friends, we must continue to live with them in a world of reality. If it is proved to us beyond doubt that they lie, steal, molest children—we have no choice but to adjust to the new information—information which is not abstract but which could have a direct bearing on our lives. Admirers of public figures, on the other hand, are under no such pressures. Damaging information about them can cause uneasiness, perhaps complete disillusion and rejection. But if the affection or need for such an ideal is strong enough, the public can make the subtle shift from the real person, their imagined "friend," to the mythic, armor-plated counterpart which cannot be harmed by unpleasant facts. When the "friendship" has no basis in reality, reality has far less chance of destroying it.

The distinction is fine between attitudes about a real but unknown person and an imaginary or mythical one. We see the fragility of this line when actors are confused with the characters they play or, conversely, when a moving film performance can generate interest in the actor's views on nuclear disarmament. Countless convicted criminals, indicted politicians and scandal-plagued film stars have been the beneficiaries of such a psychological mechanism; it seems that to a large degree Lillian Hellman was, too. Samuel McCracken, a prime Hellman denigrator, despaired of the public's ever coming to terms with the truth about Hellman and instead addressed the concluding admonition of his essay in *Commentary* to writers and academics. Confident that he had proven beyond doubt Hellman's dishonesty, he wrote: "Her eventual reputation in this regard . . . will tell us a good deal about the health, intellectual no less than moral, of our literary establishment."

Such a challenge, if its validity is acknowledged, would present knotty problems for Hellman's friends, many of whom were grand marshals of the literary establishment. But personal friendships always present special problems in moral dilemmas, and Hellman had more than her share of friends. That she was loved by large numbers of them may say simply that they knew no more of the negative side than did the readers of her books; in addition, they knew considerably more of the positive side—the sense of fun, the generosity, the thoughtful hostessing, the raucousness, the earthiness, the acts of kindness. While most of her friends had surely witnessed the terrible temper, it is unlikely they saw its ugliest manifestations: the cruelty, the bullyings, the attempts to get people fired, the discrediting falsehoods, the blackmailings. On the other hand, some very intimate friends, Peter Feibleman for one, in the last years saw so much of an ugly side, how difficult and demanding she became, that the larger accusations against her may have seemed less important. If you are receiving middle-of-the-night phone calls, listening to drunken rantings about being unloved and neglected, and you are bound by "family" honor to tolerate that sort of thing, whether or not the caller made up some stories about events in 1937 becomes of minor relevance.

As with her writing, Hellman had a good degree of control over what she wanted her friends to know, while they in turn had a degree of control over what negative information they would acknowledge—or even expose themselves to. (Why read that article everyone says is so mean to Lillian?) Most friendships involve a trade-off of positive and negative qualities, which would be particularly true in Hellman's world of names and near-names, where vainglorious attractions would frequently override profound reservations. If Hellman had been the old money of radical causes in the forties, she was, in her final years, the old money of show business and bookish celebrity—some would even argue, royalty.

Apart from the powerful lure of her fame, few people could match Hellman's record of long-lasting, solid friendships. In addition to the well-known bonds with Hammett and Dorothy Parker, she had been loved for half a century by men like Howard Bay and John Hersey, neither of whom were her lovers and both of whom are principled and perceptive and unlikely to forgive anything in the name of celebrity. As for former lovers, Ralph Ingersoll appears from his memoirs to have carried a love for Hellman to his grave, John Melby in his seventies appears to love her still, and her Lincoln Brigade longshoreman lover, Randall Smith, also in his seventies, says, "She was the greatest person I've ever known. Period."

Lillian Hellman knew how to *write* a terrific person, she knew how to *be* a terrific person—and for a great number of people she was just that for many years. For those with fuller information, the reality shows catastrophic divergences from the exemplary character she affected and depicted. For some, that may strip her of any claim to admiration; for others, it may be as irrelevant as an awareness of the ugly backstage ropes and grids to the pleasure in watching a production of *Swan Lake.*

The picture of Hellman alone at her typewriter, writing her memoirs, is haunting. The disparate motives that surely struggled within her—to write a gripping tale, to be admired, to settle scores, to justify herself, to write out the pain and humiliation, to write in the glory—all of those could have come to supersede the impulse to present an accurate record. She might have felt that not only the blank pages were "wanting" but so was her history, if only in her own eyes. Perhaps she approached the task with her well-trained dramatist's eye and sought to create a character that "worked." And sitting in that creative posture—weighing what to include, what to omit—the temptation to break loose from the confining truth may have been too great to resist. And she may have lost the ability to distinguish between what she had been and what she wished she had been.

There is little doubt that Hellman doctored, refined and expanded the image of herself that would be left in the memoirs. Yet her concern for image was a late development and had not been an overriding motivation of her life; had it been, the most elementary sense of public relations would have moved her toward reclusiveness, allowing the public to see only what she revealed in her writings. Hellman, on the contrary, kept herself highly visible for the fifty years of her prominence. Instead of creating her character and then protecting it behind a wall of privacy, she brandished it on the front lines of notoriety where it could be shot at with ease.

For all of her prodigious impact on the world—plays, books, loves, friends, politics, social criticism—there seems little doubt that her greatest contribution was the character that she created in the memoirs. So much attention has been given to the truth or falsity of the portrait that the creative feat has been overlooked. In order to be able to get such a character down on paper, a writer must have a profound knowledge of the world, of human nature and of the particular psychology being created. It requires much torturous life experience and an ensuing catharsis. It requires a rare sensitivity to what delights or repels others, an original flair to set the character apart, a strong moral sense (to be projected into the character) and a facility with words that precisely complements the personality being presented. In fact, it requires many of the skills and sensibilities that make up a great fiction writer or dramatist.

The achievement in such a creation is major and renders all but irrelevant the question of whether or not such a character actually existed. For the author to stand up at the end and say,

"This Lillian Hellman you've been reading about, this is me," is, of course, a lie. And the fraudulence must alter the perception of her integrity. But it doesn't diminish Hellman's creative achievement. The Lillian Hellman that is widely known may turn out in part to be just another admirable literary work fashioned by an author with less than admirable character. There is nothing rare about that. What is regrettable is that the real Hellman, although not as admirable, is, with her mixture of strengths and failings, far more interesting. And had she set her artistry to a frank and accurate self-portrayal, the accomplishment could have been far greater.

There was much in the character she portrayed that was true of Hellman herself. The distortions were more in the omissions, the exaggerations and the manifest conceit of some of her claims for herself. Consistent to both was a woman of fierce curiosity, ravenous for life and determined to realize her talents to the fullest. She was a woman of splendid loves, and even more splendid hatreds. In her fervor for a more just world she combined those passions—love for those she saw as abetting her vision, hatred for those she saw as opposing it. That is not to say her vision was sharp and well thought out. Even her close political allies could make little sense of her political beliefs. One old friend of Hellman's, a leading intellectual whom she greatly admired, said, "Don't rule out idiocy. With Lillian it was fifty years of *shtick*." But without analyzing her positions, or attempting to analyze them and getting nowhere, her admirers saw in her the passion—and that was what they liked. With the public it was the same. Every attempt at sorting out the fundamental beliefs from the tangle of her views, stances and actions leads to no ideological bedrock—only an overriding emotion: anger.

The playwright Marsha Norman made a pilgrimage to Martha's Vineyard in the summer of 1983 to talk with Hellman, whose anger, she said, had inspired her to become a writer. A small amount of conversation revealed that their anger—even on the most superficial psychological level—was aimed at quite different targets. It was enough for Norman that they were both angry. Perhaps that provides an important clue: that for her devotees Hellman became the household god of anger—not political anger, social anger, feminist anger, racial anger—just anger.

Hellman's anger revealed a hatred for the world, a hatred for the cruel mistakes of an unjust order, both natural and political, inflicted on her and others. So much of the thrust of her life was fueled by a desire to correct those mistakes—whether by irate dramas, political engagement or, on a more personal level, her doctorings of reality. At the same time, few people have ever loved the world as intensely, rejoiced so in its possibilities and grasped so eagerly for its rewards.

EPILOGUE

WHEN I FIRST undertook to write this book, I felt that because Lillian Hellman had written three memoirs of her own, a biography had to be objective. She had had her crack at the truth; now it was someone else's turn. I would seek her cooperation, but, doubting she would give it, I would go ahead without it. Also, knowing of efforts on her part to control what was written about her, I resolved not to yield any editorial rights in case they were requested in exchange for cooperation. (They weren't.) I also knew that Hellman, when feeling besieged, could hurl lethal thunderbolts into various power centers, causing any manner of short circuits. When one contemplates angering an individual of her fame and combative reflexes, one must also contemplate her capability to speak instantly on the phone to an editor of *The New York Times Book Review*, or the president of the company that might be interested in publishing the book.

I was convinced that the best strategy in approaching Miss Hellman, whom I had met only once, and briefly, would be to have a book contract in place before writing her of my intentions. It was based on the theory that a *fait accompli* was harder to destroy than a tentative project, however fierce the lightning.

437

Simon and Schuster, my publishers, agreed. Early in March 1984, I wrote Hellman a respectful letter expressing my gratification at being contracted to write about her, citing my admiration for her work and interest in her life, adding that I had no political axes to grind or theater history to rewrite. I concluded by saying I would be grateful for whatever cooperation she would give me. Between the lines, of course, it was implied that I would proceed with the book with or without her blessing.

Four days after I mailed the letter (she was staying in Los Angeles at the time at the home of Mrs. William Wyler), Michael Korda, the editor-in-chief of Simon and Schuster, received an angry phone call from Hellman asking how he, an old friend, could have stabbed her in the back in such a fashion? Korda, who had known Hellman since he was three years old, tried to mollify her by saying that she would be in good hands, that I was fair and was not setting out to write a hostile book. Somewhat calmed, Hellman then said that the main reason she did not want such a third-person biography was that she was planning to sponsor her own with her publishers, Little Brown, "somewhere down the line."

Two days later, on March 9, 1984, an announcement appeared in *The New York Times* that Lillian Hellman had designated her editor at Little Brown, William Abrahams, to be her official biographer. Although the timing of the news release was suggestive, I had to acknowledge that Hellman and Abrahams might have been discussing a biography for months, even years, and had only been moved to immediate action by my letter. Abrahams, in a conversation with a friend of his and mine, eliminated that possibility. He said he had received a call from Hellman "out of the blue," urging him to come to her at once to discuss initiating a third-party biography. They spent several hours considering a number of friendly authors, inevitably finding reasons to disqualify each. Seemingly stumped, Hellman announced to Abrahams she was going to lie down and "sleep on it." When she awoke, she told him she had had a dream. *He* was to be her official biographer. The announcement of his selection ran in the *Times* the next day.

While Hellman's refusal to assist my book had been anticipated—and I didn't rule out the possibility of her changing her mind—the larger question was how far would she go to obstruct it. Her hurried appointment of an official biographer seemed a substantial move in that direction. It wasn't until many weeks later that I became aware of additional steps she had taken. Talking with Hammett biographer Diane Johnson, I was told that Renata Adler had received a letter from Hellman asking her not to talk with anyone but her official biographer. That was alarming, not because I felt Miss Adler was the key to the Lillian Hellman story, but, on the contrary, because I had never heard her mentioned among the large number of names I was now coming to recognize as Hellman's friends. It conjured a picture of Hellman sending out her letter to the subscription list of *The New York Review of Books.*

I phoned Richard Wilbur, who is a friendly neighbor in Key West, and with whom I had already talked casually about Hellman. Embarrassed, Wilbur told me that he too had received first a telegram from Hellman, then "the letter." On his own generous volition, Wilbur wrote Hellman on my behalf, using an argument I had already arrived at to persuade reluctant sources: enemies are only too willing to come forward; if friends withhold positive information, the resulting picture could be unbalanced. Hellman replied to Wilbur that she might be acting foolishly and she might be taking herself too seriously, but she wanted him to abide by her wishes.

I eventually estimated that about twenty of Hellman's friends received the letter, but in the course of my research into her life, I have been gratified by the number who were either overlooked by her or who chose not to be bound by her injunction. For the most part, the recipients were members of her intimate circle in the last years of her life, the years when her important work was behind her. Many of them knew her only when she was enjoying the prolonged testimonial celebration that is the old age of a popular and gregarious celebrity.

A life with the range and force of Lillian Hellman's leaves in its wake a trail of intimates—some dead, some estranged, some merely forgotten. I found, rather than a dearth of sources, that I could spend the rest of my life talking with people who had known Lillian Hellman. In a sense her letter was a blessing; those who intended to abide by it, I discovered, were also those so devoted to her as to neutralize their testimony. It also set me to ruminating about what lay behind her call to defensive arms. Whatever her personal reasons, she risked damage to her image as a civil libertarian if her effort at censorship became known.

Why did she care so much? Such a biography, or five such books, would in no way preclude an authorized version. There was always the possibility that she feared being misunderstood by an insensitive writer or trivialized by an inept one. But, as a celebrity, Hellman had lived with that fear for fifty years and had, on balance, little to complain about: the few attacks against her, while virulent, were minuscule compared with library stacks heavy with adulatory interviews and affectionate comment. If a book was to emerge that was unfair or gratuitously hostile, reviewers, many of whom were Hellman enthusiasts, would make quick work of it. She seemed to be attempting an immunity from vulnerability to the press shared by all prominent figures, from presidents to Mafia capos.

I became intrigued by the possibility that, after a rash of exposés, Hellman still had things to hide, that she dreaded the idea of an objective researcher poking through her life and her writings. And while that possibility fired my curiosity and energized my research, I knew I had to guard against the project's becoming an inquest, a search for evidence to confirm my hunch. In fact, I soon forgot about it as the biographer's obsession gripped me to pursue every lead, whether or not it pointed toward glory or shame for my subject.

After several months of research, I made more than enough progress to dispel the fears brought on by Hellman's campaign of obstruction. I had talked with many people and been assured of cooperation by many more. As I had learned from past projects, when you begin your research you are peddling vacuum cleaners door-to-door, but somewhere in the middle of writing a nonfiction book a turning point occurs and sources come to you. That indeed happened.

Then, after a series of profitable interviews, I returned to my home in Key West to find a letter from Hellman that had arrived many weeks earlier. It consisted of only one sentence:

February 29, 1984

Dear Mr. Wright,
I do not wish a biography of me and therefore I cannot
see you.

Most sincerely,
Lillian Hellman

The letter had been typed, not on personal stationary but on
a sheet of plain white bond. "Miss Lillian Hellman" was typed
underneath her signature. The name was also typed at the top of
the page above her Los Angeles address, all neatly centered.

After Hellman's death, and about a year after receiving the
letter, I pulled it out of my files to check the exact wording. I saw
something I had not noticed before. Underneath the address a
phone number had been typed. I checked with Mrs. Wyler in Los
Angeles, and it was indeed the number for the phone Hellman
had installed in the Wyler guest quarters.

I was fascinated. If you dismiss someone as curtly as Hellman
had dismissed me, why offer a phone number? Even if her secretary added the number to her letters as a matter of course, Hellman surely would have been consulted in this case about whether
or not she wished to add her private number. If it was deliberate,
what had Hellman wanted? For me to call and plead? To offer
myself for a tongue-lashing? To match wits? To convince her of
my mettle? My persistence? Perhaps the phone number's inclusion was a clerical error, but I preferred to think it was a signal
that went unanswered and would remain, like much about Lillian
Hellman, an enigma.

NOTES

The following abbreviations have been used throughout these notes:

LH Lillian Hellman
DH Dashiell Hammett
HRC Humanities Research Center at the University of Texas
NYT *The New York Times*
NYHT The *New York Herald Tribune*
WW William Wright

Books referred to frequently:

UW *An Unfinished Woman* by Lillian Hellman (Boston: Little Brown, 1969).

PN *Pentimento* by Lillian Hellman (Boston: Little Brown, 1973).

ST *Scoundrel Time* by Lillian Hellman (Boston: Little Brown, 1976). Page numbers refer to *Three,* the edition of her combined memoirs brought out by Little Brown in 1979.

DHL *Dashiell Hammett: A Life* by Diane Johnson (New York: Random House, 1983).

SM *Shadow Man: The Life of Dashiell Hammett* by Richard Layman (New York: Harcourt Brace Jovanovich, 1981).

443

CHAPTER ONE

16
"In a magazine article": *Ladies' Home Journal,* Dec. 1963.

17
"an Italian housepainter": UW, page 17.

18
" 'did not die of natural causes' ": this anecdote and most of the information on the Newhouse and Marx families comes from Winston Smith of the Demopolis Historical Society.

19
"business prospects in Alabama": *Our Crowd* by Stephen Birmingham (New York: Harper and Row, 1967).

20
"arguments with directors": interview with Austin Pendleton.

21
"agrarian to . . . industrial": among others, Elizabeth Hardwick in *The New York Review of Books,* Dec. 21, 1967.

22
"eliminated one of the sisters": manuscripts at HRC.

22
"their own house": 1910 New Orleans Street Directory.

22
"crooked but silent": 1980 television interview with Marilyn Berger on PBS.

22
"mostly as a salesman": interview with Howard Bay.

23
"Memphis, Macon, Yazoo City": *Ladies' Home Journal,* Dec. 1963.

24
"the Hellman sisters' back door": *Eating Together* by LH and Peter Feibleman (Boston: Little Brown, 1984).

24
"open guests' mail": *Nathanael West: The Art of His Life* by Jay Martin (New York: Carroll & Graf, 1970).

25
" 'she is basically contemptuous' ": interview with Albert Hackett.

25
"she turned against the Mardi Gras": *Eating Together* by LH and Peter Feibleman.

26
"not an uncommon practice": Leon Edel in *Telling Lives,* edited by Marc Pachter (Washington: New Republic Books, 1979).

26
" 'certain love of my life' ": UW, page 24.

CHAPTER TWO

29
"not much care for cities": undated letter (1950s) from LH to Irene Worth.

30
"their patriotic vigilance": NYT, Dec. 13, 1936.

30
"Hellman was a bad influence": interview with Frances Schiff Bolton.
30
"running away from home": UW, page 30.
32
"Lillian says to Bethe": PN, page 351.
32
"Willy said to her": PN, page 398.
33
"to control Lillian": UW, page 24.
34
"she wrote a column briefly": *Lillian Hellman, Playwright* by Richard Moody (New York: Pegasus, 1972).
34
"she was cast as the villainess": ibid.
34
"A fellow student at N.Y.U.": letter from Edith Weil Smith to WW.
34
"Ann Haber, recalls Hellman": interview with Ann Haber.
35
"might well have been expelled": ibid.
37
"the extraordinary nature of the Boni and Liveright firm": most of the information about Boni and Liveright comes from *Horace Liveright: Publisher of the Twenties* (New York: David Lewis, 1970); and *No Whippings, No Gold Watches* by Louis Kronenberger (Boston: Atlantic-Little Brown, 1965).
39
"published Faulkner's first novel": *William Faulkner: His Life and Work* by Joseph L. Blotner (New York: Random House, 1974).
40
"he did not care for model employees": *No Whippings, No Gold Watches* by Louis Kronenberger.
41
"no sense of daring": UW, page 45.

CHAPTER THREE
44
"easygoing and accommodating": interview with Nan Werner.
44
"marriage as 'a disaster' ": interview with Marjorie Osterman.
45
"Hellman would climb on his back": interview with Helen Asbury Smith.
46
" 'That's who I really am' ": interview with Eileen Lottman.
46
"his freewheeling management": *No Whippings, No Gold Watches* by Louis Kronenberger (Boston: Atlantic-Little Brown, 1965).

47

"a small hotel on the Rue Jacob": *Maybe* by LH (Boston: Little Brown, 1980).

48

" 'lady-writer' stories": *Paris Review* interview with LH, winter/spring issue, 1965.

48

"remembered her book reviews": LH's tribute to Janet Flanner at the American Institute of Arts and Letters, 1981.

48

"one-night affair with an Englishman": *Maybe* by LH.

49

"Among them . . . were Hellman's letters": interviews with Rebecca Cort and Ann White, David Cort's secretary.

50

" 'fornicate and sew' ": undated letter to Helen (Mrs. Isidor) Schneider, Columbia University Library.

CHAPTER FOUR

52

"among them Arthur Kober": interview with Howard Bay.

53

"Bonn was a tranquil university town": *Malcolm Lowry* by Douglas Day (New York: Oxford University Press, 1973).

53

"a socialist youth organization": UW, page 64.

53

"Jews were isolated and clannish": *Reflections of Southern Jewry* edited by Louis Schmeir (Macon, Ga.: Mercer University Press, 1982).

54

"Faulkner . . . was paid $500 a week": *William Faulkner: His Life and Work* by Joseph L. Blotner (New York: Random House, 1974).

54

"a lengthy roster of film stars": *The Garden of Allah* by Sheilah Graham (New York: Crown Publishers, Inc., 1970).

55

"signal that the career was thriving": ibid.

55

"bottom-level screenwriter": *Nathanael West: The Art of His Life* by Jay Martin (New York: Carroll & Graf, 1970).

56

" 'I'm glamorous' ": interview with Helen Asbury Smith.

56

"Among them was Lester Cole": *Hollywood Red* by Lester Cole (Palo Alto: Ramparts Press, 1981).

57

"she attempted to organize": *Hellman in Hollywood* by Bernard Dick (New Brunswick, N.J.: Associated University Presses, Inc., 1982).

57

" 'none of us discussed politics' ": interview with Helen Asbury Smith.

58
"He sent Asbury . . . his first books": ibid.
58
"a writer the decision-makers . . . considered 'hot' ": DHL.
58
"An odd background": most of the background information about Hammett comes from SM and DHL.
60
" 'I can't stand . . . to be *touched!* ' ": interview with Emily Hahn.

CHAPTER FIVE
65
" 'his blackest silences' ": DHL.
66
" 'in Pine Street and was silly' ": UW, page 275.
68
"*In San Francisco Elfinstone*": HRC.
68
" 'AM MISSING OF YOU PLENTY' ": DHL.
70
"not have enough to eat": ibid.
70
"an award to her of $2,500": *Los Angeles Times,* June 30, 1932.
70
"West left in humiliation": *Nathanael West: The Art of His Life* by Jay Martin (New York: Carroll & Graf, 1970).
70
"Hellman had gone to bed with him": interview with Ruth Goetz.
71
"The party was aghast": interview with Helen Asbury Smith.
71
"Nunnally Johnson said": letter to Julian Symons from *The Selected Letters of Nunnally Johnson* edited and selected by Doris Johnson and Ellen Leventhal (New York: Alfred A. Knopf, 1981).
72
"trying to make art": SM.

CHAPTER SIX
75
" 'Thurber was a vicious drunk' ": television interview with Marilyn Berger, PBS, 1981.
75
"his cheeks puffed out": SM.
76
"all night talking and drinking": *William Faulkner: His Life and Work* by Joseph L. Blotner (New York: Random House, 1974).
77
"disentangled and ushered out": *William Faulkner: His Life and Times* by David Minter (Baltimore: Johns Hopkins Press, 1980).

78

"one of the best in his life": *William Faulkner: His Life and Work* by Joseph L. Blotner.

78

"publicly hailed West's book": *Nathanael West: The Art of His Life* by Jay Martin (New York: Carroll & Graf, 1970).

78

"Hellman and Hammett spent weekends there": ibid.

79

"Parker, whom Hellman met at a party": UW, page 232.

79

" 'the hue of availability' ": interview with Albert Hackett.

80

" 'She cries,' he explained": ibid.

80

"company manager for Jed Harris": *Jed Harris: The Curse of Genius* by Martin Gottfried (Boston: Little Brown, 1984).

81

"a comedy they called *Dear Queen*": *Lillian Hellman, Playwright* by Richard Moody (New York: Pegasus, 1972).

81

"the other woman was producing *something*": DHL.

81

"I Call Her Mama Now": *The American Spectator*, Sept. 1933.

82

"Perberty in Los Angeles": *The American Spectator*, Jan. 1934.

CHAPTER SEVEN

85

"admiration for the plays of Sidney Howard": a 1958 taped interview with Richard B. Stern in the Modern Poetry Collection, the University of Chicago.

85

" 'she didn't know anything else' ": television interview with Bill Moyers on PBS, April 1974.

86

"considered writing it himself": DHL.

87

"a rave from Brooks Atkinson": NYT, Sept. 30, 1926.

87

"film rights for $21,000": SM.

88

"she had been his model for Nora": interview with Albert Hackett.

88

"Many plot elements are true of both": *Bad Companions* by William Roughead (New York: Duffield and Green, 1931).

90

"In an early draft": typed manuscript of *The Children's Hour* at Boston University Library.

91
" 'an unconscious lesbian' ": HRC.

91
" 'perfect and complete villainy' ": HRC.

92
"her ruinous lie": *Bad Companions* by William Roughead.

94
"not more than a dozen lines were changed": interview with Howard Bay.

95
" 'what I'd done to make you cry' ": interview with Eugenia Rawls.

96
" 'This play could land us all in jail' ": PN, page 456.

96
" 'in quite so generous a fashion' ": PN, page 459.

96
"Brooks Atkinson . . . led the praise": NYT, Nov. 21, 1934.

96
"Robert Benchley writing in": *The New Yorker*, Dec. 1, 1934.

96
"George Jean Nathan in his monthly": *Vanity Fair*, Feb. 1934.

97
"next plane back to New York": PN, page 462.

97
"a young woman named Mildred Lewis": DHL.

98
"Hellman snapped at a fawning writer": *The New Yorker*, Nov. 8, 1941.

99
"In her essay on American women playwrights": *Plays by American Women* edited by Judith Barlow (New York: Avon Books, 1981).

100
"forbade the play's presentation": NYT, March 12, 1935.

102
"a sour note had been struck": *Lillian Hellman, Playwright* by Richard Moody (New York: Pegasus, 1972).

CHAPTER EIGHT

103
"made over $10,000 a year": *The Hollywood Writers' Wars* by Nancy Lynn Schwartz (New York: Alfred A. Knopf, 1982).

104
"all-important go-between": *William Wyler: The Authorized Biography* by Axel Madsen (New York: Thomas Y. Crowell Co., 1973).

105
"one of their Nick-and-Nora prowls": interview with Albert Hackett.

106
"as proof that he loved Lillian": DHL.

108
"an interviewer . . . asked her about the dinner": *Paris Review*, Winter/Spring 1965.

108

" 'better than Fitzgerald AND Jonathan Swift' ": *Selected Letters of John O'Hara* edited by Matthew J. Bruccoli (New York: Random House, 1978).

109

"screenplay was 90 percent hers": *Hellman in Hollywood* by Bernard Dick (New Brunswick, N.J.: Associated University Presses, Inc., 1982).

109

"out of the question for a Hollywood film": *The Search for Sam Goldwyn* by Carol Easton (New York: William Morrow & Co., 1976).

109

"the devastation caused by a lie": interview with Kim Hunter.

109

"In an interview at the time": NYT, Dec. 14, 1952.

110

"Hellman became aware of another passenger": The information about Hellman's romance with Ingersoll comes from an interview with Ralph Ingersoll and from *Ralph Ingersoll: A Biography* by Roy Hoopes (New York: Atheneum, 1985).

113

"Frank Nugent called it": NYT, March 19, 1936.

114

"Hellman had undertaken the second screenplay": *William Wyler* by Axel Madsen.

115

"Goldwyn docked his employees": *Journal of the Plague Years* by Stefan Kanfer (New York: Atheneum, 1973).

115

"two workers were killed": *The Great Depression* by Robert S. McElvaine (New York: Times Books, 1984).

116

"earned less than $2,000 a year": *The Hollywood Writers' Wars* by Nancy Lynn Schwartz.

117

"he was oppressed": ibid.

118

" 'Let's clean them out!' ": interview with Albert Hackett.

118

" 'immersed in the minutiae of it' ": *The Hollywood Writers' Wars* by Nancy Lynn Schwartz.

CHAPTER NINE

120

"West had wanted to use this title": *Nathanael West: The Art of His Life* by Jay Martin (New York: Carroll & Graf, 1970).

121

"Hackett phoned Hellman in New York": interview with Albert Hackett.

123

"they seriously considered collaborating": NYT, Dec. 13, 1936.

124

"he put on his coat and left": *Fanfare* by Richard Maney (New York: Harper, 1957).

124
"the idea for *Days to Come*": NYHT, Dec. 12, 1936.
129
"support the New Deal *and* the communists": *The Heyday of American Communism* by Harvey Klehr (New York: Basic Books, Inc., 1984).
129
"Daniel Bell makes an interesting distinction": as quoted in *Part of Our Time* by Murray Kempton (New York: Dell, 1967).
129
"he never knew her to be one as well": interview with Budd Schulberg.
130
"shunned Marxist solutions": *The New Masses*, Dec. 29, 1936.
130
"she had 'associated herself' with the communist wing of the American Labor Party": FBI report on Lillian Hellman dated June 18, 1941.
131
" 'The Motherland has been invaded!' ": *The Hollywood Writers' Wars* by Nancy Lynn Schwartz (New York: Alfred A. Knopf, 1982).
132
"He shared his classification": House Report No. 1954 of the 81st Congress.
132
"Thurber was taken aback": *Lillian Hellman* by Katherine Lederer (Boston: Twayne/G. K. Hall, 1979).

CHAPTER TEN
134
"Hellman had thought highly of the play": *Hellman in Hollywood* by Bernard Dick (New Brunswick, N.J.: Associated University Presses, Inc., 1982).
135
" 'how will I know I'm right?' ": *The Fifty Year Decline and Fall of Hollywood* by Ezra Goodman (New York: Simon and Schuster, 1961).
135
"a line-by-line refutation": *Paris Review*, Spring 1981.
136
"Hemingway put up $2,750": *Ernest Hemingway: A Life Story* by Carlos Baker (New York: Scribner, 1969).
136
" 'Which side was it on?' ": *Journal of the Plague Years* by Stefan Kanfer (New York: Atheneum, 1973).
136
"it was considered sufficiently partisan": *The Hollywood Writers' Wars* by Nancy Lynn Schwartz (New York: Alfred A. Knopf, 1982).
136
" 'MacLeish . . . is a stuffed shirt' ": DHL.
137
"on a last-minute impulse": UW, page 92.
137
"as was Martha Gellhorn": interview with Martha Gellhorn.
138
"to squelch Hellman's hankerings": interview with Howard Bay.

139

"The only other authoritative American": *Mission to Moscow* by Joseph E. Davies (New York: Simon and Schuster, 1941).

139

" 'the true charges from the wild hatred' ": UW, page 91.

139

"an advertisement endorsing them": *The New Masses,* May 3, 1938.

140

"was credited with the original story": *Lillian Hellman: Plays, Films, Memoirs* by Mark W. Estrin (Boston: G. K. Hall, 1980).

CHAPTER ELEVEN

143

"has been revived more frequently": interview with Abbott Van Norstrand of Samuel French and Co.

144

"and on one occasion Shumlin": NYT, Feb. 26, 1939.

145

" 'blackamoor chit-chat' ": *The New Yorker,* Nov. 8, 1941.

145

"considered drowning herself": ibid.

146

"insupportable sense of fraudulence": DHL.

146

"later changed the husband's ailment": HRC.

147

"a dispiriting series of flops": *Miss Tallulah Bankhead* by Lee Israel (New York: G. P. Putnam & Co., 1972).

148

"they were far from confident": interview with Howard Bay.

149

" 'It was like a Chinese box' ": interview with John Malcolm Brinnin.

150

" 'do you recognize your relatives?' ": interview with Louise Riggle (whose sister, Leah, was married to Gilbert Newhouse, Julia Hellman's only brother).

151

"Brooks Atkinson . . . had some complaints": NYT, Feb. 16, 1939.

152

"great theater rocks with violence": LH's preface to *Four Plays by Lillian Hellman* (New York: Random House, 1942).

152

"Hellman herself denies": ibid.

154

"Hellman said she never understood": interview with John Malcolm Brinnin.

CHAPTER TWELVE
156
" 'I gave it four days' ": *Paris Review,* Spring 1981.
158
"Hellman took one, Hammett the other": interview with George Hodor.
158
"like boiled skunkweed": interview with Marjorie Osterman.
158
"the happiest of Hammett's as well": DHL.
159
" 'I was afraid of competing' ": *Paris Review,* Spring 1981.
159
"Hellman's relationship with Shumlin": interview with Lola Shumlin.
159
"Rumors soon began circulating": interview with Howard Teichmann.
160
" 'We gotta save duh theatah' ": interview with Howard Bay.
160
" 'fantastic falsehood' ": *The Nation,* Aug. 26, 1939.
161
" 'suddenly become so insular' ": NYT, Jan. 20, 1940.
161
"more likely she was to cling to it": interview with Albert Hackett.
162
"to a pro-Hitler rally": UW, page 485.
162
"There was not sufficient time": *Paris Review,* Spring 1981.

CHAPTER THIRTEEN
165
"She got her B.A. from Wellesley": most of the background information
on Dr. Buttinger comes from interviews with her and from her autobiography, *Code Name Mary* (New Haven, Yale University Press, 1983).
166
"Hellman started writing": based on Hellman's having delivered the manuscript to Shumlin in January 1941 and having told an interviewer it took
nine months to write.
166
"European versus American values": NYT, April 20, 1941.
167
"Count Teck was based on": *New York Daily News,* April 28, 1941.
167
"Others such as Richard Wright": Letter from LH to Wright, April 4,
1940, Beinecke Manuscript Collection, Yale.
167
"Hammett read every word": *Ralph Ingersoll: A Biography* by Roy Hoopes
(New York: Atheneum, 1985).
168
" 'I am also a Jew' ": *New York Herald Tribune,* Jan. 10, 1940.

168
"a piece on the 1940 Republican Convention": *PM,* June 25, 1940.

168
"An FBI informant claimed": FBI file dated April 11, 1940.

170
"She heard about Zilboorg through": *Ralph Ingersoll: A Biography* by Roy Hoopes.

171
"Field and Ingersoll met": ibid.

171
"She said of his politics": UW, page 227.

171
"the approval was unrestrained": interview with Howard Bay.

171
"recommended that Hellman buy a pet": interview with Marjorie Osterman.

171
"Zilboorg ran into serious trouble": the information about Zilboorg comes from Dr. Henrietta Klein, Dr. George Goldman and Dr. Willard Gaylin.

172
"Catherine Kober recalls": interview with Catherine Kober.

172
" 'Zilboorg ended odd' ": UW, page 227.

173
"Her schedule remained fixed": *The New Yorker,* Nov. 11, 1941.

173
" 'Hammett took me aside' ": interview with Catherine Kober.

173
" 'poison in their coffee' ": HRC.

173
"the Christmas court martialing": *The New Yorker,* Nov. 11, 1941.

174
"She urged listeners": the speech was reprinted in *The New Masses,* Dec. 10, 1940.

175
"only two speeches in the play": NYT, April 20, 1940.

177
"the day's leading playwrights": *Lillian Hellman* by Doris Falk (New York: Frederick Ungar Publishing Co., 1978).

177
" 'A present for Lillian Hellman' ": *The New Yorker,* Nov. 11, 1941.

178
"convinced she could not write love scenes": interview with Albert Hackett.

179
"Wyler wanted to inject": *The Search for Sam Goldwyn* by Carol Easton (New York: William Morrow & Co., 1976).

179
"bring out the monsters": interview with Austin Pendleton.

179
"the constant fights with Wyler": *The Lonely Life* by Bette Davis (New York: G. P. Putnam and Sons, 1962).

180
" 'your hands on my play' ": interview with Austin Pendleton.
180
"fraternity of all-knowing teachers": interview with Howard Bay.

CHAPTER FOURTEEN

181
"and was 'nobody's girl' ": UW, page 207.
182
"Bette Davis was so eager": *William Wyler* by Axel Madsen (New York: Thomas Y. Crowell Co., 1973).
182
"Hal Wallis signed Hammett": *Hellman in Hollywood* by Bernard Dick (New Brunswick, N.J.: Associated University Presses, Inc., 1982).
182
"In a scathing letter": HRC.
183
"Hellman assured the President": PN, page 497.
183
"had already made a futile search": FBI report on Hellman dated June 17, 1941.
184
"the happiest day of my life": DHL.
184
"Howard Teichmann evokes": *George S. Kaufman: An Intimate Portrait* by Howard Teichmann (New York: Atheneum, 1972).
186
"filling 250 pages": NYHT, Dec. 5, 1943.
186
"she . . . went to Goldwyn": *The Moguls* by Norman Zierold (New York: Coward-McCann, 1969).
187
"Hellman bought her way out": *Hellman in Hollywood* by Bernard Dick.
188
" 'patches by Irene' ": interview with Michael de Lisio.
188
"Bosley Crowther in": NYT, Nov. 7, 1943.
189
"the film is converted": *Hellman in Hollywood* by Bernard Dick.
191
" 'I haven't had a dry shoulder' ": HRC.

CHAPTER FIFTEEN

192
"thought the film a great joke": interview with Kathleen Harriman Mortimer.
193
"he corresponded with Nancy Bragdon": HRC.

193
"a monitored radio conversation": FBI report on LH dated Oct. 16 and 18, 1944.
195
"Harriman who knew Hellman": interview with Kathleen Harriman Mortimer.
195
" 'She'll be a happy woman' ": ibid.
195
"Melby had been born": the information about Melby and about his affair with LH, unless otherwise noted, comes from interviews with John Melby.
196
"Her marvelous description": UW, page 151.
197
"dignitary 'of that type' ": interview with Kathleen Harriman Mortimer.
198
"Harriman once remarked": interview with Arthur Schlesinger, Jr.

CHAPTER SIXTEEN
201
"They chose East Hampton": interview with John Melby.
203
" 'Time is the mischief' ": letter from John Melby to WW.
203
"plans to write a trilogy": NYT, March 10, 1946.
204
"only a handful of firstrate directors": ibid.
205
"resumed the feud": interview with Edward Cooke.
205
" 'give this girl a raise' ": interview with Flora Roberts.
206
" 'Lillian wasn't interested' ": interview with Howard Bay.
206
" 'How do I tell Pat' ": interview with Edward Cooke.
206
"her interior-decorating approach": interview with Scott McKay.
207
" 'with a trace of incest' ": NYT, Nov. 21, 1946.
207
" 'an infinitely superior play' ": *The New Yorker*, Nov. 30, 1946.
208
" 'An Author Jabs Her Critics' ": NYT, Dec. 15, 1946.
209
"had him committed": interview with Howard Bay.
209
"she insisted the old woman": interview with Louise Riggle.
209
"an article appeared": *The New Masses*, Feb. 12, 1946.

211
"believed them to be temporary measures": ST, page 612.
212
" 'The Judas Goats' ": *The Screenwriter,* Dec. 1947.
214
"Barney Balaban had vetoed her": *Journal of the Plague Years* by Stefan Kanfer (New York: Atheneum, 1973).

CHAPTER SEVENTEEN
216
" 'the jargon they spoke' ": interview with Budd Schulberg.
216
"she would resign": *A Better World* by William O'Neill (New York: Simon and Schuster, 1982).
216
"Wallace pulled her aside": ST, page 687.
218
"Progressives had no further influence": Encyclopaedia Britannica (Progressive Party).
218
"Smith recounts their friendship": interviews with Randall Smith.
220
" 'The situation was ugly' ": DHL.
221
"made over a million dollars": SM.
221
"claimed to Nunnally Johnson": *The Selected Letters of Nunnally Johnson* edited and selected by Doris Johnson and Ellen Leventhal (New York: Alfred A. Knopf, 1981).
222
"the six articles she wrote": *The New York Star,* Nov. 4, 5, 7, 8, 9, 10, 1948.
223
"proof of Hellman's political independence": interview with Randall Smith.
224
" 'Lillian was a paid houseguest' ": interview with Irene Selznick.
224
"accused under the Smith Act": *The Heyday of American Communism* by Harvey Klehr (New York: Basic Books, Inc., 1984).
224
"Of particular interest to the agency": FBI file on LH dated Jan. 16, 1949.
226
"at the personal request of Stalin": *Testimony* by Dmitri Shostakovich and Solomon Volkov (New York: Harper and Row, 1979).
226
"In a scathing write-up": *Life* magazine, April 14, 1949.
226
"others knelt in prayer": *Newsweek,* April 4, 1949.
227
"heard the door slammed and bolted": NYHT, March 26, 1949.

227
" 'He rushed over to Lillian' ": *Newsweek,* April 4, 1949.
228
"smashed a dinner plate in fury": ibid.

CHAPTER EIGHTEEN
230
"The Moscow production was well received": NYT, Oct. 17, 1949.
231
" 'one of the Andrews Sisters' ": interview with Eugenia Rawls.
231
"project was in good hands": *Slings and Arrows* by Robert Lewis (New York: Stein and Day, 1984).
231
" 'I don't think Regina is a flirt' ": HRC.
231
" 'fumbling, frightened way' ": PN, page 500.
232
" 'An orange, eh?' ": interview with Howard Bay.
235
"she had defended her approach": *Four Plays by Lillian Hellman* (New York: Random House, 1942).
236
"marked in Hellman's hand": HRC.
237
" 'boneless and torpid' ": NYT, March 8, 1951.
237
" 'bursitis of character' ": *Theatre Arts,* Dec. 1951.
239
" 'too Jewish' ": *Obsession* by Meyer Levin (New York: Simon and Schuster, 1973).
239
"According to Cheryl Crawford": interview with Cheryl Crawford.
239
"Hammett invited them in": DHL.
239
"a bail fund . . . was set up": *From Left to Right* by Frederick Vanderbilt Field (Westport, CN: Lawrence Hill, 1983).
240
"he was jailed for contempt": ibid.
240
" 'He gave me two plays' ": interview with Ruth Goetz.
241
"interest had raised the figure": DHL.
241
" 'Take one of the trips to Europe' ": HRC.
241
"She sold the farm in 1951": Westchester County records.

241
"The sale price was $67,000": ibid.
242
"there was no effective blacklist": interview with Budd Schulberg.

Chapter Nineteen
244
"The ordeal began": ST, page 617.
245
"The witch-hunting mood was": *The Committee* by Walter Goodman (New York: Farrar, Straus and Giroux, 1968).
248
"you have waived your right": interview with Joseph Rauh.
248
"the constitutionality of the Smith Act": *Journal of the Plague Years* by Stefan Kanfer (New York: Atheneum, 1973).
248
" '*Scoundrel Time* is not the way it happened' ": interview with Joseph Rauh.
250
"the claim that Hellman was the first": made by LH in ST (page 619) and in a 1980 television interview with Marilyn Berger for PBS.
250
"verbal bullying from Clare Boothe Luce": *The New Yorker,* Nov. 11, 1941.
251
"The interrogation proceeded": *House Report on Committee Hearings* (Communist Infiltration into the Motion Picture Industry), May 21, 1952.
253
" 'She told me she had not been' ": interview with Joseph Rauh.
254
"HELLMAN BALKS HOUSE UNIT": NYT, May 22, 1952.
255
"Melby was never told": interview with John Melby.
255
"his crime, in their eyes": interview with Lucius Battle and Burke Wilkinson.
256
"She was flummoxed": interview with Marjorie Osterman.

Chapter Twenty
258
" 'You don't know how to talk to actors!' ": interview with Scott McKay.
258
"To each she gave a message": interview with Kim Hunter.
258
" 'That's it exactly, Kim' ": ibid.
259
"She decided not to change the text": NYT, Dec. 14, 1952.
259
"she told the group": interview with Kim Hunter.

259
" 'not about lesbianism, but about a lie' ": NYT, Dec. 14, 1952.
260
"she owed the IRS . . . $190,000": interview with John Malcolm Brinnin.
260
"The IRS will neither confirm nor deny": interview with Mark Thorn of the IRS.
260
"wiped out by the tax people": letter from LH to Theodore Roethke.
260
"no recollection of Hellman's presence": interview with Frank Alvarez of Macy's.
260
"two people close to her": interviews with Albert Hackett and John Melby.
261
"She told the director Joseph Anthony": interview with Joseph Anthony.
263
"reply from an eminent playwright": HRC.
264
" 'I'm Jewish,' she snapped": interview with John Simon.
264
" 'I needed the money' ": undated letter from LH to Sigerist, Beinecke Manuscript Collection, Yale.
264
"Hellman wrote in a letter": undated letter from LH to Irene Worth.
265
"a great part of his appeal": interview with Joseph Anthony.
267
"she went along with the idea": interview with Richard Wilbur.
267
" 'Do what you want' ": ibid.
268
" 'Out-of-date!' ": interview with Howard Moss.
269
" 'working in the Five and Ten' ": ibid.
269
" 'I was a little bit in love' ": interview with Marjorie Osterman.
269
" 'she did not make *one* change' ": interview with Thomas Hammond.
269
"Osterman recalls": interview with Lester Osterman.
271
"Wheeler . . . received a phone call": interview with Hugh Wheeler.
271
"make himself known to Osterman": this story comes from a work in progress: "Will It Win a Tony" by Marjorie Osterman.

CHAPTER TWENTY-ONE
274
"Hellman asked Lester": interview with Lester Osterman.
275
" 'Let's make a clean break' ": ibid.
275
"according to Ruth Goetz": interview with Ruth Goetz.
276
"would consult her psychiatrist": interview with Marjorie Osterman.
276
"has more pleasant recollections": ibid.
278
"Teichmann is sure she was amusing herself": interview with Howard Teichmann.
278
"two paragraphs are blacked out": FBI report on LH dated April 8, 1957.
279
"Hammett . . . gave her the idea": PN, page 508.
280
" 'one of the sexiest dames' ": interview with Howard Bay.
280
"Hellman and Bay almost fell out of their chairs": ibid.
280
" 'You should never address the troops!' ": interview with Milton Goldman.
281
" 'an anthology of bathos' ": Alan Brien in *The Spectator*, Nov. 18, 1960.
281
" 'no more . . . push than a tea trolley' ": H. A. L. Craig in *The New Statesman*, Nov. 19, 1960.
283
"It was *her* idea": interview with Marjorie Osterman.
283
" 'Hammett's taken over the whole goddamn house!' ": interview with Ruth Goetz.
283
" 'There's a dying man upstairs' ": *Nostalgia Isn't What It Used to Be* by Simone Signoret (New York: Harper and Row, 1978).
284
"When Hellman phoned John Melby": interview with Melby.
284
"took Hammett's body by train": interview with Howard Bay.
285
"and one part to Hellman": the will of Dashiell Hammett.

CHAPTER TWENTY-TWO
286
" 'wouldn't let Lillian be a celebrity' ": interview with Howard Bay.
287
"become even more a fixture in it": interview with Charlee Wilbur.

287

"a phony English accent": interview with Marjorie Osterman.

287

"was a large contributor": interview with John Malcolm Brinnin.

288

" 'he has this scar' ": interview with Marjorie Osterman.

288

"consider him dangerously crazy": PN, page 551.

289

"an active part in the intellectual social life": interview with Margo Mumford-Jones.

289

"the deluge of honors": *Lillian Hellman, A Bibliography* 1926–1978 by Mary Marguerite Riordan (Metuchen, N.J.: The Scarecrow Press, 1980).

290

"In her own memoirs": *Nostalgia Isn't What It Used to Be* by Simone Signoret (New York: Harper and Row, 1978).

290

" 'Lillian, you know perfectly well' ": ibid.

292

" 'Someday we'll do this right' ": interview with Howard Bay.

292

"Robert Brustein refused": interview with Robert Brustein.

293

"encouraged Jay Presson Allen": interview with Milton Goldman.

293

"a very upset man was on the phone": *Slings and Arrows* by Robert Lewis (New York: Stein and Day, 1984).

294

"Hellman wrote a devastating parody": *Show* Magazine, May 1964.

295

" 'Lillian came on with every man she met' ": interview with Arthur Miller.

295

" 'The picture tickles the hell out of me' ": interview with Marjorie Osterman.

296

"She wrote them several letters": interview with Jo Hammett Marshall.

296

"Hellman said that he left her his half": NYT, Sept. 23, 1973.

296

"her real reason . . . was to protect them": interview with David Wolkowsky.

296

"Hellman's agent sold the rights to *The Dain Curse*": interview with Don Congdon.

296

"At no time did Hellman ever turn over": interview with Jo Hammett Marshall.

297

"nothing more than greed": interview with Diane Johnson.

297
"a 1973 interview with Nora Ephron": NYT, Sept. 23, 1973.
297
"Hellman had it closed down": interview with Don Congdon.

CHAPTER TWENTY-THREE
300
"were overruled by Spiegel": *Hellman in Hollywood* by Bernard Dick (New Brunswick, N.J.: Associated University Presses, Inc., 1982).
300
"a film adaptation comes along that is so bad": *New Republic,* Aug. 17, 1963.
301
"Hardwick came down hardest": *The New York Review of Books,* Dec. 21, 1967.
302
"the dearth of American playwrights": *Commonweal,* Dec. 1, 1967.
302
"published a book on Hellman": *Lillian Hellman, Playwright* by Richard Moody (New York: Pegasus, 1972).
302
"The major broadside": NYT, June 18, 1972.
303
"to critic Renata Adler": NYT, July 9, 1972.
305
"interview with . . . Seymour Peck": NYT, Feb. 21, 1960.
305
"critic Kenneth Tynan replied": interview with Kenneth Tynan.
306
"In a 1942 interview she said": *World Digest,* Jan. 1942.
307
"the critic Allan Lewis": *American Plays and Playwrights of the Contemporary Theatre* by Allan Lewis (New York: Crown, 1965).
308
"in his brilliant essay": *The Crack in the Chimney* by Robert Brustein (New York: Random House, 1974).
309
"Brustein had already become friends": interview with Robert Brustein.

CHAPTER TWENTY-FOUR
311
" 'That goddamn bitch Dorothy Parker' ": interview with Howard Teichmann.
311
" 'Next time you might hurt yourself' ": *The Vicious Circle* by Margaret Case Harriman (New York: Rinehart & Co., 1951).
312
"Parker had other benefactors": interview with Marion Meade.

312

" 'Lillian was always taking umbrage' ": interview with Don Congdon.

312

"relieved when Hellman left her": ibid.

313

" 'a hundred and sixty years by being crooks' ": interview with Abbott Van Norstrand.

313

" 'frugging with Sarge Shriver' ": letter from LH to Joe Fox, Columbia University Library.

313

"Hellman sued CBS": NYT, Feb. 27, 1970.

314

"her front-page obituary": NYT, July 1, 1984.

316

"Podhoretz in his memoir": *Making It* by Norman Podhoretz (New York: Random House, 1967).

316

"Hellman spat in his face": interview with Marjorie Osterman.

316

"Diana Trilling remembers": interview with Diana Trilling.

317

"Robert Lowell spotted Bundy": interview with Howard Moss.

317

"Bundy insists . . . no such thing could have happened": interview with McGeorge Bundy.

317

"she aspired to a milieu": interview with John Malcolm Brinnin.

317

"the idea of running for President": *Making It* by Norman Podhoretz.

318

"The letters were monitored by the CIA": CIA file on LH.

318

"an open letter to Premier Kosygin": *New Republic,* Jan. 1, 1966.

318

" 'My speech was published here and in Europe' ": UW, page 207 (written for the 1979 edition, *Three*).

318

"instead she spoke of the ferment": NYT, May 31, 1967.

319

"came down hard on the Soviet Premier": interview with John Melby.

320

" ' "Prove it! Prove it!" ' ": interview with Budd Schulberg.

321

" 'wilderness of drugs' ": NYT, Aug. 23, 1969.

CHAPTER TWENTY-FIVE

324

" 'I did not fool with facts' ": UW, page 9.

325

"she never wrote about the living": interview with John Melby.

326

"as she would say elsewhere": NYT, Sept. 23, 1973.

327

"noted the enormity of Hellman's claim": *Womens Wear Daily*, Jan. 20, 1986.

328

" 'too busy with the Poles' ": NYT, March 2, 1945.

328

"told him of the invitation": interview with John Melby.

328

"She says it is unlikely": interview with Kathleen Harriman Mortimer.

329

" 'wounded in the penis' ": UW, page 99.

330

"The article differs": *Collier's*, March 31, 1945.

330

"She assured the Russian officers": ibid.

331

" 'pieces of me floating' ": UW, page 167.

334

" 'none of them are going anywhere' ": interview with Howard Bay.

334

"she had arranged to meet": interview with John Melby.

334

"Thornton Wilder, who later wrote": letter from LH to Thornton Wilder, July 31, 1972 (Beinecke Manuscript Library, Yale University).

335

"she wrote a scathing piece": NYT, Aug. 23, 1969.

335

"she wished she had done": ST, page 675.

336

"a conscious campaign on her part": interview with Barbara Handman.

337

" 'No other writer I know would know how to do this' ": *The Vineyard Gazette*, July 6, 1984.

337

"Ramsey Clark told reporters": NYT, Jan. 18, 1970.

338

"Hellman toured the country": interview with Dorothy Samuels.

338

"She was still obsessed": ibid.

339

" 'I got a frantic call from Lillian' ": ibid.

340

"Silvers . . . recalls his intercession": interview with Robert Silvers.

340
"Kramer recalls a fund-raiser": interview with Nancy Kramer.
341
"Gillers recalls talking": interview with Stephen Gillers.
341
" 'I loved her' ": ibid.

CHAPTER TWENTY-SIX

344
"Eliot Fremont-Smith cited": *New York Magazine,* Sept. 17, 1973.
344
" 'as an electron microscope' ": NYT, Dec. 2, 1973.
344
"Lehmann-Haupt in the daily *Times":* NYT, Sept. 17, 1973.
344
" 'its immense literary worth' ": *Washington Post,* Sept. 16, 1973.
346
" 'a question of moral responsibility' ": NYT, Nov. 21, 1976.
347
"eliminated several people for low marks": interview with Barbara Handman.
347
" '*that* was vintage Hellman' ": interview with Jerry Parker.
347
" 'to be held in your arms' ": ibid.
348
"In the book about food": *Eating Together* by LH and Peter Feibleman (Boston: Little Brown, 1984).
349
"Cathy's going to live with Hellman": interview with Catherine Kober.
349
"patching things up with her 'aunt' ": ibid.
350
"Hellman went into a rage": interview with Nan Werner.
350
" 'It was a beautiful picture' ": ibid.
351
" 'a foul-weather friend' ": interview with Catherine Kober.
351
"invented an imaginary character": 1980 interview with Marilyn Berger on PBS.
352
"she began hitting Mengers": interview with Betsy Seidman, to whom LH told this story.
352
"describing the stay to Ruth Goetz": interview with Ruth Goetz.
352
"Hackett remembers the sojourn": interview with Albert Hackett.

352
"a $500 down payment": interview with David Wolkowsky.
353
"doorman chased after her": interview with Marjorie Osterman.

CHAPTER TWENTY-SEVEN

357
"The opening shot came from Murray Kempton": *The New York Review of Books,* June 10, 1976.
358
"The children of timid immigrants": ST, page 607.
358
"Glazer cited numerous examples": *Commentary,* June 19, 1976.
359
"Irving Howe then joined the fray": *Dissent,* Fall, 1976.
360
" 'we were all of the anticommunist left' ": interview with Joseph Rauh.
360
"came from Sidney Hook": *Encounter,* Feb. 1977.
361
"an exchange between Dan Rather and Hellman": *Who's Who* CBS interview show, March 8, 1977.
361
"Hook went on to string out": interview with Sidney Hook.
362
"Kramer commented on the number": NYT, Oct. 3, 1976.
362
"Alfred Kazin, who groaned": *Esquire,* Aug. 1977.
363
"three other informants claimed knowledge": FBI file on LH.
364
"his father remembers Hellman": interview with Dorothy Samuels.
365
"as evidence of Hellman's official status": interview with Diana Trilling.
365
"were stated only in private": interview with Randall Smith.
365
"memoir of his Party involvement": *From Left to Right* by Frederick Vanderbilt Field (Westport, CT: Lawrence Hill, 1983).
367
"Hellman's strange introduction": *To Be Preserved Forever* by Lev Kopelev (Philadelphia: Lippincott, 1977).
368
"William F. Buckley joined the posse": *National Review,* April 29, 1977.
368
"Robert Brustein wrote": *New Republic,* Aug. 13, 1984.
370
"Hellman herself misunderstood the slogan": interview with Peter Rogers.

CHAPTER TWENTY-EIGHT

371
" 'old and respected friends' ": ST, page 650.

372
"Hellman told her friend": interview with Diana Trilling.

372
"the Trilling book was being canceled": NYT, Sept. 28, 1976.

372
"Trilling made the usual rebuttals": *We Must March, My Darlings* by Diana Trilling (New York: Harcourt Brace Jovanovich, 1977).

373
" 'a masterpiece of moral showmanship' ": ibid.

373
"Trilling claims no evidence": interview with Diana Trilling.

374
"Mailer also felt the force": *Mailer: His Life and Times* by Peter Manso (New York: Simon and Schuster, 1985).

374
"they were of no use": interview with Diana Trilling.

375
"an outburst of hostility": *Eating Together* by LH and Peter Feibleman (Boston: Little Brown, 1984).

375
"Hellman was a delightful traveling companion": interview with McGeorge Bundy.

376
"tired of her tag-along status": interview with Nancy Lady Keith.

377
"offered some sharp-edged recollections": letter from George Trow to WW.

378
"Eric Sevareid devoted part of his commentary": *CBS Evening News,* April 1, 1977 (© 1977 CBS, Inc., All Rights Reserved).

378
"to go after a private individual": interview with Eric Sevareid.

379
" 'the sexual yearnings of one girl for another' ": PN, page 414.

380
"Hellman claimed to have been surprised": 1980 television interview with Marilyn Berger on PBS.

380
"That was denied by both": interview with Jane Fonda and Alvin Sargent.

382
"Instead she phoned her agent": interview with Don Congdon.

382
" 'I think Lillian has a chip' ": NYT, Jan. 29, 1979.

382
"she went after the production": NYT, May 12, 1978.

382
"the offer was ridiculous": interview with Don Congdon.

383
" 'she didn't give a shit' ": ibid.
383
" 'decided he knew everything' ": interview with Howard Bay.
384
"She grew livid and screamed at Taylor": interview with Austin Pendleton.

CHAPTER TWENTY-NINE
386
" 'After the oily virtuosity' ": as reprinted in *Sights and Sounds* by Mary
McCarthy (New York: Farrar, Straus and Cudahy, 1956).
387
"McCarthy . . . laughed even harder": interview with Mary McCarthy.
387
"Hellman expressed surprise": NYT, March 15, 1980.
388
"a short story of McCarthy's": *The Company She Keeps* by Mary McCarthy
(New York: Harcourt Brace Jovanovich, 1942).
388
"Hellman had been an operative for the KGB": interview with Mary
McCarthy.
389
"Hellman mistook her for a student": *The Paris Metro,* Feb. 15, 1978.
389
" 'being caught red-handed' ": ibid.
389
"being Lillian, she imagined": letter from Stephen Spender to WW.
390
"Rauh recognized the fighting mode": interview with Joseph Rauh.
391
"intended to push the case to trial": interview with Betsy Schulberg.
391
"Robert Kraus, writing on the subject": *Harper's,* March 1983.
392
" 'not dishonest for an instant' ": NYT, May 11, 1980.
392
"a small book by Hellman": *Maybe* by LH (Boston: Little Brown, 1980).
392
"So the matter was researched": interviews with Joseph Anthony, Randall
Smith, John Melby and Marjorie Osterman.
394
"Bankhead's 1952 autobiography": *Tallulah* by Tallulah Bankhead (New
York: Harper and Brothers, 1952).
394
"Shumlin, who had not believed 'Julia' ": interview with Howard Teichmann.
394
"The only reviewer to question": *The Hudson Review,* Winter 1973–74.
395
"Spender told her of a woman in Vienna": interview with Mary McCarthy.

396
"was planning to write an article": interview with Martha Gellhorn.
397
"a masterpiece of vitriol": *Paris Review*, Spring 1981.
399
"incomprehension of that war": ibid.
399
" 'Hellman Word Assailed Again' ": NYT, Mar. 15, 1981.
400
"he denied that to be so": interview with George Plimpton.
400
"tried not to make any noise": ibid.
400
"A defense fund for her was established": interview with Robert Silvers.
400
"McCarthy freely acknowledged": interview with Mary McCarthy.

Chapter Thirty

401
" 'her papier-mâché chest' ": *New Republic,* Aug. 1984.
402
"I would sit with her": letter from Richard de Combray to WW.
403
"Buttinger's memoirs were published": *Code Name Mary* by Muriel Gardiner (New Haven: Yale University Press, 1983).
404
"she wrote Hellman a polite letter": interview with Muriel Gardiner Buttinger.
404
"There was no reply": ibid.
404
"O'Reilly was convinced she was Julia": interview with Jane O'Reilly.
404
" 'certainly not the model for mine' ": NYT, April 29, 1983.
405
" 'No, only "Mary" ' ": Jane O'Reilly's interview with Dr. Herbert Steiner.
405
"Gardiner volunteered": interview with Muriel Gardiner Buttinger.
405
"Gardiner had been doing it for years": ibid.
406
"verified that his father": *Washington Post,* July 6, 1983.
407
" 'we were all very curious' ": interview with Jane Fonda.
408
"Dr. George Gero phoned Muriel Gardiner": interview with Dr. Gero.
408
"she had never claimed to be Julia": interview with Muriel Gardiner Buttinger.

409
"another phone call came from Hellman": interview with David Lowe.
410
" 'Muriel Gardiner was not Julia' ": interview with Dr. George Gero.
411
" 'Julia and Other Fictions' ": *Commentary*, June, 1984.
414
" 'you're two years older than I am' ": interview with Diana Trilling.
414
" 'she certainly had those tendencies all along' ": interview with Richard de Combray.
414
"she told his . . . obituary writer": NYT, July 29, 1981.
415
"she was also the model": UW, page 290.

CHAPTER THIRTY-ONE
417
" 'Thanks a lot' ": interview with David Kalstone.
418
"he found Hellman stark naked": interview with Roger McNiven.
419
" 'you don't have to worry about the twenty-five dollars' ": ibid.
419
"MY NAME IS LILLIAN HELLMAN": *The Vineyard Gazette*, Sept. 2, 1983.
420
" 'Lillian and I led separate lives' ": interview with Mrs. William Wyler.
421
"she looked dead": interview with Michael de Lisio.
421
" 'I'd go anywhere for Pat Neal' ": NYT, May 25, 1984.
421
"give the speedboat the finger": *The Vineyard Gazette*, July 6, 1984.
422
" 'the worst writer's block I've ever had' ": *The Vineyard Gazette*, July 6, 1984.
422
" 'grabbed her by the throat' ": interview with Milton Gordon.
423
"Nancy Kramer was still troubled": interview with Nancy Kramer.
423
"the obituary on the front page": NYT, July 1, 1984.
424
" 'more fights per man and woman contact' ": *The Vineyard Gazette*, July 6, 1984.
424
" 'you are a finished woman now' ": ibid.
424
"food Hellman would have served": *Eating Together* by LH and Peter Feibleman (Boston: Little Brown, 1984).

425
" 'a believer in the doctrines of Karl Marx' ": will of LH dated May 24, 1984, filed in Surrogate's Court, County of New York.

427
"Even Muriel Gardiner admitted": interview with Muriel Gardiner Buttinger.

427
"was turned down by two . . . publishers": interview with David Lowe.

428
"is repeated (and credited to Hellman)": *Ernest Hemingway: A Life Story* by Carlos Baker (New York: Scribner, 1969).

429
"Hellman once told Yolande Fox": interview with Yolande Fox.

430
"Nora Ephron, who knew Hellman": *Heartburn* by Nora Ephron (New York: Alfred A. Knopf, 1983).

432
" 'Her eventual reputation in this regard' ": *Commentary,* June 1984.

433
" 'She was the greatest person I've ever known' ": interview with Randall Smith.

435
"A small amount of conversation revealed": NYT, Aug. 26, 1984.

INDEX

473